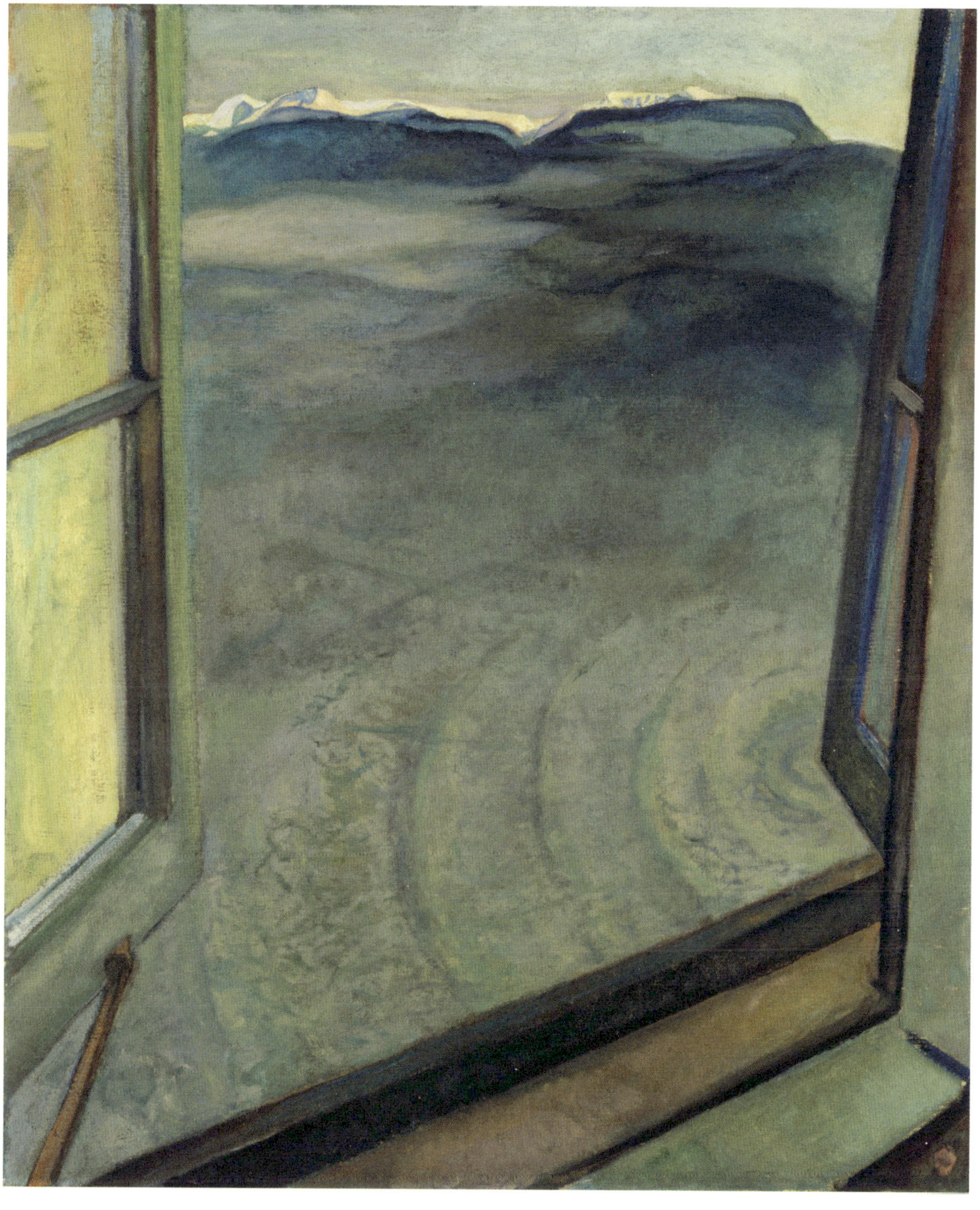

*Magnetic North
Imagining Canada in
Painting 1910–40*

Edited by
Martina Weinhart
with Georgiana Uhlyarik

SCHIRN
KUNSTHALLE
FRANKFURT

PRESTEL
MUNICH · LONDON · NEW YORK

A. Y. Jackson
*Terre Sauvage,* 1913
128.8 × 154.4 cm

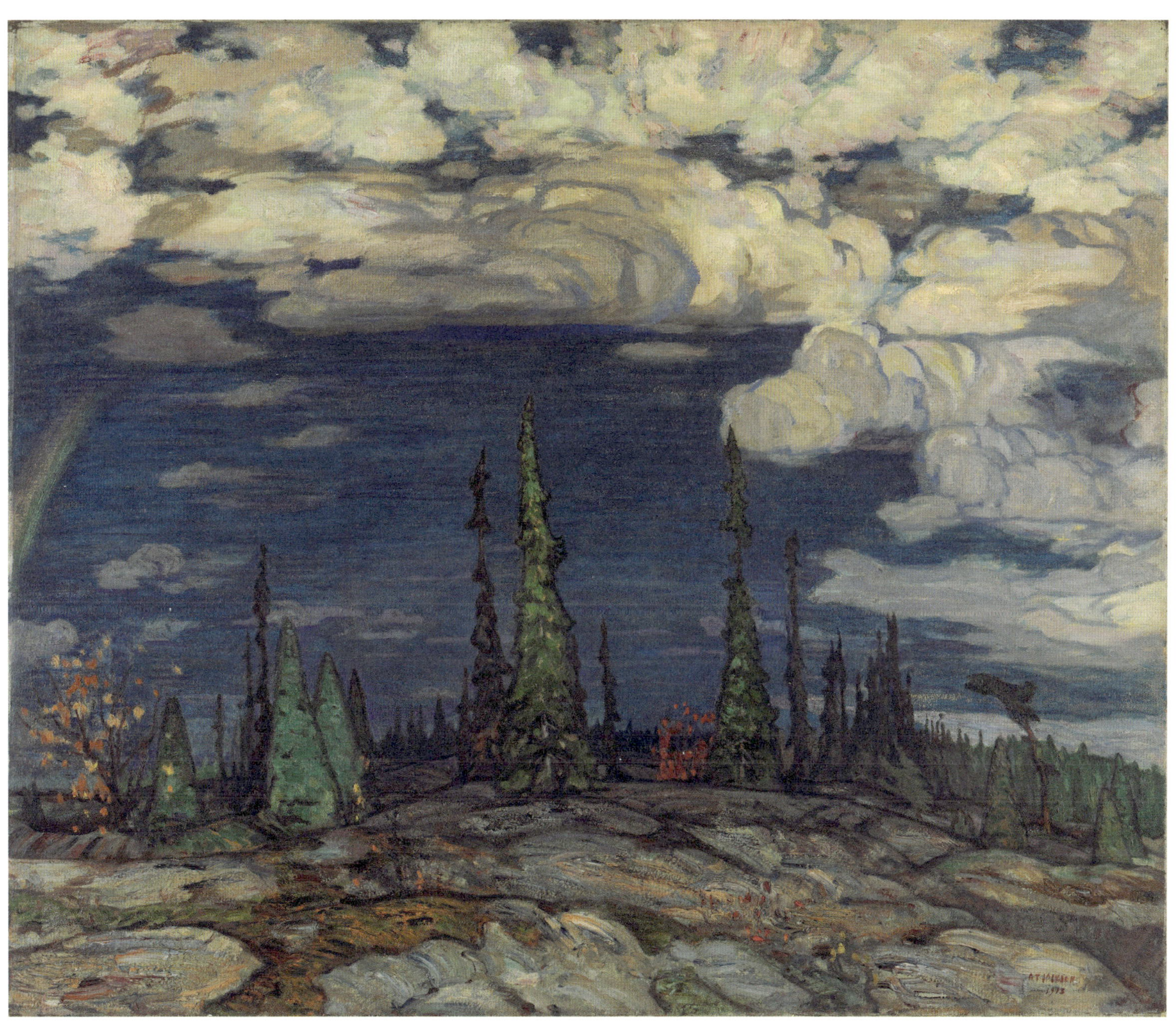

Emily Carr
*Big Raven,* 1931
87 × 114 cm

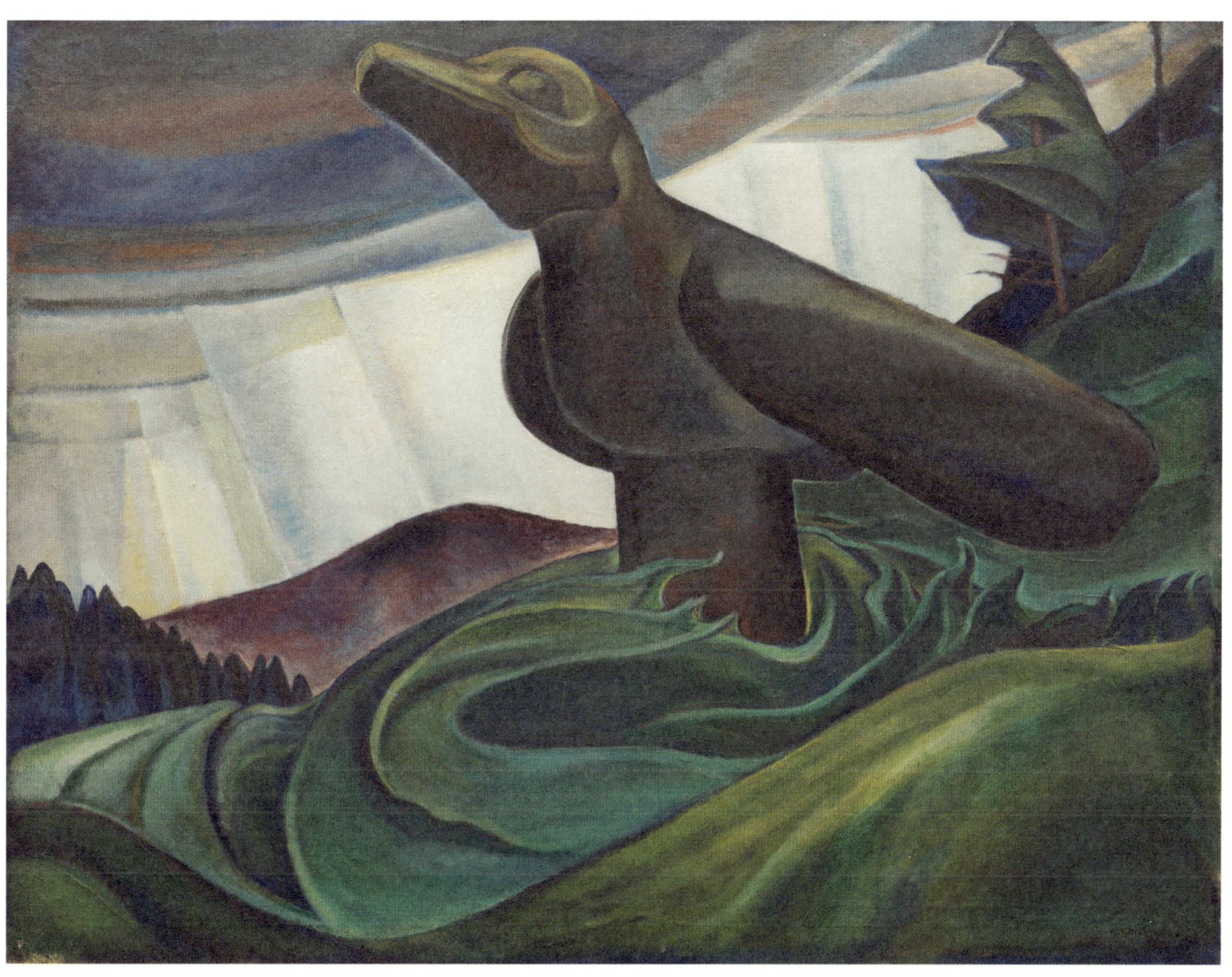

Lawren Harris
*Mt. Lefroy,* 1930
133.5 × 153.5 cm

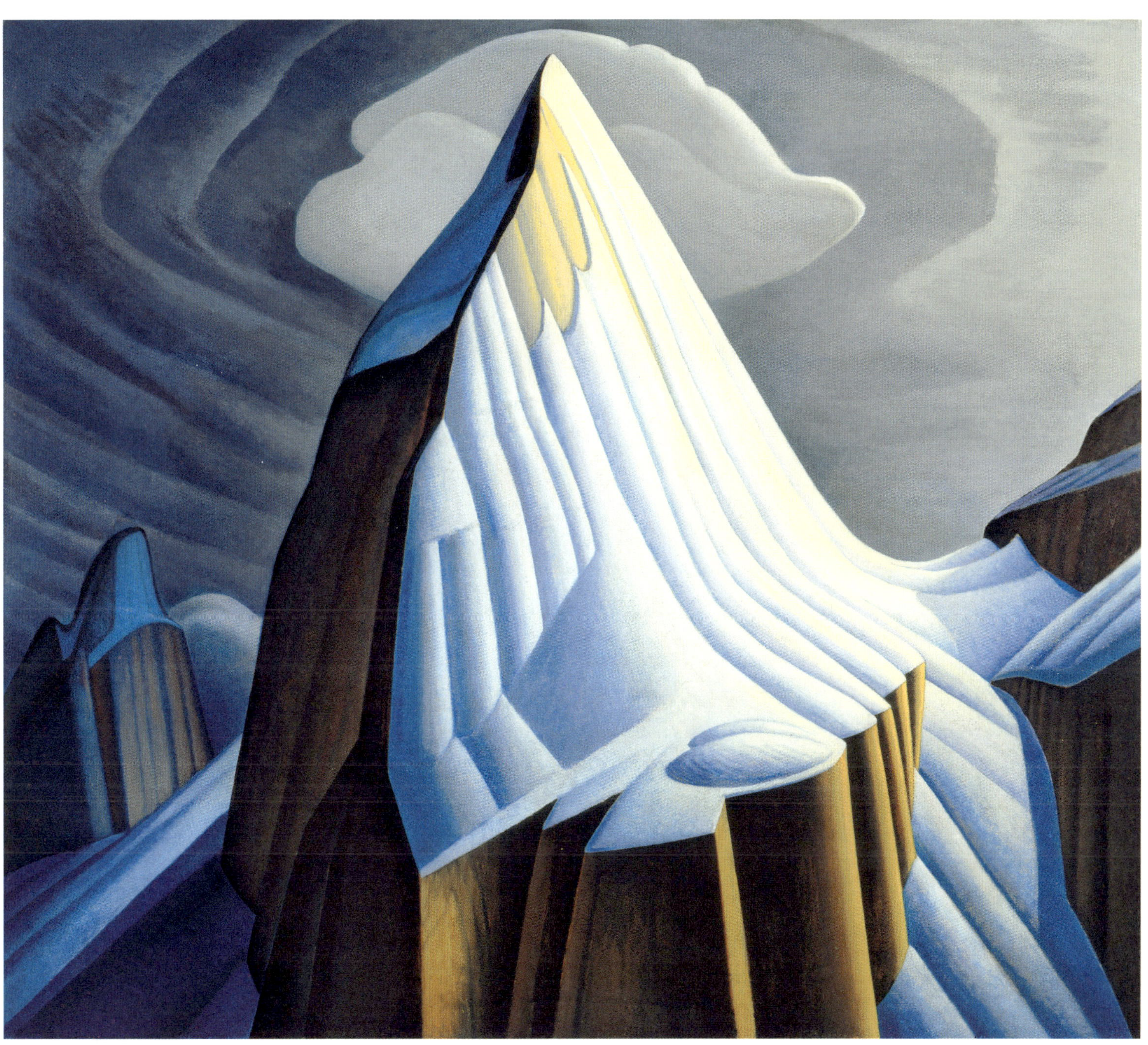

Welcoming Remarks

Canadian arts and culture reflect our country's
magnificent natural heritage and our dynamic, diverse,
and inclusive society. The Government of Canada
understands the importance of promoting Canadian
perspectives, telling Canadian stories, and sharing
our art with the world. This is why we are delighted to
be the Guest of Honour country and put our culture
in the spotlight at this year's Frankfurt Book Fair.

*Magnetic North: Imagining Canada in Painting, 1910–40*
presents visitors with an opportunity to experience
some of the most iconic and beloved Canadian paintings.
These images of distinctly Canadian landscapes, by
renowned painters such as the Group of Seven and their
contemporaries, broke with tradition and were key
in helping establish a new, uniquely Canadian style.

As Minister of Canadian Heritage, I thank everyone
who has made this celebration of Canadian art
possible. I invite you to enjoy this exhibition and learn
more about Canada's arts and culture.

The Honourable Steven Guilbeault
Minister of Canadian Heritage

With support from

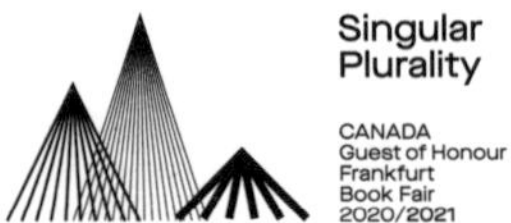
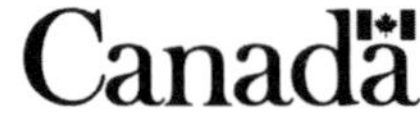
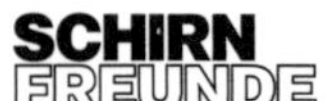

Additional support from

**Mann** Stiftung

Foreword

The early decades of the twentieth century were marked by artistic, economic, and social transformation in Canada and around the world. In Toronto, a group of young modern artists gathered to share their passion for Canada's magnificent landscape through powerful paintings of its distinctive natural features. Transformed by a newly awakened search for authenticity and pictorial experimentation, artists such as Tom Thomson, Lawren Harris, Franklin Carmichael, F. H. Varley, and J. E. H. MacDonald sought to create a new painting vocabulary for the young nation coming into its own cultural identity, together with fellow artists like Yvonne McKague Housser and Emily Carr from British Columbia.

From around 1910 and into the late 1930s, these enterprising artists ventured away from urban centers, such as Toronto and Montreal, and into the Canadian Shield to experience the sublime vistas and monumental rivers, hills, and forests around the Great Lakes, and further into northern Canada, the interior Northwest Coast, the Rocky Mountains, and the Arctic. In May 1920, they organized a historic exhibition under the name *The Group of Seven,* a collective determined to break from European stylistic traditions and reflect an increasingly Canadian sentiment. Together, their paintings imagined a mythical Canada, expansive and rugged—a symbolic identity that helped to shape Canadian settlers' sense of belonging.

In a seductive visual language, rather than portraying life, these paintings and sketches epitomize the dream of a "new" world, constructing the idyll of a vast landscape that countered the gritty reality of modern city life and expanding mining and forest industries. Such patterns of representation run deep in Canadian society, and these expressive paintings hold a powerful symbolic character within visual culture and contribute to a construction of Canadian nationhood shared around the world. While many Canadians still cherish these familiar images as emblems of national pride and self-representation, they are also criticized for their neglect of hard realities, such as violence toward and displacement of Indigenous communities and environmental devastation. As issues surrounding the construction of national identities and sovereign Indigenous relations continue to question modern landscape painting in Canada, this exhibition also brings into focus contemporary issues related to the land, nature, and impact of industry.

Through a contemporary lens, this artistic movement gains critical relevance that extends beyond their Canadian and historical significance.

When the Schirn Kunsthalle Frankfurt approached the Art Gallery of Ontario in Toronto (AGO) and the National Gallery of Canada in Ottawa (NGC), on the occasion of Canada's guest appearance at the Frankfurt Book Fair, with the idea of presenting an exhibition of the landscape paintings by the Group of Seven, both museums were thrilled. A great partnership developed across national borders. The German public now for the first time has the opportunity to become acquainted with these fascinating pictures in a comprehensive exhibition— made possible in part with generous loans from the AGO and the NGC. Both have accompanied these artists from the very beginning and now hold extensive collections of their works. Martina Weinhart, Curator at the Schirn, together with Georgiana Uhlyarik, Fredrik S. Eaton Curator, Canadian Art, at the AGO, and Katerina Atanassova, Senior Curator, Canadian Art, at the NGC, has devised a wonderful exhibition project that unites the European and Canadian perspectives, and reinterprets and recontextualizes the works of Canadian modernism from a contemporary perspective.

We would above all like to thank the artists Lisa Jackson and Caroline Monnet. Their films have made a vital contribution to this complex exhibition project and we greatly appreciate their trusting cooperation with us. We would also like to thank Rebecca Herlemann at the Schirn and Renée van der Avoird at the AGO for their commitment and valuable help in the preparation and realization of the exhibition and the catalogue.

The AGO and the NGC have played a major role in the realization of the exhibition, not only as partners and coproducers, but also through the generous provision of numerous excellent works on loan, for which the Schirn is extremely grateful. We also thank the lenders: McMichael Canadian Art Collection in Kleinburg; the Hart House Collection and the University College Art Collection at the Art Museum at the University of Toronto; Montreal Museum of Fine Arts; Museum London; the Robert McLaughlin Gallery in Oshawa; Victoria University in the University of Toronto; Firestone Collection of Canadian Art at the Ottawa Art Gallery; Vancouver Art Gallery; Judith and Norman Alix Art Gallery in Sarnia; the film archives at Library and Archives Canada / Bibliothèque et Archives Canada; Milestone Film & Video, Harrington

Park, New Jersey; Documentary Educational Resources, Watertown, Massachusetts; Moving Images Distribution Society, Vancouver; and the National Film Board of Canada.

We furthermore thank Canadian Heritage (PCH) for their support of and essential contributions to this project. Their early promise of providing substantial support for our project made the exhibition in Frankfurt am Main possible in the first place. At PCH we thank Francine Lefebvre in particular. In addition, we are grateful to the Mann Foundation, whose support has contributed to the publication of the extensive catalogue. Not least, the generous support of our 2,200 Schirn Friends has made this project possible in no small measure. We extend our thanks to Christian Strenger, chairman of the Schirn Friends, and to the entire board and the managing director Tamara von Clary. In addition, we sincerely thank the City of Frankfurt and, on behalf of all decision-makers, Mayor Peter Feldmann and Ina Hartwig, Head of the Department of Culture.

We are very grateful to Antonia Lagemann at the Schirn, as well as to Ivan Parisien (NGC) and Jim Shedden (AGO), for their support in the production of the catalogue. We also wish to thank all authors for their insightful contributions: Martina Weinhart and Georgiana Uhlyarik, Lisa Jackson and Colleen Hemphill, Caroline Monnet, Jeff Thomas, Ruth Phillips, and Carmen Robertson, as well as Rebecca Herlemann and Renée van der Avoird. We are grateful to Uta Hasekamp, Dawn Michelle d'Atri, Sarah Liss, and Valérie Mandia for their attentive and extensive editing of the German, English, and French catalogue editions, and to Amy Klement, Susie Hondl, and Bram Opstelten for their careful translations from German into English. We thank Marc Kappeler from Moiré for the creative catalogue design. Many thanks also to Prestel Publishing, and in particular to Katharina Haderer and Andrea Bartelt, for their excellent cooperation in the realization of the catalogue. We owe a debt of gratitude to the design agency VERY, Frankfurt, for the coherent graphics of the exhibition and to Marc Ulm from buero.us for the creative exhibition architecture.

We express our particular thanks to the AGO's Chief Curator, Julian Cox, and Chief of Exhibitions and Collections, Christy Thompson; Kitty Scott, Deputy Director and Chief Curator at NGC, along with Isabelle Corriveau, Director Exhibitions & Outreach, and Christopher Régimbal, Senior Exhibition Manager; and at the Schirn Kunsthalle Frankfurt to Esther Schlicht as Deputy Director and Head of Exhibitions. All of these individuals have been instrumental in facilitating and overseeing the project.

The Schirn would like to thank its entire team for their tireless dedication and commitment to the realization of the exhibition and catalogue: Karin Grüning, Elke Walter, and Luise Leyer for the complex organization of the transport, as well as the installation and dismantling of the exhibition; Christian Teltz and Oliver Taschke for technical support, and Anna Noll as assistant to the Head of Exhibitions; Andreas Gundermann and the mounting team, as well as the conservators Stefanie Gundermann and Susanne Silbernagel. In addition, we thank Luise Bachmann, Heike Stumpf, Isabel Reiche, and Angelika Schäfer for the marketing and design of the advertising campaign; Johanna Pulz, Julia Bastian, Elisabeth Pallentin, and Isabelle Hammer for the press work; Antonia Lagemann with Anuschka Berthelius for the coordination and production of this publication and for editing the Schirn Magazine. We would like to thank Chantal Eschenfelder with Simone Boscheinen, Laura Heeg, Olga Schaetz, and Anna Haag for the accompanying educational program; we also thank Ute Seiffert with Alena Flemming for the development and coordination of the events at the Schirn, and Julia Lange and Hannah Ruiz for their work with our sponsors and partners. We would also like to thank Heike Berndt, Tanja Mayer, and Boris Deckelmann at the Schirn's administrative office, as well as Samira Koch and Andrea Canthal for their assistance in a variety of matters. We sincerely thank the messenger Stefan Schell, and Rosaria La Tona with her cleaning team, as well as Bettina Beyermann and Josef Härig at the reception, and all other colleagues at the Schirn—and equally all colleagues at AGO and NGC who were involved in the elaborate preparation and implementation of this project.

We are delighted that, following the presentation in Frankfurt, the exhibition will travel to Kunsthal Rotterdam. Our sincere thanks go to Nathanja van Dijk, Director, and Eva van Diggelen, Curator, for the excellent cooperation.

All that remains is for us to wish the visitors of the exhibition, as well as the readers of the catalogue, an unforgettable encounter with some of the most beautiful and interesting works of Canadian art.

Philipp Demandt
Director
Schirn Kunsthalle Frankfurt

Stephan Jost
Michael and Sonja Koerner Director, and CEO
Art Gallery of Ontario

Sasha Suda
Director and CEO
National Gallery of Canada

# The Will to Wilderness
# An Introduction

Vast expanses, deep, dark forests where you can still get lost, high mountain ranges, majestic wilderness, the snow, the permanent ice of the Arctic, canoeing past icy-blue glaciers, trips through remote areas lasting for hours, ultimate adventures in a world otherwise dominated by humans and shaped for their purposes—in short: Canada (or how most Europeans imagine Canada). It is a place of longing for those who want to experience nature in a more primal form. A similar Canada of the imaginary was devised in the early twentieth century by a group of artists who had come together in urban Toronto in 1920 under the name Group of Seven. Seven men with one goal—to portray the beauty, the sublimity, and also the picturesque quality of the country in their own distinct way, placing it at the service of the young nation, striving to encourage the formation of a unifying identity.

It was their intention to use painting to declare their independence from Europe, to break away from traditions, and to establish their own national school of landscape painting. "Art in Canada in so far as it is Canadian is an upstart art. Its source is not the same as the art of Europe," wrote Lawren Harris, a key player in the Group of Seven.[1] The Algonquin School, as the Group had previously been called, turned away from the cities and sought its distinctive profile in the vastness of the landscape. It was a movement away from Paris, from London, from Berlin, in this case toward Toronto, or rather toward Northern Ontario, Algoma, Georgian Bay, the Rocky Mountains, or the Arctic. They organized trips, alone or in groups, in a converted boxcar or by canoe, and they would camp, fish, and hike (figs. 5-12). The artist as a bohemian—far from it, even though members of the Group shared a studio building in Toronto. "These men are robust intellectuals. They exploded studio myths and made the outdoors their workshop," reported a critic at the time.[2] Tom Thomson, the friend who drowned under mysterious circumstances in July 1917, and who had been painting in Algonquin Park, where he worked as a fire ranger and guide at the same time and spent spring to fall in nature, became the movement's poster boy. The artists would now be real tough guys who carved their way through the undergrowth and did not waste their time with five o'clock teas. The motto for this type of artist was: "less of a studio more of the forest."[3]

The resulting paintings represent excerpts of individual experiences of nature for which the Group of Seven for decades was both revered and criticized in Canada; landscape paintings that almost every child would know, and that make up the core of the work of these artists. And yes, not least of all, images that for many represent the epitome of Canada. This widely portrayed country, however, became a (more or less) independent state only in 1867 and has been founded on a long colonial history. For thousands of years before the arrival of the first settlers from Europe, it had been the territory of Indigenous peoples. Thus, the Group of Seven, with their images of sublime mountains and unspoiled nature, created the romantic vision of a preindustrial retreat, stylizing the land as an uninhabited wilderness—*terra nullius*. European powers had already used a similar approach as a legal basis for colonizing this no man's land populated only by "primitive" peoples. The Group of Seven created not only beautiful landscapes, but their practice of excluding Indigenous peoples from the images also denied the paintings any social reality. Their painting is thus certainly both product and testimony of cultural hegemony within postcolonial society.

# The Value of the Woods

The forest as idea and ideal has many roots. "We can never have enough of Nature,"[4] wrote the American Henry David Thoreau, who, with his radical experiment of spending a year alone far from civilization, exemplified the dream of a simple life in nature. Like that of few other nineteenth-century philosophers, Thoreau's thinking in and about nature had a decisive influence on the Group of Seven.[5] "A taste for the beautiful is most cultivated out of doors, where there is no house and no housekeeper,"[6] he wrote in his account *Walden*—considered a cult book by some and still to this day a classic of counterculture. Thoreau wanted to escape the increasing hustle and bustle of the industrial age and concentrate on the essential things in life. Getting along with little, while searching for meaning in nature and giving it expression, was his main motivation. He formulated his belief with passion: "I wish to speak a word for Nature, for absolute freedom and wildness, as contrasted with a freedom and culture merely civil …"[7] The Group of Seven's aesthetics includes reflections of these ideas; the rather typical images by its members Arthur Lismer, J. E. H. MacDonald, F. H. Varley, Franklin Carmichael, Lawren Harris, and A.Y. Jackson are removed from civilization and quite emotive, as are the outdoor sketches by Tom Thomson and the forest views by Emily Carr, who was close to the Group not just in these works.

Like Thoreau, his friend Ralph Waldo Emerson also called for a life in harmony with nature. Both shared an anti-materialistic worldview. The combination of the imagery with the transcendental, found primarily in works by Lawren Harris, but also in those of Emily Carr, is consistent with Emerson's thinking, whereby nature is always seen in alliance with the divine in which humans can participate through observation. Harris's towering mountains reflect Emerson's aesthetics of the sublime, through which, when he looks at nature, "the Universal Being" transmits itself into his consciousness.[8] Nature allows us to sense the absolute. And Emerson was certain: "In the woods, we return to reason and faith."[9]

Emerson also wrote: "Art cannot rival this pomp of purple and gold."[10] But it seems that the painters of the Group of Seven were willing to take up such a challenge and set themselves the goal of depicting Emerson's "nature glorious with form, color, and motion."[11] Indeed, it is precisely the representations of woods, such as Franklin Carmichael's *Autumn Hillside* (1920, p.39), A.Y. Jackson's *Lake Superior Country* (1924, p.41), or Tom Thomson's *Autumn's Garland* (winter 1915–16, p.51), in particular, which are like fireworks of brilliant colors and shapes. Their depiction of the variety of forms and colors of the autumnal trees in the depths of the dense woodland is striking and impressive. Emily Carr, similarly captivated by the poetics of the forest, said of herself: "I spent all the time I could in the forest."[12] She captured her particular sensitivity to nature in vivid pictorial representations of the forests of British Columbia, for which she was also able to find appropriate words: "still forest, black-green and mysterious, layer upon layer of marching trees, climbing trees, trees burned, trees fallen, myriad millions of trees and loneliness intertwisted."[13]

# Landscape as a Construct

In the paintings by the Group of Seven, we quite often encounter, in addition to the deep forest, the image of a single tree growing out of rocky terrain. It defies storms, the cold, the elements, and withstands all kinds of adversity. This is the case in Tom Thomson's *The West Wind* (winter 1916–17, p.223), but also in its counterpart *The Jack Pine* (winter 1916–17), or in Arthur Lismer's *A September Gale, Georgian Bay* (1921). F. H. Varley introduced this motif in 1921 with *Stormy Weather, Georgian Bay*. As the cultural chronicler David P. Silcox declared: "Thomson's great paintings *The West Wind* and *The Jack Pine* are the visual equivalent of a national anthem, for they have come to represent the spirit of the whole country."[14]

The German Romantic artist Caspar David Friedrich likewise painted his symbolic landscapes against the background of a transcendent and meaningful experience of nature. Connecting the actual landscape with the possibility of using it as a symbol proved a momentous discovery in the history of art. Yet, the political was already inherent in German Romanticism, and a tree in Friedrich's work would not only reflect loneliness, but could also be read as a national symbol of freedom (fig.1). Time and again, landscape elements were inserted as political metaphors. "In the literature and journalism of the late Enlightenment, winter, glaciers and ice were frequent symbols of the old despotic order, which would inevitably be followed, in accordance with the laws of nature, by the thaw and the warming sun of liberty."[15] Martin Warnke emphasizes the political aspects of the depiction of any landscape, one that offers a wealth of projection possibilities: "… permanent topographical phenomena too, which to an enlightened view might appear 'sublime,' were often credited with political significance."[16] This can also be linked to the majestic mountains of Lawren Harris. Warnke points out: "Transferred to the political plane, 'sublimity' becomes the possibility of binding people emotionally through a show of greatness and force, making them subservient,

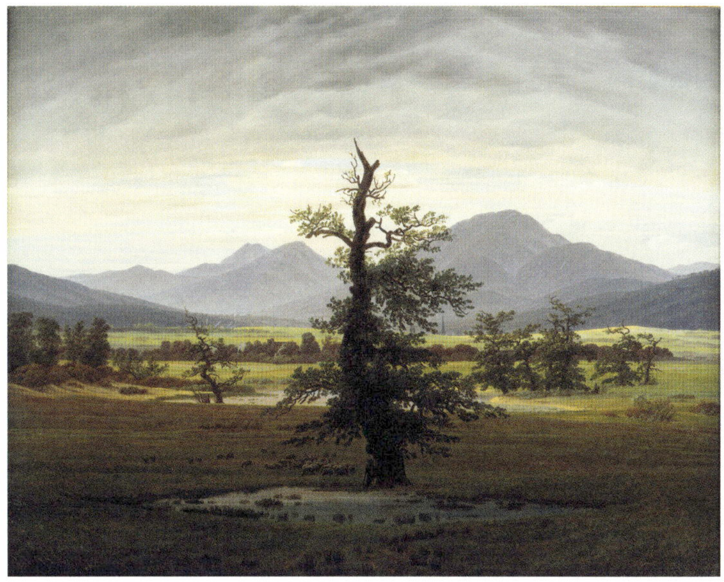

Fig. 1—Caspar David Friedrich, *Der einsame Baum*
(The Lonely Tree), 1822, oil on canvas, 55 × 71 cm, Staatliche Museen
zu Berlin, Alte Nationalgalerie

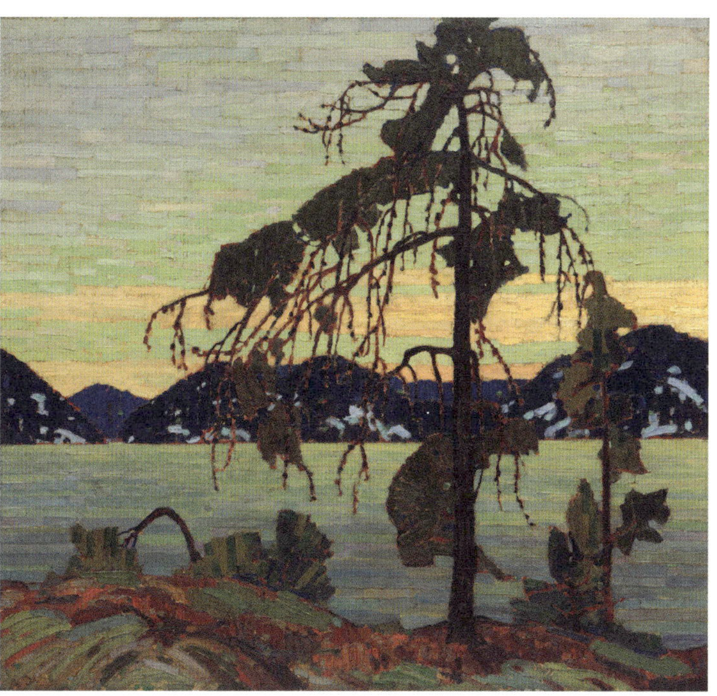

Fig. 2—Tom Thomson, *The Jack Pine,* winter 1916–17, oil on canvas,
127.9 × 139.8 cm, National Gallery of Canada, Ottawa

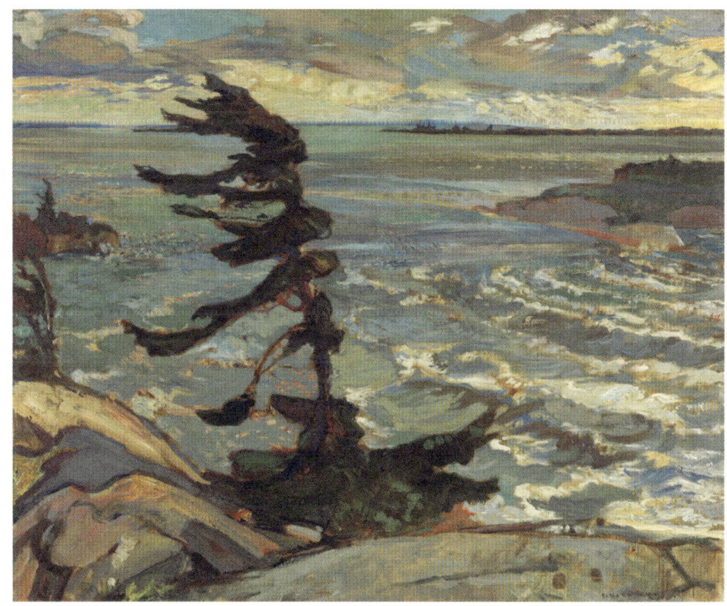

Fig. 3—F. H. Varley, *Stormy Weather, Georgian Bay,* 1921,
oil on canvas, 132.6 × 162.8 cm, National Gallery of Canada, Ottawa

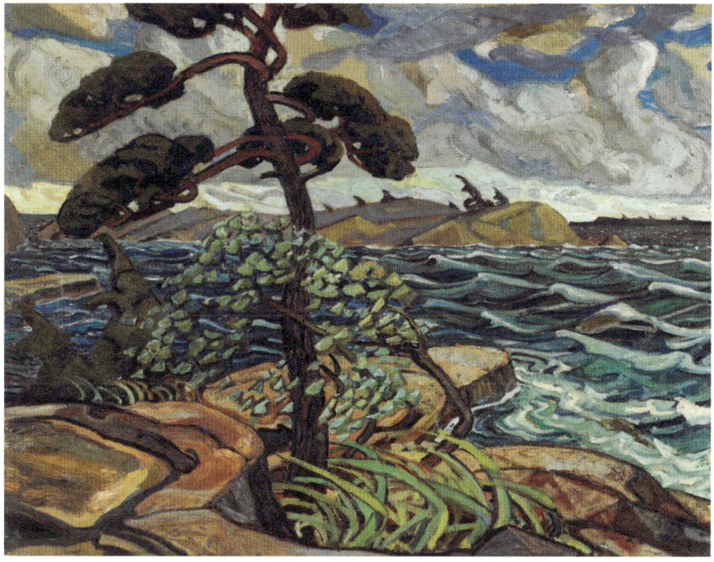

Fig. 4—Arthur Lismer, *A September Gale, Georgian Bay,* 1921,
oil on canvas, 122.4 × 163 cm, National Gallery of Canada, Ottawa

psychically if not legally."[17] The American expert on visual culture W. J. T. Mitchell denies landscape representation any innocence when he writes: "Landscape is a particular historical formation associated with European imperialism."[18]

The Group of Seven is certainly not alone in its patriotic aspiration to establish a (Canadian) identity as a national school of landscape painting. Even if these artists wanted to distance themselves from the European tradition of the nineteenth century, their art was nevertheless still deeply rooted in it. In the neighboring settler nation of the United States, the Hudson River School had developed a comparable connection between nature and nation. These artists, too, used the exploration of the American landscape as an expression of cultural and national identity. Much like the artists of the Group of Seven, they roamed through nature with their sketchbooks, in their case the area around the Hudson River or the Catskills and Adirondacks, with the intention of establishing an American way of looking at the landscape.

# Art for the Nation

Time and again, there have been exhibition projects and publications on the Group of Seven that have examined its national character and its widely held claim to representation in an affirmative but also critical manner.[19] The Group wanted to create "Canadian Art for the Canadians."[20] This had already been tenaciously asserted in their early exhibitions. One of the advocates of an art in the service of the nation was A. Y. Jackson: "The great purpose of landscape is to make us at home in our own country."[21] Exhibitions were organized to this end throughout the country. It is also interesting in this context that the work of the Group of Seven is often discussed from a topographical perspective. That is not altogether surprising, since most of their work titles consist of a place name, a region, or an area with a landscape

formation, and they are often completed by a season. Lawren Harris emphasized the complex ambition behind the Group's travels: "That adventure, as it turned out, was to include the exploration of the whole country for its expressive and creative possibilities in painting."[22] Looking at the works of the Group of Seven, the impression of a visual cartography of Canada tends to quite readily come to mind. The individual landscape painting, however, is far more than a precisely, or less precisely, reproduced section of a specific topography. As a whole, the paintings are meant to combine both patriotic and aesthetic goals, with the aim of reaching the largest possible audience. Clearly, this approach mirrored the aesthetics of the Group. These artists created, if you will, the Pop Art of their time. This art was intended to be anti-elitist and easily understood by everyone, even though the target audience was the English-speaking part of Canada.[23] The images of the Group of Seven share a boldness and an immediacy—linked by their goals, ideals, themes, and motifs instead of by a unified style rooted in Post-Impressionism, Art Nouveau, Expressionism, or Romanticism.

# Wilderness and the "True North"

Margaret Atwood noted how little the Group of Seven's paintings had in common with European landscapes, pointing to the wildness of nature in Canada: "And these paintings are not landscape paintings. Because there aren't any landscapes up there, not in the old, tidy European sense, with a gentle hill, a curving river, a cottage, a mountain in the background, a golden evening sky. Instead there's a tangle, a receding maze, in which you can become lost almost as soon as you step off the path … And the trees themselves are hardly trees; they are currents of energy, charged with violent color."[24]

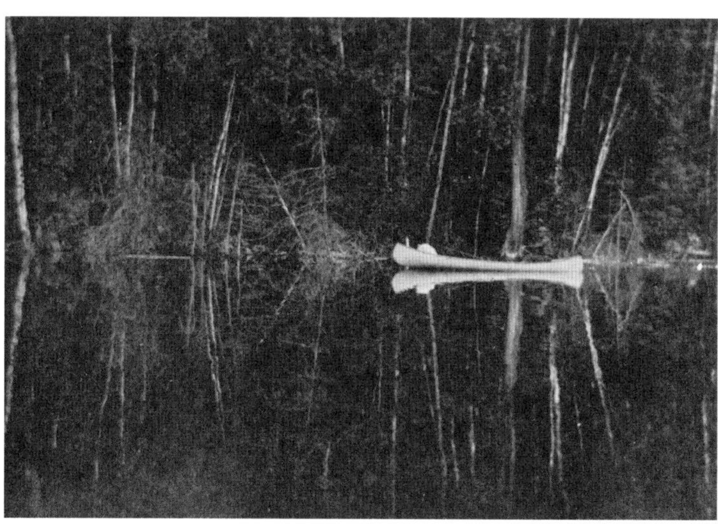

Fig. 5—Tom Thomson, 1914

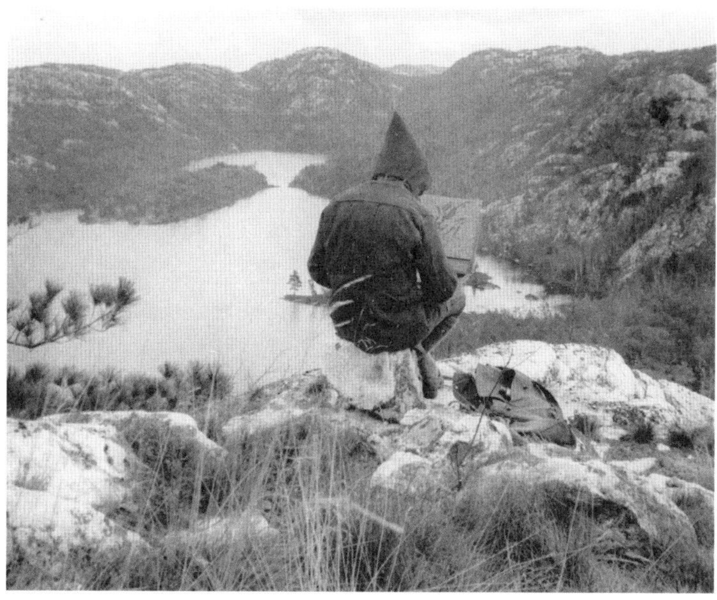

Fig. 6—Franklin Carmichael at Grace Lake, Killarney Provincial Park, Ontario, October 1935

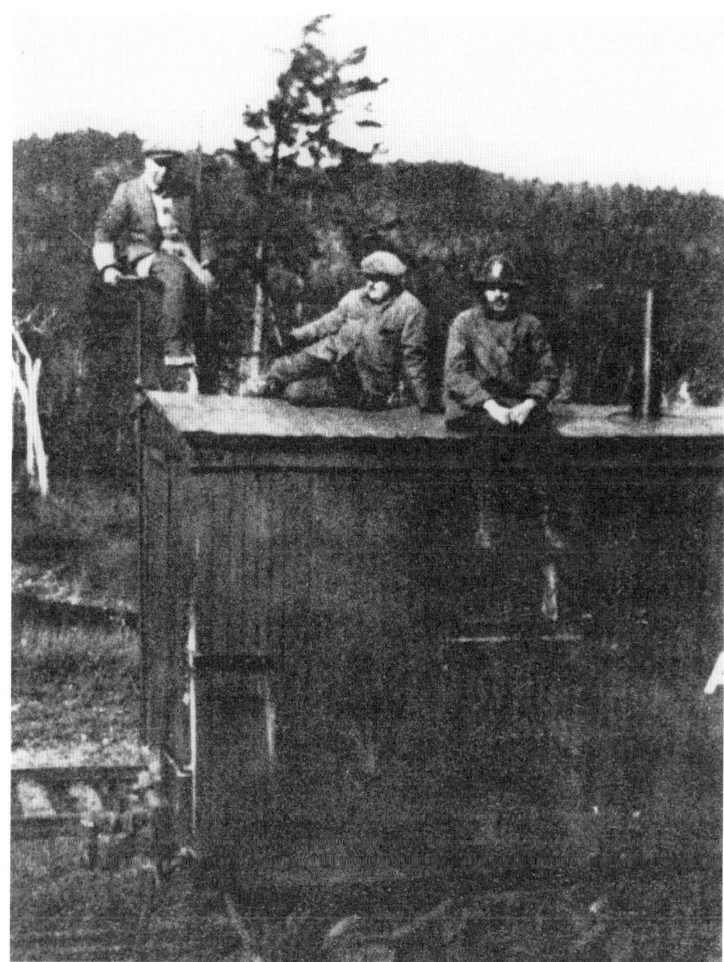

Fig. 7—A.Y. Jackson, Frank Johnston, and Lawren Harris on the boxcar, which the artists used for several trips to the Algoma District in Northern Ontario as of 1918, ca. 1920

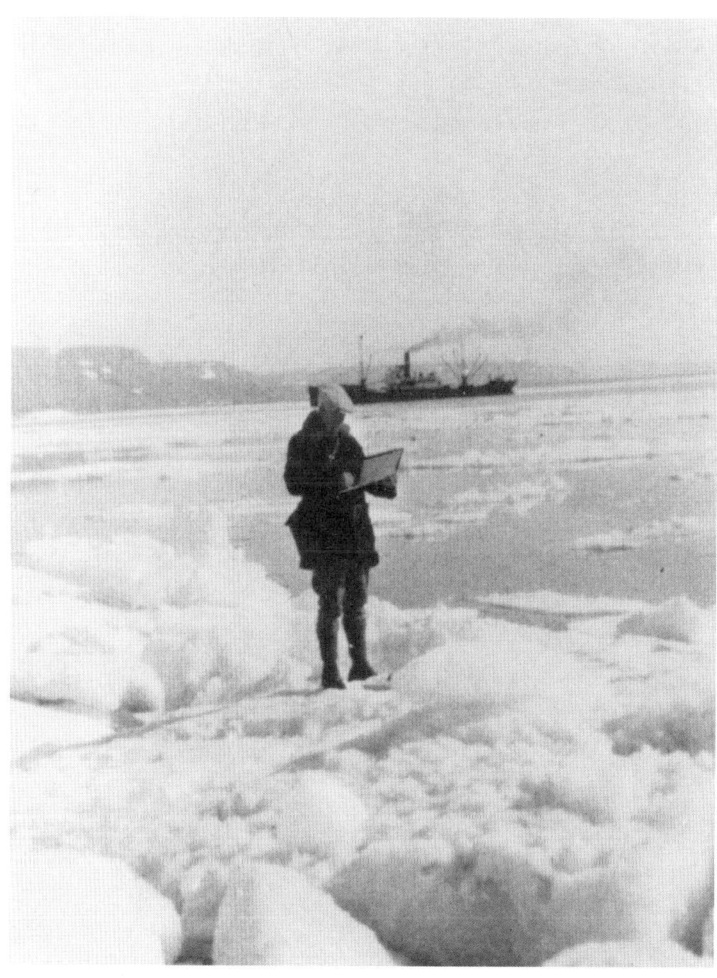

Fig. 8—A.Y. Jackson in the Arctic, the supply ship *S. S. Beothic* in the background, on which the artist traveled, 1927

Wilderness is a rarity today. It is threatened by man, population growth, environmental destruction, global warming—in short: it is an invaluable treasure. At the time of the Group of Seven, large sections of Canada were sparsely populated, and in 1915, the *Atlas of Canada*[25] still indicated a population density of only one person per square mile even in the southern half of the country. People lived mostly along the coasts, the rivers, and in the eastern provinces. "Canada's vastness took my breath away," wrote Emily Carr in her memoirs.[26] Yet with its timber industry and the exploitation of its rich mineral resources, Canada was nonetheless still a budding industrial nation. The seemingly boundless expanses of the North American continent seemed to offer the country two things: a glorious future of economic prosperity and the preservation of the last impenetrable wilderness. The wilderness and the "True North" are powerful fictions within the Canadian self-conception. "We are in the fringe of the great North and its living whiteness, its loneliness and replenishment, its resignations and release, its call and answer—its cleansing rhythms," wrote Lawren Harris.[27] And elsewhere: "This emphasis of the north in the Canadian character that is born of the spirit of the north and reflects it, has profoundly affected its art and its art in turn clarifies and enhances the quality of Canadian consciousness."[28] The North is visually defined by icebergs, majestic peaks, trees, colors, and cold light. John O'Brian quite aptly calls the respective paintings "wildercentric."[29]

In the Group of Seven's world of ideas, wilderness is placed alongside the "True North" as a realm of possibility. Indeed, wilderness is fascinating. "Life consists with wildness. The most alive is the wildest,"[30] Thoreau had written and clairvoyantly predicted that "in Wildness is the preservation of the World."[31] The exploration of wilderness in art as an experiential space reflects this fascination, yet at the same time it creates a stylized counter-world and embodies a complex relationship with reality—particularly when considering that the Group of Seven's access to the "wilderness" had already been facilitated by modern technology and transport. So the question remains: What does this imagined wilderness stand for? Similar to the landscape, it, too, is a cultural construct of longing and projection, but also of coveting. A.Y. Jackson's *Terre Sauvage* (1913, p.7), the depiction of an autumnal scene at Georgian Bay, is one of the most famous pictures claiming a wilderness already in its title, although the area—as O'Brian emphasized—had been used for tourism even then and was dotted with summer houses.[32] Jackson brought the scene to a point, with a blank space resulting from the removal of any signs of human civilization, making it an almost extramundane, timeless allegory of the North.

# Land(scape)

The depiction of a deserted landscape insists on being seen as wilderness, and not as a cultural landscape. Long before today, the Group of Seven had been reproached for creating a myth about the Canadian wilderness, and the evocation of a Canadian identity that excluded Indigenous peoples who had lived on the land for thousands of years. In the 1960s, the perception of the Group's paintings had changed, demanding that they be viewed from social and political perspectives. As Charles Hill already remarked: "The appropriation of Native culture by associates of the Group of Seven has been criticized, and their depiction of an unpeopled landscape described as a weapon in the cultural genocide of the aboriginal population."[33]

The voices of Indigenous critics have become more insistent in the course of decolonization. They rightly oppose the portrayal of Canada as an unspoiled country. The Anishinaabe filmmaker Lisa Jackson calls them the "territories now called Canada."[34] "Nothing about us without us"—this is the maxim under which Indigenous people resist the representation and appropriation of their culture by non-Indigenous artists, which is why, for instance, Emily Carr's depictions of totems have been the subject of controversial debate since the 1990s.

"There is no word for 'landscape' in any of the languages of the ancient one still spoken. In Ojibwa whenever the word *uhke* is pronounced, it is more an exaltation of humanness than a declaration of property," writes the Saulteaux-Anishinaabe artist Robert Houle.[35] Today, from a historical distance, we view modernism in a new light. The paintings of the Group of Seven are legendary, and they embody the myth of Canada. However, myths are projections and do indeed harbor ideological pitfalls. A critical view of certain myths should now be a matter of course. Following such a change of perspective, the landscape becomes the land that tells a different story.

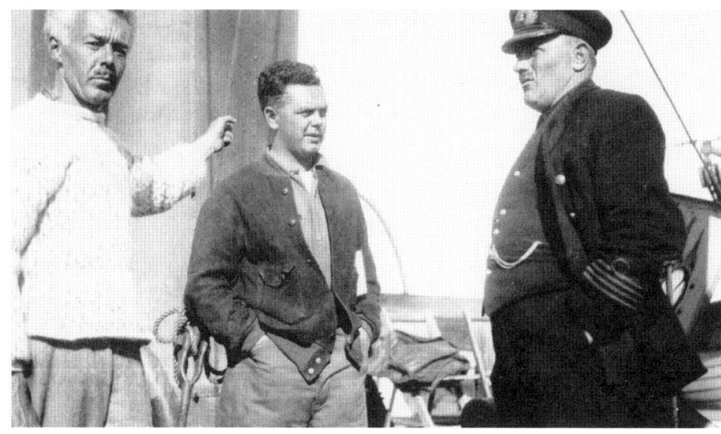

Fig. 9—Lawren Harris, unknown person, and the captain of the
*S. S. Beothic* during Harris's and Jackson's second trip to the Arctic, 1930

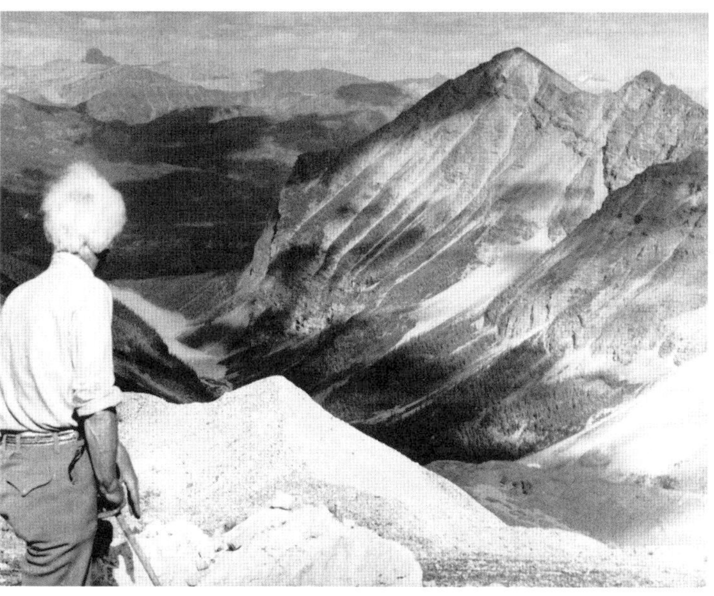

Fig. 10—Lawren Harris above Lake Louise at Banff National Park,
Canadian Rocky Mountains, August 1946

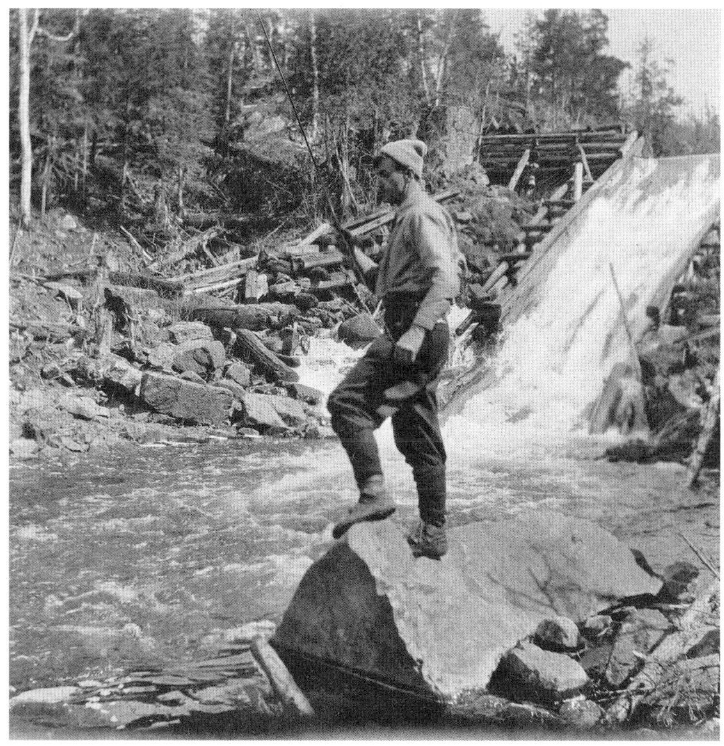

Fig. 11—Tom Thomson at Tea Lake Dam, Algonquin Provincial Park, 1916

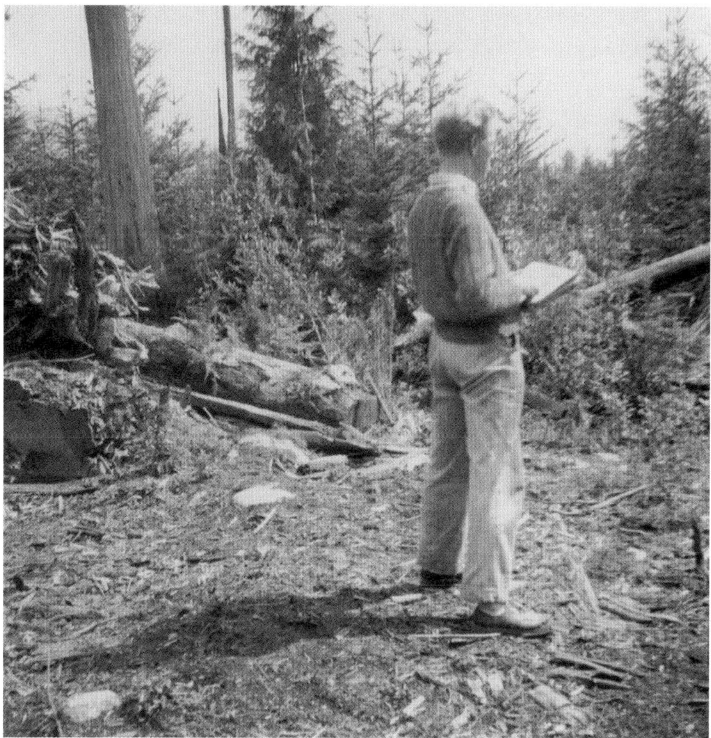

Fig. 12—F. H. Varley in Lynn Valley, British Columbia, 1937

In the historical dialogue, both overlap and comment on one another. It should remain our task to continually re-examine the archive. In this way, the blind spots become visible in the images, and with them the human being in the landscape, which is not a landscape but the land.

1—Lawren Harris, "Creative Art and Canada," *Yearbook of the Arts in Canada (1928–29)*, p. 184.
2—Blodwen Davies, "The Canadian Group of Seven," *The American Magazine of Art* 25, no. 1 (July 1932), p. 19.
3—Gregory Clark, "Canadian Artists Must Cut Loose from Old World Ideals," *Toronto Star Weekly*, December 2, 1914; quoted from Charles C. Hill, *The Group of Seven: Art for a Nation*, exh. cat. National Gallery of Canada, Ottawa, Art Gallery of Ontario, Toronto, et al. (Toronto: NGC, 1995), p. 58.
4—Henry David Thoreau, *Walden* (London: Penguin Classics, 2016), p. 295.
5—One of the painters of the Group of Seven, J. E. H. MacDonald, named his son after Thoreau.
6—Thoreau, *Walden*, p. 36.
7—Henry David Thoreau, "Walking," *Atlantic Monthly* (June 1862), https://www.theatlantic.com/magazine/archive/1862/06/walking/304674/ (accessed in November 2020).
8—R. W. Emerson, *Nature* (Boston and Cambridge: James Munroe & Company, 1849), p. 8.
9—Ibid.
10—Ibid., p. 17.
11— Ibid., p. 38.
12—Emily Carr, *Growing Pains: The Autobiography of Emily Carr* (Oxford: Oxford University Press, 1946), p. 306.
13—Ibid., p. 113.
14—David P. Silcox, *The Group of Seven and Tom Thomson* (Richmond Hill, ON: Firefly Books, 2003), pp. 49–50.
15—Martin Warnke, *Political Landscape: The Art History of Nature*, trans. David McLintock (London: Reaktion Books, 1994), p. 95.
16—Ibid.
17—Ibid.
18—W. J. T. Mitchell, "Imperial Landscape," in *Landscape and Power*, ed. W. J. T. Mitchell (Chicago and London: University of Chicago Press, 2002), p. 5.
19—See Hill, *The Group of Seven: Art for a Nation*. Critically examined in: John O'Brian and Peter White, eds., *Beyond Wilderness: The Group of Seven, Canadian Identity, and Contemporary Art* (Montreal: McGill-Queen's University Press, 2007).
20—Dennis Reid, *The Group of Seven*, exh. cat. The National Gallery of Canada, Ottawa, and Musée des Beaux-Arts de Montréal (Ottawa: NGC, 1970), p. 12.
21—Quoted from ibid., p. 132.
22—Lawren Harris, "The Story of the Group of Seven" (1964), in Joan Murray, *The Best of the Group of Seven* (Edmonton: Hurting Publishers, 1984), p. 26.
23—Charles C. Hill, in Hill, *The Group of Seven: Art for a Nation*, p. 20.
24—Margaret Atwood, "Death by Landscape," in *Wilderness Tips* (New York: Doubleday, 1991), pp. 97–118, esp. pp. 117–18.
25—Charles C. Hill, in Hill, *The Group of Seven: Art for a Nation*, p. 23.
26—Carr, *Growing Pains*, p. 112.
27—Lawren Harris, "Revelation of Art in Canada," *The Canadian Theosophist*, July 15, 1926, pp. 85f.
28—Harris, "Creative Art and Canada," p. 182.
29—John O'Brian, in O'Brian and White, *Beyond Wilderness*, p. 24.
30—Thoreau, "Walking."
31—Ibid.
32—John O'Brian, in O'Brian and White, *Beyond Wilderness*, p. 25.
33—Charles C. Hill, "Introduction," in Hill, *The Group of Seven: Art for a Nation*, p. 16.
34—See p. 114 in this catalogue.
35—Robert Houle, "The Spiritual Legacy of the Ancient Ones," in *Land, Spirit, Power: First Nations at the National Gallery of Canada*, exh. cat. National Gallery of Canada, Ottawa (Ottawa: NGC, 1992), pp. 60f.

On the Stylization of the Word Indigenous
The term "Indigenous" is frequently capitalized—by Indigenous peoples who assume a sovereign position within settler societies (see p. 106 in this volume), and by the non-Indigenous who wish to express solidarity. The authors of this catalogue have capitalized the term as well.

# Raw Materials Canada's Painted Landscapes

In the early 1910s, a few young Canadian artists began painting alone and together in the rural outskirts of Toronto and then further north in Algonquin Park, Ontario's first provincial park.[1] They gained momentum, purpose, and notoriety, regularly exhibiting their work in Toronto, Ottawa, and Montreal, through established artists' societies and professional clubs. Their development was interrupted by the First World War and personal tragedies—in particular, the death of the artist Tom Thomson in 1917. A woodsman and painter with limited formal training, Thomson had inspired these artists to paint in Algonquin, to spend extended time in the woods, camping and sketching. His adventurous spirit and exuberant visions, along with the mysterious circumstance of his drowning in Canoe Lake, fed the myth of a new type of Canadian artist: heroic, bold, self-reliant, and deeply connected to nature. Emboldened by the shared artistic vision to develop "a way of painting dictated by Canada itself,"[2] these artists joined together and sought inspiration on camping trips, in the hardwood forests and along the shores of glacial bays and lakes in Ontario's north, surveying lands scarred by fires and decades of logging.

Around 1918, and continuing for the next four years, Lawren Harris, along with artists who would soon form the Group of Seven—J. E. H. MacDonald, A. Y. Jackson, Frank Johnston, Arthur Lismer, Franklin Carmichael, and A. J. Casson—spent a month each autumn exploring the Algoma region and painting the expansive views.[3] Located in Northern Ontario on the north shores of Lake Superior and Lake Huron, Algoma is a vast area of old-growth forests, rivers, and lakes, as well as rich mineral deposits.[4] The Algoma Central Railway, built to support mining and logging in the region since the late nineteenth century, offered a network of train tracks that facilitated the travels and camping of these artists. They had an old boxcar refurbished with windows, water tanks, and cooking, eating, and sleeping areas.[5] The artists used "a one-man handcar" to move along the tracks, a canoe for the lakes, and they camped in a tent even in below-freezing weather.[6] As Harris recalled in 1948, in Algoma they found "a wild richness and clarity of colour" and skies of "singing expansiveness and sublimity." It was "a rugged, wild land packed with an amazing variety of subjects … a veritable paradise for the creative adventurer in paint in the Canadian North."[7] Ontario's northern lake and forests energized what Harris characterized as "the creative life … [that] resulted from a love of the land."[8]

Landscape is the "raw material" of Canada.[9] Graham McInnes, author of *A Short History of Canadian Art,* employed this industrial terminology in 1939 to explain and champion the persistent appeal of landscape to artists who sought to establish a distinct school of Canadian painting in an international context. The creative individuals whom McInnes identified as the first to be "painting Canada … through Canadian eyes"[10] were those associated with the Group of Seven. It is his invocation to "raw" natural resources in reference to art that points to the dual source and conduit of creative productivity for these Canadian "artistic pioneers."[11] More explicitly, this assessment captures the paradox at the core of imagining Canada in painting: nature and industry. Canada's history of industrialization frames the country's landscapes.

These artists officially launched their association in May 1920 at the Art Museum of Toronto (today, Art Gallery of Ontario), with the first Group of Seven exhibition. In the accompanying brochure, they put forward their shared vision of a kind of art that would be "original and vital," work that would effectively capture the ethos of the fast-growing nation.[12] As the Group further elaborated in 1922, "the thought of today cannot be expressed by the language of yesterday … new material demands new methods."[13]

In McInnes's account, written six years after the Group disbanded in 1933, he contended that it was the Group's fervent presence and bold vision that had laid the principal ideals of a unique Canadian art.[14] The notion of establishing a distinct national art has since been critically unraveled and discredited as enforcing and advancing the colonial ideology of assimilation and extinction of Indigenous life and culture in Canada. In the early 1900s, these foundations were professed to be necessary and essential to the process of the new nation articulating its own sense of autonomous identity and national unity.[15] Indeed, in those foundational decades, as the Canadian art historian Joyce Zemans explained, "National unity, the promotion of a common understanding of Canadian life, along with the expression of 'national feeling' and vigorous Canadianism would be the motivating factors in the establishment of each new national institution at this time. The visual arts … were believed to have the capacity to mold public taste, to create proper moral values and identify the basic truths required to establish a sense of nationhood."[16]

From the 1920s through the early 1930s, the Group of Seven artists actively participated in this process of "molding" through their paintings and exhibitions, as well as writings and lectures that framed and articulated their vision of the role of art and the artist in Canada. In their second exhibition brochure in 1921, the members of the Group declared their belief "whole-heartedly in the land" and in "the artist … as a real civilizing factor in the national life."[17] In 1928, in his essay "Creative Art and Canada," Lawren Harris hauntingly elaborated his notions of Canadian art as founded on a "oneness with the informing spirit of the whole land" and the artist as the creator of "an art and home for the soul of a people."[18] As these artists traveled across the country, they sought views and compositions that captured these ideals and manifested the Canadian "spirit."

Paintings such as A. Y. Jackson's *Terre Sauvage* (1913, p. 7), Thomson's *The West Wind* (winter 1916–17, p. 223), and Harris's *Beaver Swamp, Algoma* (1920, p. 43), were deemed by artists and writers to exemplify the nation's aspirations as strong, resolute, and majestic.[19] The row of young pines coming out of igneous rock reaching toward a clearing sky in Jackson's canvas speaks to the determination of growth and survival in the face of adversity. Harris's screen of trees depicted in changing light evokes a primordial territory filled with potential. The image of the solitary tree, exemplified in *The West Wind* as silhouetted against a darkening sky and threatening clouds, its roots clinging to rock on the edge of a cold lake, is emblematic of the rough yet steadfast Canadian identity.

Many Group artists, as well as Thomson, were trained and earned a living as graphic designers working for Grip Limited, a commercial design firm in Toronto. This advertising background made them keenly aware of the ways in which disseminating their images and participating in popular events could serve as critical channels to connect with as wide of an audience as possible. It not only informed them of the potential inherent in mass distribution and popular appeal, but it made them acutely aware of the ways in which distilled images and symbols could be harnessed to communicate ideological and aspirational notions, translating images of place into a sense of belonging to a nation. Astutely, the Group extended their reach through the wide distribution of commercial reproductions of their work,[20] as well as through affiliations with national enterprises such as the development of a trans-Canada railway, in partic-

ular as it expanded in Western Canada,[21] and by securing representation at world fairs. As Canada increasingly thrived industrially and economically, so did the Group's ambitions extend beyond Toronto. McInnes credited the young nation's "rapid industrialization and development" with contributing to the production of a "national" art.[22]

To fully grasp this, the history of this art must be traced through that of the resources whose extraction helped shape the nation—and inscribed its symbolic narrative. Put another way, land and water are the raw materials of Canada. Its lakes and rivers are extensive, cold, and fresh, marking the vast land with ancient striations, forming watersheds which pour into three northern oceans. With the arrival of Europeans in the late 1490s, this network of waterways made possible the exploration, conquest, and eventual colonization of this new nation, from the Atlantic to the Pacific and into the Arctic. At the turn of the twentieth century, hydroelectric power in Ontario held the promise of a new and improved age of industrialism.[23] Water in the province was valued as abundant, clean, and a source of vast productivity and technological progress. Since the late 1890s, Niagara Falls has been the most iconic and powerful hydraulic power generator in North America.[24]

Resource extraction has long driven Canada's economy. The country's advancement required the violent removal and dispossession of Indigenous communities from their territories. This systemic expulsion and assimilation intensified after Confederation in 1867, when the former British colonies united to form the self-governing Dominion of Canada. As more provinces and territories joined this new country, the federal government instituted the Indian Act[25] in 1876 and began to negotiate treaties that relocated and displaced Indigenous nations. These measures effectively cleared the land for settlement, agricultural expansion, and the ongoing exploitation of the land's rich natural materials.[26]

Over time, industrial development catalyzed growing concern for nature's preservation. Banff National Park in the Rocky Mountains, the first in Canada, was established in 1885 (inspired by Yellowstone National Park in the United States).[27] These mountains located in Western Canada are the northern portion of the North American Continental Divide, parting the watersheds west to the Pacific and east toward the Atlantic. Just as Banff protects that region of Rocky Mountain peaks and valleys,

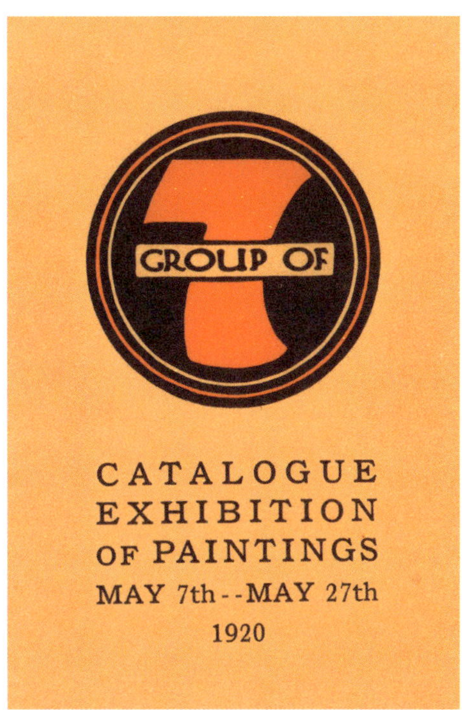


Fig. 1—Group of Seven exhibition catalogue with logo designed by Arthur Lismer, Art Gallery of Toronto, May 1920

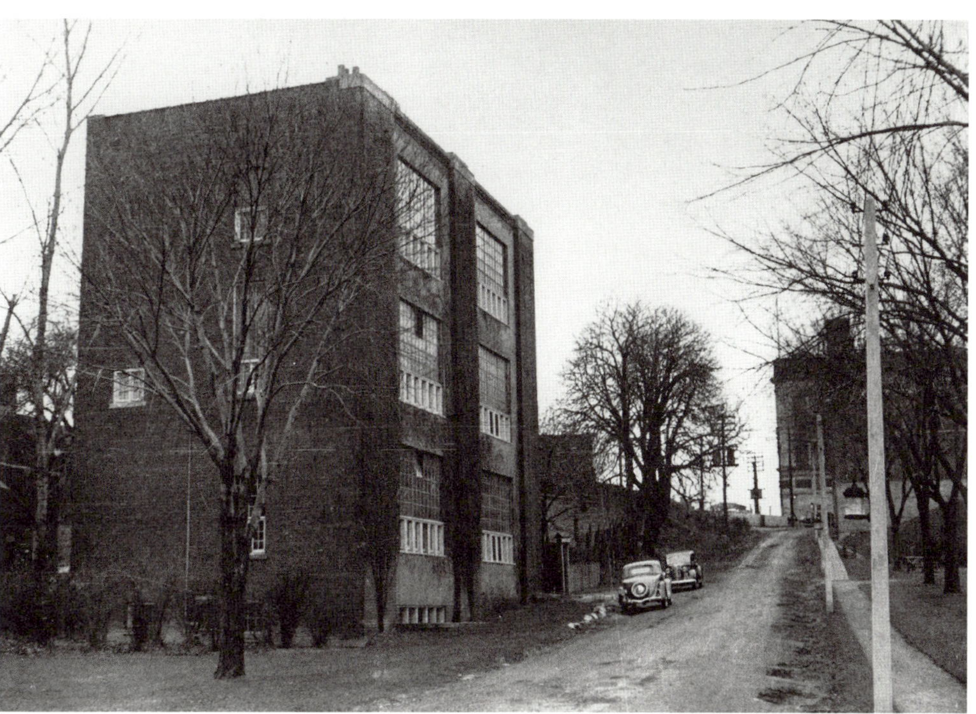

Fig. 2—The Studio Building in Toronto, financed by Lawren Harris and Dr. James M. MacCallum, completed in 1914

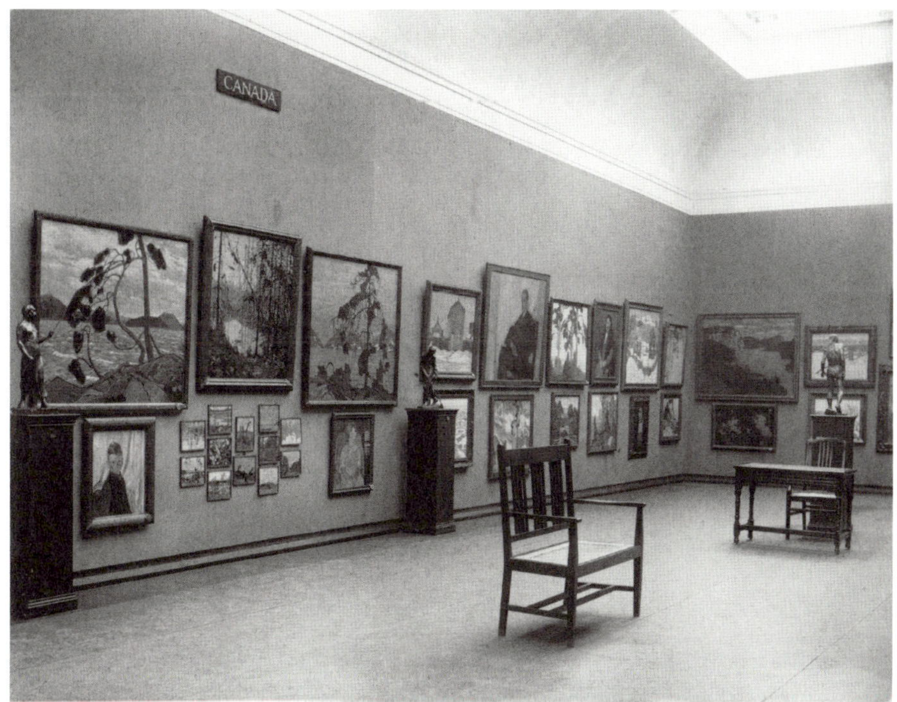


Fig. 3—Canadian Section of Fine Arts, *British Empire Exhibition,* London, 1924; on the left, Tom Thomson's paintings *The West Wind, Northern River,* and *The Jack Pine*

Algonquin Park was celebrated in 1893 by *Scientific American* as "an important advance in the development of Ontario," to be "cherished as one of the most precious possessions of the province."[28] While the establishment of forest reserves and national parks restricted unregulated logging, such legislation also forcibly evicted Indigenous communities and prohibited or limited their hunting and fishing rights—their very livelihood. This was openly acknowledged with doleful passivity, as the article concludes by making reference to the naming of Algonquin Park to perpetuate "the memory of the powerful Indian nation who held sway over this territory centuries ago."[29] The same year that Banff National Park was founded, the Canadian government executed Louis Riel, the charismatic and inspiring Métis leader, in the town of Regina, to the east of Banff across the wide, flat prairie. Riel had led his people in the North-West Resistance, an uprising against the federal army demanding Métis land rights, which had been negotiated as part of the establishment of the province of Manitoba in 1870. The defeat of the Resistance and Riel's execution was to suppress Indigenous efforts to achieve sovereignty for decades to come.[30] The government's victory was due in part to its newfound ability to swiftly deploy soldiers to the disputed area by way of the Canadian Pacific Railway (CPR), the transcontinental train line that had been completed in 1885 as well. Built to connect East and West—an aspirational nod to Canada's official motto, *A Mari usque ad Mare* (From Sea to Sea)—the railway accelerated the movement of goods and people across the extensive breadth of the country, facilitating and advancing settlement as well as the logging, mining, and tourist industries. The CPR had been a deciding factor in British Columbia joining the Confederation in 1871.[31]

It was this expanding network of train tracks that brought the Group of Seven artists to the monumental vistas of the Algoma region in the late 1910s and 1920s (and, for that matter, to the Rocky Mountains between the mid-1920s and 1930s). Each responded differently to Algoma. MacDonald was impressed by the waterfalls and the canyons. In a letter from his first trip in 1919, Jackson describes the changing colors; the immense forests made up of pine, spruce, and birch; and the compulsion of the artists to paint furiously despite rain and bad weather ("the box car is very cosy and one can soon get dried out").[32] Drawing from dozens of painted sketches on small wood panels they had completed on site (up to four a day), the members of the Group produced some of their most compelling canvases in their studio in

Toronto (fig. 2), such as MacDonald's intensely intricate *The Beaver Dam* (p. 65) and *The Wild River,* both 1919, along with Harris's many Lake Superior paintings, including the majestic *Above Lake Superior* (ca. 1922, p. 133), and Jackson's high-keyed *Lake Superior Country* (1924, p. 41).[33] This "rugged scenery," to use Harris's phrase,[34] stirred an exultation expressed in their 1922 exhibition brochure: "Artistic expression is a spirit, not a method, a pursuit, not a settled goal, an instinct, not a body of rules … Art must take the road and risk all for the glory of a great adventure."[35]

In plainer terms, Lismer described the Group of Seven's aim "to make people see what the land looked like and to make them understand that it was not just a place to be exploited industrially."[36] Tom Thomson produced hundreds of sketches in Algonquin Park, the majority described by McInnes as "attempting to distil, in one spontaneous painting, the feeling of his beloved North Country."[37] Yet Thomson captured with the same immediacy and force the full range of activities in the park, including logging, camping, and fishing. Among his few large canvases, *The Drive* (winter 1916–17, fig. p. 177), completed in the last year of his life, captures the beauty and the danger of the place.[38] The Toronto artist Mary E Wrinch employed a similarly impressionistic style in *Saw Mills, Muskoka* (1906, p. 183), a work based on her travels to nearby Muskoka, which she exhibited in 1907, some years before Thomson started painting. MacDonald's early sketches of 1911 included several of log drives.[39] They inspired Harris to paint one of his first Canadian landscapes, *The Drive* (1912), a dramatic atmospheric treatment of a logging drive, likely on the Humber River near Toronto.[40] Taking up the same subject, Lismer painted *Logging in Nova Scotia* (1920, p. 180), while he was living on the Sackville River near Halifax. By imagining Canada in painting, these artists sought to reframe such industrious sites as inspiring.

After these artists reached Algoma in 1918, their landscapes subsumed subject matter into fundamentally formal concerns. This new visual language included "strong rhythmic lines and swirling patterns, clarity of atmosphere, brilliance of color, and decorative simplicity and forcefulness,"[41] even when painting mining sites in the 1930s (pp. 192-201). The art and activities of the Group thus fostered a conflation of nature and industry in their search for "spiritual awareness," with "roots in the very soil a people tread upon … here and now."[42] This conflation is the foundational myth of Canada's "national" art.

Scholarship that is not swayed by the Group's elegies of their pictorial search for a new visual language focuses instead on the ways in which these artists were complicit with state institutions and industry in the development of that foundational myth. As the art historian Paul H. Walton asserted in 1990 (and many scholars have elaborated on since), their paintings evoke a "romantic communion with the 'wilderness' … in a modernist … style that had evolved within the cultural processes of industrialized urban life."[43] These artists brought "enthusiastic originality and a rebellious creative spirit,"[44] as McInnes characterized it, to sites profoundly marked by forestry, mining, and tourism. Carmichael, Harris, and Jackson, along with Yvonne McKague Housser, an artist who was later invited to exhibit in Group of Seven exhibitions, painted in Cobalt and other mining towns in Northern Ontario in an attempt to capture their own subjective, strong aesthetic and emotional reactions to these sites.[45] Their views of "worked" lands are imbued with monumental beauty and elegant form, transcending the industrial subject matter. Walton argues that in this way they "humanize" and make "emotionally accessible" Canada's extraction industry.[46] This is the sustained paradox of the inexhaustibly rich land: at once abundant in its natural beauty, in and of itself a "raw" resource of spiritual energy, and plentiful in its mineral resources so ripe for the exploitation that permanently scars the land.

The distinctiveness of a nation's identity and the development of its supporting myths are articulated from within and without. The new nation of Canada distinguished itself at the *British Empire Exhibition* (fig. 3) at Wembley, England, in 1924 as a persuasive balance of "the scenic and the industrial."[47] Actively promoted by the National Gallery of Canada, paintings by Thomson and the Group of Seven were included in this international fair, along with a working model of Niagara Falls, a large sample of silver ore from a mine near Cobalt, a mural tribute to national parks, and a tableau of a cattle ranch in Alberta at the foothills of the Rockies, sculpted in 1,360 kilograms of butter.[48] Incorporated into this scenic display, the section featuring Canadian modern painting included two works by Tom Thomson, *Northern River* (winter 1914–15, p. 49) and *The West Wind* and Franklin Carmichael's *Autumn Hillside* (1920, p. 39). The paintings were very well received by British critics, the public was impressed by the ample butter, and Canada was popularized in the British imagination as "a place of peace and plenty."[49] These artists understood the need for such symbiotic

perspectives. Up until then, when they referenced "the North," they were referring primarily to the areas where they had been painting in Northern Ontario. Buoyed by their critical success in England in 1924 and seeking new challenges, the members of the Group broadened their ambition to convey the fulsome range of the Canadian experience, extending their search for the "informing spirit of the whole land" by traveling west; later, they would journey to the Arctic.

In a number of critical essays written between 1926 and 1933, Harris articulates his search for an authentic Canadian art informed by the creative "spiritual flow" which emanates from the "great North."[50] He seeks to clarify the paradox of the particular ("the north") and the universal ("the spirit"), proposing that "[t]he creative faculty is the means of communion between these two, the immediate and the eternal."[51] For Harris, that "spirit" manifested most profoundly in the Rocky Mountains, which he painted between 1924 and 1931 (pp. 139, 141), and culminated in his eventual release into painting abstraction from the mid-1930s on. While in the past curators and scholars have accepted and honored Harris's search for an awakened consciousness in his writing and his paintings from this period, recent scholarship offers a commanding counter-narrative of essentialism.[52]

It is untenable to argue for an enduring national art, as though it were a static or completed project, yet the paintings of the Group of Seven and their contemporaries persist. These images endure because, from the outset, the endeavor of these artists to create "art for a nation" expanded nationally and internationally. It was disseminated through many commercial and scholarly publications, exhibitions, documentaries, and reproductions. Although more precisely characterized as a regionalist art movement of English-speaking urban artists, their work is imprinted in the Canadian imagination, mythologized in recurrent revivals over the past century.[53] These painted views persuasively projected onto the land a feeling of ownership and communion. Perhaps such sentiments still resonate for those whose life and identity are tied to a means of belonging to a vista, a dominion, and seek a view that is aspirational, comforting, and familiar. And yet, it cannot be denied that these effects obscure the conditions under which they were achieved: the history of loss, dispossession, and natural destruction. As we confront these paintings today, we understand these territories as contested. Their vitality remains in the land and water.

1—Statutes of the Province of Ontario: "An Act to establish the Algonquin National Park of Ontario," ratified on May 27, 1893, https://archive.org/details/statutesofprovin1893onta/page/32/mode/2up (all URLs accessed in September 2020). Algonquin Park is the traditional territory of the Algonquin nation.

2—Lawren S. Harris, "The Group of Seven in Canadian History," *Canadian Historical Association, Report of the Annual Meeting* [held at Victoria and Vancouver, June 16–19, 1948] 27, no. 1 (1948), pp. 28–38, esp. p. 29.

3—F. H. Varley is the only original Group of Seven member who did not travel to Algoma. A. J. Casson joined the Group after Franz Johnston had left it in 1921.

4—Algoma Region is the traditional territory of the Anishinaabe, Cree, and Métis nations.

5—Harris, "The Group of Seven in Canadian History," p. 34.

6—Ibid.

7—Ibid.

8—Ibid., p. 36.

9—Graham McInnes, *A Short History of Canadian Art* (Toronto: The Macmillan Company of Canada Limited, 1939), p. 81.

10—Ibid., pp. 74 and 80.

11—Ibid., p. 80.

12—Group of Seven, 1920 exhibition publication, n.p.

13—Group of Seven, 1922 exhibition publication, n.p.

14—McInnes, *A Short History of Canadian Art,* p. 2.

15—For a general outline of these national sentiments, see Frederick Housser, *A Canadian Art Movement: The Story of the Group of Seven* (Toronto: The MacMillan Company of Canada Limited, 1926) and also McInnes, *A Short History of Canadian Art*, chapters 1 and 8 in particular.

16—Joyce Zemans, "Establishing the Canon: Nationhood, Identity and the National Gallery's First Reproduction Program of Canadian Art," *The Journal of Canadian Art History* 16, no. 2 (1995), pp. 7–35, esp. p. 11.

17—Group of Seven, 1921 exhibition publication, n.p.

18—Lawren S. Harris, "Creative Art and Canada," reprinted in *Yearbook of the Arts and Canada 1928–1929,* ed. Bertram Brooker (Toronto: Macmillan, 1929), pp. 177–86, esp. pp. 185–86.

19—For an in-depth discussion, see Charles C. Hill, *The Group of Seven: Art for a Nation,* exh. cat. National Gallery of Canada, Ottawa, Art Gallery of Ontario, Toronto, et al. (Toronto: McClelland & Stewart, 1995), in particular chapters 5 and 6. Also see Matthew Teitelbaum, "Sighting the Single Tree, Sighting the New Found Land," in *Eye of Nature,* exh. cat. Walter Phillips Gallery (Banff: Walter Phillips Gallery, 1991), pp. 71–88.

20—For example, in 1925, the Group of Seven produced a portfolio of twenty photolithographs of drawings included in their exhibition that year, to accompany the show.

21—For a discussion of the artists' close association with state-coordinated tourism, see Lynda Jessup, "The Group of Seven and the Tourist Landscape in Western Canada, or The More Things Change …," *Journal of Canadian Studies* 37, no. 1 (Spring 2002), pp. 144–79.

22—McInnes, *A Short History of Canadian Art,* p. 3.

23—H. V. Nelles, "Hydro as Myth," chapter in *The Politics of Development: Forests, Mines & Hydro-Electric Power in Ontario, 1849–1941* (1974; repr., Montreal and Kingston: McGill-Queen's University Press, 2005), pp. 215–55.

24—Niagara Falls is on the traditional lands of the Haudenosaunee Confederacy.

25—The Indian Act ("An Act to amend and consolidate the laws respecting Indians"), ratified on April 12, 1876 by the Parliament of the Dominion of Canada. Current Act: https://laws-lois.justice.gc.ca/eng/acts/i-5/; and the 1876 Act: http://www.canadiana.ca/view/oocihm.9_08051_5_1/213?r=0&s=1.

26—Since the 1970s, treaties between Canada and Indigenous communities have been the subject of ongoing land claims and disputes, many not yet settled. Several nations claim their lands as unceded Indigenous territories.

27—Banff National Park is located in Treaty 7 territory, the traditional lands of the Stoney Nakoda, Blackfoot, and Tsuut'ina Nations.

28—"Algonquin Park," *Scientific American* 69, no. 9 (August 26, 1893), p. 140. It was also in 1893 that the flow of the Horseshoe Falls at Niagara was first diverted toward a newly built electrical power plant to service the region.

29—Ibid., p. 140.

30—The uprising began in 1884 and asserted Métis rights; it instated a provisional Métis government with Riel as its President.

31—The railway connecting Canada "from sea to sea" was also critical in abetting the advancing interests of the United States to annex western territories, especially following the Alaska purchase of 1867.

32—A. Y. Jackson, letter of 1919, quoted in Hill, *The Group of Seven: Art for a Nation,* p. 80.

33—See entries on these paintings and also J. E. H. MacDonald's *The Beaver Dam* in this catalogue, p. 64.

34—Harris, "The Group of Seven in Canadian History," p. 34.

35—Group of Seven, 1922 exhibition publication, n.p.

36—Arthur Lismer speaking to the Massey commission, ca. 1950, quoted in Zemans, "Establishing the Canon," p. 16.

37—McInnes, *A Short History of Canadian Art,* p. 74.

38—See the entry on *The Drive* in this catalogue, p. 174.

39—See, for example, J. E. H. MacDonald, *By the River (Early Spring),* 1911, Government of Ontario Art Collection, https://www.ola.org/en/photo/river-early-spring-jeh-macdonald.

40—Jeremy Adamson, *Lawren S. Harris: Urban Scenes and Wilderness Landscapes 1906–1930,* exh. cat. Art Gallery of Ontario (Toronto: Art Gallery of Ontario, 1978), p. 44.

41—McInnes, *A Short History of Canadian Art,* p. 80.

42—Lawren S. Harris, "Revelation of Art in Canada," *Canadian Theosophist* 7, no. 5 (July 15, 1926), pp. 85–88, esp. pp. 86–87.

43—Paul H. Walton, "The Group of Seven and Northern Development," *RACAR: Canadian Art Review* 17, no. 2 (1990), pp. 171–79, esp. p. 173.

44—McInnes, *A Short History of Canadian Art,* p. 89.

45—Yvonne McKague Housser, "Excerpts from Letters to Fred Housser, Cobalt, 1934," *Northward Journal: A Quarterly of Northern Arts* 16

(June 1980), pp. 29-38, esp. p. 31.

46—Walton, "The Group of Seven and Northern Development," pp. 175-76.

47—Anne Clendinning, "Exhibiting a Nation: Canada at the British Empire Exhibition, 1924-1925," *Social History* 39, no. 77 (May 2006), pp. 79-107, esp. p. 89.

48—Ibid., pp. 89-93.

49—Ibid., p. 95.

50—Harris, "Revelation of Art in Canada," pp. 85-86.

51—Harris, "Creative Art and Canada," p. 180.

52—On this, see Lynda Jessup's various publications, especially "Art for a Nation?," *Fuse Magazine* 19, no. 4 (Summer 1996), pp. 11-14; and "Bushwhackers in the Gallery: Antimodernism and the Group of Seven," in *Antimodernism and Artistic Experience: Policing the Boundaries of Modernity,* ed. Lynda Jessup (Toronto: University of Toronto Press, 2001), pp. 130-52. More recently, see Jessup's discussion with contemporary artist Deanna Bowen regarding her project *God of Gods: A Canadian Play* at The Art Museum, Toronto, November 6, 2019, https://artmuseum.utoronto.ca/video/deanna-bowen-and-lynda-jessup-in-conversation/; and Deanna Bowen and Maya Wilson-Sanchez, "A Centenary of Influence," *Canadian Art,* April 20, 2020, https://canadianart.ca/features/a-centenary-of-influence-deanna-bowen/.

53—See Lynda Jessup's characterization of the Group in "The Group of Seven and the Tourist Landscape in Western Canada, or The More Things Change …," pp. 144-79.

# Tangled

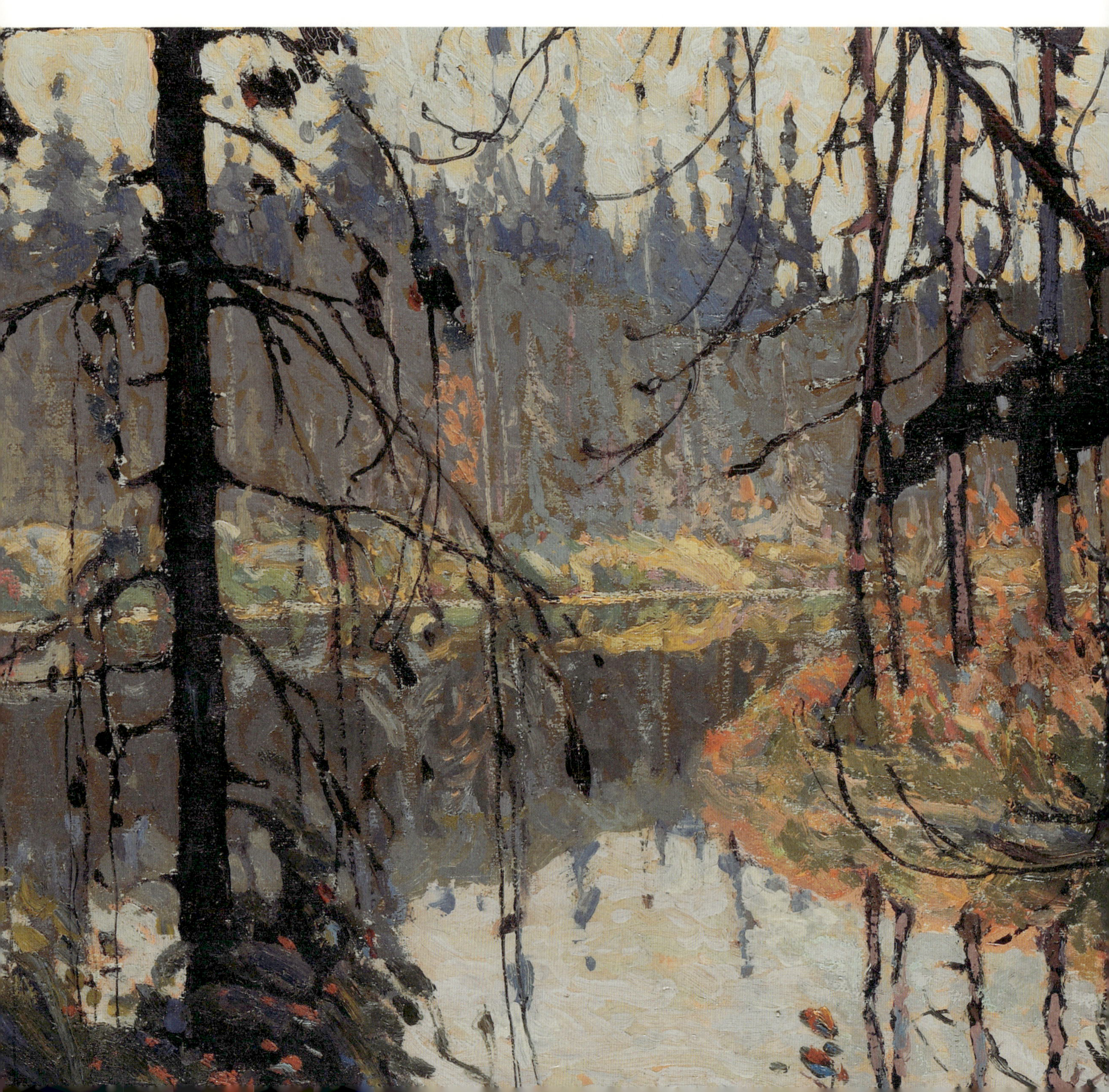

# Woods

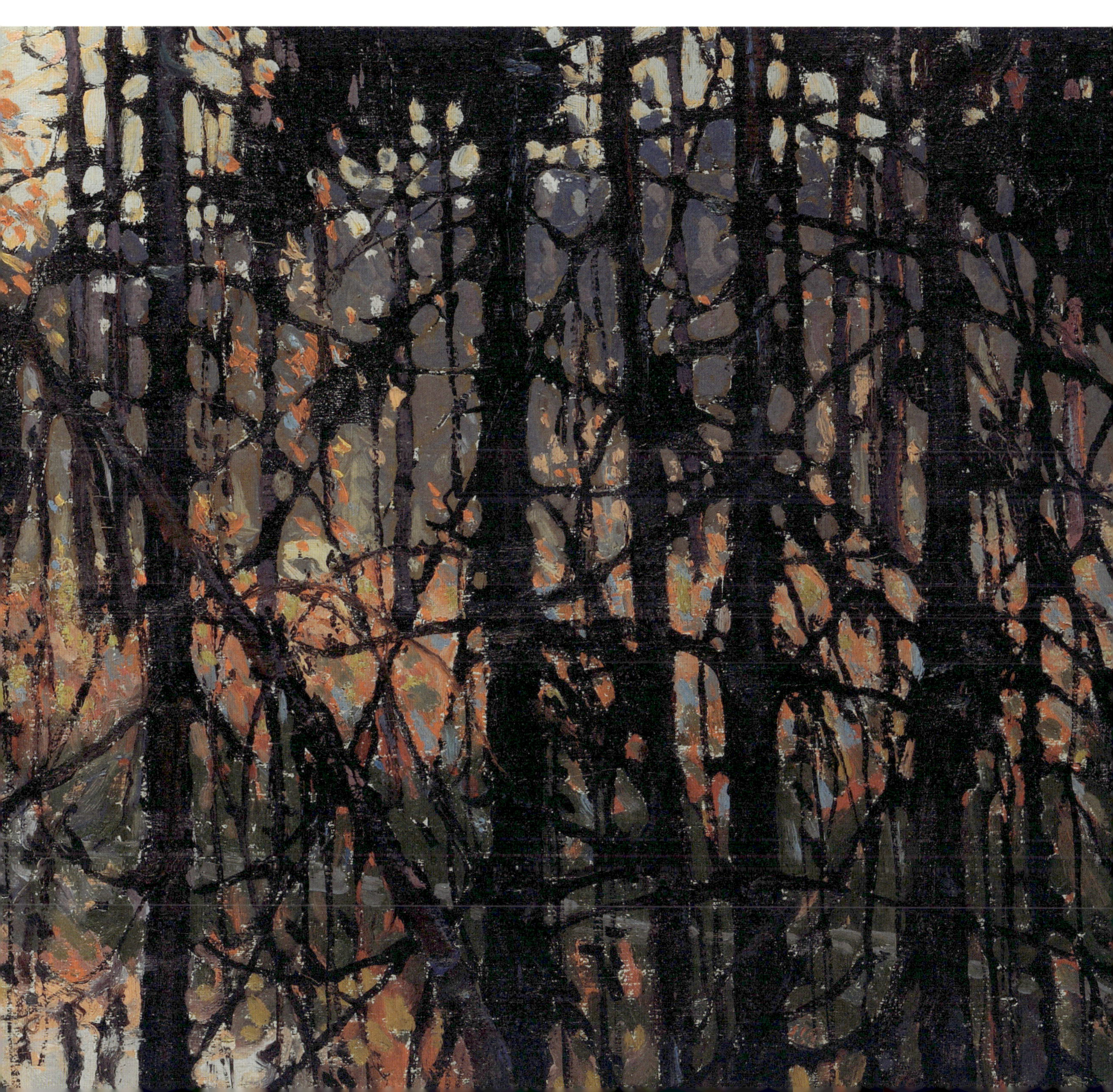

Artists associated with the Group of Seven spent much of their time in the woods, camping and sketching on extended painting trips—in tangled territory, not always easily accessible. They found ample inspiration in Ontario's vast forests, in their characteristic play of light and shadows and glorious seasonal colors. Tom Thomson depicted deep woods with dense foliage and a twisted screen of trees in his *Northern River* (winter 1914–15) to conjure up a sense of silence and pristine isolation. Lawren Harris's anthropomorphic silhouetted trees in changing light, in turn, evoke a primordial territory filled with potential in *Beaver Swamp, Algoma* (1920). A close-up view of the water's edge in his *Beaver Pond* (1921) reveals dead tree trunks, partially submerged, standing sentinel on the margins of impenetrable, dark woods.

In contrast, Arthur Lismer and Franklin Carmichael painted resplendent trees dappled with sunlight and infused with vivid colors as an offering of dazzling optimism. F. H. Varley's singular work *Magic Tree* (1924) is a portrait of a swirl of sinuous branches entwined around a thick trunk engulfed in a bed of fallen autumn leaves. A small, rousing painting, it is infused with power and emotion, conveying the artist's vivacious vision of Canadian woods.

Collectively, these canvases reveal the artists' search for new ways of expressing their relationships to place and their exuberance for simplified forms and energetic colors. They chose to focus on the stirring beauty of Ontario's majestic trees and forests, despite the relentless presence of the logging industry. Spending time in the midst of tangled woods, they experimented with fundamentally formal concerns of painting and created a unique visual language that proves essential to understanding the development of the modernist painting tradition in Canada.

Georgiana Uhlyarik

Franklin Carmichael
*Autumn Hillside*, 1920
76 × 91.4 cm

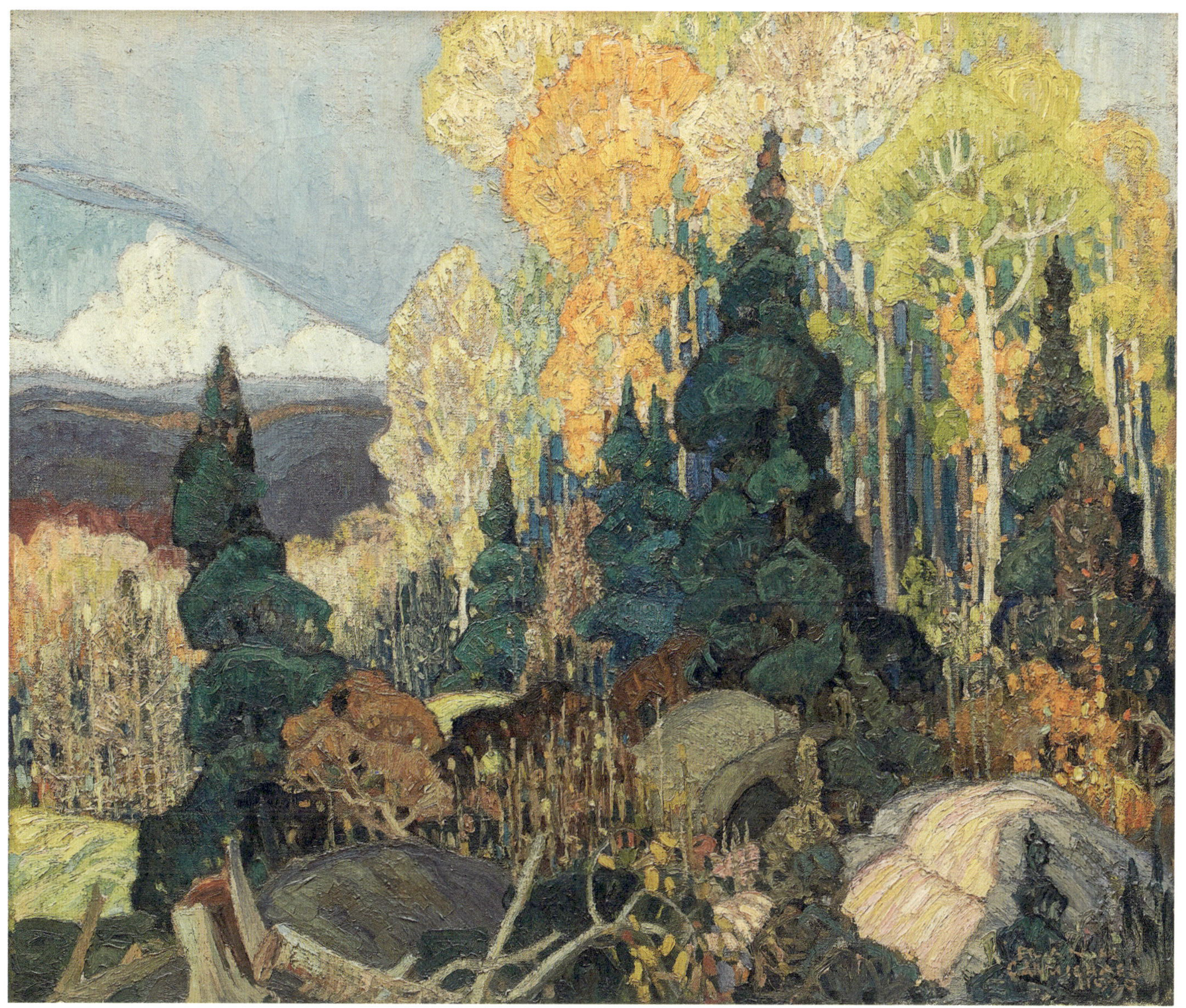

A.Y. Jackson
*Lake Superior Country*, 1924
117 × 148 cm

"I know of no more impressive scenery in Canada for the landscape painter,"[1] remarked A.Y. Jackson, describing the north shore of Lake Superior. The largest of the Great Lakes, Superior was a key destination for Jackson and other Group of Seven painters, Lawren Harris in particular, throughout the 1920s. While Harris focused on the lake's expansive waters, Jackson turned inland, capturing with vigor the topography of the Precambrian Shield.

*Lake Superior Country* is one of several important canvases by Jackson that respond to this distinctive Northern Ontario terrain. Shaped by ancient flows of hot magma, the rolling basalt arcs and ridges appealed to the artist's penchant for rhythmic natural forms. "There is a sublime order to it, the long curves of the beaches, the sweeping ranges of hills, and headlands that push out into the lake," the artist mused in an autobiographical reflection. "In autumn the whole country glows with colour."[2]

The flamboyant palette and eccentric stylization make this an unusual work for Jackson—and for the Group of Seven in general. Sloping rock layers are rendered in a symphony of magenta, mauve, vermillion, and burnt ocher. In the foreground, established spruces and golden birches appear as conical and rounded masses. Wispy green-gold tamaracks spring up from the rock face in the middle ground, signaling new growth where so much land had been burnt years earlier. A frieze of darkened, semi-skeletal spruces looms in the distance. Are they the charred remains of a forest after the destruction of a fire?

*Lake Superior Country* is a testament to Jackson's command of landscapes, and his ability to play within this genre. He dedicated his career to observing Canada's topography; by the 1920s, he had already developed a deep understanding of and passion for the underlying structures of the land. To his Group of Seven compatriot Arthur Lismer, Jackson "gives the conviction to anybody who will see that he can, and does, grasp the breadth and depth of … vast stretches of lonely terrain in a sweep of fervent affection for all that it means to him."[3]

Indeed, despite its spirited coloration, *Lake Superior Country* is a lonely scene, devoid of the human habitation and industry that existed in the area. One of Jackson's most radical departures from a realistic landscape, the painting with its isolated and vaguely postapocalyptic atmosphere reinforces the myth of the northern stretches of Canada as *terra nullius*.

Renée van der Avoird

1—A.Y. Jackson, *A Painter's Country: The Autobiography of A.Y. Jackson* (Toronto: Clarke, Irwin & Co. Ltd., 1958), p. 48.
2—Ibid.
3—Arthur Lismer, "A.Y. Jackson," in *A.Y. Jackson: Paintings, 1902–1953,* exh. cat. Art Gallery of Toronto and National Gallery of Canada, Ottawa (Toronto: Art Gallery of Toronto, 1953), p. 6.

Tangled Woods

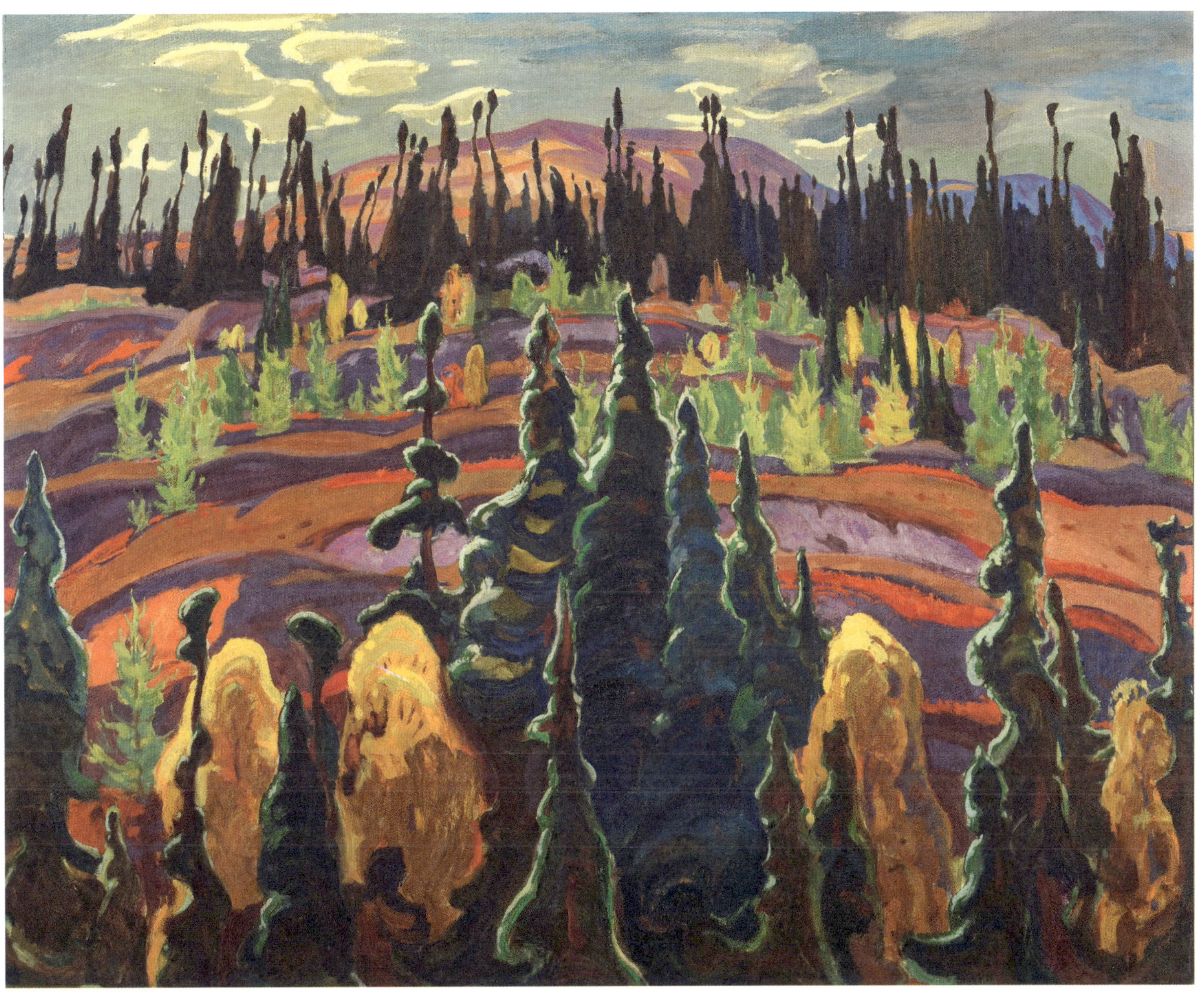

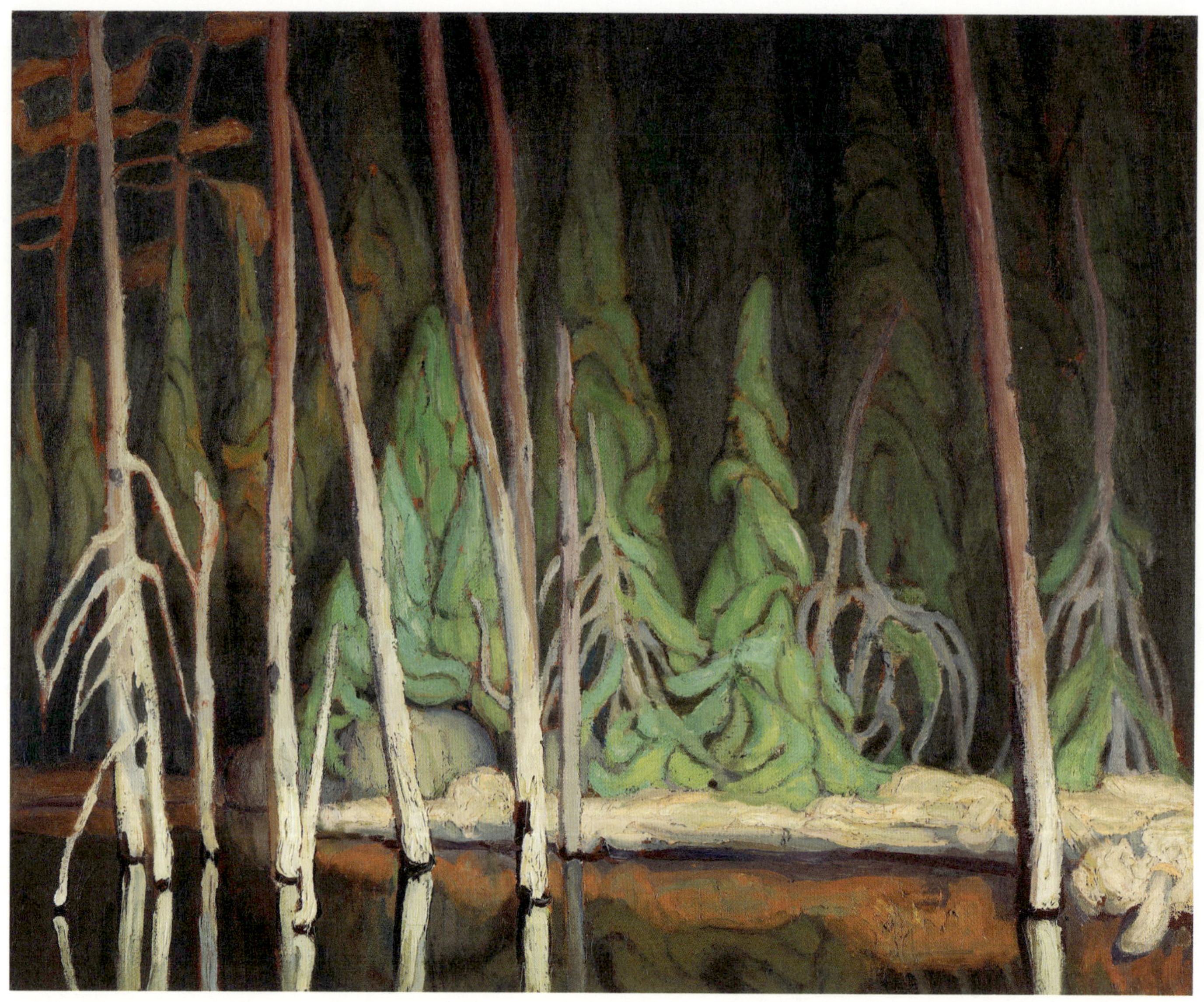

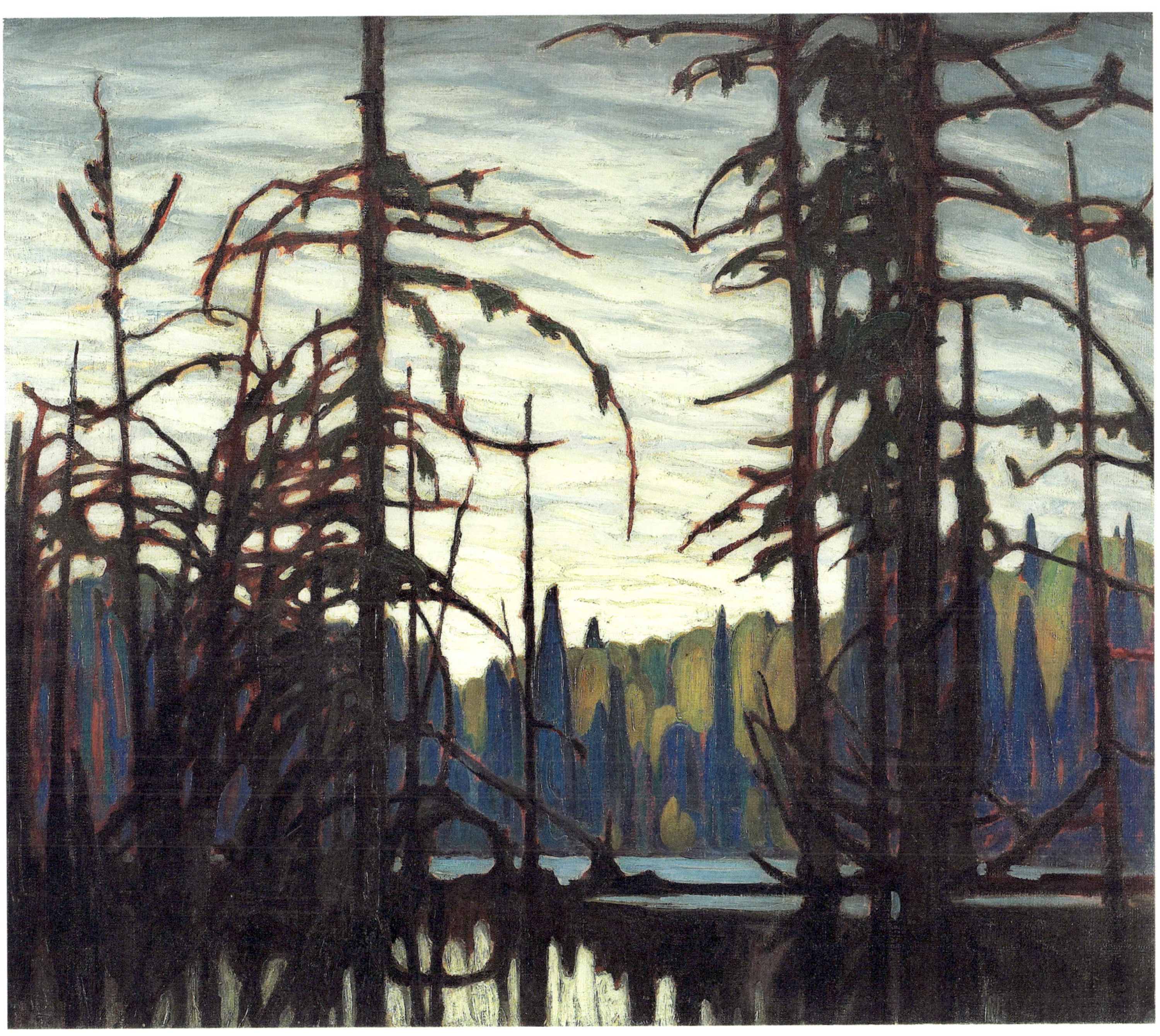

Lawren Harris
*Beaver Pond,* 1921
81.7 × 102 cm

Lawren Harris
*Beaver Swamp, Algoma,* 1920
120.7 × 141 cm

Arthur Lismer
*Sunlight in a Wood,* 1930
91.4 × 101.6 cm

Throughout the 1920s and 1930s, Arthur Lismer and his family spent summers at a cottage on McGregor Bay in Ontario. The family would visit secluded locales where Arthur would sketch, and his wife and young daughter, Esther and Marjorie, would read. Part of Anishinaabe territory, the McGregor Bay settlement and archipelago of the same name are situated on the north shore of Lake Huron. The region's plentiful islands are rocky and wooded, and covered by wildflowers in the summer. Over the years, Arthur Lismer's interest had shifted from the region's majestic island panoramas to the complex inner workings of its boreal forest.

*Sunlight in a Wood,* one of Lismer's earliest woodland interiors, celebrates the richness of the forest floor. Ferns, lichen, and roots are woven into a vibrant quilt of color and pattern in the foreground. "Even in such minute forms there is vastness," the Group of Seven artist once wrote, describing the complexity of the natural world.[1] "There are vistas and design unsurpassed, at least to my myopic eyes." Lismer's focus on such details was a challenge that lent itself to a more abstract treatment of forms: his rocks and pine boughs became buoyant and globular, his sunbeams thick, diagonal shards. The sunlight—a recurring subject in his work—dissects the background, illuminating robust tree trunks. Vigorous brushstrokes and saturated, striking hues suggest that this work is as much about the artist's appreciation of form and color as it is a depiction of an actual landscape.

*Sunlight in a Wood* was painted from a crayon sketch that Lismer had made the previous year.[2] The earlier work is a chaotic array of vertical trunks and horizontal branches interspersed with dense vegetation. In the subsequent painting, the foreground is a more direct focus, shifting the viewer's attention to the coniferous forest's natural cycles of generation and decay. Lismer places a fallen tree in the very center of the painting, its sprawling roots a fertile setting for new growth. He saw in art the same vitality he saw in nature: a great productive force, a unifying element. "Life is much richer for all people if they can see further and deeper than others into the meaning and beauty of life,"[3] he once remarked.

Renée van der Avoird

1—Marjorie Bridges Lismer, *A Border of Beauty: Arthur Lismer's Pen and Pencil* (Toronto: Red Rock Publishing, 1977), p.140.
2—Arthur Lismer, *Study for "Sunlight in a Wood,"* 1929, Art Gallery of Ontario, Toronto, gift of the artist, 1946.
3—Bridges Lismer, *A Border of Beauty,* p.139.

# Tangled Woods

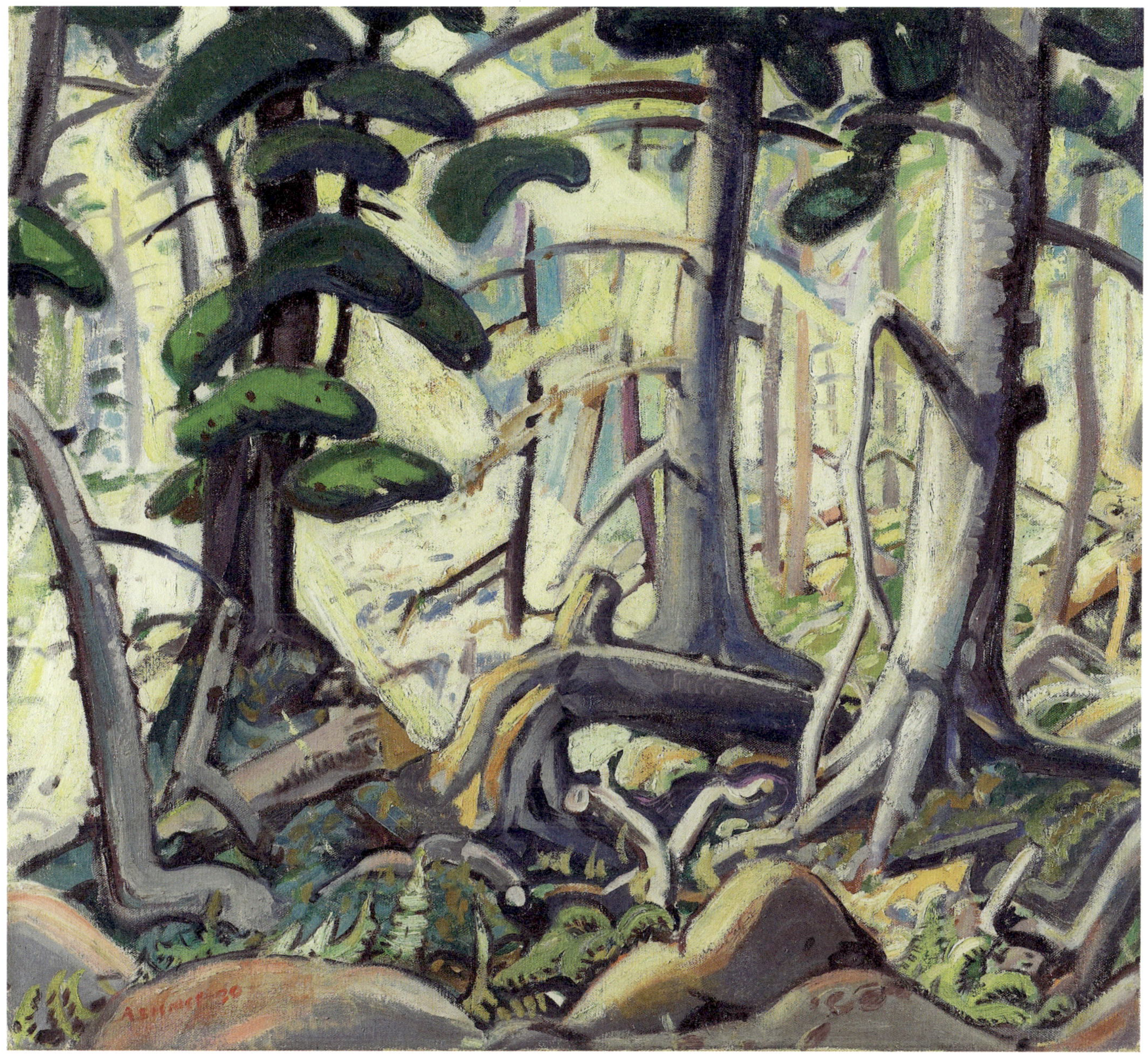

Arthur Lismer
*Pine Wrack,* 1933
92.1 × 106.9 cm

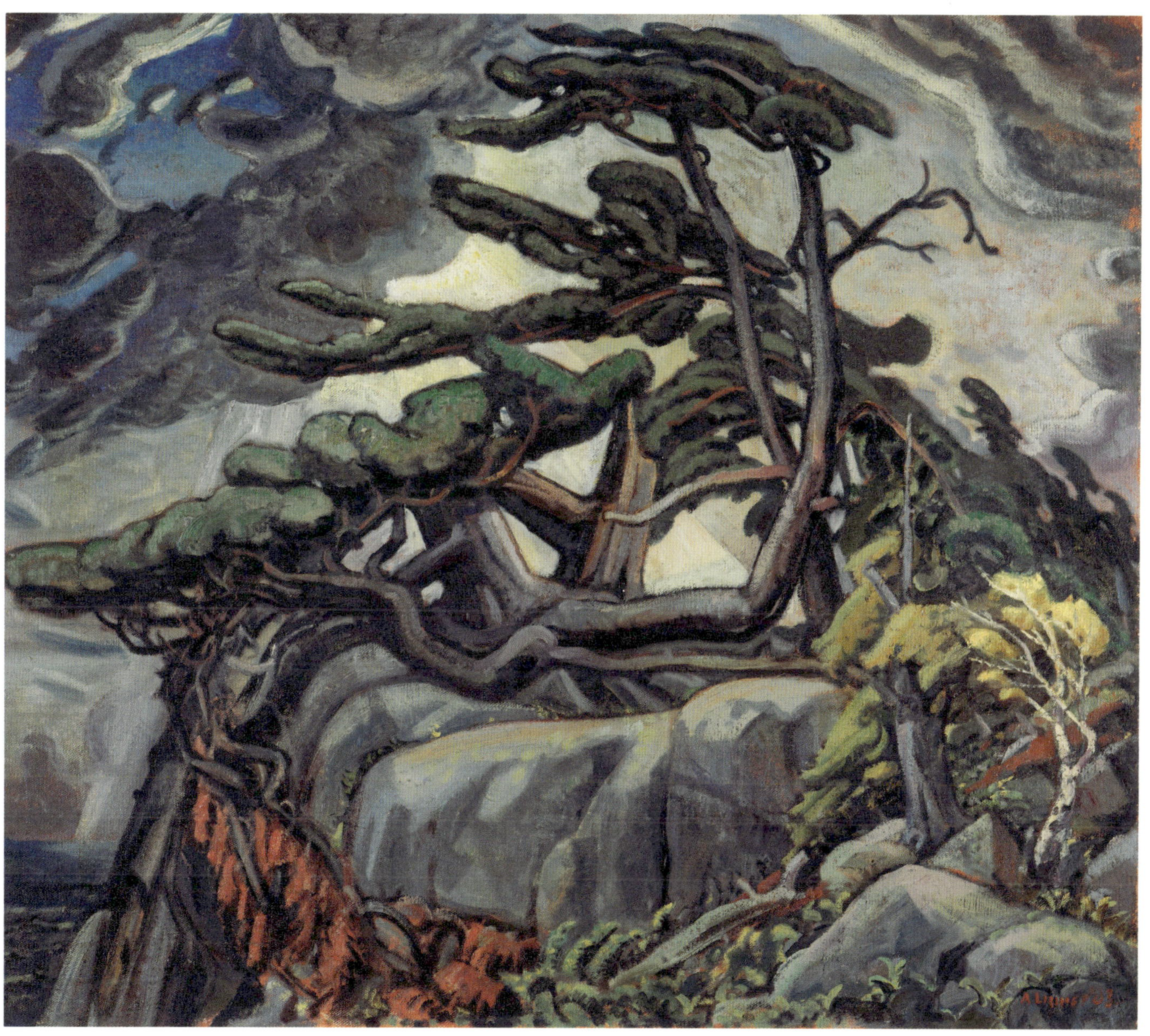

Tom Thomson,
*Northern River,* winter 1914–15
115.1 × 102 cm

Tom Thomson painted *Northern River,* one of his rare large canvases, from the perspective of a canoeist who has perhaps just docked his boat. A quiet mood prevails and there is a sense of enclosure, of privacy. The artist referred to this as his "swamp picture."[1] With the low horizon emphasizing the forms of mid-Northern Ontario shores, *Northern River* is indeed a love letter to that murky, transitional zone between land and water. In Ontario, swamps are typically shallow and grant access only to lightweight, non-motorized boats. In this work, one of Thomson's best-known paintings, viewers can imagine (and, perhaps, vicariously experience) the artist's privileged entry as he stealthily paddles through wooded channels to arrive at this pristine moment.

A darkened curtain of black spruce trees frames the foreground, the interlaced branches lyrical and almost decorative. Thomson's interest in the sinuous forms of Art Nouveau is evident in this picture, as is his training as a graphic designer. Prior to creating this oil on canvas, he painted a small study in gouache and ink on illustration board.[2] Because of its opaque quality, gouache was commonly used in advertising materials, and *Northern River* may well have been conceived as a poster or illustration. The vertical format and flattened background further link this work to commercial art, and the graphic lines made it a good candidate for mass reproduction. In 1943, the National Gallery of Canada produced a silkscreen print of *Northern River* which was widely distributed throughout the country.[3] Consequently, Thomson's swamp picture became a familiar and cherished work of art in the Canadian consciousness.

As influential as it may have been, the silkscreen of *Northern River* fails to express what is so remarkable about the painting: energetic gestures, decadent textures, and complex buildups of color. Arguably, the real subject of this work is the act of painting itself: it is a prime example of Thomson's mastery of his brush, the kind of control earned only by a fervent dedication to one's craft. The artist's expertise was aptly summarized by the Canadian abstract painter Harold Town: "Thomson could manipulate a brush with easy virtuosity, hesitating in the middle of a stroke, turning abruptly during sweep, flattening and extending the width, contracting, rolling the hair to its edge … without losing his rhythm."[4] If in *Northern River* we recognize Thomson as a painter's painter, then we also witness, through his romanticized rendering of the riverscape, his quest for authentic and sacred experiences within nature.

Renée van der Avoird

1—Tom Thomson, letter to J. M. MacCallum, April 22, 1915, National Gallery of Canada Archives, MacCallum papers.
2—Tom Thomson, *Study for "Northern River,"* 1914–15. Collection of the Art Gallery of Ontario. Purchase, 1982.
3—The National Gallery of Canada purchased *Northern River* in 1915, and it released the silkscreen version of the painting in 1943 as part of the Sampson-Matthews print program. This program, which ran from 1942 to 1963, included many works by the Group of Seven and other modernist painters. It played a major role in shaping the collective national sense of Canadian art.
4—Harold Town, quoted in David P. Silcox and Harold Town, *Tom Thomson: The Silence and the Storm* (Toronto: McClelland & Stewart Ltd., 1977), p. 25.

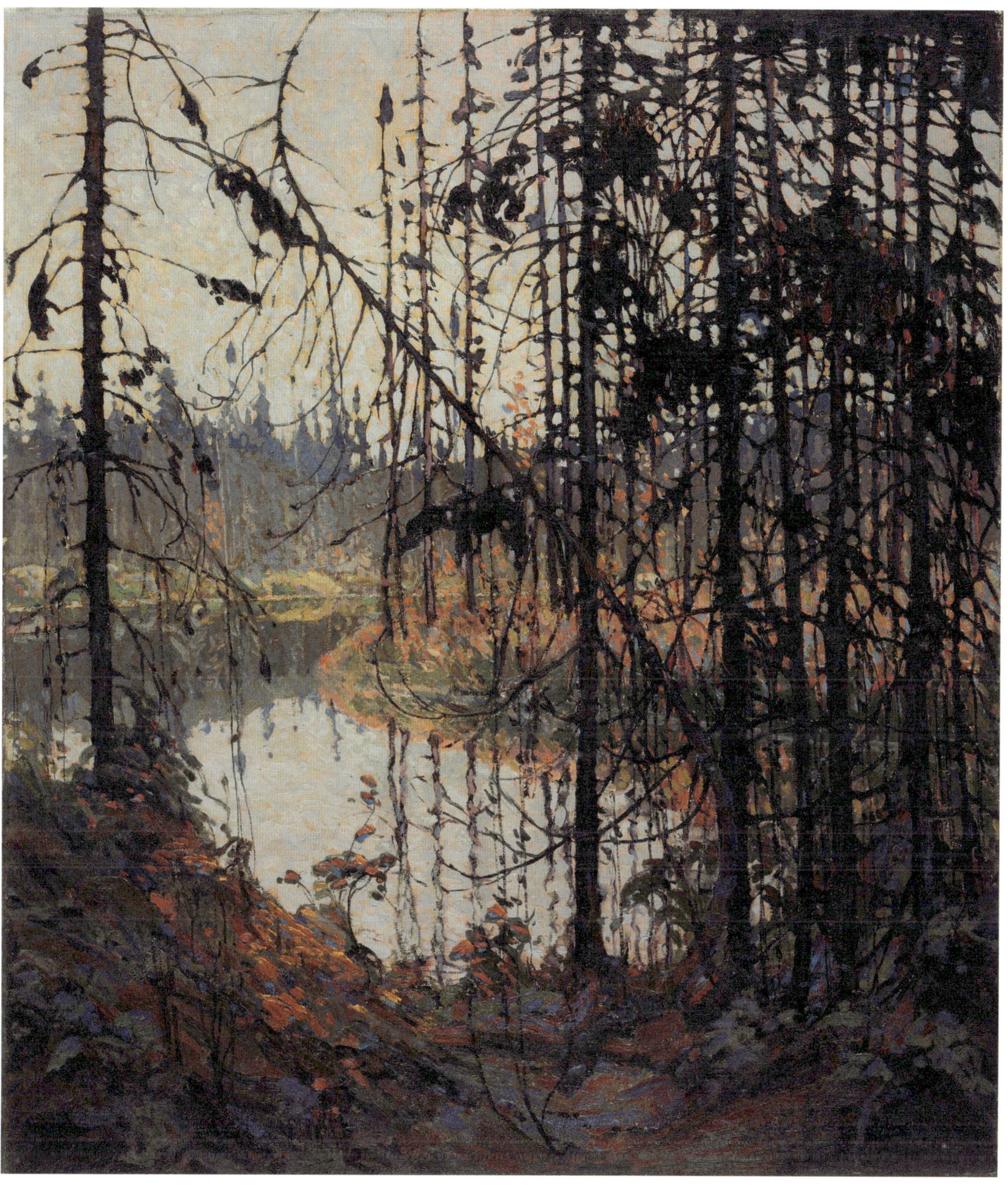

Tangled Woods

Tom Thomson
*Autumn's Garland,* winter 1915–16
122.5 × 132.2 cm

Tangled Woods

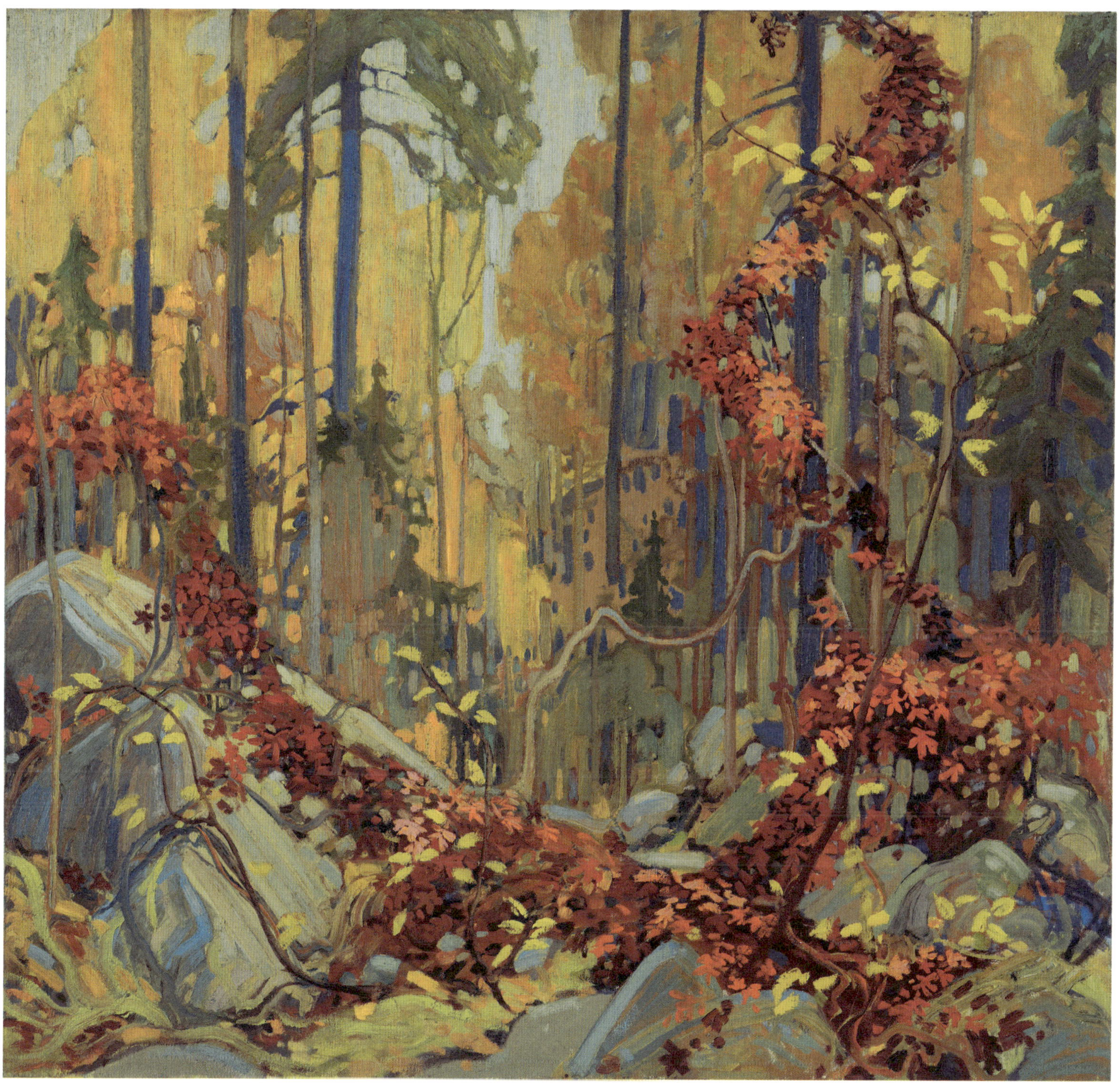

F. H. Varley
*Magic Tree*, 1924
52.7 × 52.7 cm

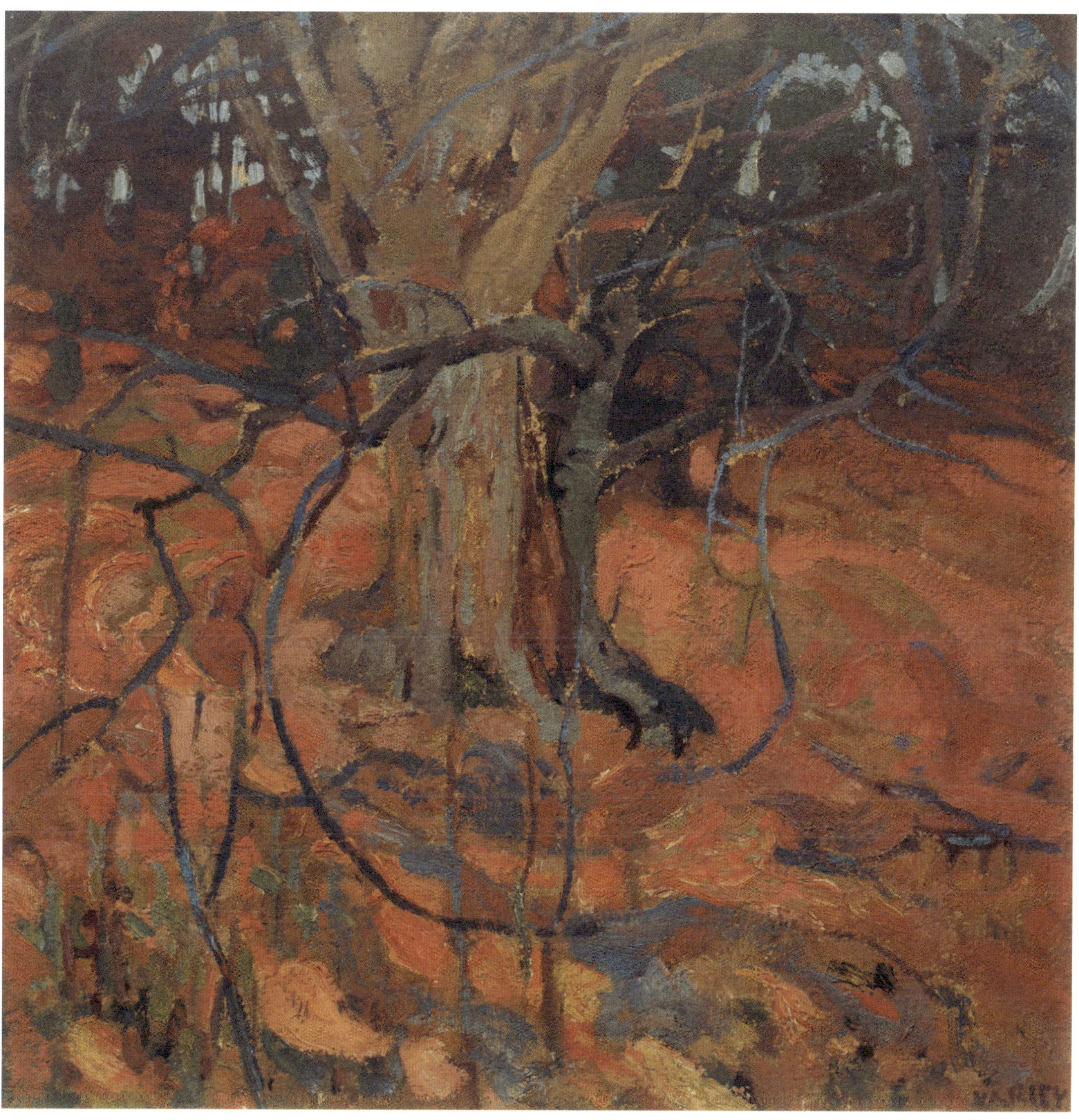

# Trip into

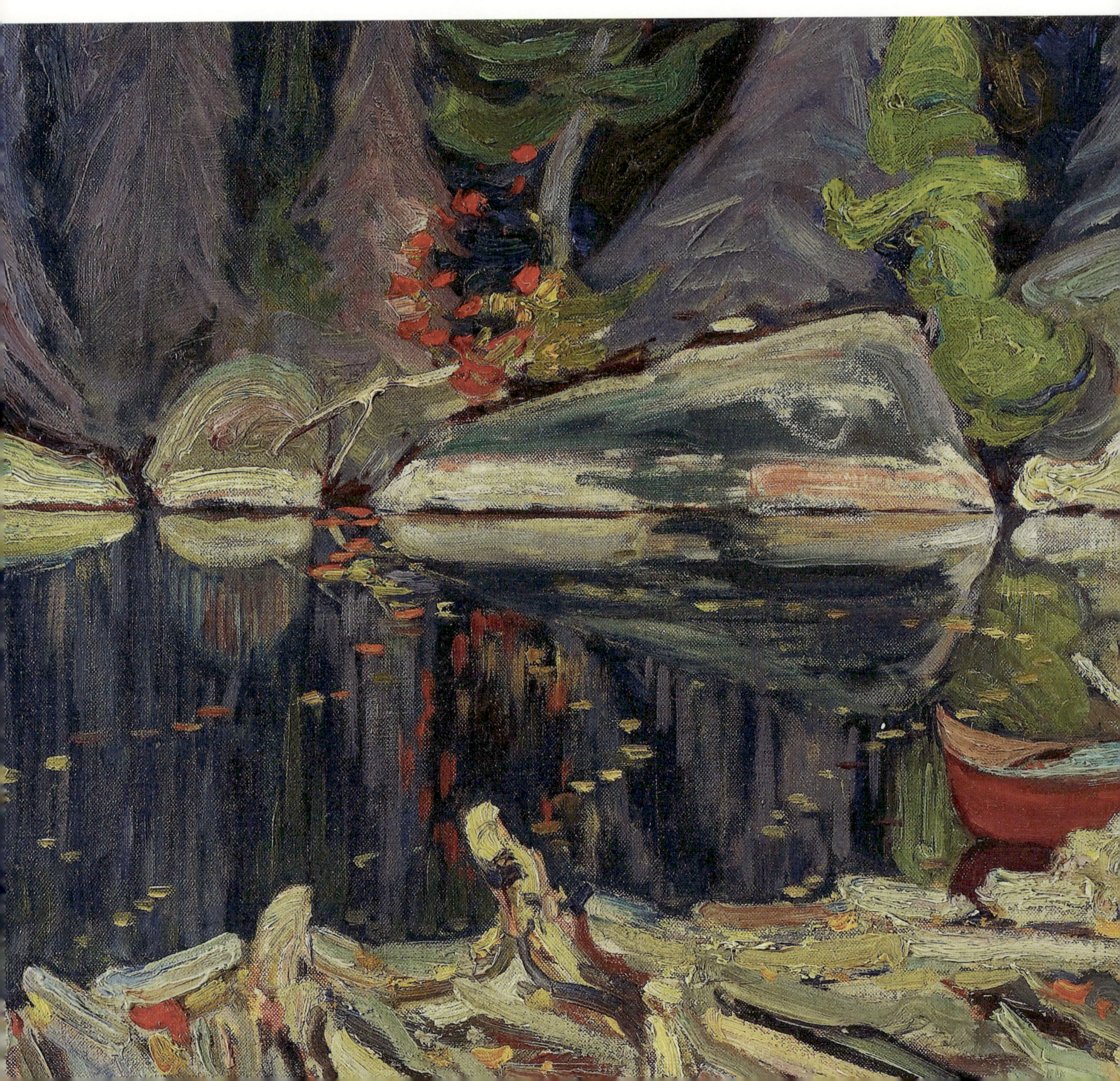

# the Wild

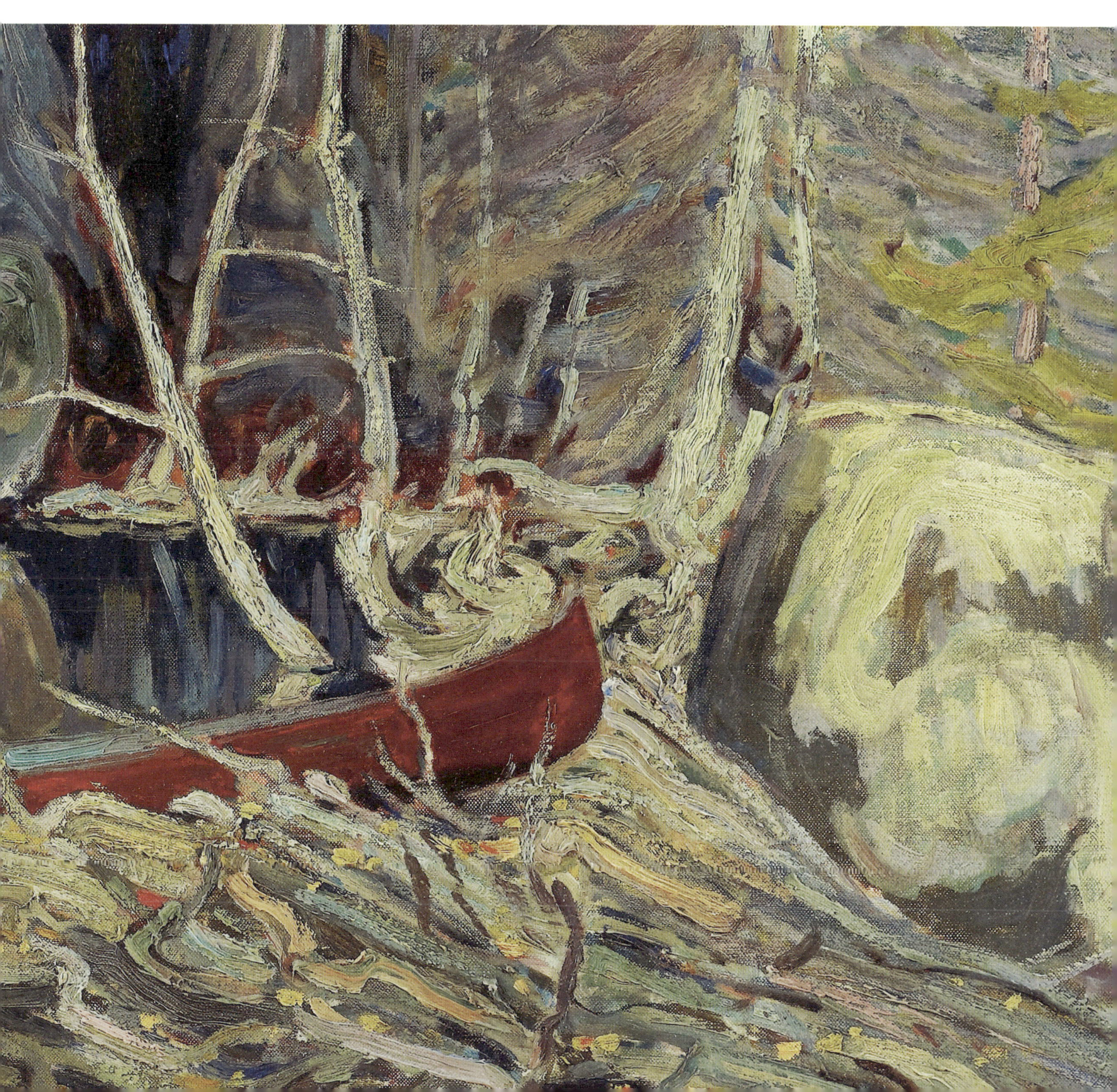

From around 1910 and into the late 1930s, a number of artists based in Toronto—transformed by a newly awakened search for authenticity and pictorial experimentation—traveled away from urban centers in favor of hiking, camping, and painting outdoors. Lakes and rivers have always been a principal way for people to move across the vast land and into the dense woods of Northern Ontario. Traveling by canoe, these waterways opened up the territory and allowed these enterprising artists to venture into the Canadian Shield to experience the sublime vistas and monumental rivers, hills, and forests around the Great Lakes, and further into the interior of the Rockies. Confronting the challenges of the terrain and enduring the inclement weather was a critical aspect of their artistic identity: "The new type of artist ... puts on the outfit of the bushwhacker and prospector; closes with his environment; paddles, portages and makes camp; sleeps in the out of doors under the stars; climbs mountains with his sketch box on his back."[1]

Tom Thomson and J. E. H. MacDonald often painted the canoe moored on the shores and natural dams of Algonquin Park's lakes and rivers, indicating the remoteness of their painting sites. Traveling together in groups, these artists camped in tents and portaged from site to site, seeking new views across hills, lakes, and river canyons to sketch on the spot. Arthur Lismer and F. H. Varley captured these activities, offering insight into the physical demands necessary on these painting trips. Mac-Donald's and Varley's inclusion of figures absorbed by a land-scape of considerable clouds, rocky shores, and rushing water, and more notably of the artist himself painting on the side of a glacial lake, actively evokes the endurance and tenacity of the "mythical" stature of this new kind of intrepid Canadian artist. This image of the artist as heroic explorer has persisted in the Canadian imagination, despite its colonial vestiges.

Georgiana Uhlyarik

1—F. B. Housser, *A Canadian Art Movement: The Story of the Group of Seven* (Toronto: Macmillan Co. of Canada, 1926), p. 15.

J. E. H. MacDonald
*The Elements,* 1916
71.1 × 91.8 cm

Trip into the Wild

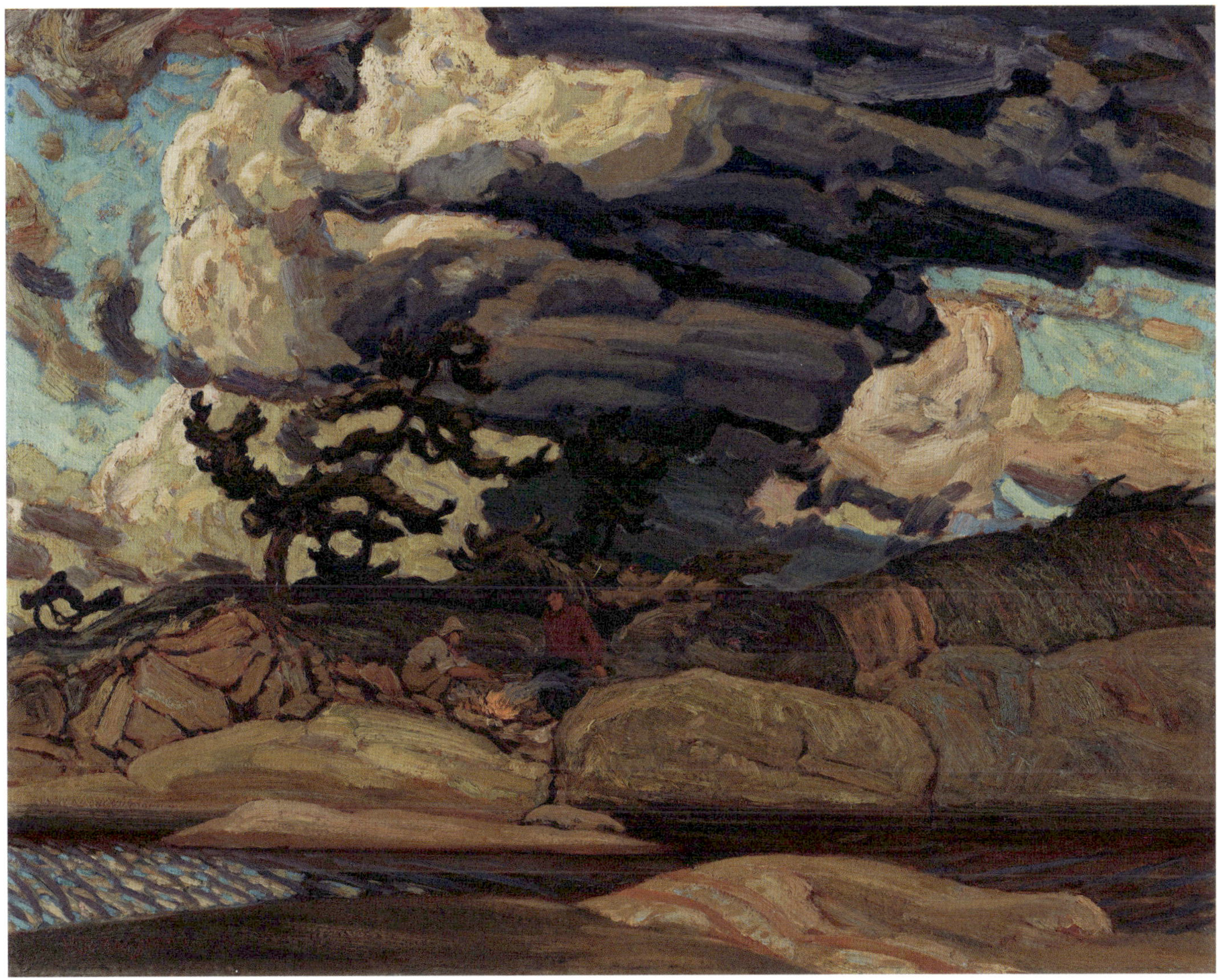

J. E. H. MacDonald
*Falls, Montreal River,* 1920
121.9 × 153 cm

When J. E. H. MacDonald traveled by train with a small group of
painters to Ontario's Algoma
district in 1918, he fantasized that
he and his peers were the first
to set foot on that land. In a letter
to his wife, he reported: "We felt
we could understand something of
the feeling of the early Canadian
explorers. The whole scene seemed
so primeval and unspoiled, and the
great broad [Montreal] river
another St. Lawrence waiting for
discoverers."[1]

The artist's profound appreciation
of nature, particularly hills and
mountains, stemmed from his upbringing in picturesque Kirkby
Stephen in North West England,
where he had lived until his early
teens. Perhaps these European
roots made his "explorer" musings
seem apropos. In reality, Algoma
was neither uninhabited nor unspoiled at the time of MacDonald's
visit, but its dramatic scenery provided the artist with his greatest
inspiration to date, pushing him to
the height of his career.

MacDonald's Algoma paintings are
a testament to the exhilaration
he felt in nature. He was enraptured
by rushing rivers, old-growth
forests, steep slopes, and prominent terraces, which provided him
with a source of spiritual energy.
"The smooth glimmering infinity of
waters was like a glimpse of God
himself,"[2] he exclaimed as the train
of artists passed Lake Superior.

Painted in Toronto from an oil
sketch, *Falls, Montreal River* is Mac-
Donald's liveliest canvas from this
period. His high-keyed palette
reveals a keen attention to the early
autumn foliage, which he described
in an Arts and Letters Club article
as "a great concert of colour" con-
taining "every shade from palest
yellow to deep crimson against the
big blue-gold hills of the Montreal
Valley."[3] In addition to his passion
for the land, the jostling panorama
evokes MacDonald's post–First
World War optimism, a lens that informed his view of Canada as a
resilient country in the process of
growing into itself.

Renée van der Avoird

1—From a letter to his wife, Joan MacDonald,
September 24, 1918. Cited in E. R. Hunter,
*J. E. H. MacDonald: A Biography and Catalogue
of His Work* (Toronto: The Ryerson Press,
1940), p. 21.
2—From an undated letter to Joan MacDonald,
September 1918. Cited in Hunter, *J. E. H.
MacDonald,* p. 21.
3—J. E. H. MacDonald, "A. C. R. 10557," in *The
Lamps* (Arts and Letters Club), December 1919.

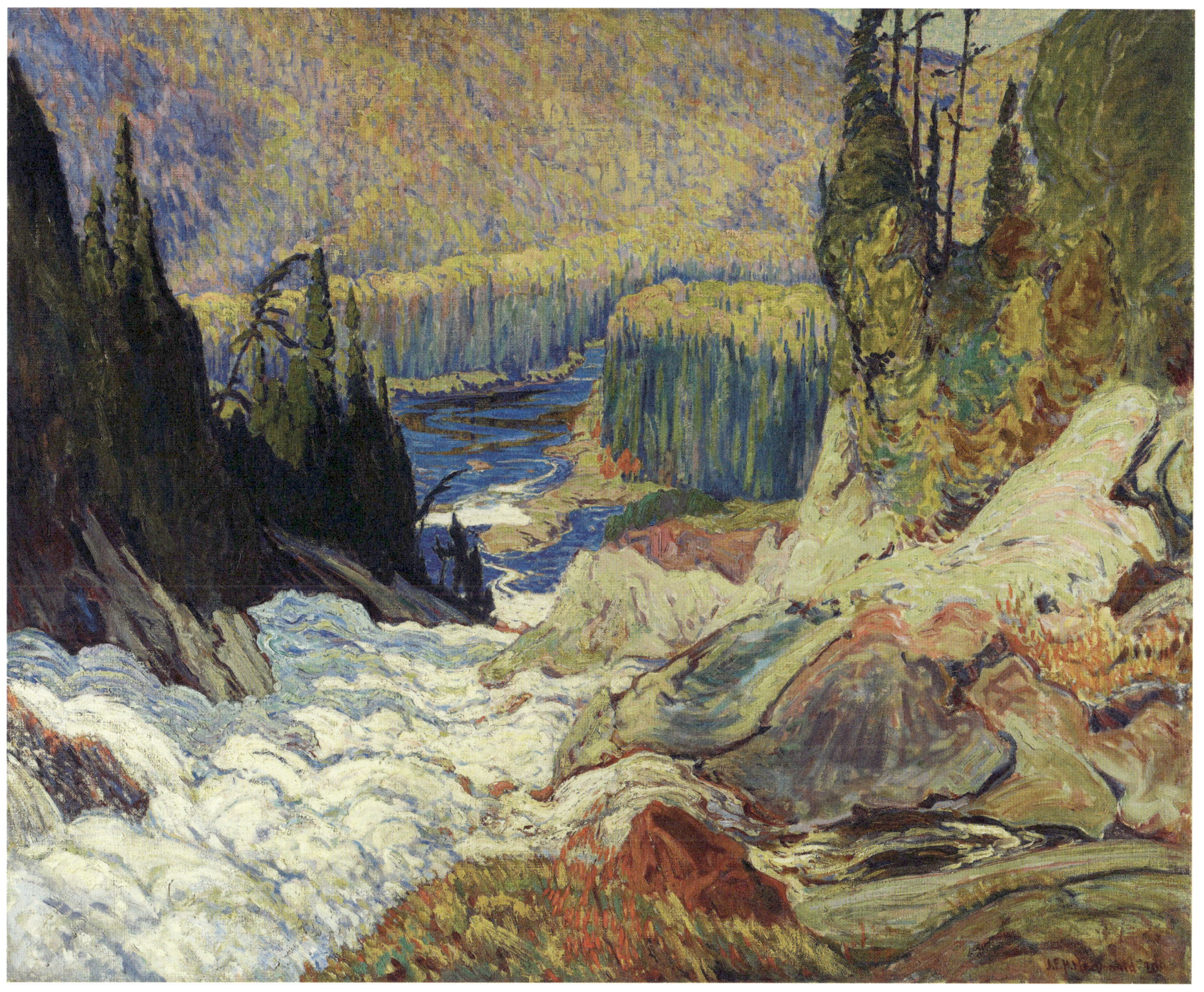

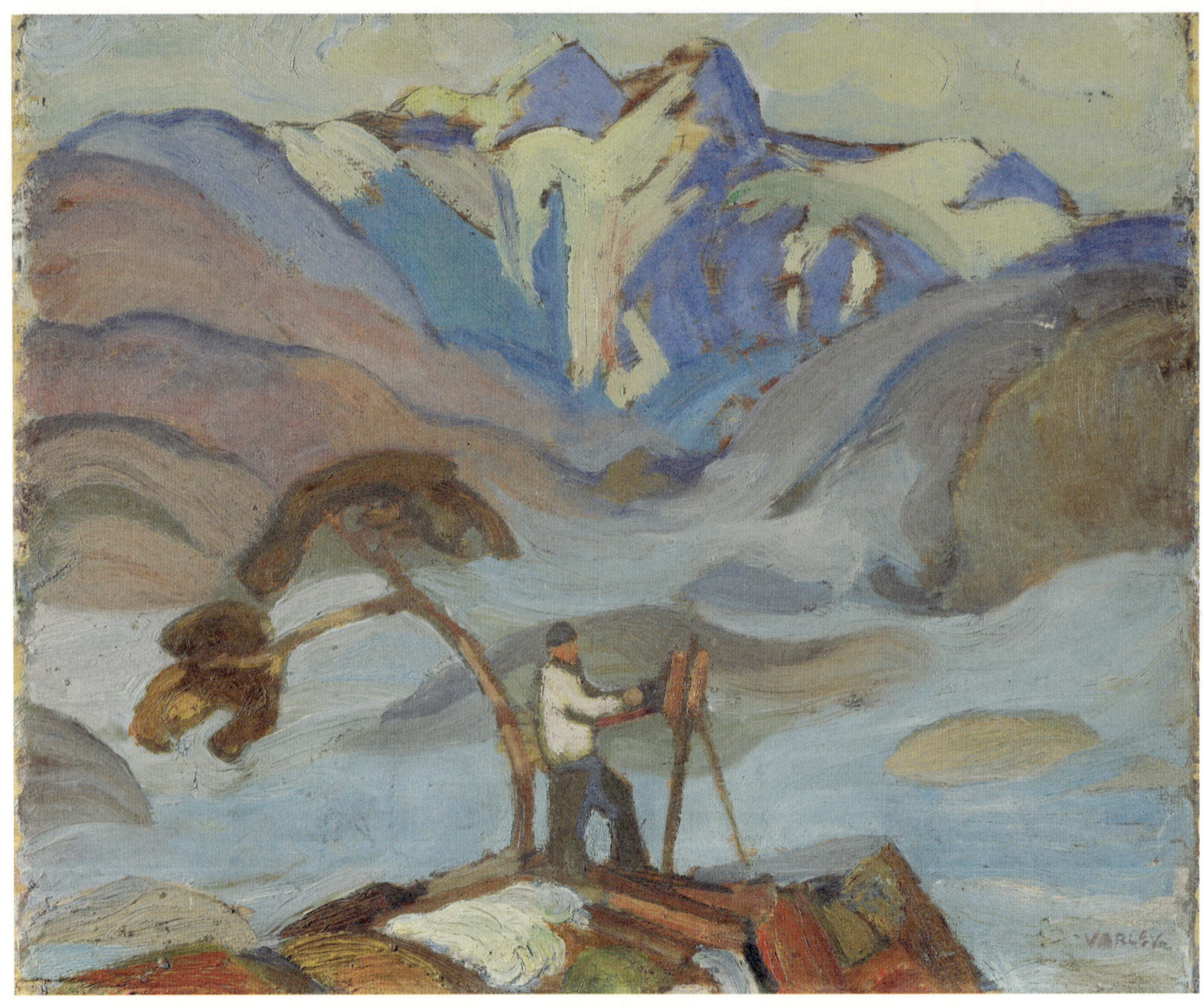

F. H. Varley
*Mountain Sketching*, ca. 1929
30.5 × 38.1 cm

F. H. Varley
*Mountain Portage*, 1925
50.5 × 61 cm

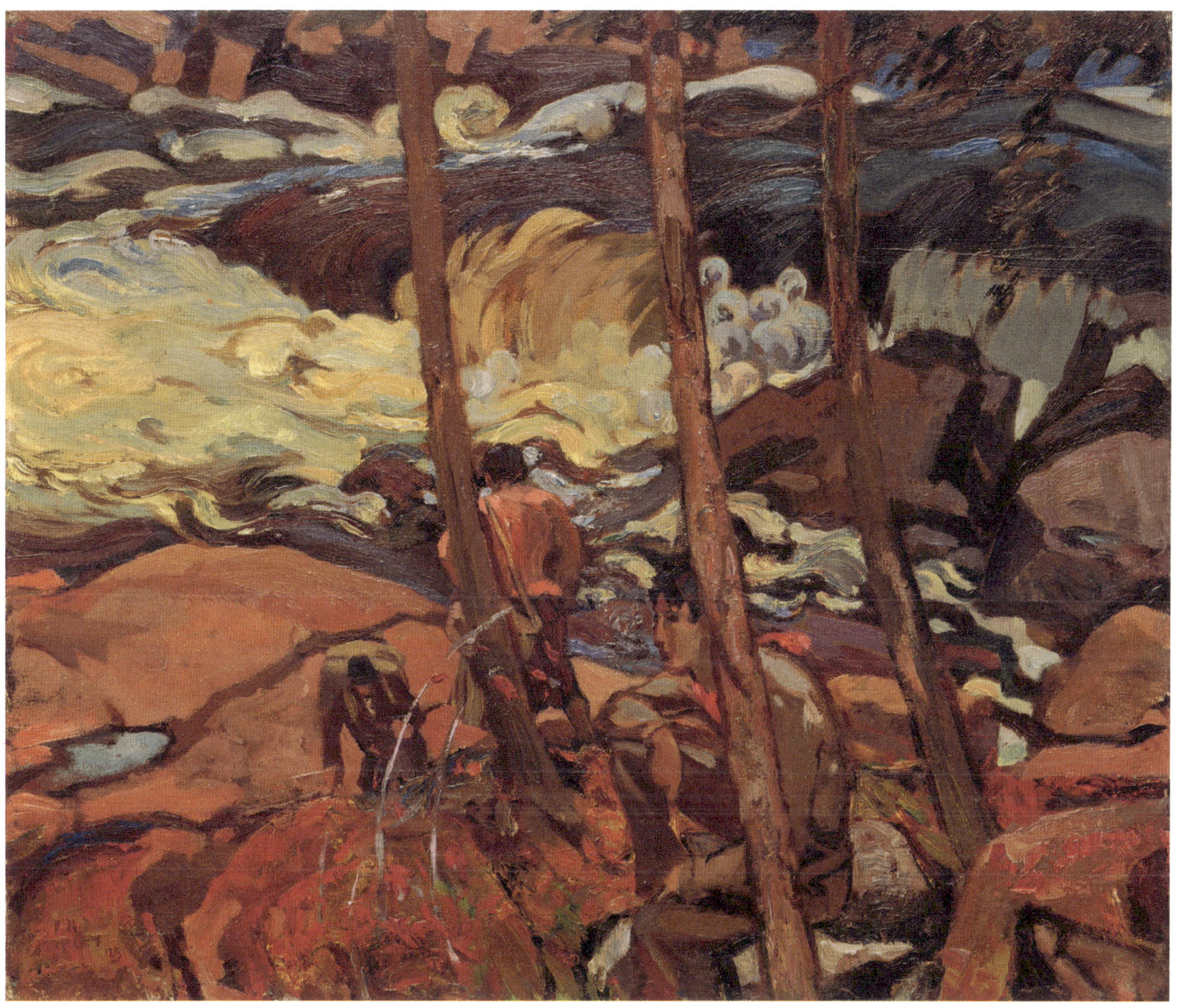

J. E. H. MacDonald
*The Beaver Dam,* 1919
81.6 × 86.7 cm

Carefully constructed of gnawed timber, dredged mud, and boulders, a beaver dam is a marvel of animal engineering. The semiaquatic rodent was at the crux of the North American fur trade from the seventeenth to nineteenth centuries. Ever since, the beaver's ingenuity has been widely admired, especially in Canada, where, in 1975, it was named the national animal. The symbol, however, is a loaded one, as the beaver—whose pelts were used in the Victorian era for popular felted top hats—was nearly driven to extinction by settlers. Although beaver populations have been restored in North America, the animal remains a symbol of fraught relations between Indigenous peoples and settlers, and of the ongoing colonization of Canada.

J. E. H. MacDonald doesn't engage directly with the political history of the beaver, but his attraction to the animal's industriousness is evident in his major canvas *The Beaver Dam*. Painted from a sketch done on a train trip to Algoma, Ontario, the composition highlights the structure and textures of the dam as a tapestry of color woven into its surroundings. Fallen leaves pepper the scene, signaling the end of summer. The bulk of the dam and the corresponding depth of the pond reveal an exquisite balance: the deep water is held in place by a wall of interlocked wood that is as precarious as it is strong.

A canoe (another fraught colonial symbol) gently rests on the dam. The red boat appears small and unstable amid rock outcroppings and looming forests that evoke the superiority of nature over humankind. Overall, *The Beaver Dam* is lyrical and serene, but it is also foreboding, speaking to the inherent duality of harmony and chaos that underpins all nature. Two years before MacDonald painted this work, his close friend and colleague Tom Thomson mysteriously drowned while canoeing in Algonquin Park. The tragedy certainly affected the way MacDonald reckoned with Ontario's vast and powerful backcountry.

Renée van der Avoird

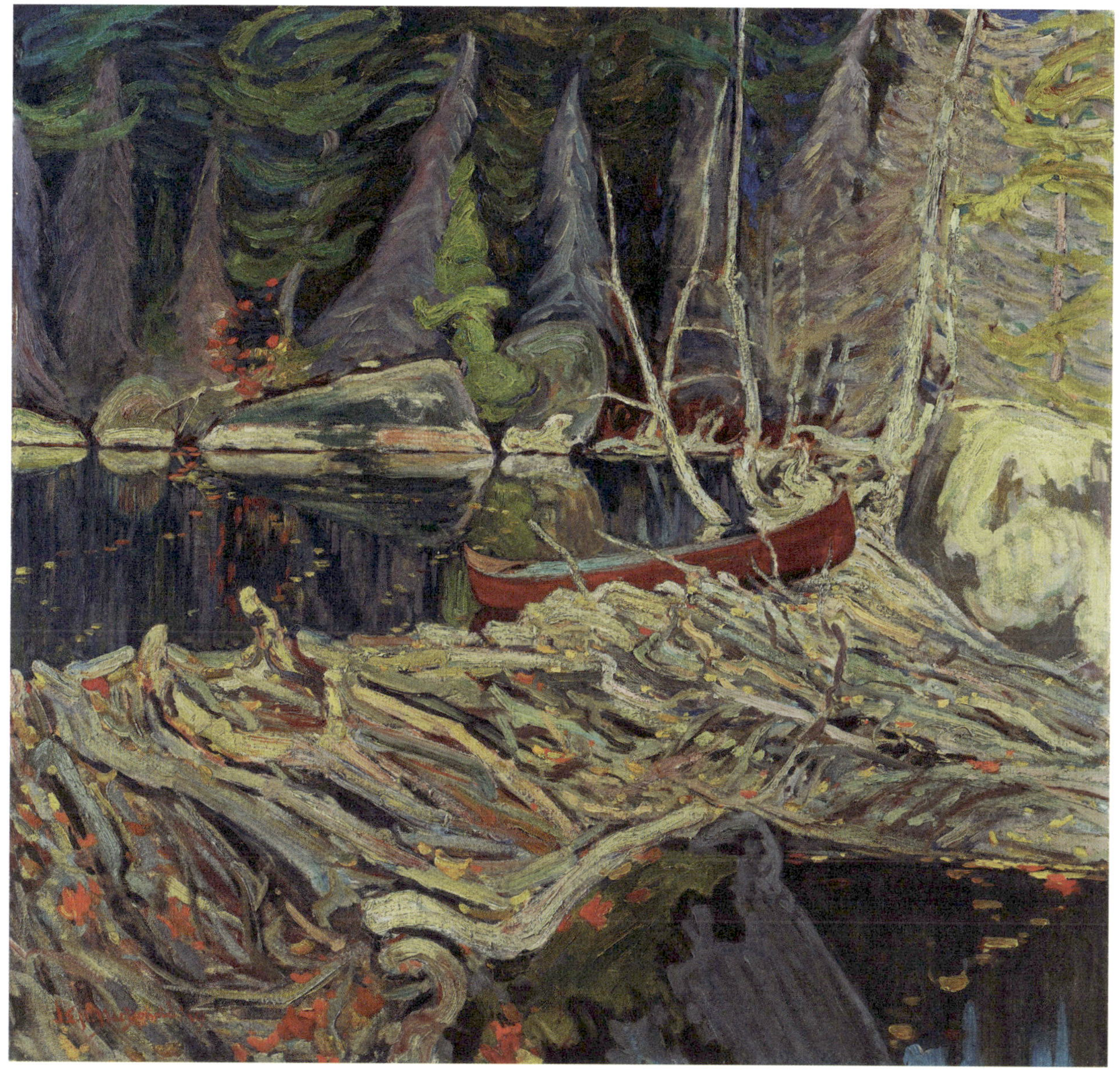

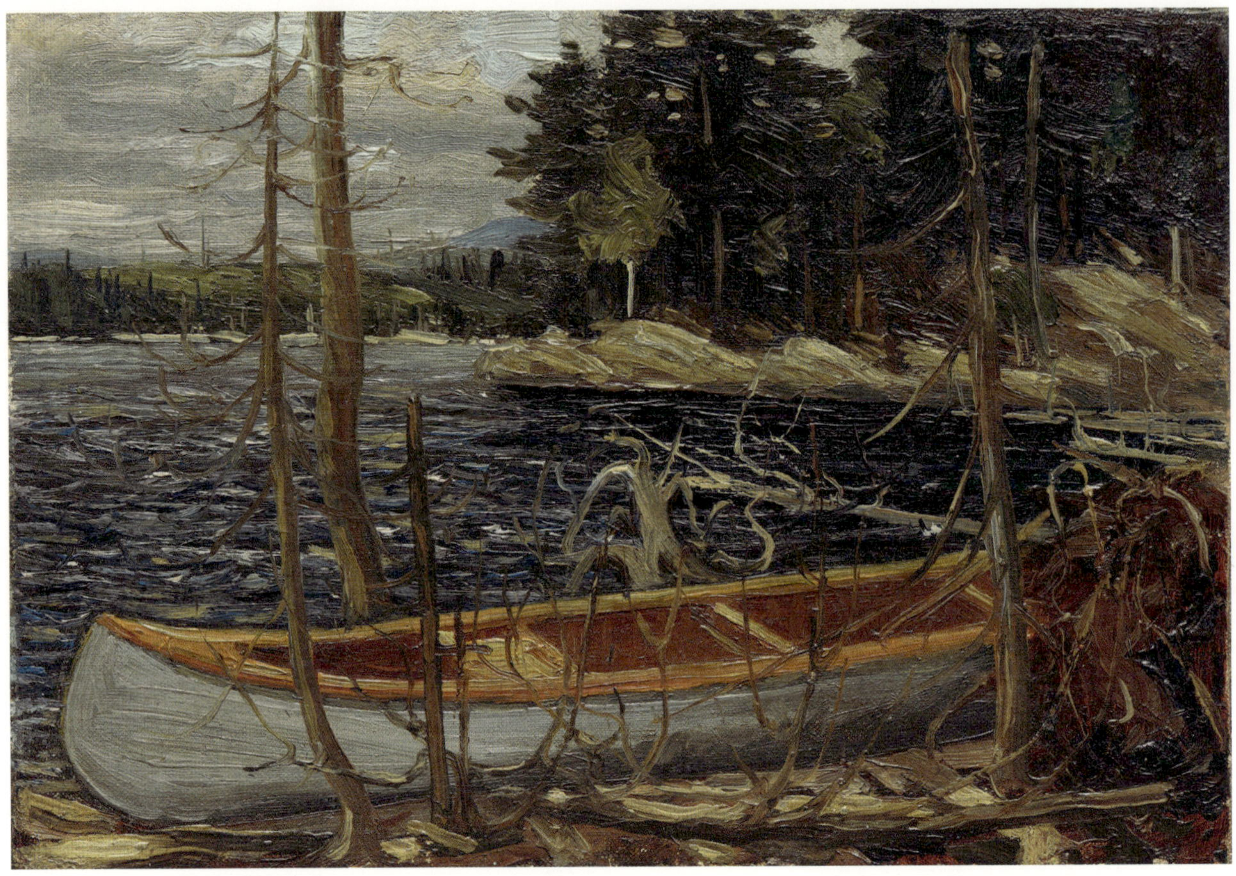

Tom Thomson
*The Canoe,* spring or fall 1914
17.3 × 25.3 cm

Arthur Lismer
*Tom Thomson's Camp,* 1914
30.8 × 23.4 cm

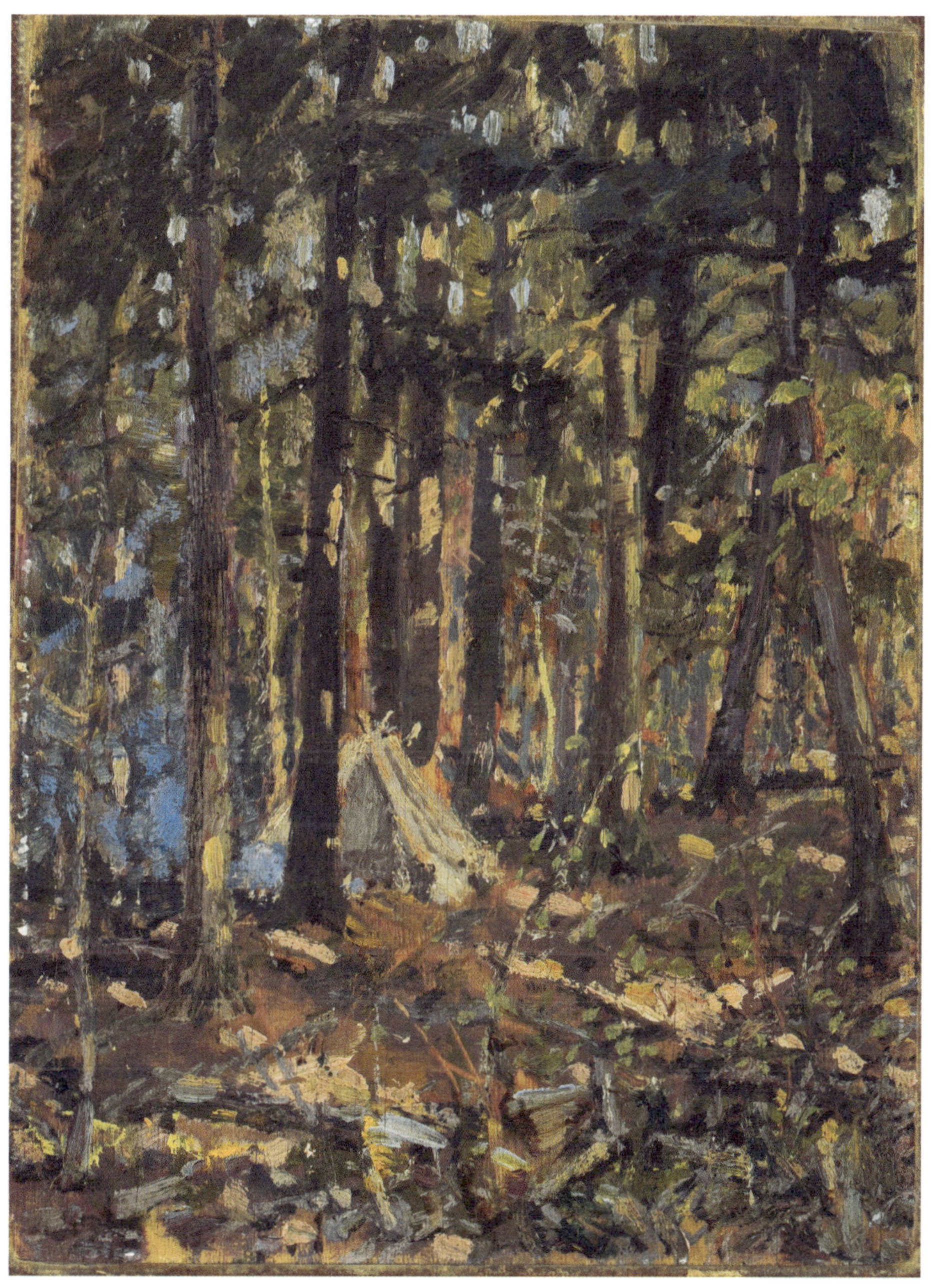

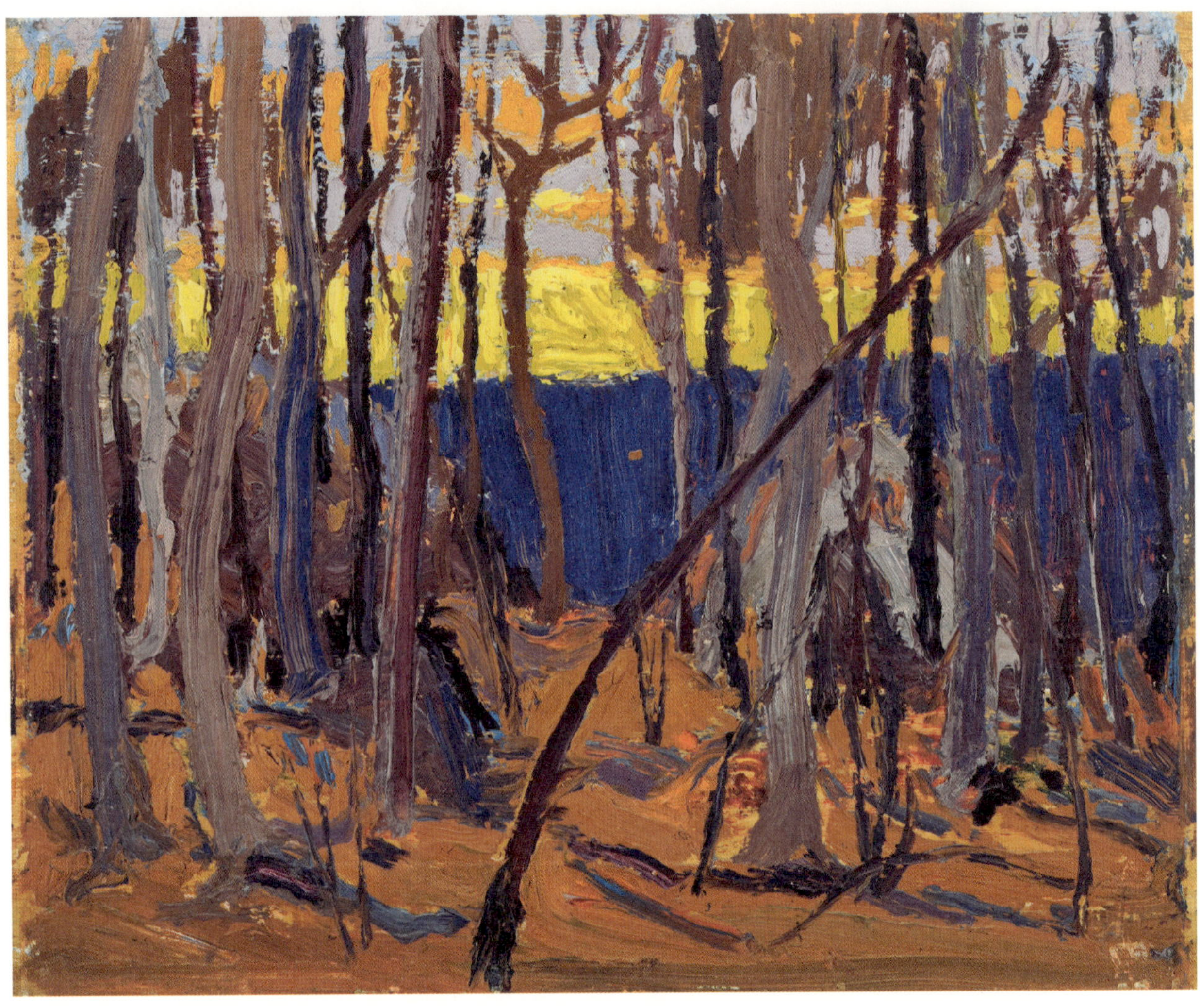

Tom Thomson
*Phantom Tent,* fall 1915
21.4 × 26.7 cm

Tom Thomson
*Bateaux,* summer 1916
21.5 × 26.8 cm

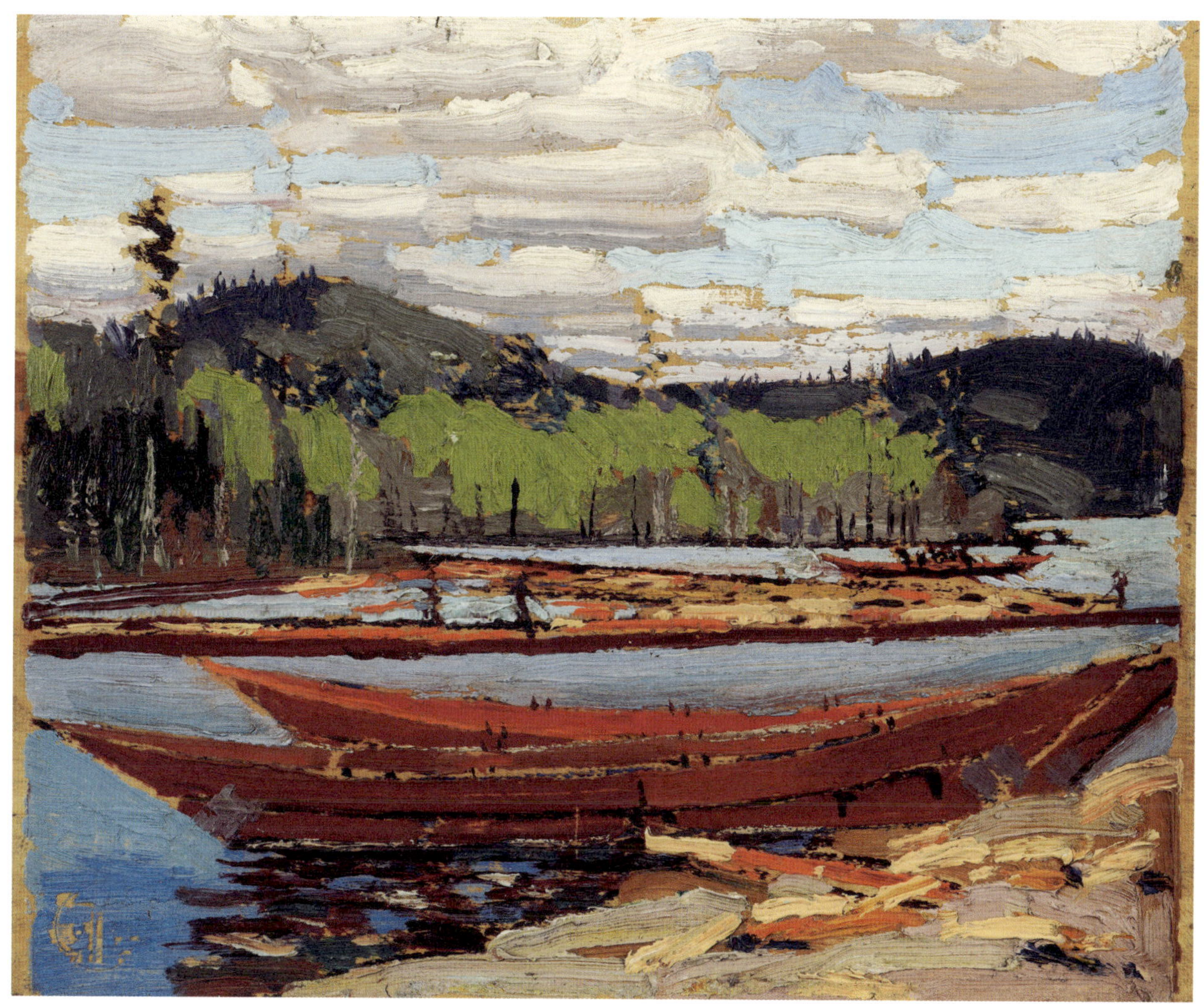

# Emily

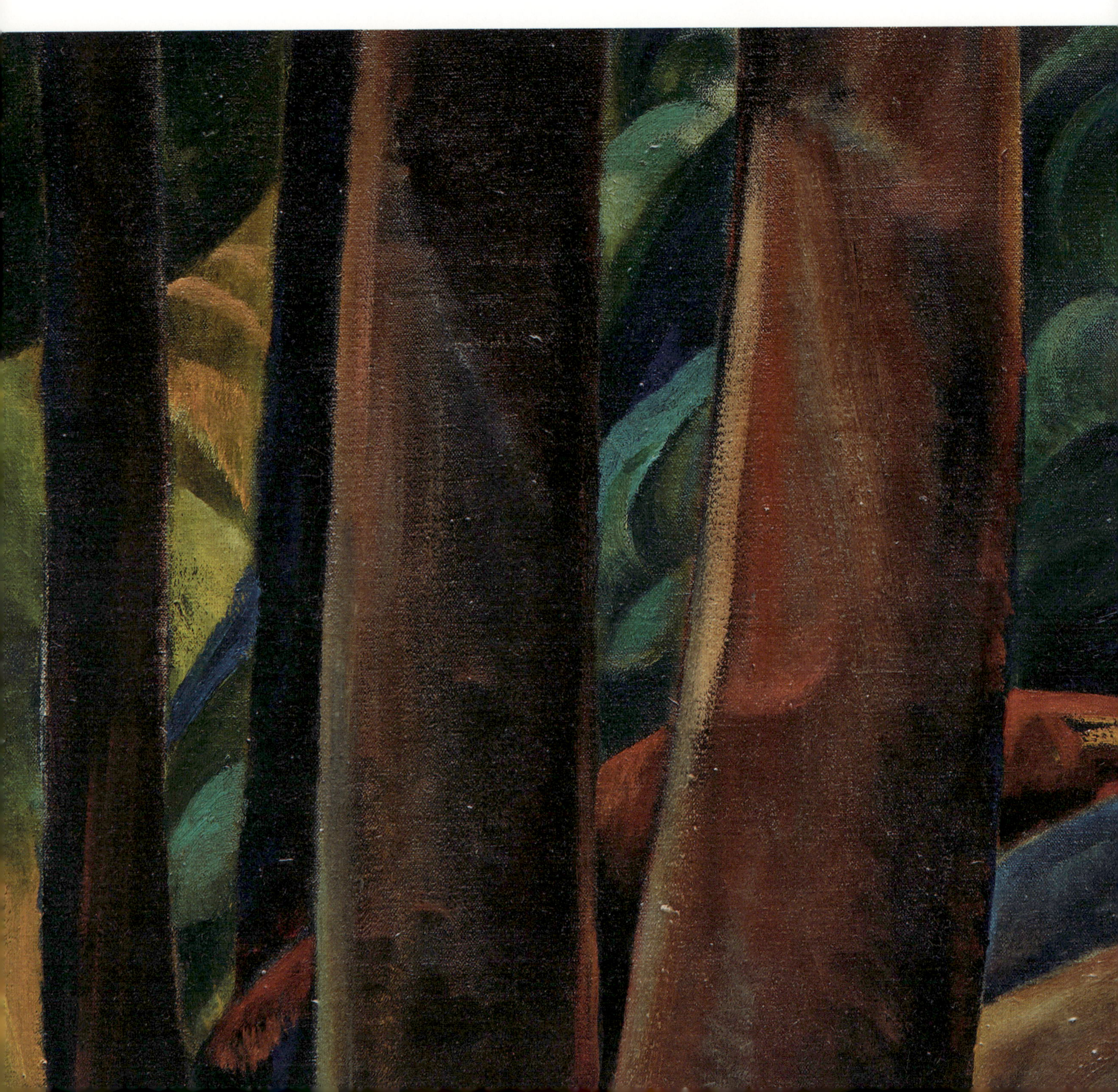

# Carr

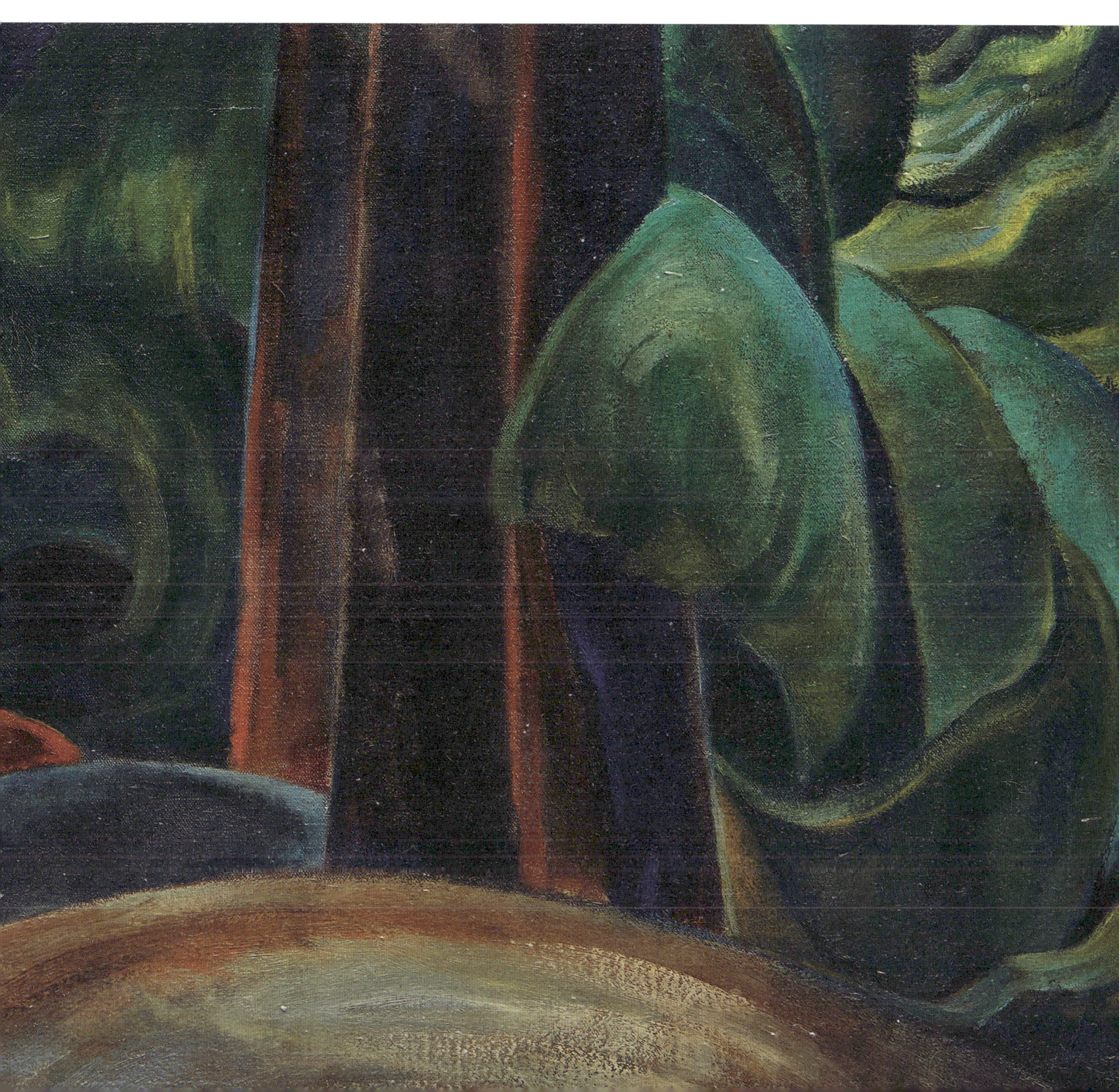

Celebrated for her dense paintings of forest interiors from the 1930s, Emily Carr spent the early decades of her career painting the Indigenous villages of the Northwest Coast. Having traveled from her hometown of Victoria, British Columbia, to Alaska, she was fascinated with their monumental carvings, later on writing extensively about her experiences. Carr repainted the views she found particularly inspiring, such as Cumshewa on Haida Gwaii, the site of her powerful painting *Big Raven* (1931). Other times, she used photographs as a source of her compositions, such as *Blunden Harbour* (ca. 1930). These pictures reveal a foundational shift in Carr's painting. While in the 1910s she had painted Indigenous villages and carvings with the vibrant colors of Post-Impressionism and Fauvism absorbed during her time studying in England and France, these later canvases exhibit the confident fluidity and form that articulate her own distinctive painting vocabulary.

Carr's preoccupation with Indigenous art and people is radically different from the work of artists associated with the Group of Seven who deliberately evacuated their landscapes of any Indigenous presence. Yet, her attitude was shaped by her Victorian upbringing. Despite her stated admiration, Carr's paintings of this period are fittingly viewed today as indicative of colonial thinking, and of participation in the forced assimilation of Indigenous peoples as dictated by restrictive Canadian laws, such as the Indian Act, intended to rupture and destroy life in the villages.

It was her friendship and artistic exchange with Lawren Harris in the 1930s, after a fourteen-year hiatus from painting, that transformed Carr's work, along with her own maturity as an artist on a spiritual quest. "What I am after is out there in the woods," Carr declared.[1] In luscious paintings such as *Wood Interior* (1929–30), *Western Forest* (ca. 1931), and her enigmatic *Forest* (ca. 1930–39), Carr's commitment to evoking the inner life force of the old-growth temperate rainforest reveals a profound spirituality and connection to the land.

Georgiana Uhlyarik

1—Emily Carr, letter to Eric Brown, director of the National Gallery of Canada (NGC), March 2, 1937, NGC files, Ottawa.

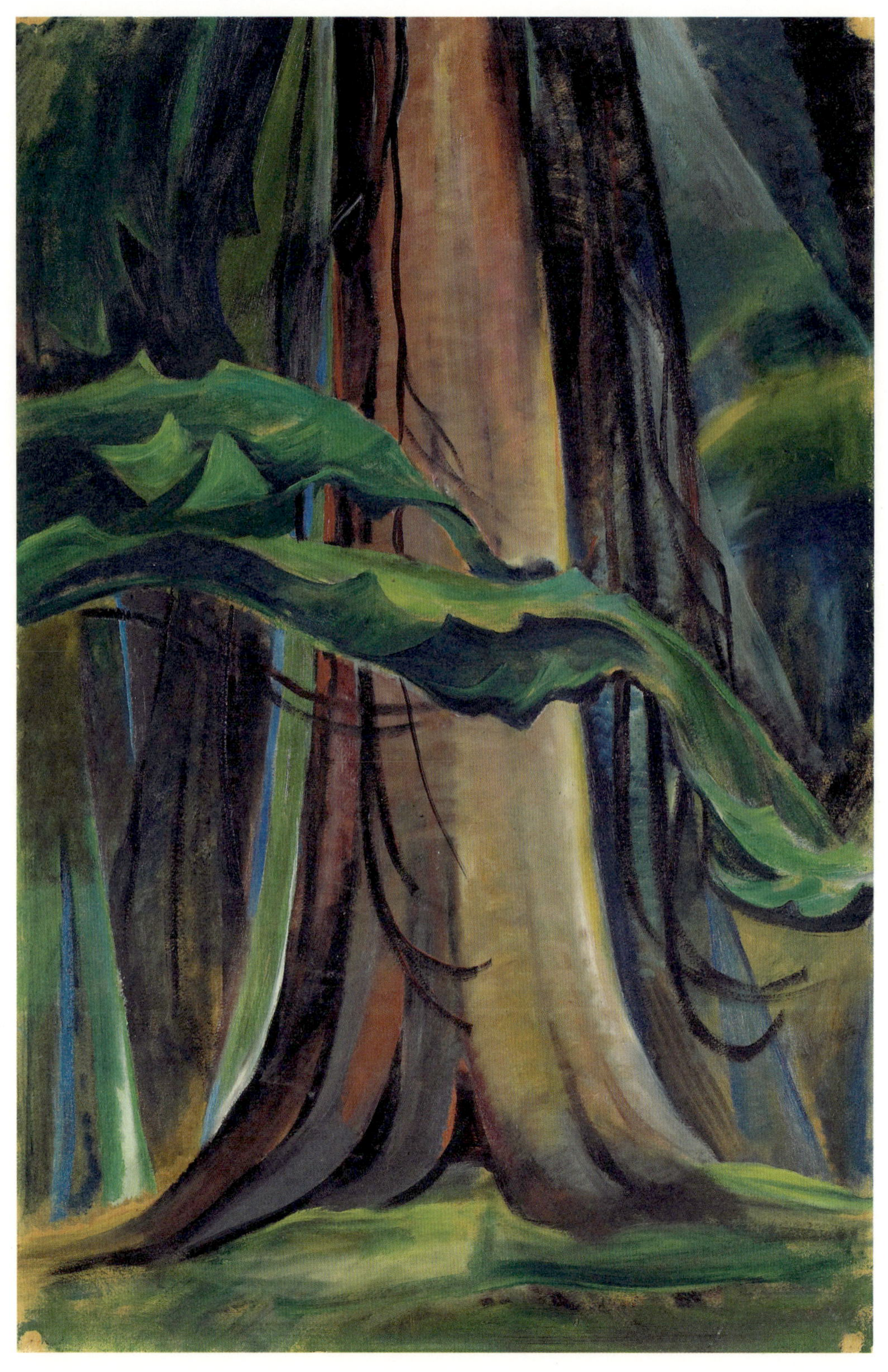

Emily Carr
*Red Tree,* ca. 1938
91.8 × 61.2 cm

Emily Carr
*Guyasdoms D'Sonoqua,* ca. 1930
100.3 × 65.4 cm

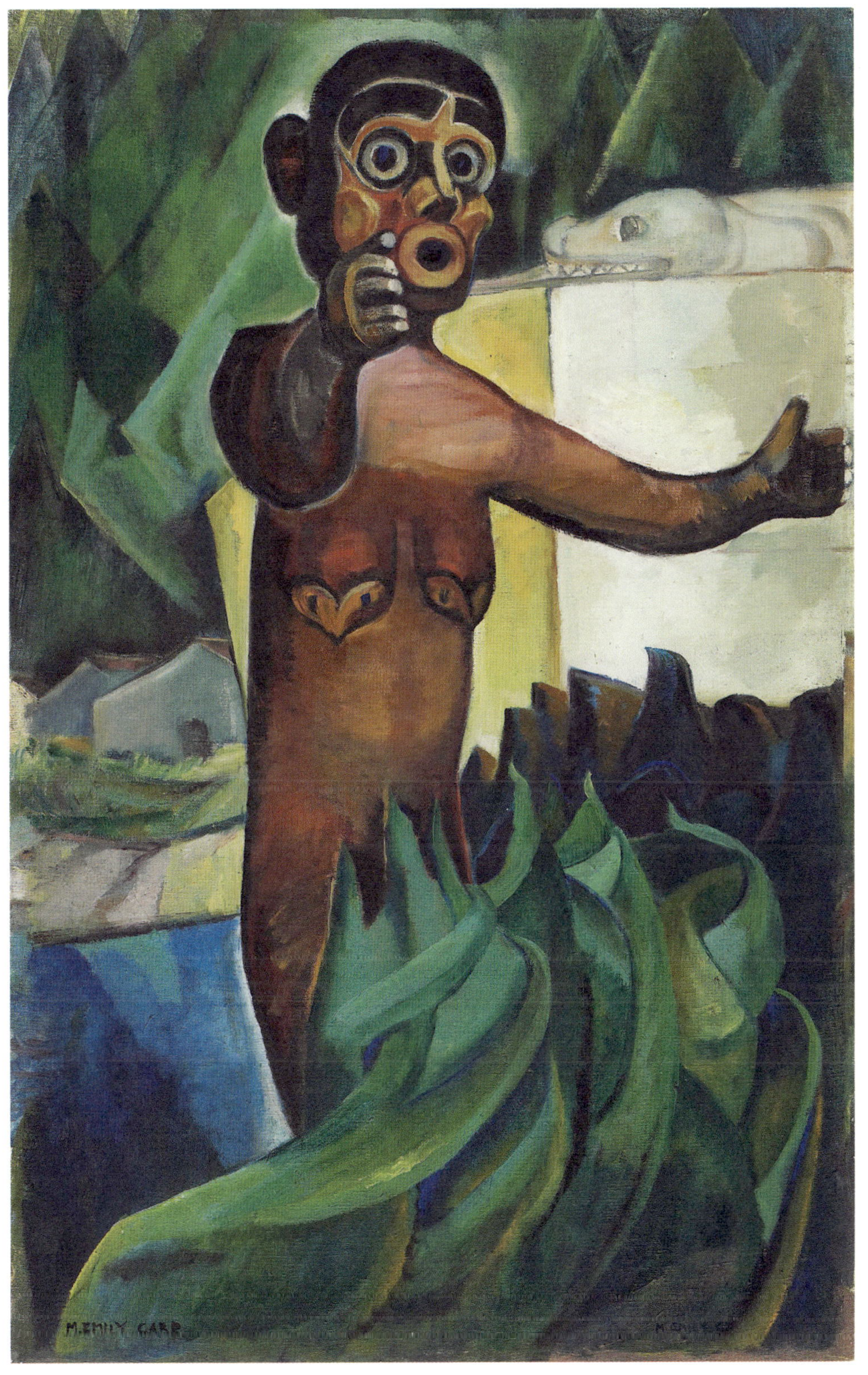

Emily Carr,
*Blunden Harbour,* ca. 1930
129.8 × 93.6 cm

In 1907, Emily Carr saw totem poles at their original locations for the first time on a trip up the coast of Alaska.[1] In her autobiography, she later wrote how important this experience had been for her, and for her artistic development.[2] Thereafter, she visited coastal villages of First Nations in British Columbia, such as the Haida and the Kwakwaka'wakw,[3] studying their artwork in detail.

"You must be absolutely honest and true in the depicting of a totem, for meaning is attached to every line," Carr wrote. This was linked to a desire to catalogue all remaining totem poles with the greatest possible accuracy,[4] but she lacked the financial means to fund the expensive trips. In 1912, Carr offered to sell about 200 paintings to the Ministry of Education of British Columbia, but the officials rejected the offer, for they felt the depictions were too individual to be considered ethnological studies.[5] Carr's work was infused by the Fauvism she had encountered in Europe, and she had strong and colorful expression in her painting. Disappointed and financially unable to support her art, Carr stopped painting until around 1928. Now in her fifties and reinvigorated by her friendship with Lawren Harris, Carr returned to painting with a distinct new style and vision.

*Blunden Harbour* really differs from her earlier paintings in terms of style and color. It shows a wooden landing with three monumental totem poles installed to welcome, or deter, visitors. The canvas is painted in a unified color palette, with browns and grays for the landing and the figures, and with blues and greens for the landscape and sky. While the elements of the composition are vivid and dynamic, the image exudes a deep calm.

The title of the painting states the English name of the Kwakwaka'-wakw village called Ba'as, home of the 'Nakwaxda'xw, some 500 kilometers north of Vancouver—a place that Carr never visited. Instead, *Blunden Harbour* was created after a photograph by Charles Frederick Newcombe that Carr had seen around 1930.[6] Yet her painting presents a lonely landing in expressive colors rather than the jetty bustling with people seen in the photograph. The source of light behind the scenery gives everything a dramatic glow, and the totems are filled with an aura of power and spirituality. Carr's ambition to create faithful representations of totems seems to have shifted. By that time, she was no longer traveling to the Indigenous villages and would soon give up her preoccupation with related art. Exploring her own expression and interpretation of the world around her,[7] she subsequently turned to depictions of nature.

Rebecca Herlemann

1—Jay Stewart and Peter Macnair, "Reconstructing Emily Carr in Alaska," in *Emily Carr: New Perspectives on a Canadian Icon,* ed. Ian M. Thom, Charles C. Hill, and Johanne Lamoureux, exh. cat. National Gallery of Canada, Ottawa, Vancouver Art Gallery, and Art Gallery of Ontario (Vancouver: Douglas & McIntyre, 2006), pp. 12–42. Her illustrated journal has been recently found (2014): https://www.gallery.ca/magazine/books/lost-and-found-emily-carrs-sister-and-i-in-alaska.
2—Emily Carr, *Growing Pains* (Toronto: Clarke, Irwin & Co., 1946).
3—Carr visited villages of, among others, the Gitxsan, Haida, Heiltsuk, Kwakwaka'wakw, Nisga'a, Nuu-chah-nulth, Nuxalk, Wet'suwet'en, and Tsimshian.
4—Emily Carr, "Lectures on Totems" (April 1913), in *Opposite Contraries: The Unknown Journals of Emily Carr and Other Writings,* ed. Susan Crean (Vancouver: Douglas & McIntyre, 2003), p. 195. The Indian Act of 1876 forbade the raising of totem poles.
5—See Dr. C. F. Newcombe, Victoria, in a letter dated January 17, 1913, to F. Kermode, curator at the Provincial Museum in Victoria. Newcombe Family Papers, BC Archives, Add MSS 1077, vol. 52, file 19, as quoted by Charles Hill, "Blunden Harbour: Between Photography and Painting," in *From the Forest to the Sea: Emily Carr in British Columbia,* ed. Sarah Milroy and Ian Dejardin, exh. cat. Art Gallery of Ontario, Toronto, and Dulwich Picture Gallery, London (Fredericton: Goose Lane Editions, 2014), pp. 171–74, esp. p. 172.
6—See the entire essay by Charles Hill, "Blunden Harbour: Between Photography and Painting," in Milroy and Dejardin, *From the Forest to the Sea,* pp. 171–74.
7—Emily Carr to Eric Brown, June 30, 1938, National Gallery of Canada Library and Archives (NGC Arch.), 7.1-Carr, as quoted in Marcia Crosby, "A Chronology of Love's Contingencies," in Thom et al., *Emily Carr,* p. 158.

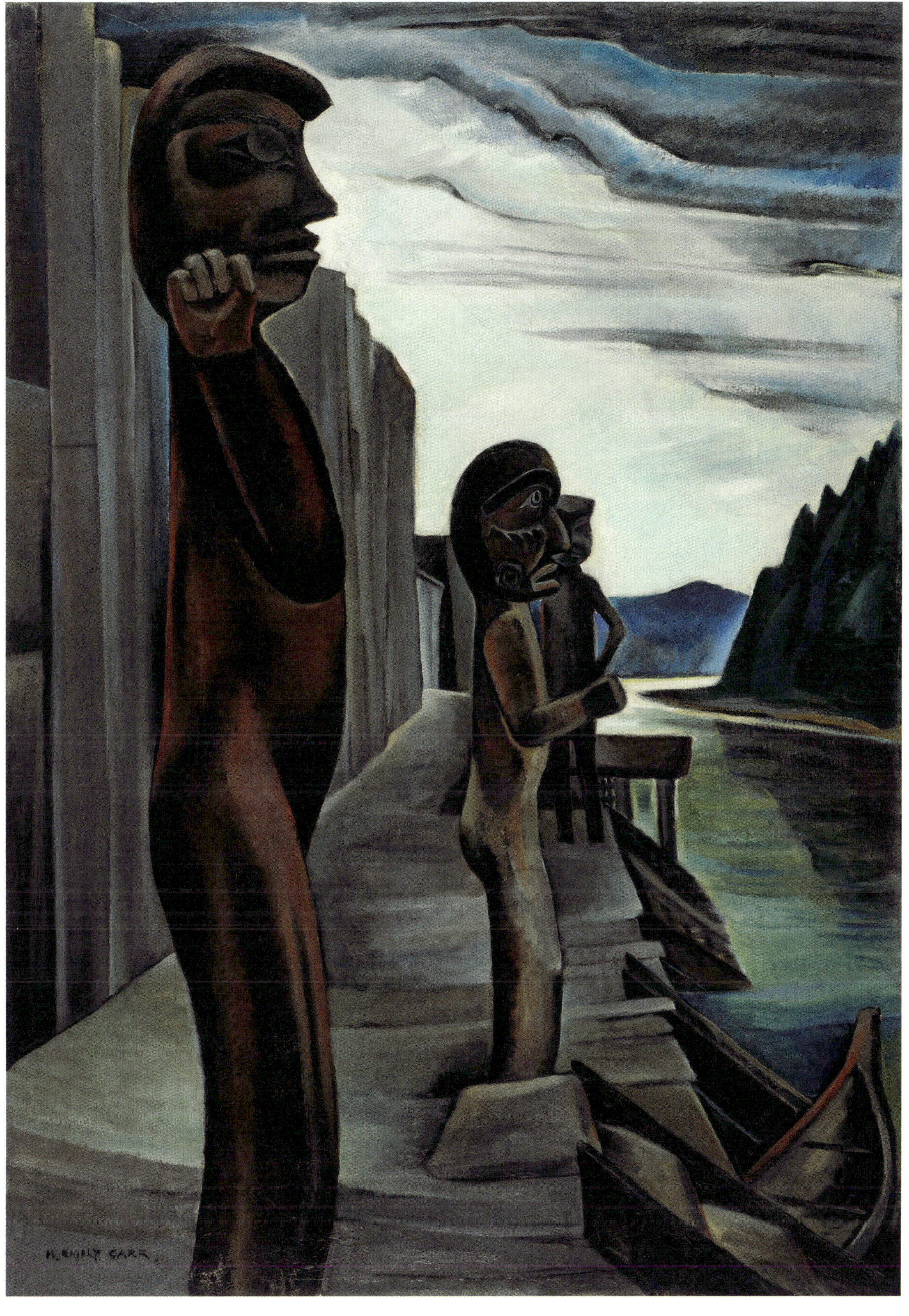

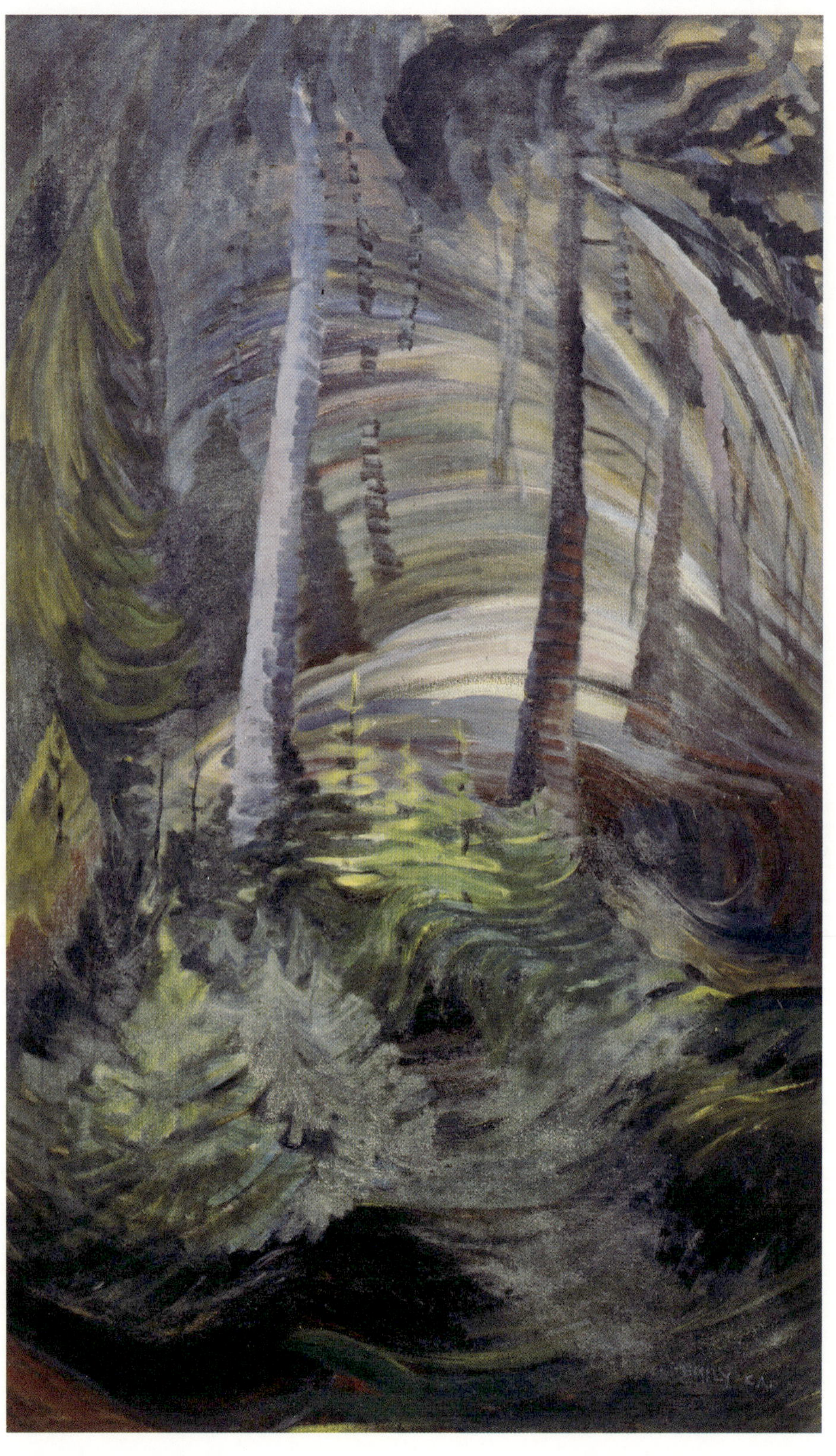

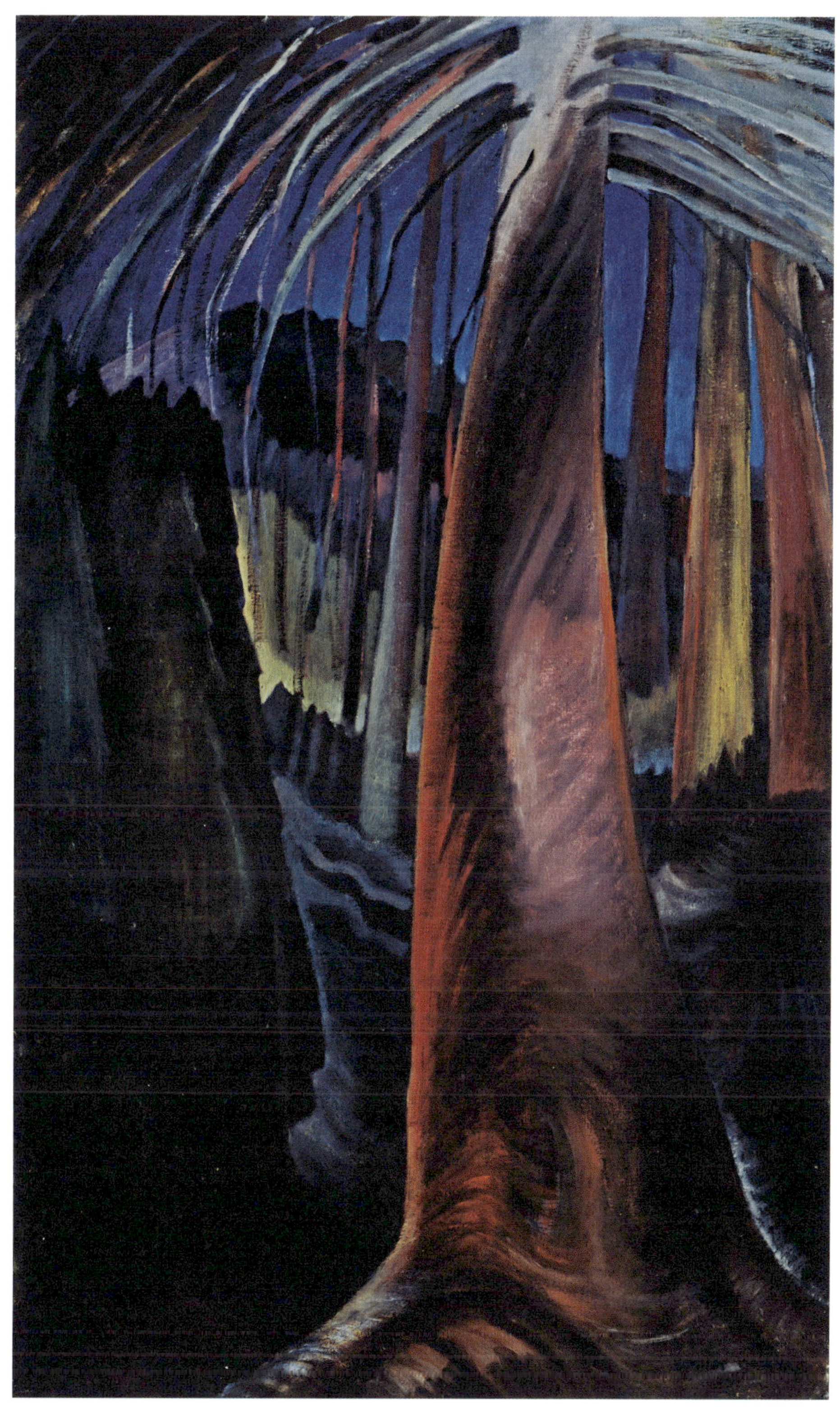

Emily Carr
*Forest,* ca. 1930–39
111.7 × 68 cm

Emily Carr
*Old Tree at Dusk,* ca. 1932
112 × 68.5 cm

Emily Carr
*Wood Interior,* 1929–30
106.9 × 70.2 cm

In 1927, following a recommendation from the ethnologist Marius Barbeau, the artist Emily Carr was invited by Eric Brown, the director of the National Gallery of Canada in Ottawa, to participate in the exhibition *Canadian West Coast Art: Native and Modern.*[1] The show was a great success for Carr, and the trip to Ottawa (with a stopover in Toronto) also connected her with the Group of Seven, whose works she had previously known only from Fred Housser's 1926 publication *A Canadian Art Movement: The Story of the Group of Seven.*[2] She found great inspiration in their painterly approaches and their relationship to nature. Her meeting with fellow artist Lawren Harris, in particular, would lead to a deep connection and close friendship.

Carr shared with Harris a religious feeling about nature. He encouraged her to turn to the forests and seascape of Vancouver Island, instead of focusing on Indigenous villages and totems of the region.[3] From about 1930 on, Carr devoted herself exclusively to painting sea, sky, and forests, leaning more and more toward abstraction while trying to capture the spirit of nature. In trees and woods "you can find strength," as she put it: "The juice and essence of life are in them."[4] Guided by a strong wish to be in nature in order to paint it, she undertook extended trips into the areas surrounding Victoria, British Columbia, her place of residence.[5]

The paintings that Emily Carr created of the forests of British Columbia are charged with energy and full of movement. For all of her tree pictures, she chose the portrait format, which leads the view of the spectator upward and makes one seem small in front of the monumental growth. *Wood Interior* directs the gaze into a thicket of green shapes, with only a few smooth brown tree trunks standing out against it. The bushes, leaves, and treetops seem to be caught in a wild vortex and carried upward to where a clearing opens up between the branches. In painterly terms, the canvas continues the tradition of European art movements like Cubism, with which Carr had been able to acquaint herself during study trips to England and France. The image is broken up into geometric structures; individual pictorial elements can no longer be clearly distinguished, and rather than create an actual pictorial space, the suggestive colors evoke a poetic space that draws the viewer into its spell. The breakdown of the motif into cubes is very rare in Emily Carr's work and sets *Wood Interior* apart from most of her forest paintings. It is an experiment in form which she was not to pursue again, leaving the painting to be one of the most remarkable of her works.

Rebecca Herlemann

1—Charles C. Hill, "Backgrounds in Canadian Art: The 1927 Exhibition of Canadian West Coast Art; Native and Modern," in *Emily Carr: New Perspectives on a Canadian Icon,* ed. Ian M. Thom, Charles C. Hill, and Johanne Lamoureux, exh. cat. National Gallery of Canada, Ottawa, Vancouver Art Gallery, and Art Gallery of Ontario, Toronto (Vancouver et al.: Douglas & McIntyre, 2006), pp. 92–156.
2—Alicia Boutilier, "Mapping an Artist's Identity: The Life, Work and Writing of Yvonne McKague Housser" (master's thesis, Carleton University, Ottawa, 1998), p. 76.
3—Doris Shadbolt, *The Art of Emily Carr* (Toronto: Clarke Irwin / Douglas & McIntyre, 1979), p. 76.
4—Emily Carr, as quoted by Ian Dejardin, "A Life of Emily Carr," in Milroy and Dejardin, *From the Forest to the Sea,* ed. Sarah Milroy and Ian Dejardin, exh. cat. Art Gallery of Ontario, Toronto, and Dulwich Picture Gallery, London (Fredericton: Goose Lane Editions, 2014), pp. 19–32, esp. p. 28.
5—Ibid. Carr purchased a caravan for this purpose in 1933, which she dubbed "Elephant." It allowed her and her pets to travel flexibly and comfortably.

# Emily Carr

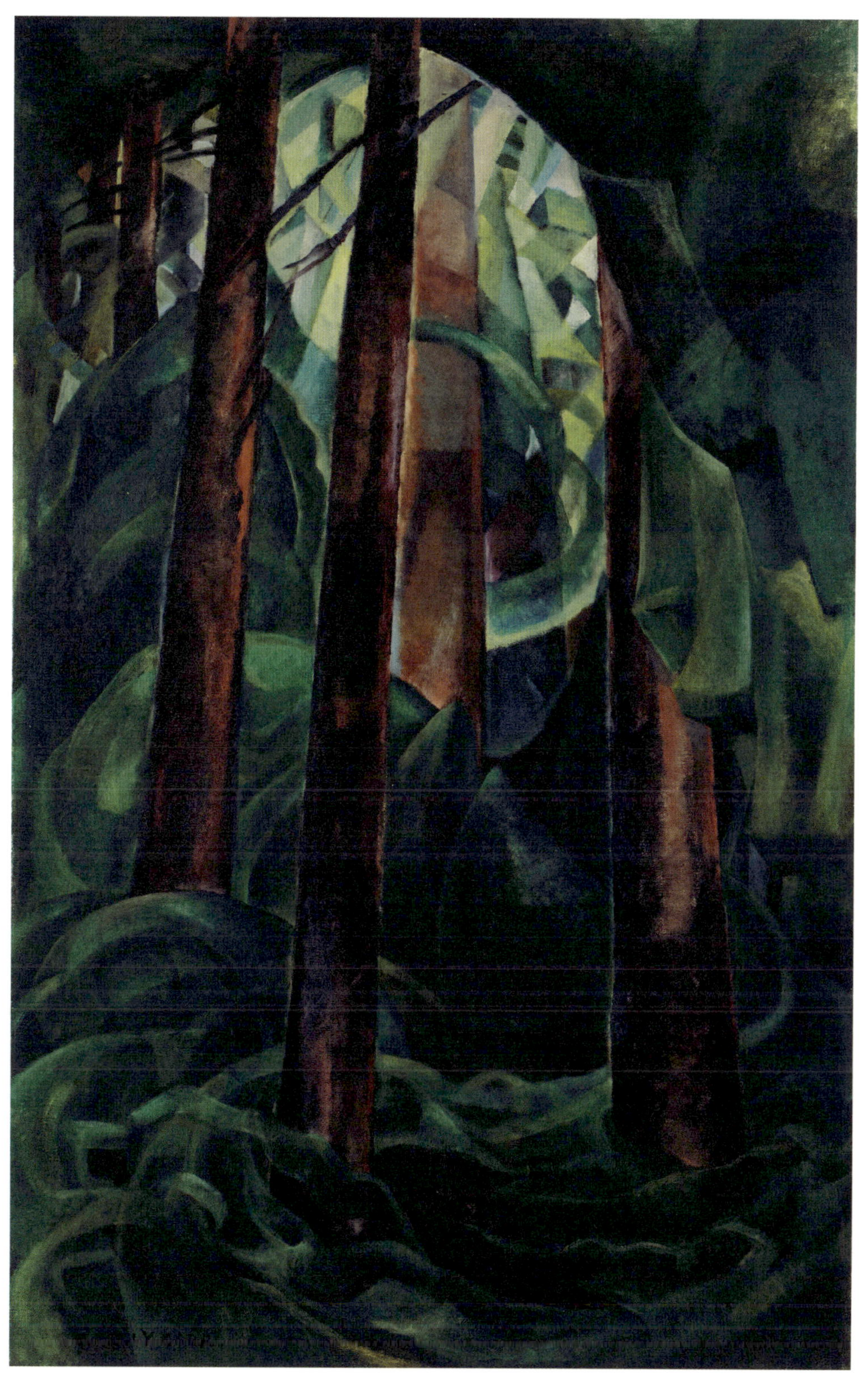

Emily Carr
*Western Forest,* ca. 1931
128.3 × 91.8 cm

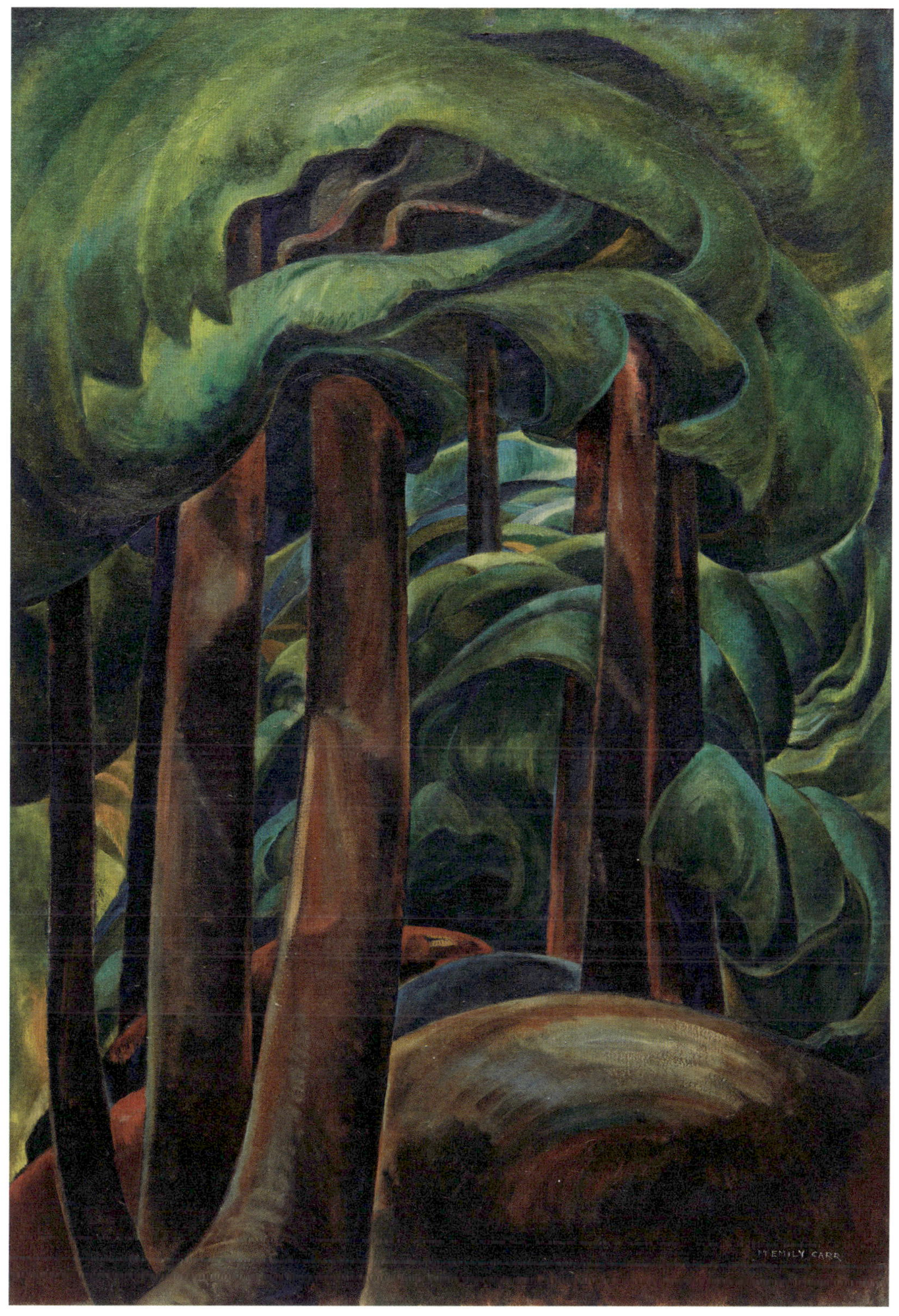

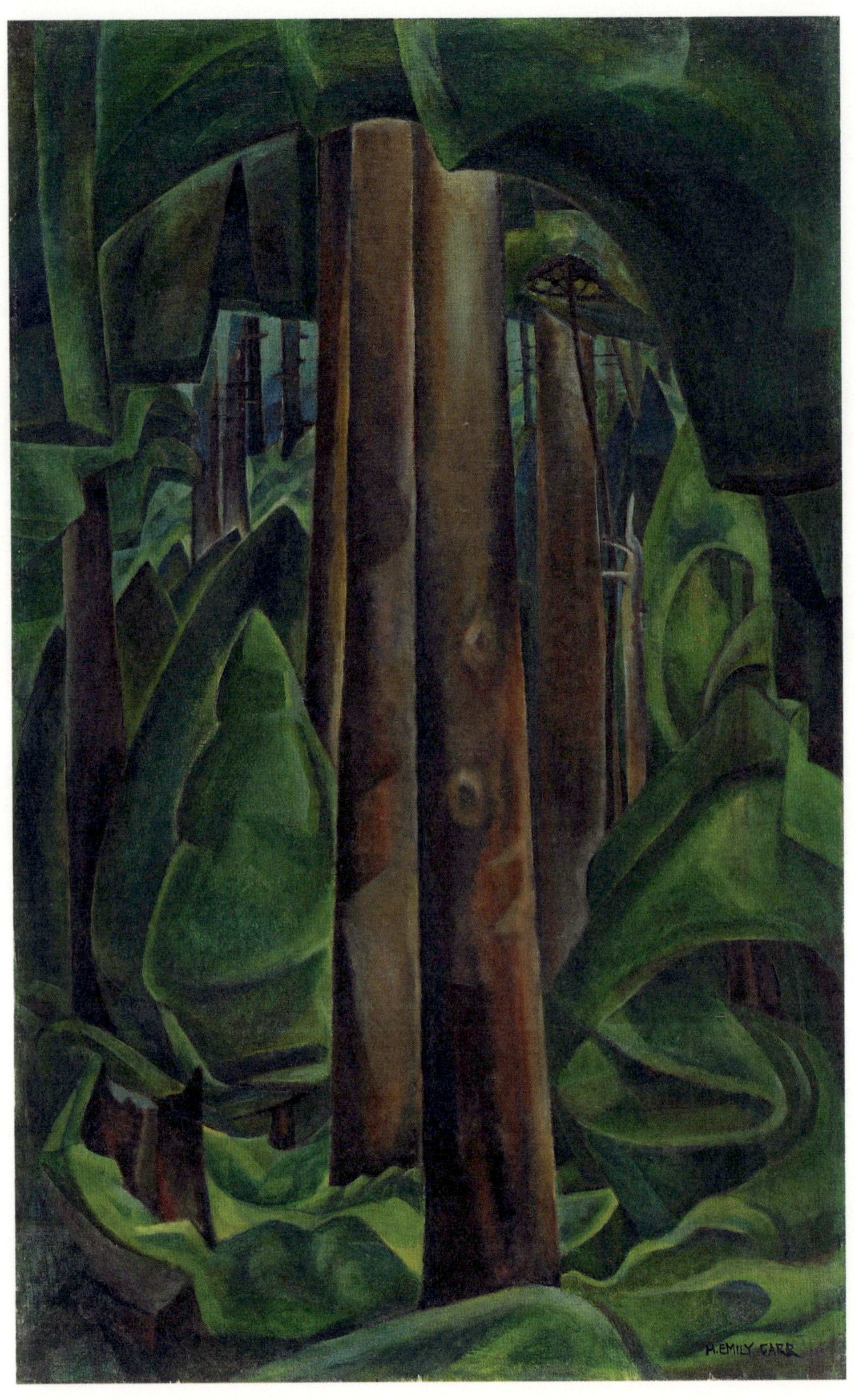

Emily Carr
*Inside a Forest II*, 1929–30
109.9 × 69.8 cm

Emily Carr
*Heina Q.C.I.*, 1928
129.6 × 91.2 cm

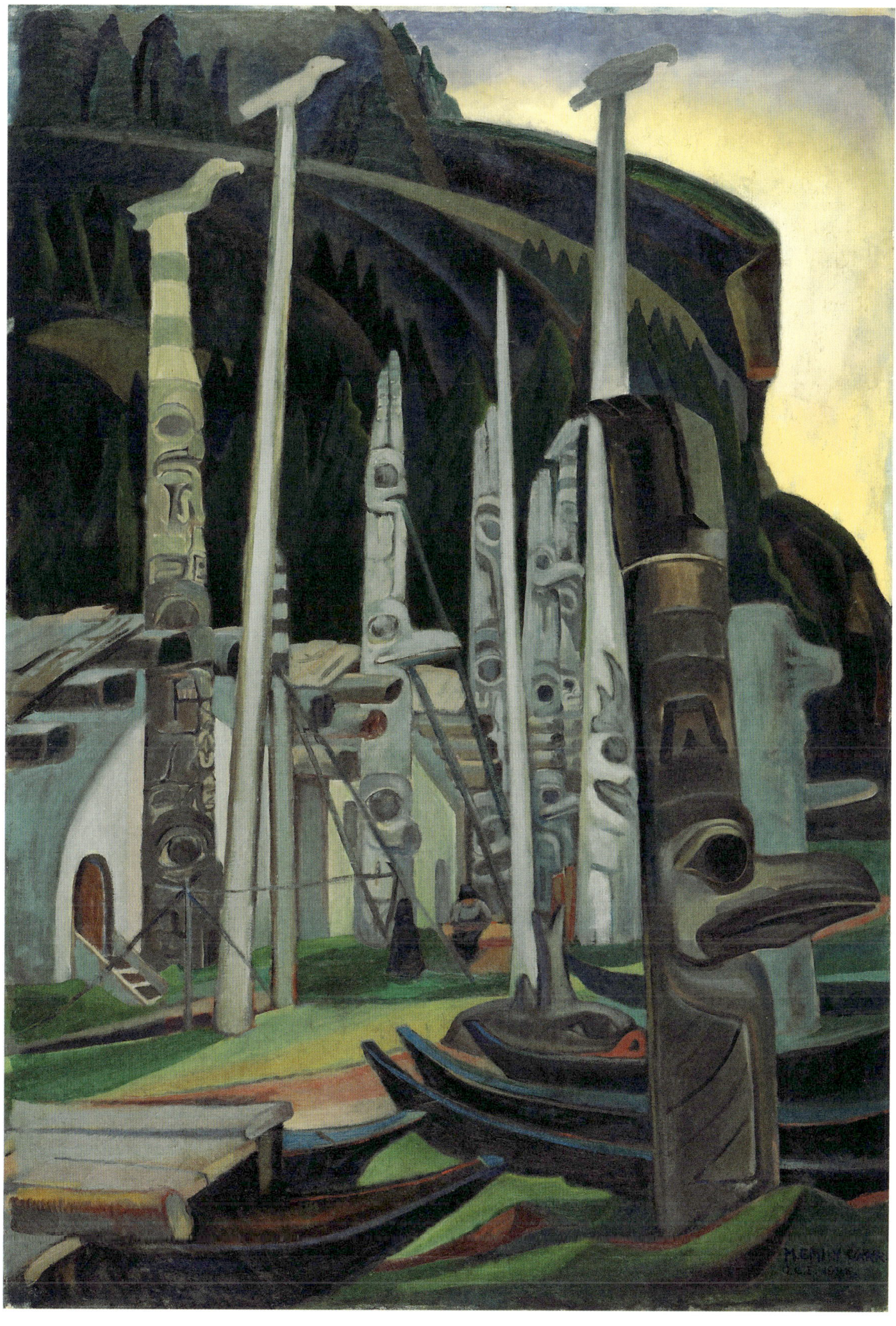

# Land vs

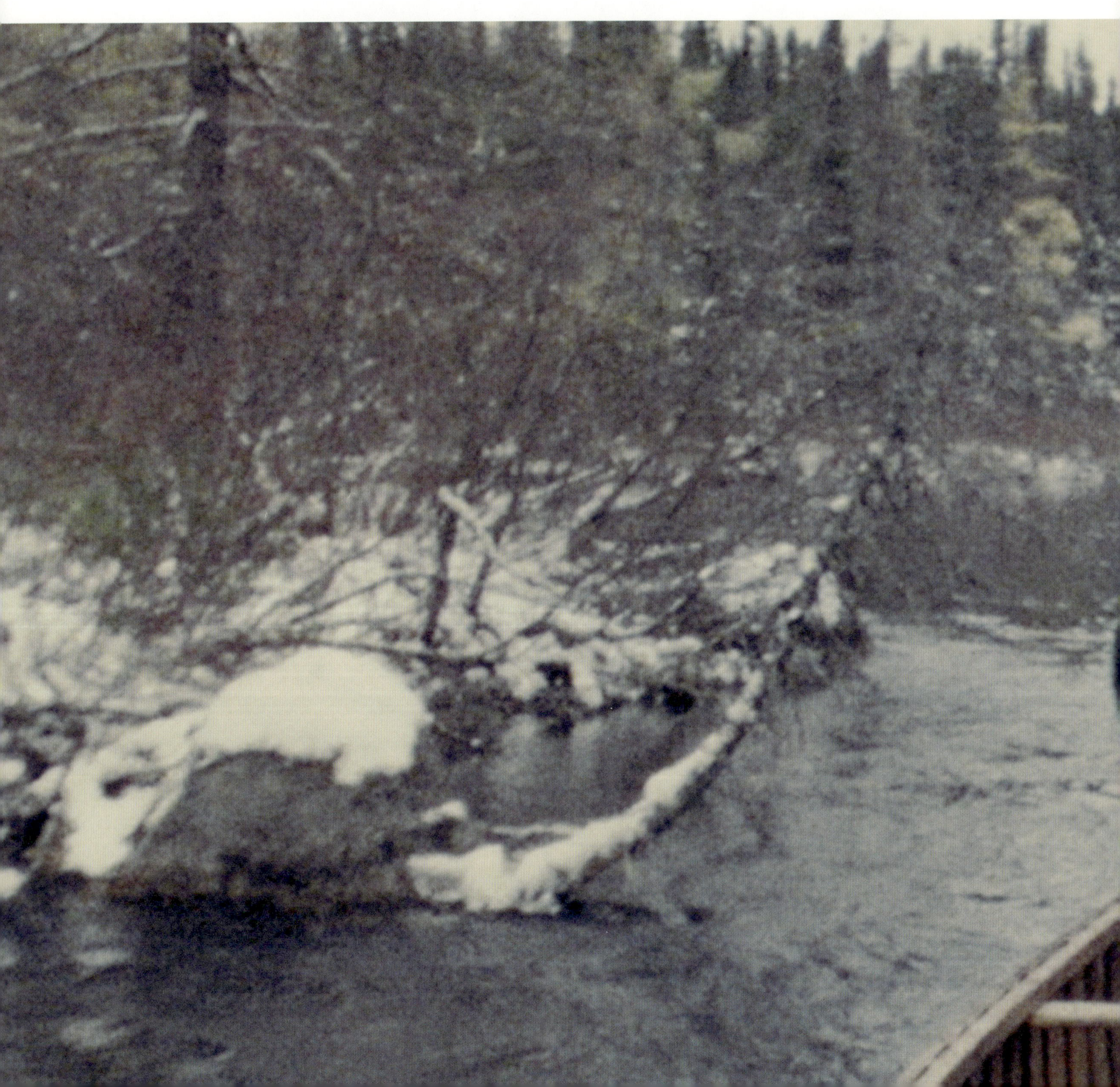

# Landscape

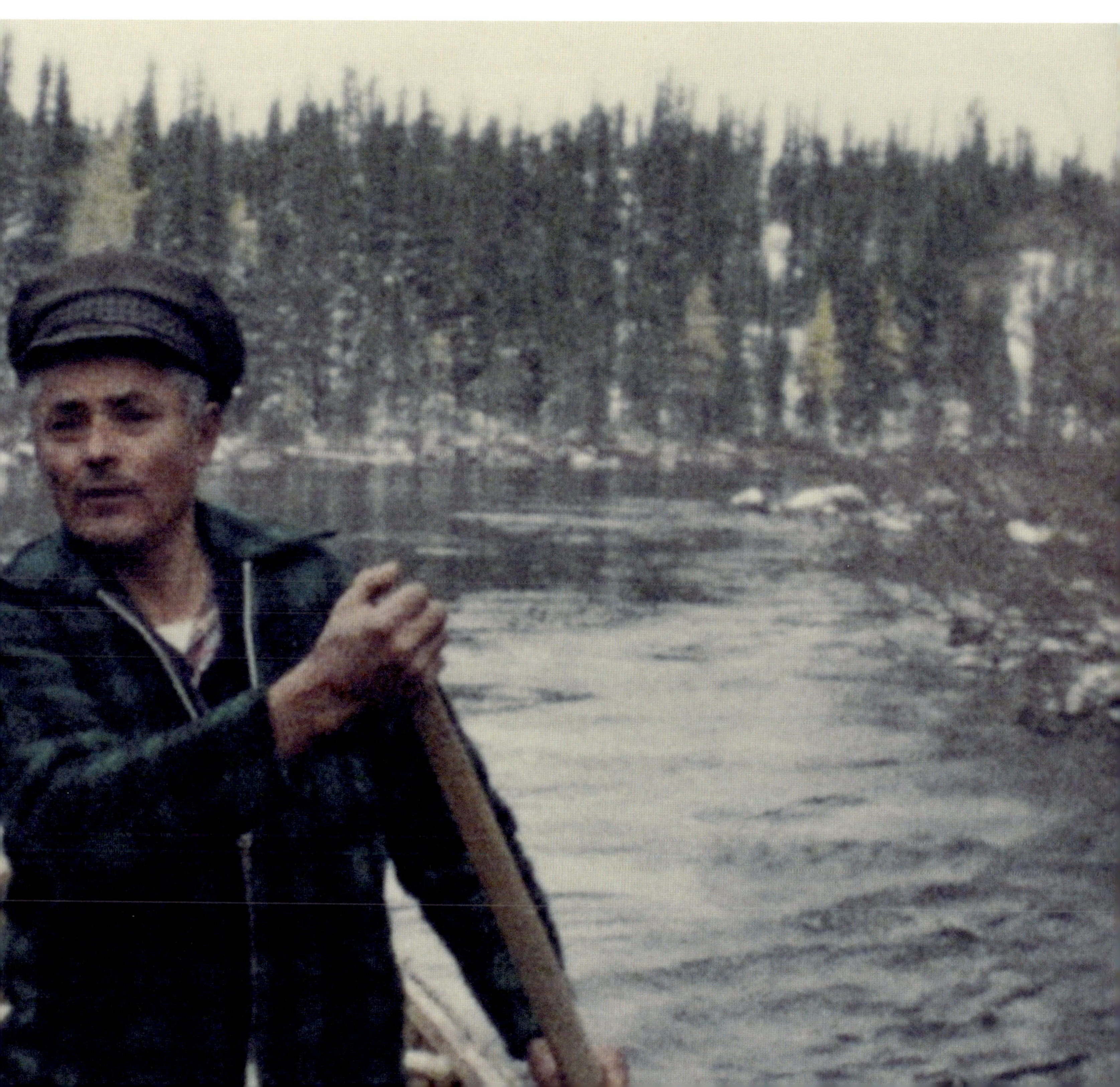

All official members of the Group of Seven were white men, some raised in England. The few women who exhibited alongside the Group were also of European descent. During their years of training in Europe, many of these artists had absorbed the various trends in art there, yet they all shared the idea of wanting to create genuinely Canadian art. They were further united by their social and cultural context. Completely absent, however, both in their art and in the era in general, was an awareness of the colonial perspective inscribed within their images of Canadian landscapes. This remained a blind spot in the art of the time. The search for a visual representation of Canada was also a process of exclusion. The paintings would construct a wilderness that was quite often not there, for this supposedly uninhabited landscape was, and always had been, home to many Indigenous peoples. The essentially European concept of an aesthetically ordered landscape, be it sublime, picturesque, or romantic, is opposed by Indigenous connection to land as one of kinship—humans are bound with the land and are in relation to all nonhuman beings. Unlike Eurocentric no-tions of human ownership and dominance of the land, the Indig-enous world places land "at the root of all our relations" (Caroline Monnet). It is the ancestral land that settlers annexed and from which Indigenous communities were removed through resettlement.

This chapter bands together positions of Indigenous critique of knowledge informed by colonialism. Time periods are presented using the example of a region in British Columbia. Thus, different voices reveal how the depiction and representation of this region has changed. A famous painting by Emily Carr is titled *Blunden Harbour* (ca. 1930). It was painted after a photograph by Charles F. Newcombe and depicts three monumental totem poles. The same place, with the actual name Ba'as, is the setting of the first silent film by a white director with an Indigenous cast, *In the Land of the Head Hunters* (1914), as well as the documentary *Blunden Harbour* (1951). We trace the shift in narrative perspective to the present day, to *Mobilize* (2015) by the Algonquin-French artist Caroline Monnet; and in Lisa Jackson's film *How a People Live* (2013), we reappraise the traumata of an Indigenous community following the Indian Act. These films and the photographs by Jeff Thomas—all works by Indigenous artists—form a counternarrative to the landscapes of the Group of Seven.

Martina Weinhart

Edward S. Curtis
*In the Land of the Head Hunters /
In the Land of the War Canoes,* 1914
Film (restoration with original
musical score, tinted, sound,
66 min.)

The silent film set among the Kwakwaka'wakw, an Indigenous people who live around the Queen Charlotte Strait on the coast of British Columbia in the northwest of Canada, is a fictionalized love story set amidst warring clans. Written and directed by the American photographer Edward S. Curtis, with George Hunt as his Kwakwaka'wakw advisor,[1] it is considered to be the first film with an entirely Indigenous cast. Stanley Hunt and Maggie Frank star in the principle roles. Hunt's second wife, Francine, a noblewoman from the 'Nakwaxda'xw nation, familiarly known as Tsak'wani, made the robes, advised on details, and played several roles. George Hunt's grandchildren Margaret, Frank, and Robert Wilson, as well as Helen Wilson Knox, were also given parts. The elaborate production was filmed on Kwakwaka'wakw territory and was intended for a broad audience. Its reception has focused predominately on its perceived "documentary" aspects, which is why it is quite frequently (mis)understood as an ethnographic document.

Despite the criticism of Curtis, who was accused in particular of stylizing and historicizing Indigenous peoples and subjecting them to the romantic cliché of a declining "primitive" culture, the film provides, as a result of its photographic quality, insights into the culture of the Kwakwaka'wakw that had otherwise barely been possible. The film

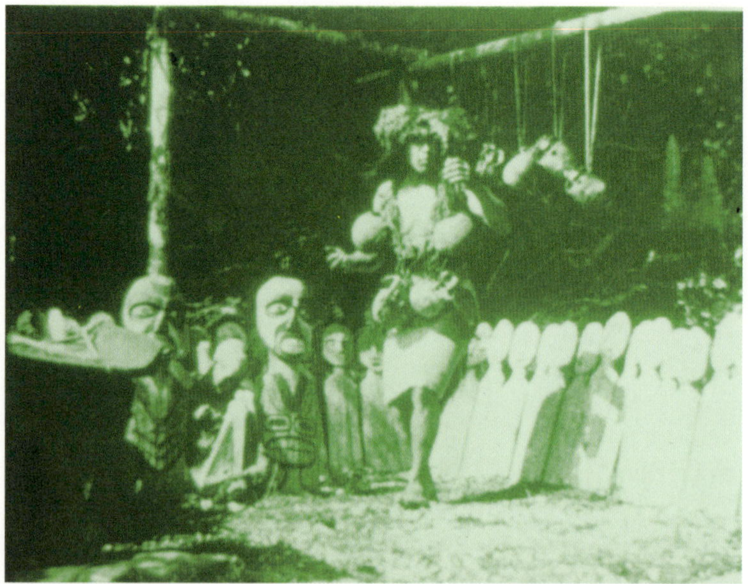

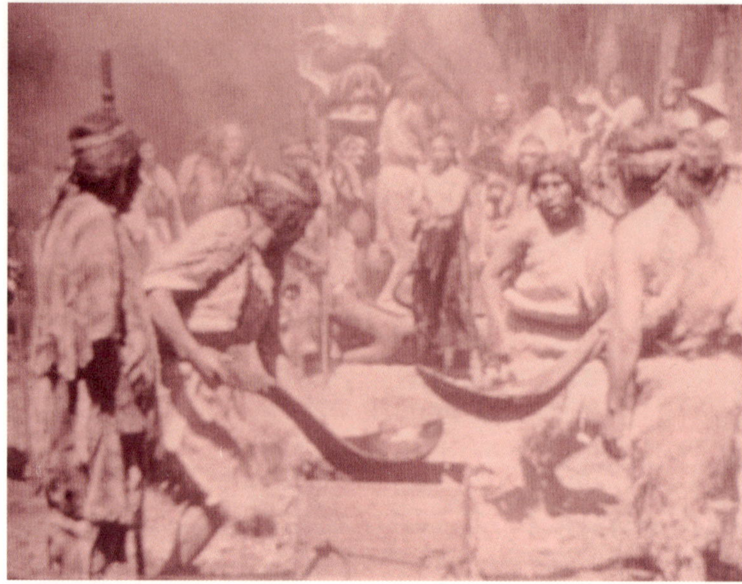

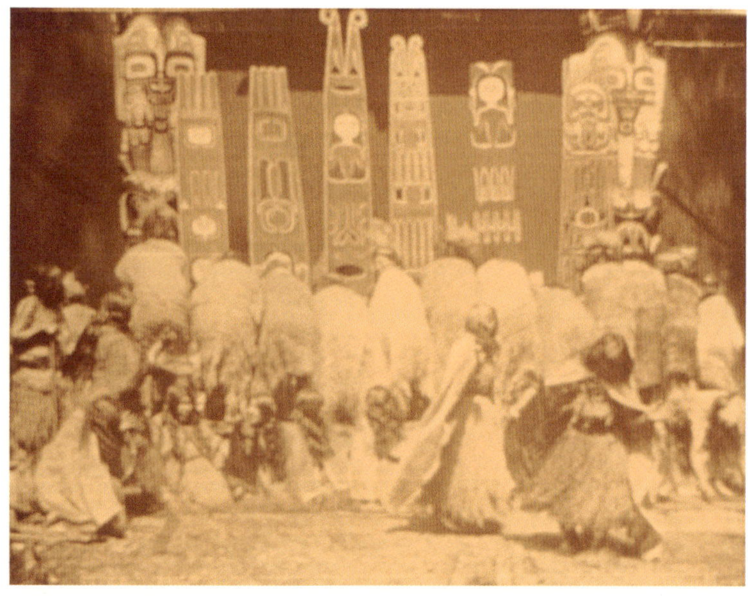

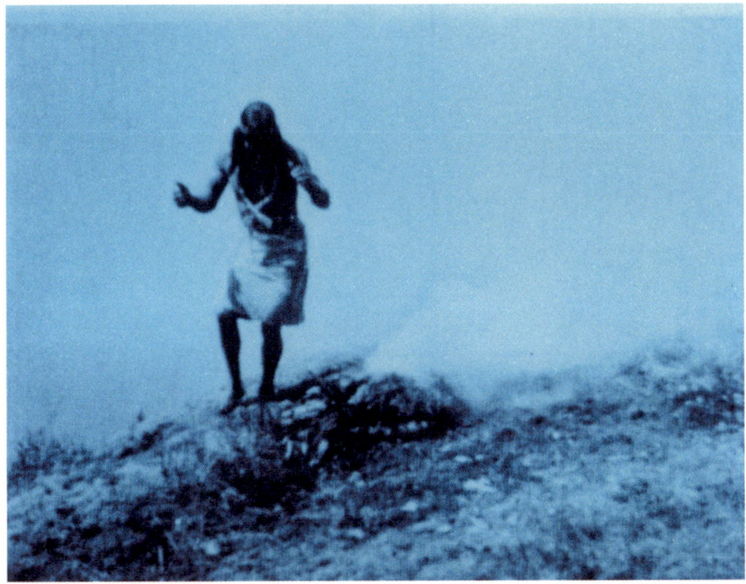

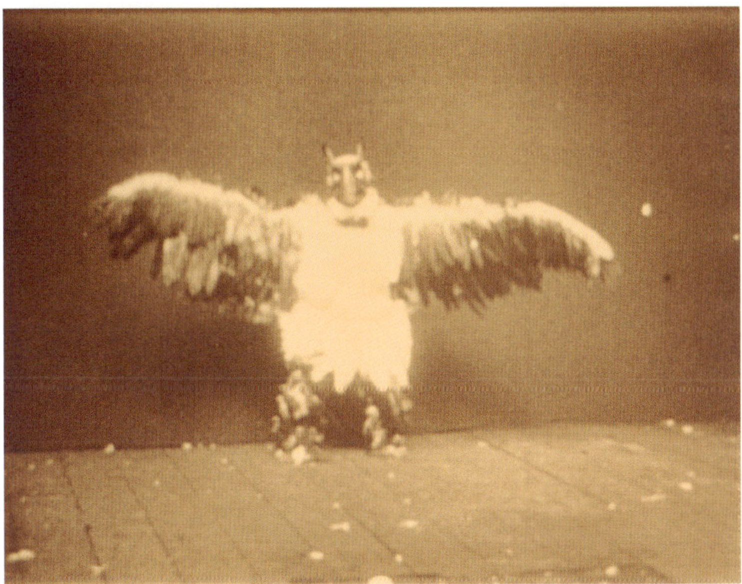

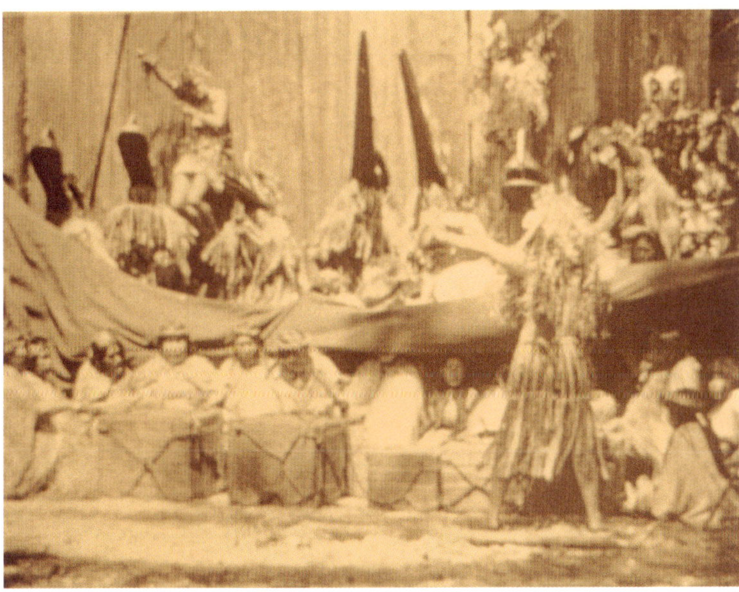

includes totems, war canoes, masks, and a potlatch, a ceremonial feast banned from 1885 to 1951 as part of the Indian Act. The filmed potlatch was celebrated specifically for the production. The anti-potlatch ban was otherwise rigidly enforced; eight years after the filming, twenty-two Kwakwaka'wakw people went to jail for participating in a potlatch.[2]

The film had limited success at the box office and was then long thought to have been lost. It was rediscovered in the late 1960s, reedited in 1972 on the initiative of Bill Holm and George Quimby, in consultation with some of the Indigenous people who had originally worked on the film. It was subsequently supplied with a soundtrack by a large group of Kwakwaka'wakw, who had gathered in the auditorium of the British Columbia Provincial Museum in Victoria, and then released in 1973 under the title *In the Land of the War Canoes.* The original version was reconstructed in 2008 with the revival of the original orchestral score.[3] The original film title and intertitles were restored, and color tinting was re-created from rediscovered footage.

Martina Weinhart

1—Before working with Edward S. Curtis, George Hunt had been the Kwakwaka'wakw guide and interpreter for Franz Boas, the founder of the field of ethnological field research.
2—Bill Holm, "Foreword," in *Return to the Land of the Head Hunters: Edward S. Curtis, the Kwakwaka'wakw, and the Making of Modern Cinema,* ed. Brad Evans and Aaron Glass (Seattle and London: University of Washington Press, 2014), p. xvii.
3—See Evans and Glass, *Return to the Land of the Head Hunters.*

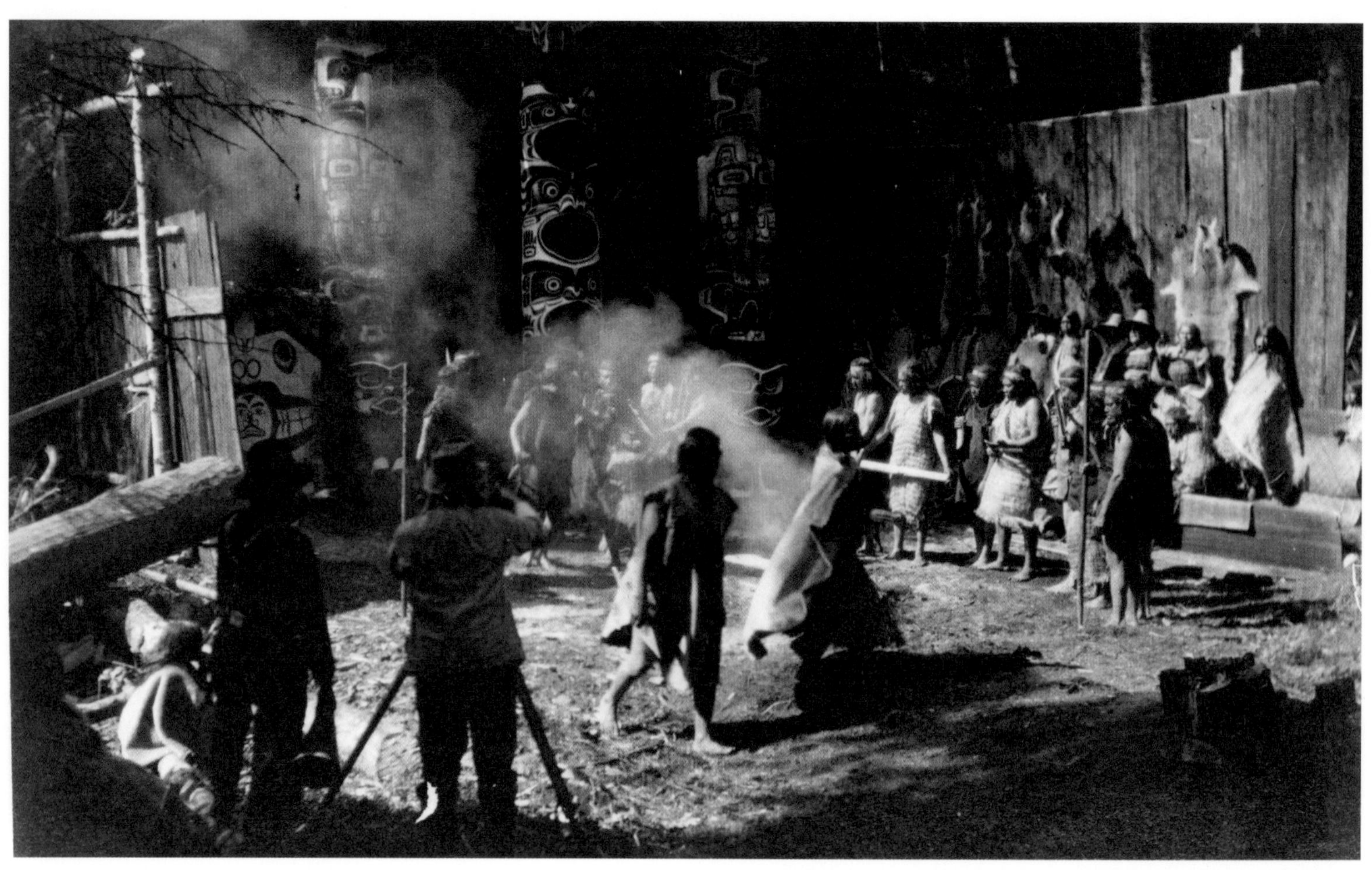

Georg Hunt (with megaphone),
Edward S. Curtis, and actors
filming *In the Land of the Head
Hunters,* 1914

Kwakwaka'wakw dancers in 1910
simulating a Hamatsa winter
ceremonial dance, with bird masks
related to the Baxbaxwalanuksiwe
myth

Dancers of the Nan (Grizzly Bear)
dance, Kwan'wala (Thunderbird)
dance, and Hamasalal (Wasp) dance
appear in a Kwakwaka'wakw "capturing the bride" ceremony, ca. 1914

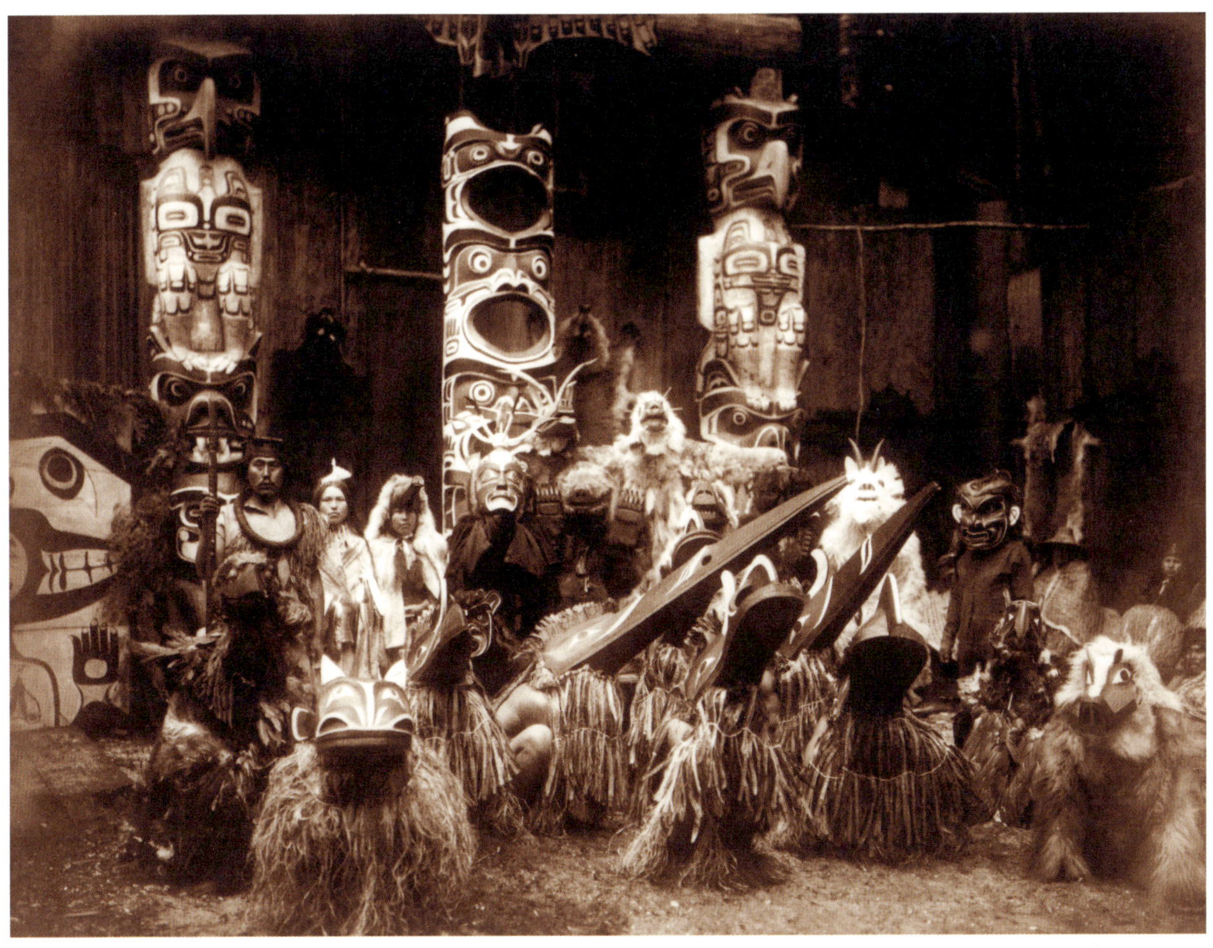

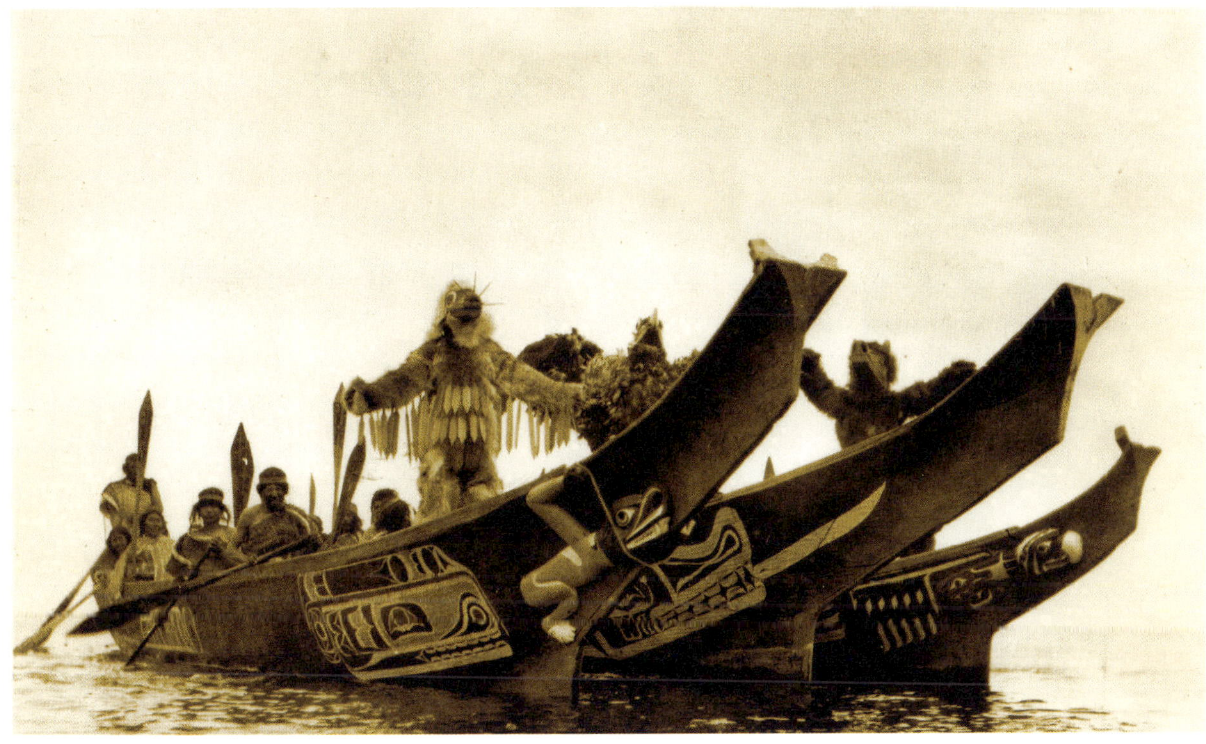

# Reexploring the Archive
# An Indigenous Artist's View on Stereotyping Indians

Like so many children growing up in the 1960s, I watched Western movies on television and found myself rooting for the "good" guys, the rugged cowboys played by actors like John Wayne and Gary Cooper. They were positioned as heroes within a narrative of good versus evil, fighting Indians that stood in the way of colonial expansion and progress. While I was preparing for an exhibition of my work some years ago, I asked my mother if she could recall when my Indigenous identity began to take shape. She told me that when I was a young boy of five or six, she heard me crying in the living room. When she asked what was wrong, I pointed at the television and said I was afraid of the Indians. She replied, "You are an Indian and you don't have to be afraid." When I cried harder, she said, "You're not *that* kind of Indian."

*What is an Indian?* This question has been central to my career as a photo-based storyteller and researcher. While doing my early research, I found deeply entrenched and myopic stereotypes of Indianness. "Indians" were not depicted as real people, but as characters in a Western, forever frozen in a time of great conflict for Indigenous people. Numerous non-Indigenous image-makers, such as Edward S. Curtis (1868–1952), produced representations of Indianness that appealed to non-Indigenous audiences. The Indians he depicted were not the war-whooping threats to colonial settlers, but symbols of a vanishing race meant to evoke pathos in the viewer. Between 1900 and 1930, Curtis traveled throughout the North American West photographing more than seventy Indigenous tribes. His project resulted in *The North American Indian*, a twenty-volume work of narrative text and photogravure images. Each volume is accompanied by a portfolio of large photogravure plates (figs. 1, 2). The photographs were intended to present daily activities, customs, and religions of trial-based people.

In the late 1970s, Curtis's work was in the midst of a revival, perhaps linked to the burgeoning environmental movement and the positioning of Indigenous people as guardians of the land. Lucrative prints of his original negatives were produced for the fine art audience, and his images could be found in pop culture on gift cards, calendars, posters, and T-shirts. In recent decades, Curtis's work has come under fire. He has been accused of manipulating his images to exclude any sign of modernity, of editing to create a seamless picture shrouded in mystery, with the soft-focus sepia tones of the photo-gravure printing process. Curtis's images do not address the harsh realities, both economic and political, that each community had to endure. These realities include not being able to leave the reserve (in Canada) or reservation (in the United States) without permission from an Indian agent (a local government representative), authorities removing children to be reeducated at residential and government-run boarding schools, and the taking of treaty lands and land rights. Communities that had enjoyed freedom on the land were forced by colonial governments to become farmers and work for non-Indigenous people. By the time Curtis began his project in 1900, tipis had been replaced by log houses and headdresses by Western-style clothing. The artist often resorted to staging his scenes in an effort to depict a way of life that had largely vanished. Was he complicit in perpetuating stereotypes?

One day in the early 1980s, while taking a photo-walk in downtown Buffalo, New York, I noticed a gift shop displaying large-format gift cards with images of Indians taken by Curtis in the window. I bought five cards, put them in my camera bag, and continued on my search for sites to photograph. When I went to the reserve, I gave one of the cards to my family elder Emily General, who noted that the man in the photograph must have been very important. Emily didn't see the man as a symbol of what was lost; she immediately recognized his dignity and power.

Her reaction changed the way I look at archival photographs. I realized that we, as Indigenous people, can reposition images of Indianness made by non-Indigenous people. We can start new conversations to find some resolution or compromise as to the viability of using archival images as part of today's quest for self-determination. I began to recognize the potential of using my own photography as a counterpoint within those conversations. I was convinced that by working with the sitters in mind, I could make an argument for the value of Curtis's work. It was an instinctual assumption based on one thing: when you take away the tribal clothing and the tipis, you're left with the faces—faces that remind me of my elders. I wanted to sit down with them and hear their stories, just as I did when I was a young boy listening to my elders.

My relationship with Curtis further shifted when I learned that Library and Archives Canada in Ottawa, Ontario, had two complete sets of *The North American Indian*.

I moved to Ottawa and began my study of the collection. I discovered that each volume was devoted to a geographic area and comprised both images and narrative texts. Each tribal group was described in detail, as both an ethnographic and a historical study. This was a significant discovery because, unlike the isolated images circulating in the art market and popular culture, the text places each tribal group in a specific place and time and includes information on history, culture, and practices—largely thanks to community elders who contributed their knowledge.

One could argue that the people may not have provided Curtis's field work team with precise information about the more sensitive ceremonies. But I would put forward another possibility: perhaps the elders knew what was happening to their world and cared about their future generations. Perhaps they were compelled by the same question that drove me when I first began my research: What if there were no Indigenous histories in the archives? Here was a way to preserve their culture and history at the same time as government policies and religious orders were dismantling the social order within Indigenous communities during large stretches of the twentieth century. This targeted breakdown can be seen in the example of the Indian residential school program in Canada, which removed Indigenous children from their families and communities to "reeducate" them based on the cultural norms of the now dominant society. The effects of forcefully separating a child from the people and places that anchor their identity and replacing those elements with an alienating foreign education, not to mention the cruel acts of physical, mental, and sexual abuse, still reverberate in Indigenous families and communities. While Curtis only hinted at this social and political landscape in his work, elders may have permitted the artist to photograph their communities based in part on a desire to preserve their history for future generations.

I believe that Curtis envisioned a conversation where the text was more prominent than the images. Yet the reality is that the images had more value; the photogravure pages were cut out of the volumes and sold as fine art prints. I began to imagine a project of rebinding the Curtis volumes. Rather than reinserting the cut-out pages, I would insert my own work to bridge past and present and call attention to a new reading of Curtis's images—and, in turn, to a reinterrogation of antiquated stereotypes. The first example, *Self-Determination* (2009/2017), is an exploration of what might have been seen behind the backdrop that Curtis used for fieldwork portraits (fig. 3). My son Bear poses in front of the heavily industrialized area in my hometown of Buffalo. The Buffalo River signifies the former Buffalo Creek Reservation, upon which the current city of Buffalo was built.

The second example juxtaposes the Curtis image of Swallow Bird with two images of Joseph Crowe that I took at the Sioux Valley powwow in 1990 (fig. 4). Crowe was a mentor and role model: when I approached to ask permission to photograph him, he was surrounded by a crowd of young children. As Crowe posed for me, three boys started dancing around us. I remember thinking that small details like this can add a conversational dimension to a portrait, and it made me wonder what Curtis could have told me about photographing Swallow Bird.

My conversation with Curtis further expanded when I was approached by Ali Kazimi, then a documentary film student who wanted to make a film about my work. Our conversations on Indianness resulted in the film *Shooting Indians: A Journey with Jeffrey Thomas* (1997). The film begins with Ali's immigration to Canada from India and the stereotypes he encountered about Indigenous people. Ali (who is now an established filmmaker, writer, and professor at York University in Toronto) was interested in my work not only with Curtis's images, but also with the artist's silent film *In the Land of the Head Hunters* (1914, pp. 90-93), which combines fact and melodramatic fiction to depict the world of the Kwakwaka'wakw (Kwakiutl) peoples of the Queen Charlotte Strait region of the Central Coast of British Columbia. Curtis wrote and directed this film, which featured Kwakwaka'wakw individuals as actors. The film follows the precarious marriage of two young lovers, Naida and Motana, the latter a son of a great chief; the pair is thwarted by an evil sorcerer and headhunter who covets Naida's dowry. The film, which was restored based on consultation with the Kwakwaka'wakw and released in 1974 under the name *In the Land of the War Canoes,* also corresponds to the work that Curtis was producing for volume 10 in *The North American Indian*. As part of Ali's project, he and I traveled to Vancouver Island, British Columbia, to meet Mary [Margaret] Frank, the last surviving participant in the Curtis film. We spoke of Curtis, and she shared her memories of working on the film. When I asked to photograph her, she told me that she had also been photographed by Curtis, in the year 1914.

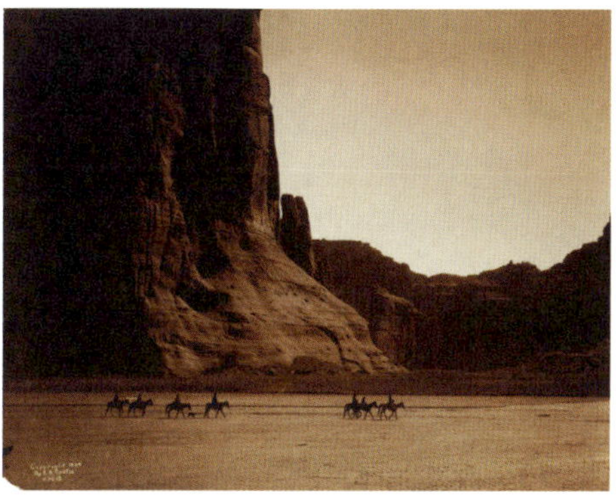

Fig. 1—Edward S. Curtis, *Navajo riders in Canyon de Chelly,* 1904, in *The North American Indian,* vol. 1, portfolio plate no. 28

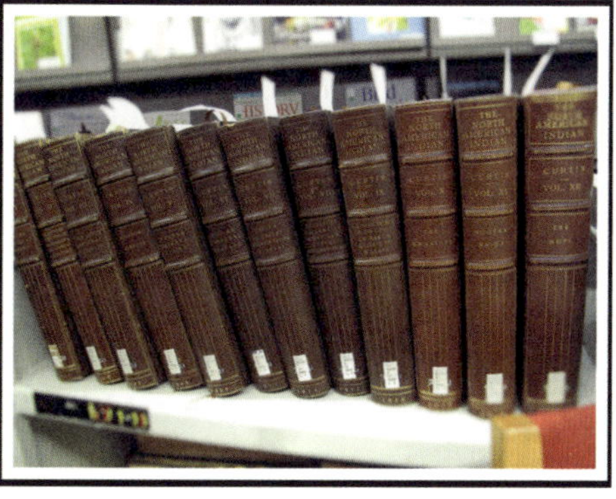

Fig. 2—Book cart holding volumes of *The North American Indian* at the Royal Ontario Museum in Toronto, 2005

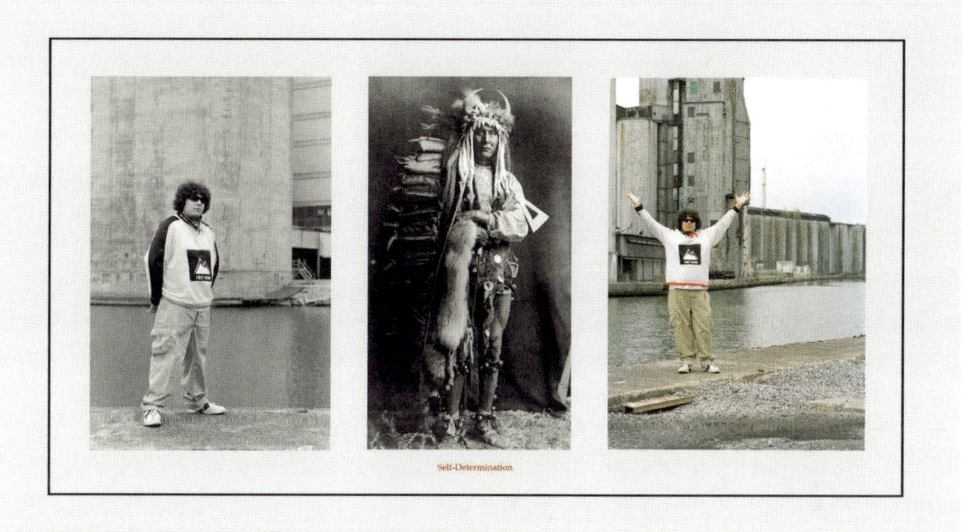


Fig. 3—Jeff Thomas, *Self-Determination,* 2009/2017
Left: Jeff Thomas, *Bear Thomas,* Buffalo Creek, Buffalo, New York, 1997
Middle: Edward S. Curtis, *Iron Breast, Piegan,* ca. 1900
Right: Jeff Thomas, *Bear Thomas,* Buffalo Creek, Buffalo, New York, 1997

When I gave the Curtis postcard to my elder Emily General, I didn't know anything about the man in the image; I had just begun my relationship with the artist's work. In hindsight, I have imagined what it would have been like if I'd brought more images for my conversation with Emily. I would have liked to tell her about meeting Mary Frank. I would also have liked to show her the portrait of the two young Zuni women I used in *Where the Rivers Meet* (2014–15, fig.5). The portrait was not published in *The North American Indian*, but I find it to be very powerful because of the direct eye contact between the girls and the photographer, which reflects the subjects' notable confidence. When I considered the two Zuni girls for this panel, I wondered what Emily might have said about them.

Setting up a conversation between the past and the present can be seen in the juxtaposition of *In the Land of the War Canoes* with *Blunden Harbour* (1951, pp.100-103). The latter is a twenty-two-minute documentary film made by Robert Gardner (1925–2014) in 1951, set in the small Kwakwaka'wakw village on the British Columbia coast. Gardner was an American academic, anthropologist, and documentary filmmaker, and the director of The Film Study Center at Harvard University from 1956 to 1997. This film remains one of the few accounts of the Kwakwaka'wakw people. It is a glimpse into a community that could have looked very much like the Alert Bay community that Curtis worked with in 1914. Yet the 1951 film is untethered from Curtis's fanciful story line, with a social message about the plight of a people trying to manage their (now) impoverished lives in the wake of colonialism. Although the film offers only a glimpse of that broader context, it nevertheless raises important questions about authorship and social relevancy in an age of Indigenous self-determination.

One area of experience common to so many Indigenous people that is often overlooked is the migration from reserve to urban communities. Curtis had photographed his first Indigenous sitters, many of whom he had seen on the city streets selling craftwork, in his portrait studio in Seattle in 1895. Yet ironically, these are not the works that are valued or known. He ended up spending thirty years traveling to reservations across the North American West to capture or recreate the past. Caroline

Monnet, in turn, is an Algonquin/French filmmaker who produced *Mobilize* (2015, pp.116, 117), a three-minute short film, using archival film footage from the National Film Board. The film journeys from a remote Indigenous community to Montreal. The Anishinaabe filmmaker Lisa Jackson offers another counterpoint to the Curtis legacy with her hour-long film *How a People Live* (2013, pp.110, 111). The documentary traces the history of the Gwa'sala-'Nakwaxda'xw First Nation, whom the Canadian government forcibly relocated from their homeland on the British Columbia coast to the Tsulquate Reserve in 1964. Unlike the previous films, we can now listen to the Indigenous people tell their own stories. Jackson also includes archival film footage and still images.

Viewers of these four very different films can see a progression from an outsider's voice to Indigenous people telling their own stories, a vital element of self-determination. Equally important, both Monnet and Jackson approach the archive, as I do, with a view toward creating new conversations.

Like Curtis, the dominant society continues to be preoccupied with an Indianness that adheres to visual cliché. For me, shining a light on the urban experience is particularly important, as I am the first person in my immediate family to be born in a city. My grandparents and parents had moved to Buffalo, New York, to find work. I am also an enrolled member of the Six Nations of the Grand River in southern Ontario. Growing up, I was intrigued by the contrast in community between the city and the reserve, and this generated a lot of questions about my Indianness. Being a self-identified urban Iroquois did not carry the same cachet of authenticity; there was no interest in studying or documenting urban Indian experience. As I think back to my mother's comment "You're not that kind of Indian," I realize that *I am that kind of Indian*—one who is fighting to retain Indigenous autonomy, homelands, histories, and stories. At the dawn of the twentieth century, it was widely believed that the "Indian race" was going to vanish because the death rate had overtaken the birth rate. Curtis and others sought to capture that "vanishing race." But we are still here. We did not vanish. And we are reexploring the archive to address not only our survival, but how we can move forward.

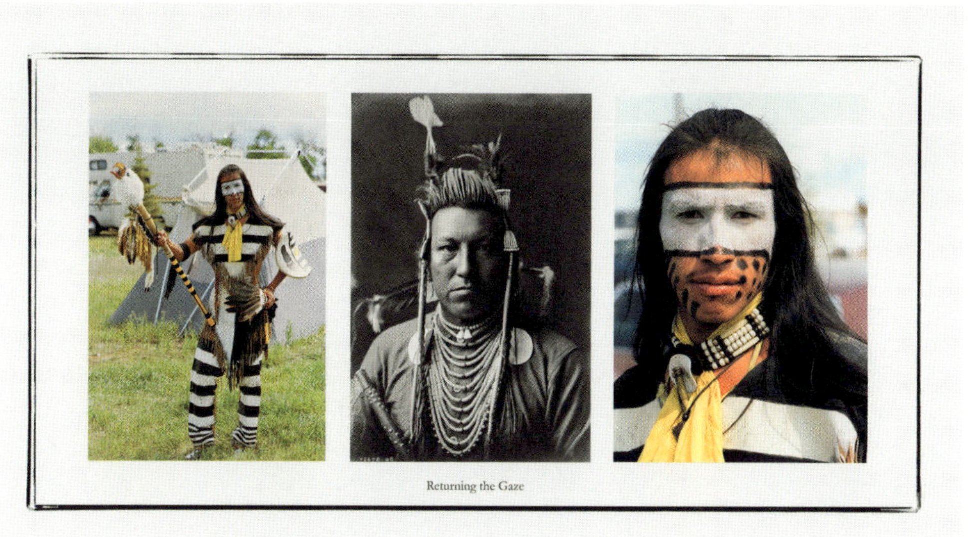

Fig. 4—Jeff Thomas, *Returning the Gaze, Swallow Bird and Joseph Crowe,* 2009/2015
Left: Jeff Thomas, *Joseph Crowe, Saulteaux tribe,* Sioux Valley Powwow Grounds, Manitoba, 1990
Middle: Edward S. Curtis, *Swallow Bird, Apsaroke (Crow tribe),* Crow Reservation, Montana, ca. 1900
Right: Jeff Thomas, *Joseph Crowe, Saulteaux tribe,* Sioux Valley Powwow Grounds, Manitoba, 1990

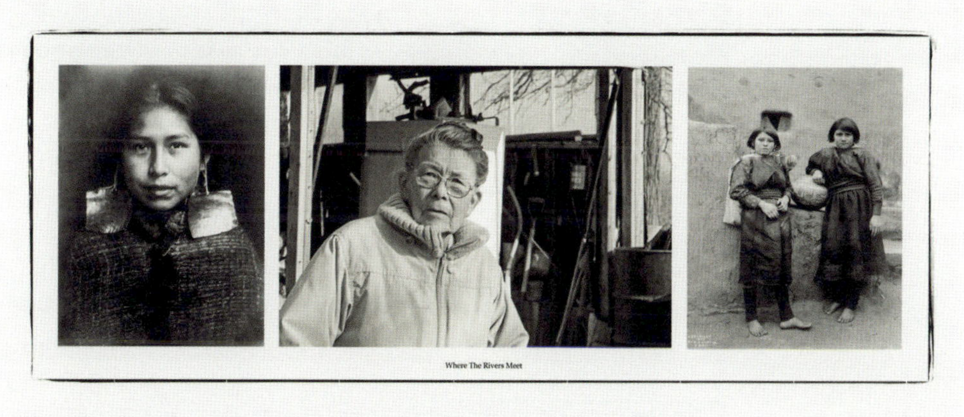

Fig. 5—Jeff Thomas, *Where the Rivers Meet,* 2014–15
Left: Edward S. Curtis, *Tsawatenok girl (Margaret Frank),* ca. 1914
Middle: Jeff Thomas, *Emily General,* Six Nations of the Grand River, 1985
Right: Edward S. Curtis, *Two Zuni girls standing in front of pueblo buildings,* ca. 1903

Robert Gardner
*Blunden Harbour,* 1951
Film (digital video transfer, black and white, sound, 22 min.)
Richard Selig (casting),
W. H. Heick, P. Jacquemin (camera),
M. E. Dowd (sound)

The US anthropologist and filmmaker Robert Gardner, who established the Film Study Center at Harvard University, was still a young student at the University of Washington in Seattle when he set off for Blunden Harbour to do research for an extensive film project about the Kwakwaka'wakw (Kwakiutl). He was inspired by Ruth Benedict's studies of the Kwakiutl and by her teacher Franz Boas, the founder of the discipline of ethnological field research. The opportunity to make this short documentation, for which the American photographer William Heick did the camerawork, arose during Gardner's stay in the village. *Blunden Harbour* was Gardner's debut film. The more extensive film project was never realized.

Blunden Harbour (Paas or Ba'as) was a small Kwakwaka'wakw harbor village on the mainland side of the Queen Charlotte Strait in British Columbia. It is well known due to the 1901 photographs taken by the British ethnographer Charles F. Newcombe, and as one of the locations for *In the Land of the Head Hunters.* In his documentary sketch, Gardner depicts the day-to-day life of the Kwakwaka'wakw, which is characterized by fishing and life near the water. To a soundtrack consisting of singing and rhythmic rapping, we see people collecting mussels and hauling in nets, cooking, carving, and doing other woodwork, and also children at play. The narration tells of the legends of the

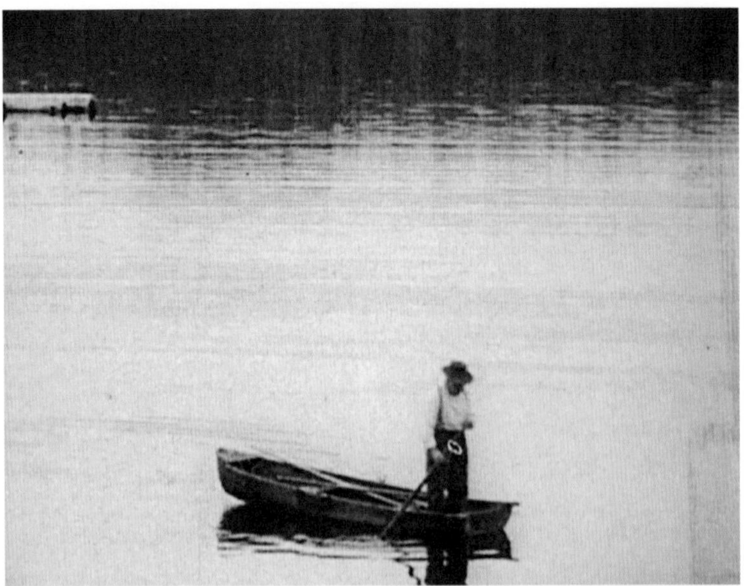

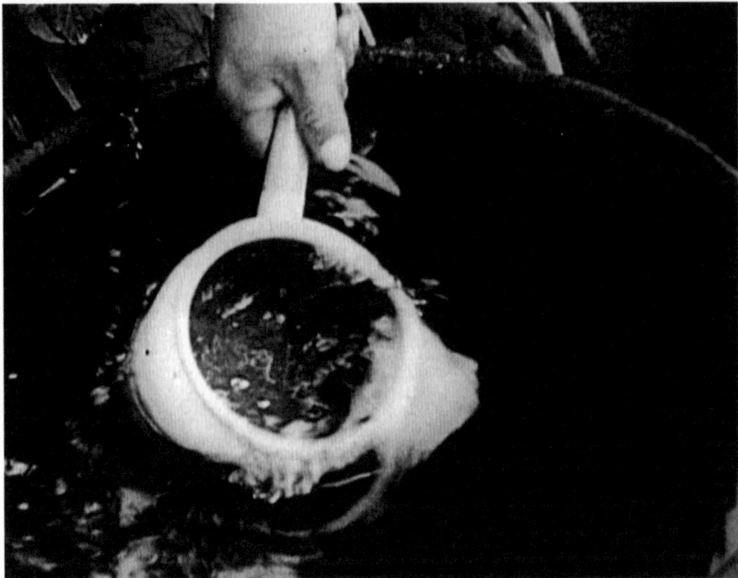

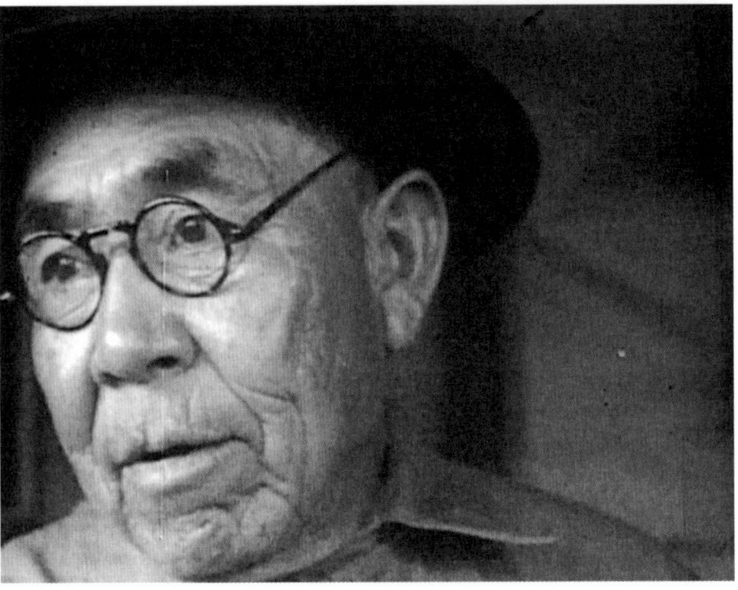

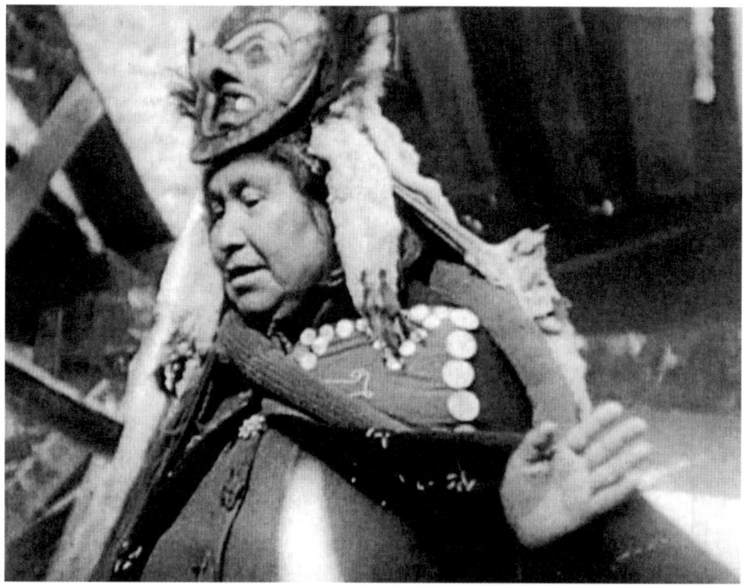

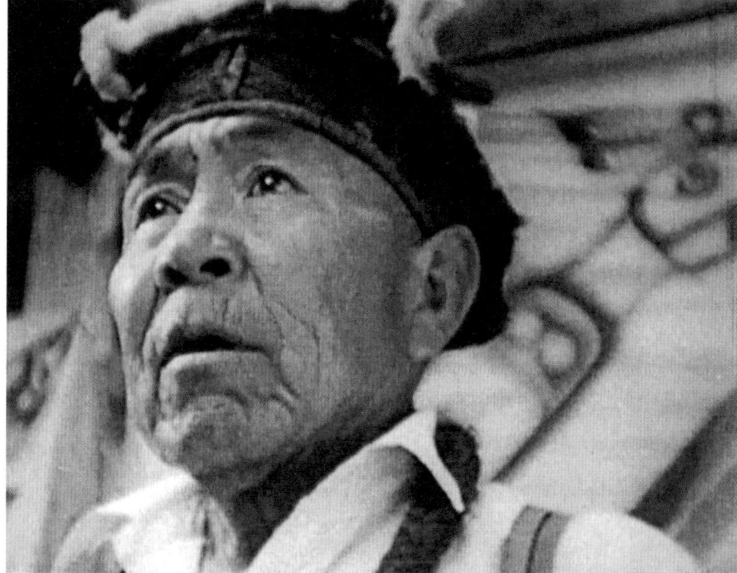

Kwakwaka'wakw and describes a peaceful coexistence impacted by modern life, but nonetheless defined by tradition. Among other things, the film shows an older man painting masks, and its final sequence is a ceremonial dance in traditional clothing. That same year, Gardner and Heick also shot *Dances of the Kwakiutl*.

Martina Weinhart

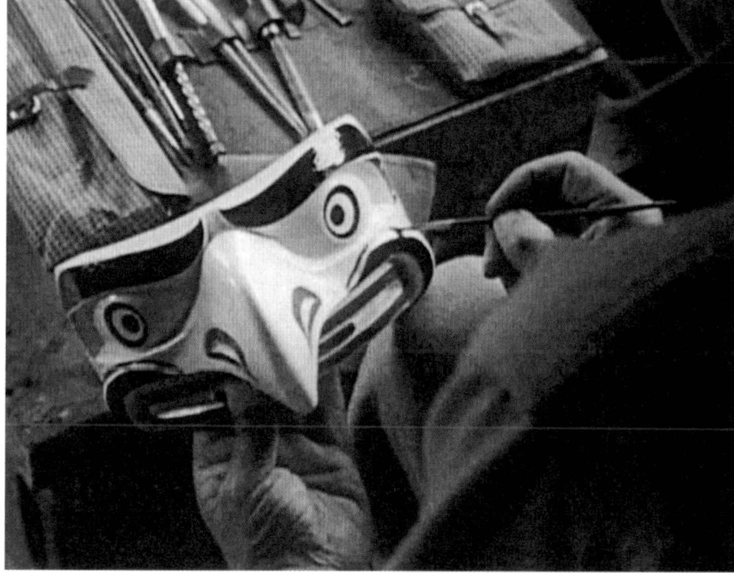

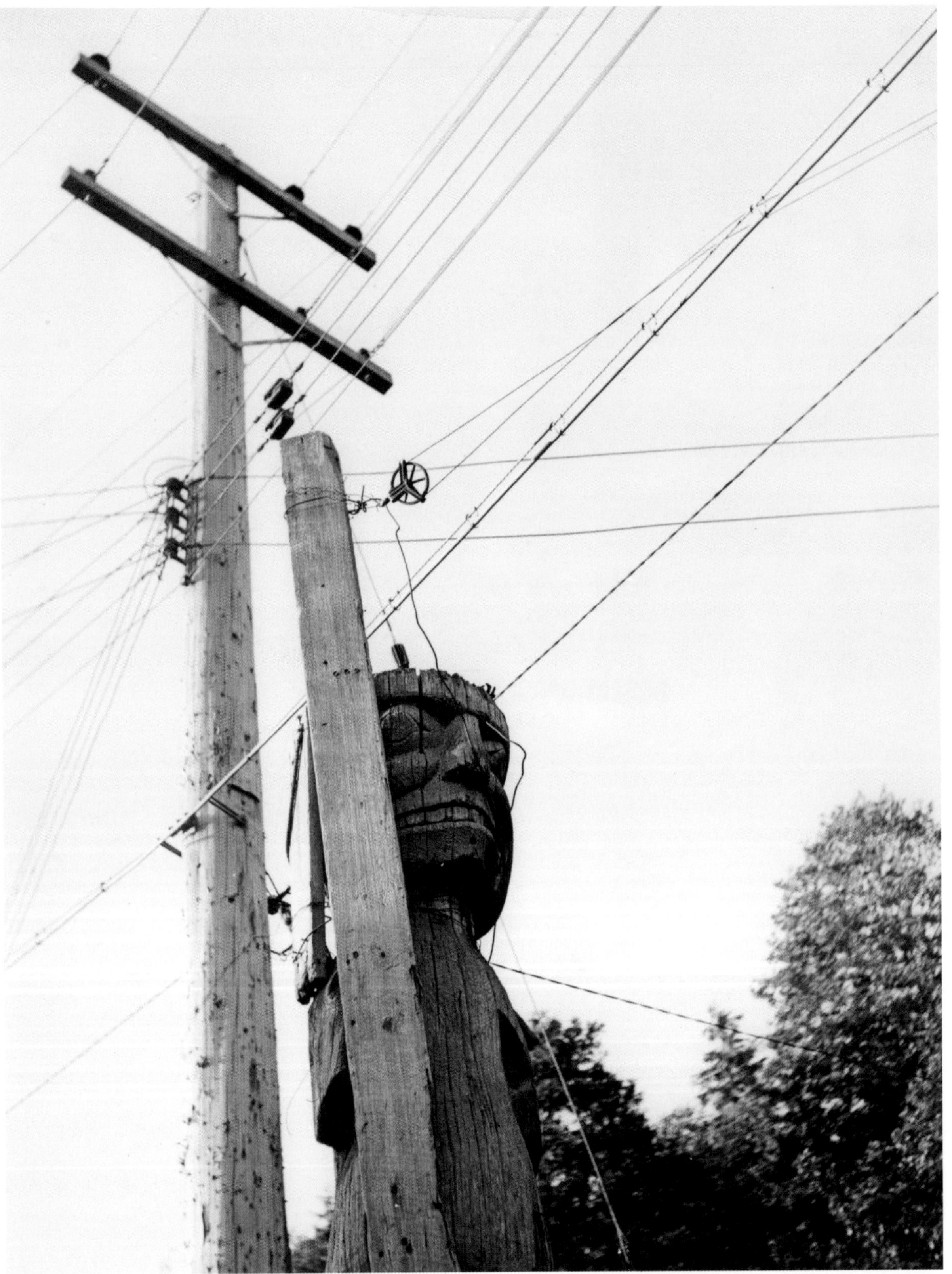

Set photographs from *Blunden Harbour*

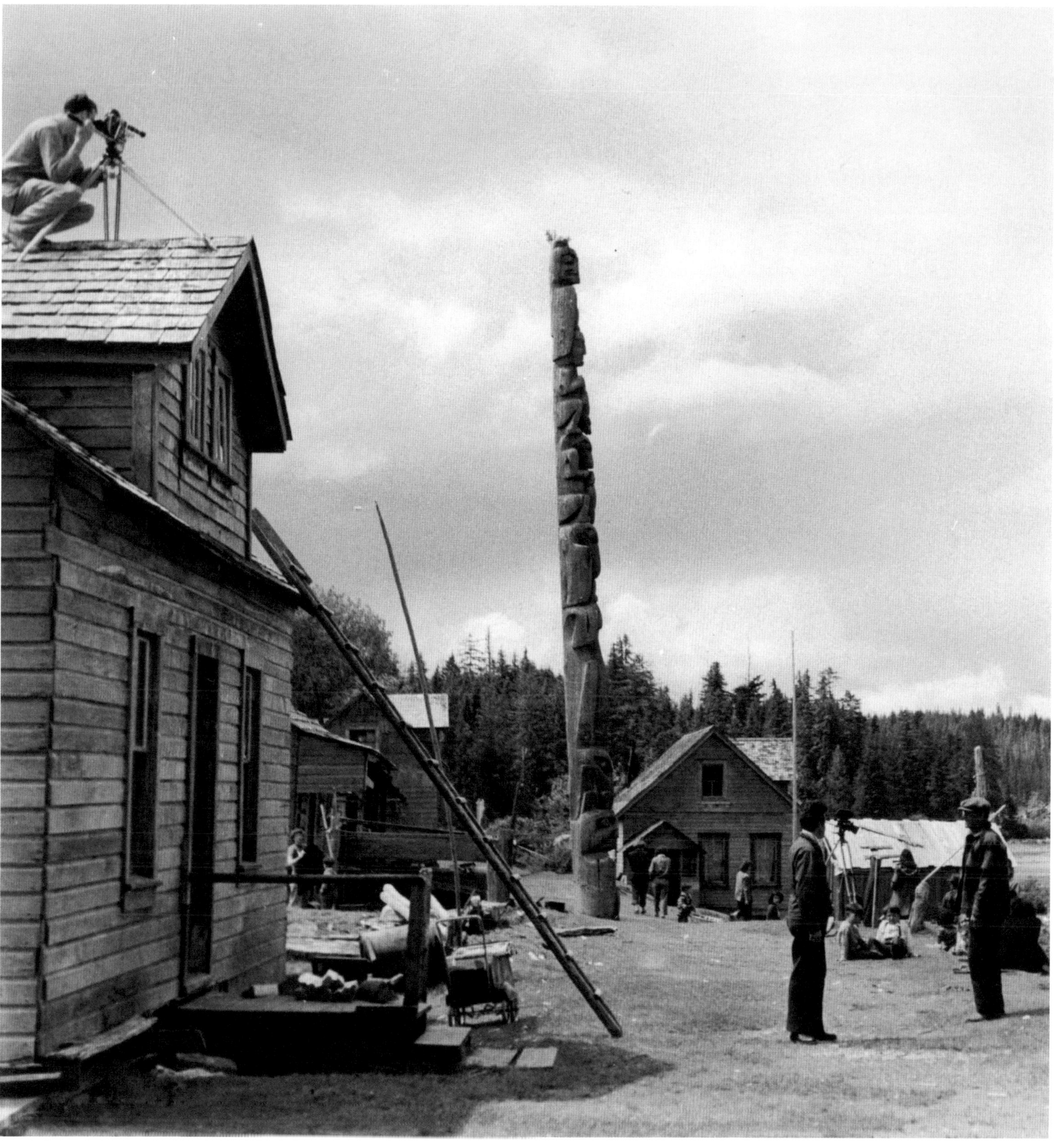

# Indigenous Art in Canada and Beyond

Historic First Nations arts made their first appearance at the National Gallery of Canada (NGC) in the *Exhibition of Canadian West Coast Art, Native and Modern,* which opened in December 1927. Celebrated for their aesthetic qualities as "primitive art," these works were appropriated as precursors of the modern Canadian arts of the Group of Seven and Emily Carr.[1] The direct link between these arts was, however, political rather than formal; Northwest Coast carvings and textiles had, in the words of the curator and National Museum of Canada (today: Canadian Museum of History) ethnologist Marius Barbeau, "sprung up wholly from the soil and the sea within our national boundaries."[2] Until the late twentieth century, however, the NGC's mandate excluded Indigenous arts, and examples of historic objects appeared only sporadically with several notable exceptions. Modern Inuit sculptures and prints began to enter the NGC's collections in the 1950s and 1960s, and two major traveling exhibitions initiated by outsiders were organized there. The 1969 *Masterpieces of Indian and Eskimo Art from Canada* was developed through an overture made by the Friends of the Musée de l'Homme Society in Paris to the National Museum of Canada but mounted by the NGC in 1969–70 because the latter's building was being renovated.[3] *The Comfortable Arts: Traditional Spinning and Weaving in Canada* was proposed to the National Gallery of Canada by Dorothy Burnham, the recently retired pioneering curator of Canadian textiles at the Royal Ontario Museum. In 1981–82, it celebrated the woven and embroidered arts of Indigenous peoples alongside the textiles of settler Canadians.

During the 1980s, the National Gallery of Canada came under mounting pressure from the Society of Canadian Artists of Native Ancestry (SCANA) to collect and exhibit the Indigenous arts that had come to national prominence during the preceding twenty-five years. The NGC's 1986 purchase of the monumental work *The North American Iceberg* (1985) by the Anishinaabe artist Carl Beam broke the long period of exclusion. It was featured in the NGC's first major exhibition of contemporary North American Indigenous art, *Land, Spirit, Power: First Nations at the National Gallery of Canada,* which opened in 1992 to mark the 500th anniversary of Columbus's arrival in the Americas. During these same years, the NGC's collections of Inuit art were greatly amplified by donations and, most importantly, by transfers from the Department of Indian Affairs and Northern Development (today: Indigenous and Northern Affairs Canada). A suite of small galleries was assigned for regular displays of these collections.

Although the NGC had considered incorporating First Nations arts into the new building it opened in 1988, it was not until 2002 that Indigenous arts entered the permanent Canadian Galleries until then exclusively dedicated to arts made by settlers from the seventeenth through the mid-twentieth centuries. For the next fifteen years, the retitled *Art of this Land* exhibits juxtaposed Indigenous and settler arts in a series of periodic rotations organized as a chronological survey.[4] In 2017, marking Canada's sesquicentennial, the Canadian and Indigenous Art galleries were once again remounted and again renamed as the Canadian and Indigenous Galleries. The new exhibits present a series of interrelated stories of Canadian and Indigenous art in Canada dating from 5,000 years ago to 1967. Although the 2002 and 2017 initiatives signify notable gestures of inclusion, they have also generated critique from artists and scholars advocating "visual sovereignty" in exhibitions and institutions.[5]

With the establishment of its Indigenous Section and the appointment of Greg Hill as the Audain Curator of Indigenous Art in 2007, the National Gallery of Canada was able to take up the challenges of collecting and curating modern and con-temporary Indigenous arts in critical ways. In 2006, Hill curated *Norval Morrisseau, Shaman Artist* for the NGC—its first retrospective exhibition of an Indigenous artist. This breakthrough show led to further solo and retrospective exhibitions featuring such artists as Daphne Odjig (2009–10), Carl Beam (2011–12), and Alex Janvier (2018). The exhibition *Sakahàn: International Indigenous Art,* mounted in 2013, served to signal a new commitment by the NGC to showcase the contemporary arts of Indigenous peoples from around the world. *Sakahàn,* meaning "to light [a fire]" in the language of the Algonquin peoples, was followed up in 2019 with *Àbadakone / Continuous Fire / Feu continuel,* its second survey of International Indigenous contemporary arts.[6] Both exhibitions were large and ambitious—*Sakahàn* was the largest ever mounted in the history of the National Gallery of Canada, and a record overflow crowd attended the opening of *Àbadakone.* The collaborative curatorial teams went beyond mere surveys to situate the chosen works within particular cultural ways of knowing and to highlight shared values and experiences, as well as distinctive histories and cultural traditions. Both have added a level of critical engagement to the discourses surrounding contemporary Indigenous arts.

Indigenous, as a term and as an organizing concept, connotes both a global and a local sense of connectivity that resonates through art and beyond. Since 1977, when Elders from Six Nations of the Grand River in Canada joined a delegation that marched on Geneva, Switzerland, to gain a seat at the United Nations (UN), the concept of the Indigenous has served to politically unify a global community, many of whose members remain internally colonized within settler nations. The United Nations Declaration on the Rights of Indigenous Peoples (UNDRIP) was adopted by the UN General Assembly in 2007 as an instrument to protect and promote Indigenous rights worldwide. Central to this declaration are the rights to language, artistic expression, intellectual and cultural property, and other aspects of expressive culture. As stated in Article 43, it affirms the rights that "constitute the minimum standards for the survival, dignity and well-being of the Indigenous peoples of the world." In 2016, Canada finally removed its objector status and declared support for UNDRIP, in the context of the Truth and Reconciliation Commission of Canada (TRC). Formed to undertake an "overall holistic and comprehensive response to the Indian Residential School legacy,"[7] the commission recommended that the Canadian government adopt UNDRIP as the broad framework for reconciliation. Specific TRC recommendations ask that UNDRIP's principles and affirmation of Indigenous rights inform the work of museums, universities, and cultural institutions.

It is helpful, in considering the contemporary nuances and negotiations entailed by bringing together global art traditions under the umbrella of "Indigenous art," to reflect briefly on the genealogy of the term. The category "indigenous people"—uncapitalized—is an artifact of colonial rule that has continued to evolve over the past fifty years. Derived from the Latin term meaning "born in the place," it was first used to distinguish "natives" from colonizers and settlers. With the establishment of colonial regimes, defining peoples as "indigenes" or "natives" quickly became a tool of oppression and cultural genocide. Yet different histories of liberation and decolonial activism have given rise to a bifurcation in the use of the term. During the second half of the twentieth century, with the retreat of imperial powers from Africa, Asia, the Caribbean, and elsewhere, the terms "native" and "indigenous" quickly dropped from use and were re-

placed by new national and tribal identifiers. In contrast, the term "Indigenous"—now capitalized—has been embraced by peoples who remain internally colonized within settler societies like Canada.

Christine Lalonde and Jolene Rickard have explored the productive instability of the term Indigenous today. As Lalonde wrote in her introduction to the exhibition catalogue *Sakahàn: International Indigenous Art,* "essential to the value and function of Indigenous is the word's built-in capacity to accommodate self-definition in terms of cultural distinctions, duplicity and hybridity."[8] Rickard stresses the need to recognize the fundamental and political entanglement of "nation-states, international law and Indigenous peoples"[9] and the implication of this political lens for a definition of Indigenous arts. For her, Indigeneity is not simply a matter of "blood" or "race," as had been true in the colonial era. Rather, only "those artists whose works show an acknowledgement of the ongoing conditions of colonial settler nations, the continuing dispossession of land and resources, and an awareness of Indigenous worldviews as part of the future of global cultures" should be included in this category.[10]

Change and recognition of these historical shifts and differences have, however, been slower to penetrate Western institutions of art. The advent of modernism during the early twentieth century brought with it the promotion of "primitive" arts by innovative European artists bent on countering and displacing Western classical and academic traditions. Their fantasies of the "primitive" were informed by desires not only for radical formal innovation but also for the more authentic relationships to the natural world, the life of the body and the subconscious psychic experience that they imagined to be expressed in the arts of Africa and of the Pacific and North American Indigenous peoples. Inevitably, the modernist artistic promotion of the "primitive" was also informed by the hierarchical and racist premises of the theories of cultural evolution that had been formalized during the nineteenth century and used to justify colonial regimes.[11] The result was the artificial grouping together in books, museums, and university courses—both in anthropology and art history—of world arts coming from a range of geographically distant and historically unconnected peoples.

The Second World War, as a global conflict, engaged colonized peoples alongside politically empowered ones. It dislodged people all over the world from the familiar and the local and flung them into new geographic and cultural contexts to which they had to respond. Many of the thousands of Indigenous soldiers who fought in Europe during this war had not previously left the reserves to which they were confined by law. Canadian Indigenous soldiers, mixed on near-equal terms with other recruits, made the same sacrifices and experienced the same horrors. As the Métis filmmaker Loretta Todd found, they returned to a Canada where patterns of discrimination and injustice increased rather than diminished; veterans' programs were denied to them, and even more of their land was taken.[12] The period of political activism that followed the war led to the repeal of some of the most restrictive laws and ongoing fights for land reclamation and justice. Modernist ideologies and theories of the primitive slowly began to erode.

The new awareness of the absolute evils of racism and genocide produced by the war also led the United Nations to formulate the 1948 Universal Declaration of Human Rights and thus to open a path that would lead, fifty years later, to UNDRIP. And the war also set in motion a small army of European refugees who spread the universalist ideologies of modernism around the globe. In a number of significant instances, this diaspora combined with the struggles for nationhood and independence to catalyze the emergence of the first generations of Indigenous contemporary artists.[13] A third factor in the rise of these pioneering generations was Cold War politics itself, which induced the American and Canadian governments to circulate Indigenous arts internationally—Pueblo paintings and Inuit sculptures—to promote the "liberal" and "tolerant" protection of minorities that contrasted to Communist repression.[14]

Yet despite these developments, there remained a persistent disconnect between anti-colonial political activism and shifts in academic anthropology and institutionalized art world practices that has lasted into the early twenty-first century. Although the categorization of African, Pacific, and Native American arts as "Primitive" dropped from use during the 1960s, these arts remained conjoined in museums and university courses under the new rubric of Africa, Oceania, and the Americas. Perhaps even more difficult to dislodge has been the taste for "primitive art" that continues to be tightly linked to the history of artistic modernism and its modes of museological representation. Of equal significance was the refusal within art museums and art history courses to recognize the "authenticity" of

Indigenous modern arts until the late twentieth century. Up to this point, these modernisms had been consigned, if collected or exhibited at all, to museums of anthropology and are only unevenly shown today within installations of modern art.[15]

What, then, does Indigenous art mean today in Canada? First, because Canada remains a colonial power, politics infuse all discourses related to Indigeneity. Since the institution of the Indian Act in 1876, the nation has officially decided who is and who is not legally considered to be Indigenous. The legal term "Indian"—a misnomer dating back to the days of Christopher Columbus and assigned to those people who have fallen within the narrow, patriarchal rule set down by the federal government—started a process that has led to a long and problematic process of naming. Assigned terminology has resulted in a shifting list of descriptors that in Canada has included "native," "Aboriginal," and "First Nations." Positionality therefore serves as a significant way to unify when faced with government assimilationist effort. Indigenous is currently embraced as a term charged with expediency. It fosters community building and solidarity, providing a needed unifying language. Yet, a change is currently underway with regard to the term Indigenous in Canada. As part of a larger decolonizing and sovereignty movement, and with the adoption of UNDRIP, Original Peoples now increasingly identify themselves by their original nations. Indigenous, as a term, is little more than a catchall. Using one's actual national identity demonstrates ongoing efforts to articulate sovereign rights and responsibilities.

Decolonizing art institutions, as with decolonizing anything, remains a complicated process. The term alone requires some unpacking within a settler-colonial nation context like Canada. In the now famous essay "Decolonization Is Not a Metaphor," Eve Tuck and K. Wayne Yang caution against efforts to turn "decolonization" into a metaphor.[16] They remind readers that the language of decolonization has been adopted and adapted in ways that merely "decentre settler perspectives," but at times do little to critically examine the ease with which decolonizing language has been problematically employed in and assigned to multiple situations.[17] Structural change underway in art institutions cannot escape such scrutiny because, as Tuck and Yang assert, "decolonization is not accountable to settlers."[18]

*Authors' note: We wish to acknowledge that the thinking around this contribution derived from a larger collaboratively written essay titled "World-Making: Indigenous Art and Worlding the Global" by Birgit Hopfener, Heather Igloliorte, Ruth Phillips, Carmen Robertson, and Ming Tiampo, in* Àbadakone / Continuous Fire / Feu continuel, *ed. Rachelle Dickenson, Greg A. Hill, and Christine Lalonde, exh. cat. National Gallery of Canada, Ottawa (Ottawa: NGC, 2020), pp. 114–23. In his essay "Making Tomorrow from Long Ago," in the same publication, Greg A. Hill preferenced the Kanien'kéha (Mohawk language) word* Onkwehónwe *over the word "Indigenous" in a decolonizing action in order to move away from the always problematic and contested colonial naming of the Peoples who have always been here and who have always had their own names for themselves.*


1—The exhibition was co-organized by the National Museum of Canada and curated by one of its staff ethnologists, Marius Barbeau. See Diana Nemiroff, "Modernism, Nationalism, and Beyond," in *Land, Spirit, Power: First Nations at the National Gallery of Canada,* ed. Diana Nemiroff, Robert Houle, and Charlotte Townsend-Gaults (Ottawa: NGC, 1992), pp. 15–42.

2—Marius Barbeau, "West Coast Indian Art," in *Exhibition of Canadian West Coast Art, Native and Modern,* exh. cat. National Gallery of Canada, Ottawa (Ottawa: NGC, 1927), p. 4.

3—See Ruth B. Phillips, "Modes of Inclusion: Indigenous Arts at the National Gallery of Canada and the Art Gallery of Ontario," in *Museum Pieces: Towards the Indigenization of Canadian Museums* (Montreal: McGill-Queen's University Press, 2011), pp. 252–76.

4—See Phillips, "Modes of Inclusion" (ibid.); and Anne Whitelaw, "Placing Aboriginal Art at the National Gallery of Canada," *Canadian Journal of Communication* 31, no. 1 (2006), special issue: "Culture, Heritage, and Art," pp. 197–214.

5—For a critique of inclusion, see Glen Coulthard, *Red Skin, White Masks: Rejecting the Colonial Politics of Recognition* (Minneapolis: University of Minnesota Press, 2014); on visual sovereignty, see Jolene Rickard, "Visualizing Sovereignty in the Time of Biometric Sensors," *South Atlantic Quarterly* 110, no. 2 (Spring 2011), pp. 465–86.

6—Greg A. Hill, Candace Hopkins, and Christine Lalonde, eds., *Sakahàn: International Indigenous Art,* exh. cat. National Gallery of Canada, Ottawa (Ottawa: NGC, 2013); and Rachelle Dickenson, Greg A. Hill, and Christine Lalonde, eds., À*badakone / Continuous Fire / Feu continuel,* exh. cat. National Gallery of Canada, Ottawa (Ottawa: NGC, 2020).

7—Truth and Reconciliation Commission of Canada, "Our Mandate," www.trc.ca/about-us/our-mandate.html (accessed April 28, 2020).

8—Christine Lalonde, "Introduction: At the Crossroads of Indigeneity, Globalization and Contemporary Art," in Hill et al., *Sakahàn,* p. 15.

9—Jolene Rickard, "The Emergence of Global Indigenous Art," in Hill et al., *Sakahàn,* p. 54.

10—Ibid.

11—The literatures on cultural evolutionism and modernist primitivism and their influence on museums are too vast to be listed here. For helpful introductions and critiques, see, for example, Robert Goldwater, *Primitivism in Modern Art* (Cambridge, MA: Harvard University Press, 1986), Susan Vogel, ed., *Art/artifact: African Art in Anthropology Collections* (Munich: Prestel, 1988), James Clifford, *The Predicament of Culture: Twentieth-Century Ethnography, Literature, and Art* (Cambridge, MA: Harvard University Press, 1988), Shelly Errington, *The Death of Authentic Primitive Art and Other Tales of Progress* (Berkeley: University of California Press, 1998), and Sally Price, *Primitive Art in Civilized Places* (Chicago: University of Chicago Press, 1989).

12—*Forgotten Warriors,* directed by Loretta Todd, National Film Board of Canada, 1997.

13—Among many examples, the pioneering Denesuline modernist Alex Janvier was introduced to Klee, Kandinsky, and other modernists in Edmonton, Alberta, by the refugee German artist Carl Altenberg in the early 1950s; see Jaime Koebel, "Chronology: The Life and Work of Alex Janvier," in *Alex Janvier,* ed. Greg Hill, exh. cat. National Gallery of Canada, Ottawa (Ottawa: NGC, 2016). Ulli Beier, who fled with his family from Germany to the British Protectorate of Palestine and was educated at the University of London, played a key role in the emergence of modern visual art and literature in both Nigeria and Papua New Guinea during the 1950s and 1960s. See Chika Okeke-Agulu, *Postcolonial Modernism: Art and Decolonization in Twentieth-Century Nigeria* (Durham: Duke University Press, 2015), pp. 131–82, and Nicholas Thomas, "'Artist of PNG': Mathias Kauage and Melanesian Modernism," in *Mapping Modernisms: Art, Indigeneity, Colonialism,* ed. Elizabeth Harney and Ruth B. Phillips (Durham: Duke University Press, 2018), pp. 163–86. The curatorial work of another refugee, the German ethnographer Leonhard Adam, was instrumental in bringing Australian Aboriginal art into major art institutions for the first time.

14—Norman Vorano, "Inuit Art in the Qallunaat World: Modernism, Museums, and the Popular Imaginary, 1949-1962" (PhD diss., University of Rochester, New York, 2007).

15—Harney and Phillips, "Inside Modernity: Indigeneity, Coloniality, Modernisms," in *Mapping Modernisms,* pp. 15–19.

16—Eve Tuck and K. Wayne Yang, "Decolonization Is Not a Metaphor," *Decolonization: Indigeneity, Education & Society* 1, no. 1 (2012), pp. 1–40.

17—Ibid., p. 2.

18—Ibid., p. 35.

Lisa Jackson
*How a People Live,* 2013
HD video (color, sound,
59 min., 5 sec.)

The film was created as a work commissioned by the Gwa'sala-'Nakwaxda'xw First Nation, whose members were forcibly resettled by the Canadian state in 1964. They had no choice but to move from their ancestral land on the coast of British Columbia to Tsulquate, a newly established native reserve near Port Hardy in the territory of the Kwakiutl. Based on interviews and historical film material, the Anishinaabe filmmaker Lisa Jackson hauntingly documents the history of this community and the trauma connected with this resettlement, along with its consequences: hardship, illnesses, alcohol dependency, and the forced internment of children in the education system for schools. The filmmaker accompanies the members of the surviving people on a journey back to their home, during which they reencounter their memories and traditions.

Martina Weinhart

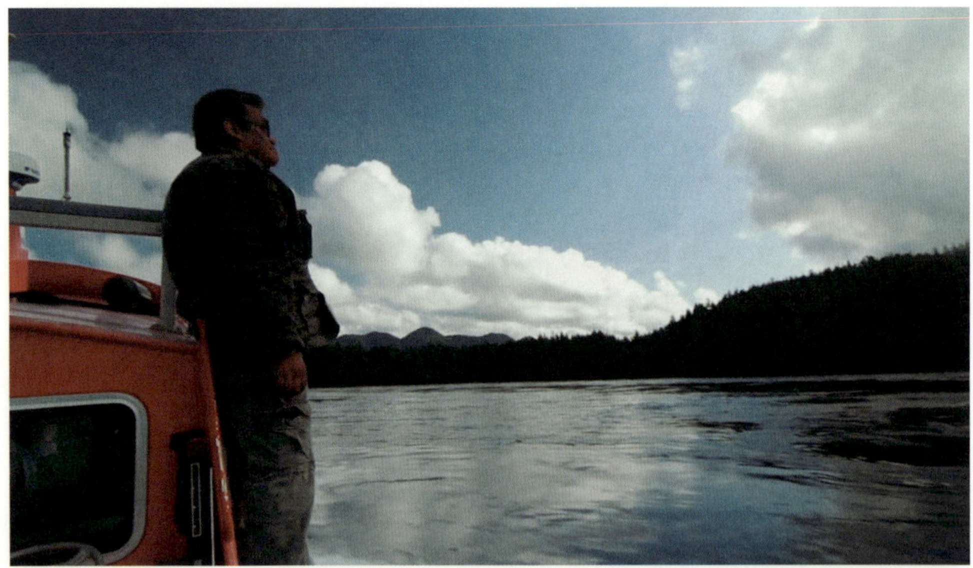

1

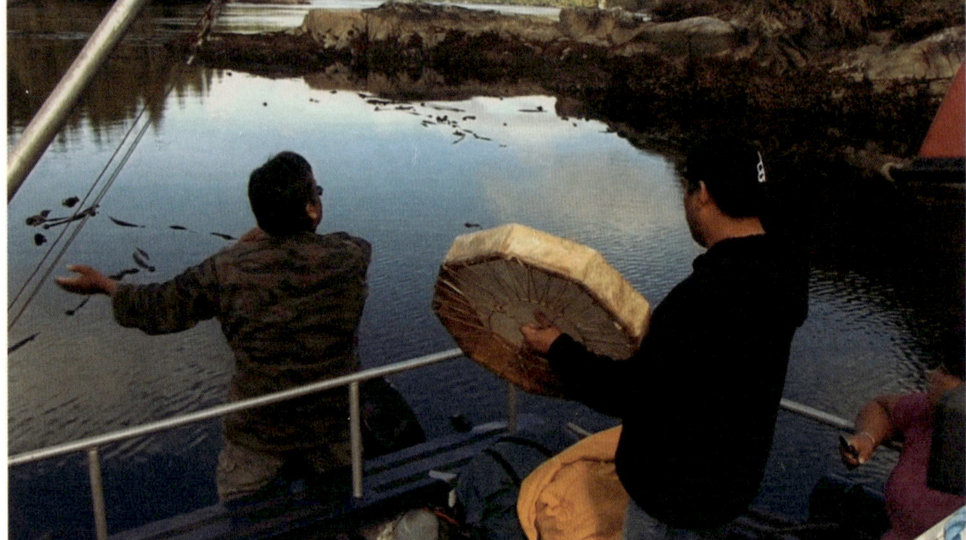

2

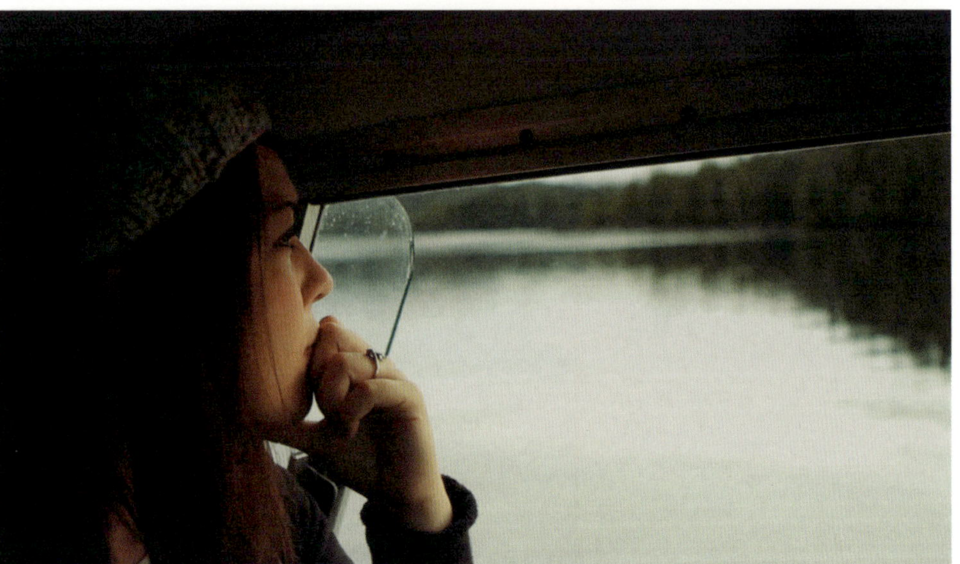

3

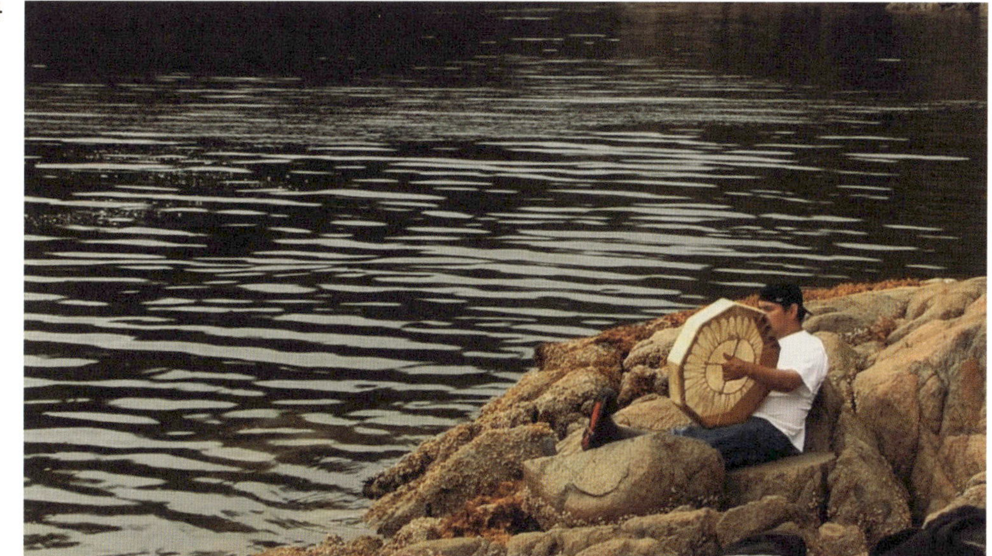

1—Chief Tom Henderson on a boat near traditional territory (Homelands)
2—Chief Tom Henderson and Chief Buddy Walkus in traditional territory (Homelands)
3—Jessie Hemphill, 'Nakwaxda'xw, Ligwitlda'xw, and Métis, on a visit to traditional territory (Homelands)
4—Chief Buddy Walkus on shore, in traditional territory (Homelands)
5—Children's potlatch, 2011, Gwa'sala-'Nakwaxda'xw First Nations
6—Tom Henderson, Hereditary Chief, 'Nakwaxda'xw First Nation

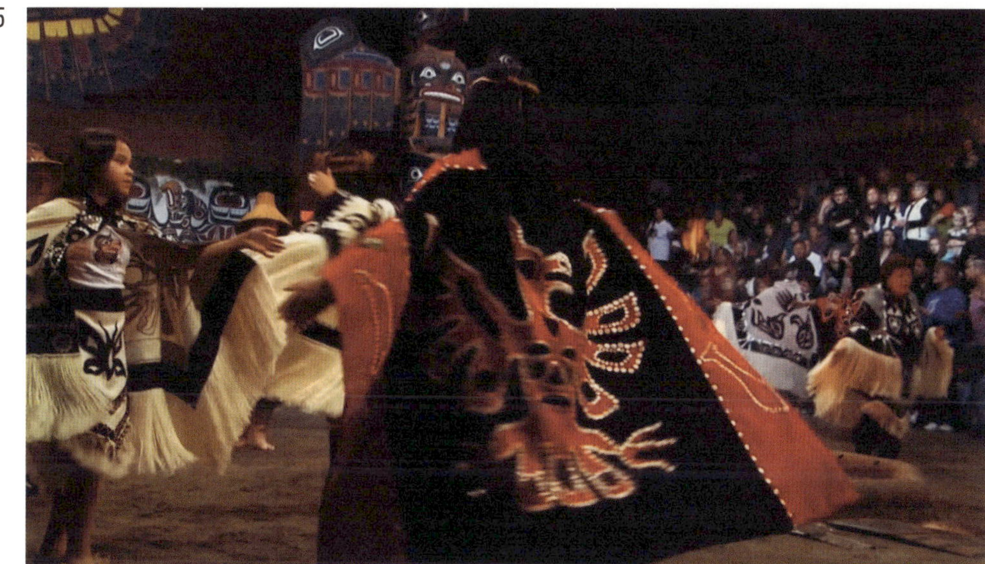

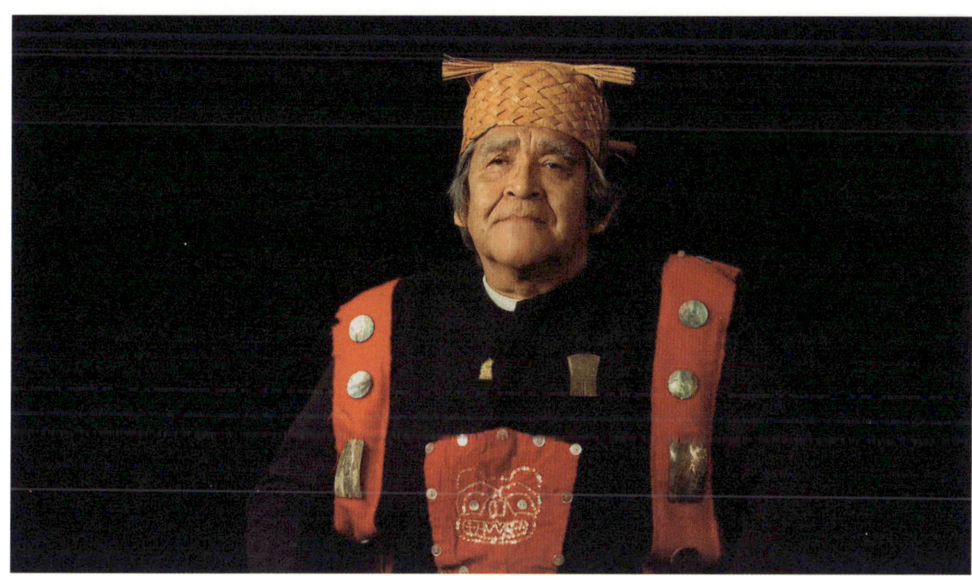

# "Nothing About Us Without Us" Lisa Jackson and Colleen Hemphill in Conversation with Martina Weinhart

Martina Weinhart of the Schirn Kunsthalle Frankfurt spoke with Lisa Jackson, an Anishinaabe documentary filmmaker, and Colleen Hemphill, a representative of the Gwa'sala-'Nakwaxda'xw First Nations, in October 2020 about their project *How a People Live*.

Martina Weinhart (MW): The documentary film *How a People Live* (2013, pp. 110, 111) was commissioned by the 'Nakwaxda'xw and Gwa'sala First Nations. It reports on the forced relocation of these Indigenous peoples to the Tsulquate Reserve in 1964, from their traditional territories of the Smith and Seymour Inlets and surrounding islands on the coast of British Columbia. Let's start from the beginning: How did this project get started?

*Colleen Hemphill (CH): This project was started in response to the call and need of the Gwa'sala-'Nakwaxda'xw Nations (GNN) Elders and community to record our own history by speaking with Elders who remembered and experienced the horrendous government action that caused the tragic relocation in 1964. We had made an unsuccessful attempt to put this film together in the early 1990s. By the time the film came about, the GNN were prepared, with funds available, to work with a historian and with Lisa Jackson, a highly respected Anishinaabe director.*

Lisa Jackson (LJ): The Gwa'sala-'Nakwaxda'xw reached out to me, having seen my previous film work on television. To begin with, I participated in a week-long youth media-making workshop in the community, Tsulquate, put on through a program called Our World. Over the course of the workshop, several community members made films with the support of mentors (including me). I also spent time digging into the extensive visual and written archives that the community had sourced.

The workshop took place in a building at the heart of the reserve of Tsulquate, so community members could stop by any time to meet and chat. At the end of the week, there was a well-attended community screening and dinner to showcase the new films. During that event, I screened a couple of my short films and discussed the upcoming documentary I had been asked to direct, inviting questions and conversation. Given that I was from a different Nation/territory, it was important that there be a fulsome opportunity for people to connect with me as a director, but also as a person whom they were entrusting with a sensitive and traumatic history.

I was tasked with telling the story of the GNN from their perspective. There had been much media coverage and ethnographic study of these Nations since the beginning of colonization, but always from an outsider/colonial gaze, which was often damaging. It was important that this film tell the story of the GNN from their point of view. It would tell their history with a particular focus on the relocation, which had caused so much suffering. As for the audience, the younger community members could learn much, the Elders' experiences would be honored, and, as well, for outsiders there would be a true document of what the GNN had experienced, no longer mediated through a colonial lens.

I drew up a short outline of what the film could look like, and when that was agreed on, I spent a month poring over 1,000 pages of archival documentation as well as dozens of images. Then, I drafted a detailed film outline with the three threads you now see in the film: archival sources, a boat journey to the Homelands, and community member testimonies.

MW: The new destination was Tsulquate. One sentence in the film stayed with me especially: "We lived off the land, knowing that this was our country. Everything comes from the land." Could you describe this notion of the land that seems to be quite different from European societies?

*CH: From the land and seas comes our ability to thrive in this part of world. The ancient histories and legends portray early ancestors working with the lands and seas to establish the Nations, the clans, and the original ancestors. Our ancestors were given principles of harmony, love, sustainability, respect, and family to live by. One only needs to witness our ancient ceremonies to find these essential land- and sea-based ordinances at play in songs, dances, and speeches in our language today. These laws apply to every living being, even those without motion, such as rocks. For example, the Metsa legend "When Mink Marries the Rock."*

MW: The interviews with the Elders are incredibly moving: the traumas they experienced as a result of the relocation, as well as other restrictions like the banning of the potlatch or the children being forced into residential schools, among other measures. Did you experience the filming as part of a healing process?

*CH: This is an interesting question, and, yes, we did see the beginnings of healing during the film process. It still continues today as GNN folks see and reflect on their own beginnings, and on the impact of colonization and the ways that we need to move forward—in fact, on our responsibility to protect what was given to our Nations, societies, at the beginning of time.*

MW: How did you arrive at the title of this film?

CH: *The title of the film came about in two ways. Firstly, there was a book written by a former Canadian government employee in charge of the districts of various First Nations—and based on the government program and the GNN relocation, the employee felt our Indigenous Nations would soon disappear. He wrote a novel that was published here in Canada in the early 1970s called* How a People Die. *In some ways, our film* How a People Live *was a response to that former dire prediction.*

*Secondly, in the film a hereditary chief states at a traditional 'Nakwaxda'xw village Sagwoombalah, after a sacred song of love and respect has been sung by young Buddy Walkus, "This is how our people lived." Our very insightful director Lisa took it from there and proposed the name at one of our early views of the upcoming film, and the name seemed to stick.*

MW: The journey back to the land is also a journey back into history, which leads to very crucial and complex questions of tracing a history that had been told before in a different manner. *How a People Live* combines interviews with Elders, as well as footage from a recent journey back to the ancestral village, with archival material. Could you tell us a little bit about your research, about what material was to be found, and where and how you made your selection?

LJ: As mentioned earlier, the visual and written archive was extensive and had already been sourced by the GNN. I have always loved working with historical materials, and I dove into the opportunity to reappropriate and employ the archive in a way that would recenter the GNN as the authors of their own story. No longer passive observational imagery, the film and photographs now bring to life this history from the community's perspective. And the historical written documents convey in hearbreaking detail the attitudes and harm wrought by the arrival of the colonizers and their systems meant to contain and control the Indigenous peoples of the territory they were entering. In terms of my approach, I drew up an extensive outline of these historical materials that would be useful in the film before we started shooting, so that I really knew that history intimately before we shot any new footage.

MW: You have used very interesting footage. Edward Curtis's film *In the Land of the Head Hunters*, released in 1914, was filmed on location in British Columbia with an all-Indigenous cast in the hope of impressing popular audiences with the pagentry of the Kwakwaka'wakw (Kwiakutl) people. Today, this groundbreaking filmic endeavor raises a lot of critical voices. What is your view of this loaded material that you have integrated into your film?

LJ: We have learned how subjective archival materials are and how often tainted with the biases and implicit assumptions of the outside collectors of such imagery. In the case of Edward S. Curtis, I spent time researching him and the history of the making of this film in particular, which has received a lot of attention. And while the film can be criticized as presenting a skewed version of the reality of the Kwakwaka'wakw people he was filming at the time—the salacious title, erasing all indications of modern life, shaping the storyline to create a populist "drama" for a wide audience—there is also value in seeing these traditional ways enacted over 100 years ago by the ancestors of the very community portrayed in *How a People Live*. The creation of costumes and props was carried out by the Kwakwaka'wakw under the guidance of George Hunt, who is now considered to be a key Indigenous collaborator of Curtis's in the three years of preparation for and filming of *In the Land of the Head Hunters* (since renamed *In the Land of the War Canoes*).

MW: "Who is speaking?" is always an interesting question, including whose voice is heard in a society. We will show your film in the context of Canadian modernism with the intention of creating a polyphonic and multilayered context to open new and differentiated perspectives on image production in that field. How do you relate to the patterns of representation in Canada?

CH: *I love the work of the Group of Seven for portraying the beautiful landscape of the country of Canada. However, the paintings are absent of the people who lived on those lands for thousands of years and who had maintained the lands and seas in the pristine state that the Group of Seven had the benefit of portraying in their paintings. Later, Emily Carr, from the West Coast, did include a few people …*

LJ: The narrative of the Indigenous peoples in these territories now called Canada has been told for most of history through a colonial lens—and continues to be, though things are changing. This has been deeply damaging to the many Indigenous Nations living here and has deprived generations of Canadians from knowing the truth about their country, whose colonial aims required the displacement, dehumanization, and erasure of Indigenous peoples.

Our representation in film and media is improving, and there are now many Indigenous filmmakers creating powerful films that receive accolades in Canada and internationally—from Alanis Obomsawin's films to Zacharias Kunuk's *Atanarjuat: The Fast Runner,* to Elle-Máijá Tailfeathers's *The Body Remembers When the World Broke Open.*

However, there is still a tendency toward treating Indigenous peoples as the "Other" in representations, which can romanticize us, reduce our experience to that of trauma and victimization, or present other portrayals that rob us of our agency and full humanity. "Nothing about us without us" is a phrase often used when discussing narrative screen sovereignty. Canada is slowly moving forward on the path of creating a more equitable screen culture that supports the voices of those so often left behind in the storytelling of this country, from Indigenous peoples to immigrants and others whose stories have rarely been shared—yet.

Caroline Monnet
*Mobilize,* 2015
Single-channel video
(color, sound, 3 min.)

The short film collage is a montage from the holdings of the archive of the National Film Board. It was established in Canada in 1939 and has the task of promoting projects that give expression to the culture and society of the country. Its archives are correspondingly wide-ranging. For the initiative "Souvenirs," the organization invited four Indigenous filmmakers to address questions of identity and representation using existing material, to interpret the history of Canada, and to portray it anew from their specific perspective. Besides Caroline Monnet's film, works were also created by Kent Monkman, Michelle Latimer, and Jeff Barnaby.

Monnet takes viewers on a journey from the high north to the urban south, in pictures that shed light on the interplay between tradition and modernity. A tree is felled, stripped of bark, a canoe is built, and there are swift trips across the water again and again, first with a paddle, then motorized. In the course of the film, modern life intrudes: high-rise buildings are erected, and the journey continues by airplane or subway. The idea of progress or striding forward is conveyed by the propulsive sound of the throat singing of the Inuit performer Tanya Tagaq, whose piece "Uja" gives the rapid sequence of images its own urgency.

Martina Weinhart

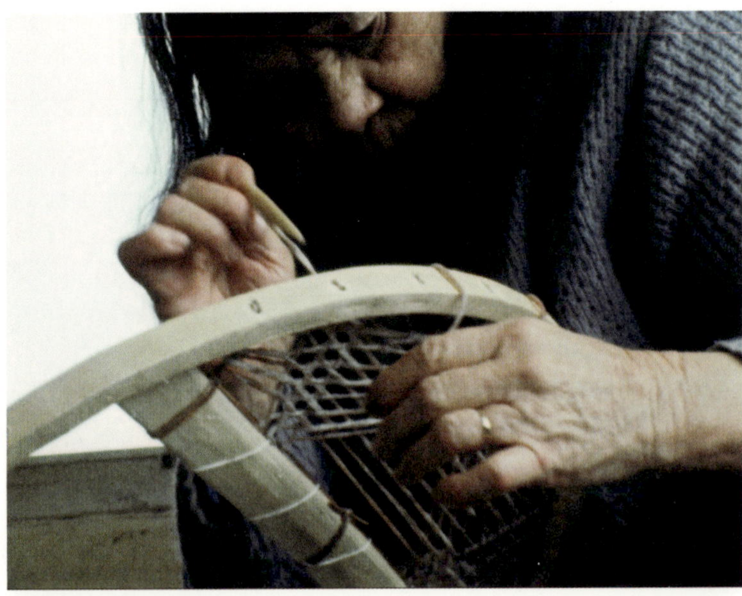

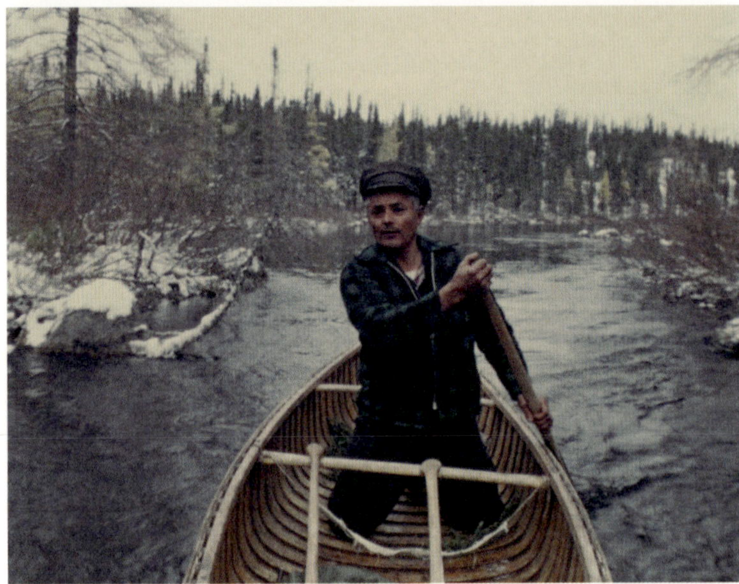

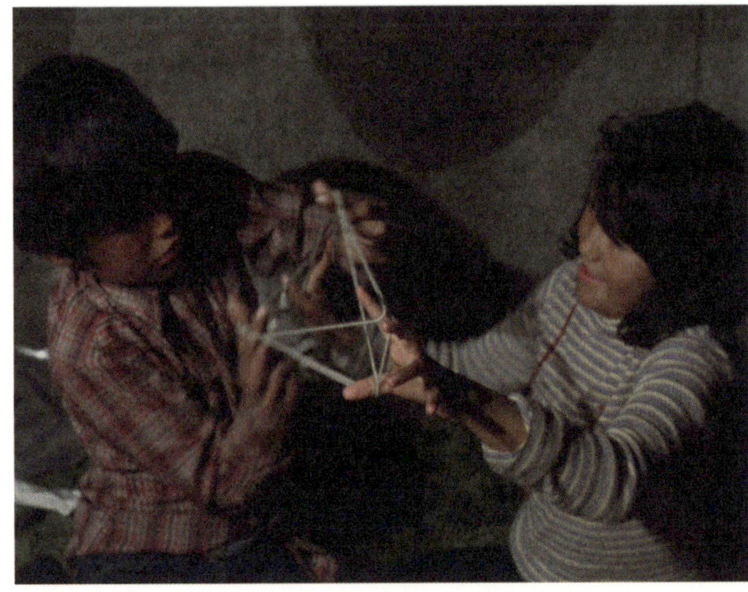

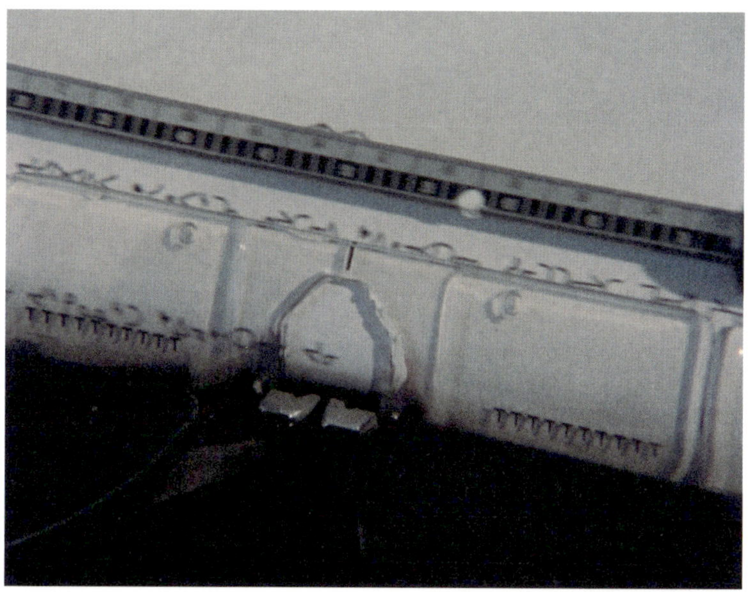

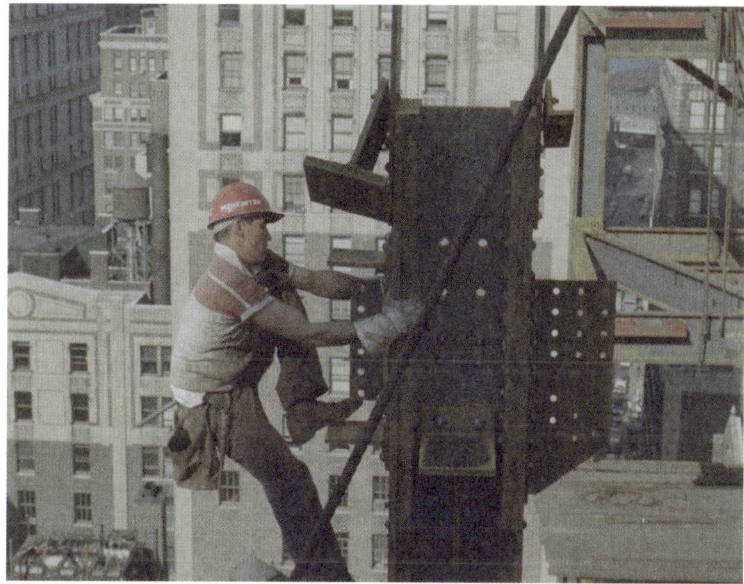

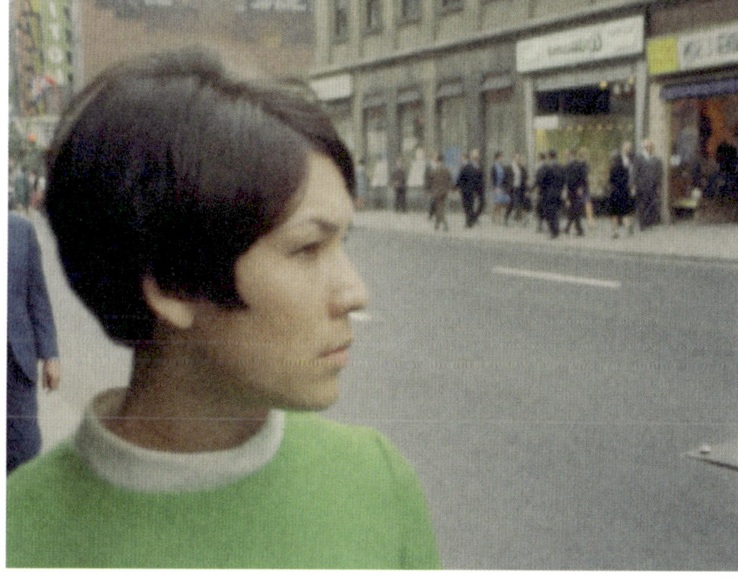

# "I'm Uncovering a Different Side of the Story"
## Caroline Monnet in Conversation with Renée van der Avoird

Caroline Monnet is an artist of Algonquin-French heritage based in Montreal, working in sculpture, installation, and film. Her practice focuses on the representation of Indigenous people and culture in contemporary society; this theme resonates in *Mobilize* and *Transatlantic,* the two works by Monnet included in *Magnetic North.* Both films celebrate Indigenous knowledge and engage with canonical works by the Group of Seven by offering subtle yet critical commentary on the ongoing colonial dynamics between Europe and North America.

Renée van der Avoird (RvdA): Caroline, your work adds critical context to the *Magnetic North* exhibition and publication and opens up a space for dialogue about ongoing colonial legacies. How do you view your work in relation to the understanding of the Group of Seven as a national treasure?

Caroline Monnet (CM): My work has often focused on responding to the environment that surrounds me. Much like the Group of Seven, I am sensitive to the vastness and grandeur of landscape and territory. However, the members of the Group of Seven have received criticism for the ways in which their work reinforces the notion of *terra nullius,* and for their omission of the Indigenous presence in the country's narrative. It is crucial to include more diverse voices in dialogue with the Group of Seven, as its members' perspectives on Canada at the time were unidirectional. Clearly, the fight for inclusion of Indigenous artists in Canadian mainstream galleries and museums is still ongoing—and highly relevant—today.

RvdA: How are land and territory connected to Indigenous identity?

CM: Land and territory are everything. Language, culture, and identity are connected to those core concepts. People need to realize that not all First Nations are the same. We vary from one nation to the next; the diversity of our respective territories influences all aspects of our lifestyles and cultures. And land is at the root of all our relations.

RvdA: Strategically, your practice is centered around giving visibility to Indigenous people. This is especially clear in *Mobilize* (2015, pp. 116, 117), a fast-paced short film that splices together archival footage from Canada's National Film Board (NFB), a government-funded agency that produces and distributes film and digital media to the public. I see the film as an assertion or celebration of skill—very specialized skills—rooted in valuable Indigenous knowledge. Is your representation of these skills a political call to action?

CM: My work is about bringing Indigenous stories to the fore and presenting positive messages that counter what is usually portrayed in the media—stereotypical narratives such as stories of poverty, of abuse, of addiction. I'm uncovering a different side of the story, asserting the presence of strong, resilient, beautiful, eccentric, and elegant Indigenous women and men.

When the National Film Board approached me to make *Mobilize,* using footage from their archives, they specifically asked for a representation of Indigenous identity. I immediately knew I wanted to create something dynamic that would counter the potential for stagnation and nostalgia. I centered my process around key verbs—building, moving, walking, running—and the concept of forward motion. I chose to focus on Indigenous excellence, highlighting specialized skill sets like building canoes, snowshoes, or even skyscrapers. The film celebrates the key role that Indigenous people have played in building the world around us and how Indigenous knowledge has been passed down through generations to inspire all nations.

I'm not necessarily presenting such knowledge as a conscious call to action, but it is certainly a strategy for taking up space. I want to put forth an accurate representation where, as Indigenous individuals, we can feel confident in who we are and gain a sense of pride in our knowledge and skills. Maybe it's a way of reclaiming the valorization that was once taken away from us.

RvdA: What was the original intent of the NFB archival footage?

CM: The NFB footage was documentary and ethnographic in nature. It's important to note that these archives are most often, if not always, generated from a white male perspective. I wanted to dig into them and recreate a film through my own lens, as a way of using the archives in a productive and relevant way decades after they were made.

RvdA: I read your approach as a gesture of reclamation, or reappropriation.

CM: My approach brings Indigenous perspectives into a context that was developed without them. The act of collage implies that the artist can be selective in what they choose to show; they can create associations through images that retell a different story than the one that was originally intended. This is a gesture of visual sovereignty as well as a way of reclaiming the power of the image.

RvdA: Several Group of Seven and Tom Thomson paintings feature the image of the canoe, a loaded symbol of colonialism and cultural appropriation. In *Mobilize*, we see a birchbark canoe being fabricated by hand. We're able to observe how the creation of a canoe is highly technical and rooted in traditional Indigenous knowledge and the land.

CM: Indigenous knowledge has proven to be extremely relevant and useful in today's global reality. It is something to be proud of. The man paddling his canoe down the rapids is in total control. I wanted to portray him as a true expert, and for people to feel energized seeing Indigenous people like him on screen showing off their skills. The energy from this scene comes from the soundtrack, but also from the canoeist's incredible skill, strength, and confidence.

RvdA: In a public artwork you made in Toronto in 2018, *History Shall Speak for Itself,* you use photography, collage, and reclaimed archival material to honor Indigenous women filmmakers. What does it mean for you to be a part of this legacy? What do you appreciate about film as a medium?

CM: I aim to change the representation of Indigenous women in our collective consciousness. I believe that image-based work is often the most appropriate way to challenge those perceptions. When conducting research in the NFB archives, I noticed that Indigenous women were portrayed as passive protagonists, busy with daily chores. I took action by weaving a different narrative into that representation, where, through my lens, women would face the camera, projecting royalty, elegance, exuberance, pride, and strength. I come from a long line of strong Indigenous women; so many came before me and worked hard in allowing us to be who we are today. There is a legacy that will continue for generations to come. The medium of film is a great way to document this legacy in action.

RvdA: You also bring Indigenous women into your practice as collaborators. You feature "Uja," a song by the Inuit throat-singing innovator Tanya Tagaq, as the soundtrack to *Mobilize*.

CM: Indigenous women are still the most marginalized group in our society. I feel a sense of responsibility to counteract the preconceived notions that are, to this day, so often highlighted in mainstream media. At the end of *Mobilize*, you see a fashionable woman confidently walking down the streets of Montreal—for me, it is important to include this kind of representation as part of that cityscape. *Mobilize* begins in the Northern Canadian bush and then migrates south to Montreal. It is a met-

aphor for my family's trajectory: my grandfather leaving the reservation, Kitigan Zibi, and moving to Ottawa, and then me ending up in Montreal, an even bigger city.

I was excited to use archival images to refer to the future, which resonates with Tanya Tagaq's song "Uja," because her sound is just that: past and future. It is culturally specific and rooted in tradition, but it also has a metal-punk sound that I absolutely love. To juxtapose her music with the NFB clips anchors *Mobilize* in contemporaneity. It also makes the film somehow urban, but still very much attached to land, the landscape, and territory.

RvdA: *Transatlantic* (2018, pp. 122-25), a non-narrative video documentation of your voyage on a cargo ship from a port in Europe to your current hometown in Montreal, picks up on this context in a modified way. Can you explain how this film relates to your own family history and to the journey that settlers took from Europe to North America around the time of contact?

CM: My father is from France, and my mother is Algonquin from Maniwaki, Quebec, two hours north of Ottawa. I grew up between Brittany, France, and Outaouais, Canada. For me, the Atlantic Ocean became the symbol of a middle ground for both sides of my ancestors, a liminal space for understanding who I am. That's how the project originally started.

My father left France to settle in Canada, where he married my mother who is Anishinaabe. I guess it could be seen as the same story that built New France, as if history repeats itself. My journey across the Atlantic also connects to a larger context in the sense that it represents those people who left Europe in search of a better world in North America. It takes courage to leave a country behind and step into the unknown, but for my mother's ancestors, the arrival of those settlers caused great trauma. The journey from Europe to North America remains a conflicted symbol, from both settler and Indigenous perspectives.

RvdA: When viewing *Transatlantic,* one has the experience of being overwhelmed by the universe—or perhaps by nature itself. The work also sparks in the viewer a powerful sense of destabilization, not only as a result of its mirrored images, but also through the soundtrack.

CM: *Transatlantic* is about communication, or rather the lack of communication between nations. At the time of developing the concept, I wanted to talk explicitly about mixing identities, but the work later evolved to suggest more of an emotional journey. It captures the shifts between excitement, boredom, fear, tranquility—moods which, at sea, all feel the same day after day, but are never exactly the same.

For the soundtrack, I collaborated with Simon Guibord, a very talented artist from Gatineau, Quebec. We discussed ways to create messages through sounds, using radio frequencies, electronic waves, and Morse code as references to communication devices. Overall, we sought to create a soundtrack that brought rhythm to the editing.

RvdA: I am curious to hear more about your experience on the cargo ship. Is it true that you were the only woman on board for the duration of the twenty-two-day journey?

CM: The experience was isolating, and being disconnected from civilization was a challenge. I boarded the ship in an industrial park with a Polish, all-male crew who barely spoke English. I was terrified at first, but gradually I felt comfortable enough to move freely around the ship. I was treated with a lot of respect, and most crew members were curious about my intentions with the project. Because there was no Internet or phone connection, I was alone with my thoughts. There is something very meditative and transcendental about being at sea for that long.

RvdA: How did that sense of isolation affect the making of the project?

CM: It was a very slow process, which is reflected in the rhythm of the film. In the fifteen-minute piece, there are some very quiet moments, and a lot of serenity.

In my full immersion, I began to consider the Atlantic Ocean as a symbol for greater phenomena. I thought about how Europe got rich on the back of Canada, on the back of Indigenous people, to be more precise. I also felt extremely small in front of the elements, and the teachings I have received on the cosmos and the tides started to make sense on a different level.

RvdA: Your work incorporates image and sound, but not words, placing it outside or beyond spoken language. The installation of *Transatlantic* at the Schirn Kunsthalle Frankfurt will be the first time it is shown outside of Canada. How does the journey shift when it is shared with an audience close to its point of origin? Who are the imagined passengers on this voyage?

CM: I like that *Transatlantic* is not culturally specific to Indigenous identity. Viewers unfamiliar with my work will not see it as Indigenous right away. It has been shown in Ottawa and Banff, where it was specifically anchored in an Indigenous narrative. However, at the Schirn it will be read in a very different context, and this change in perception will be interesting. In Europe, the fascination with the Canadian landscape and its Indigenous people is still strong. Viewers might be enthusiastic about the journey—the notion of arriving in a land of plenty, a land that in our imagination remains untouched and wild.

Caroline Monnet
*Transatlantic,* 2018
Multichannel HD video installation
(color, sound, 15 min., 10 sec.)
Courtesy of the artist

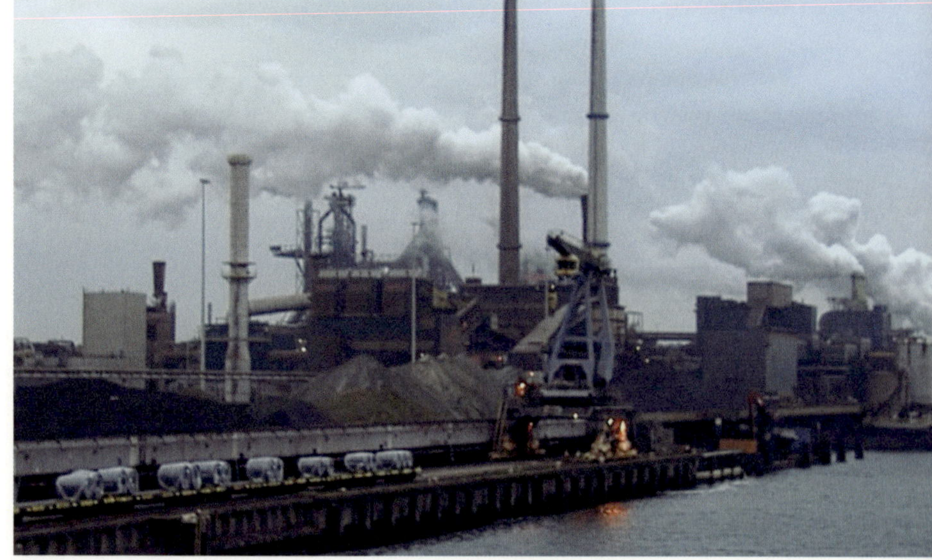

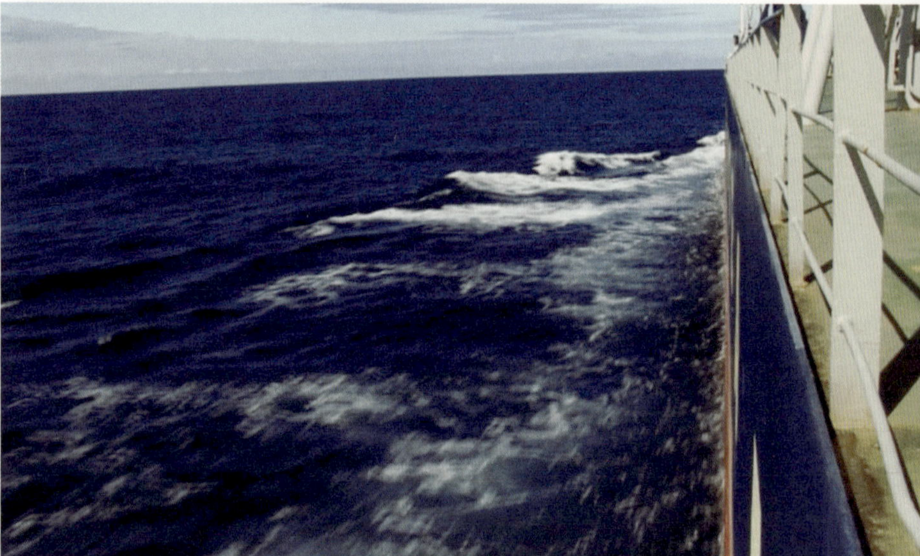

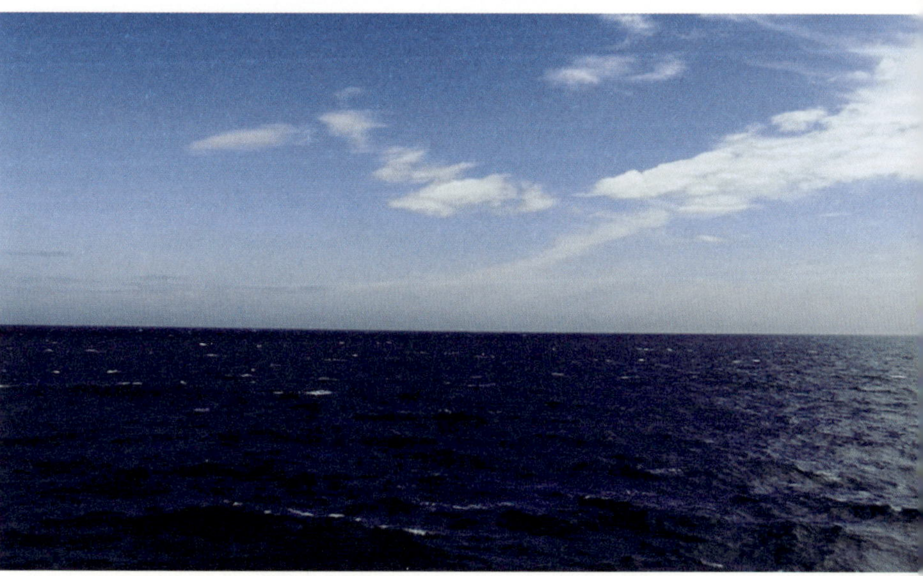

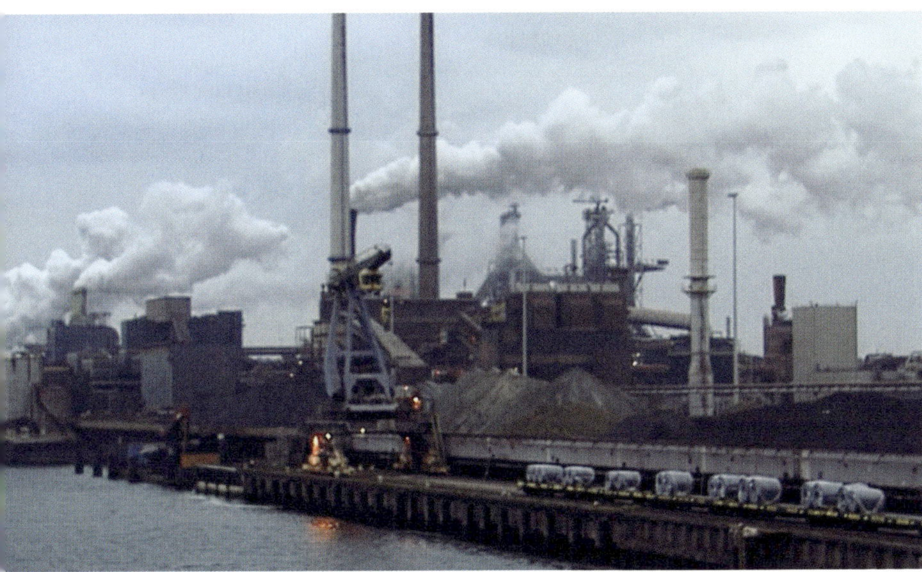

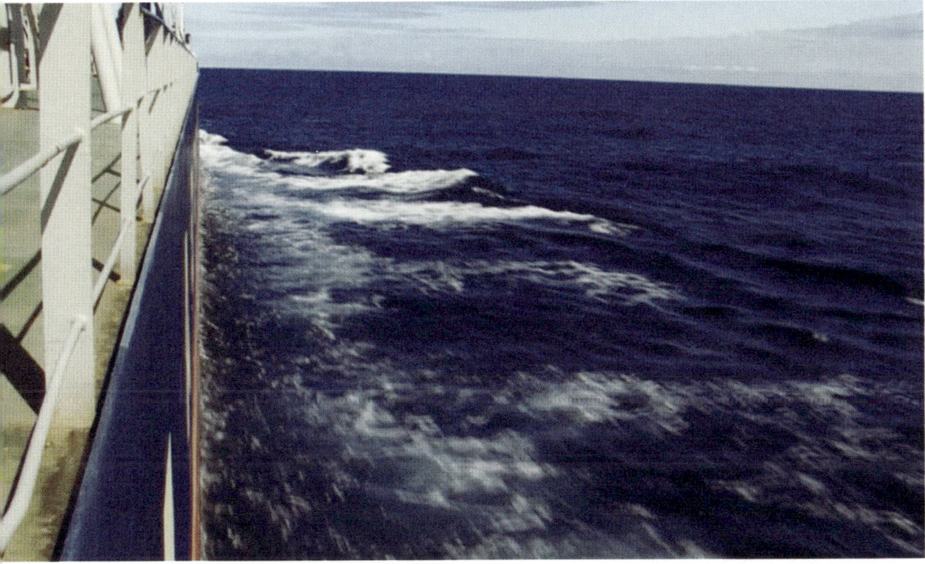

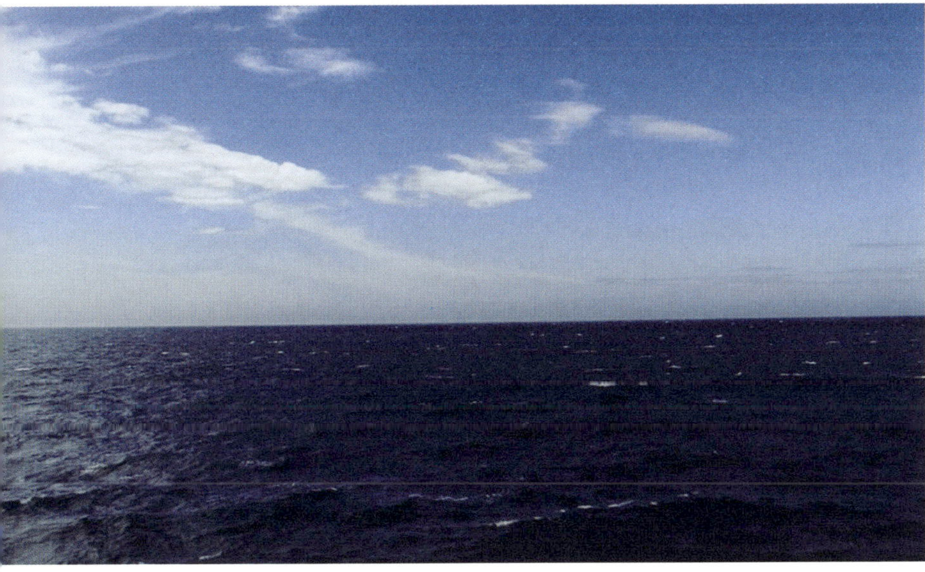

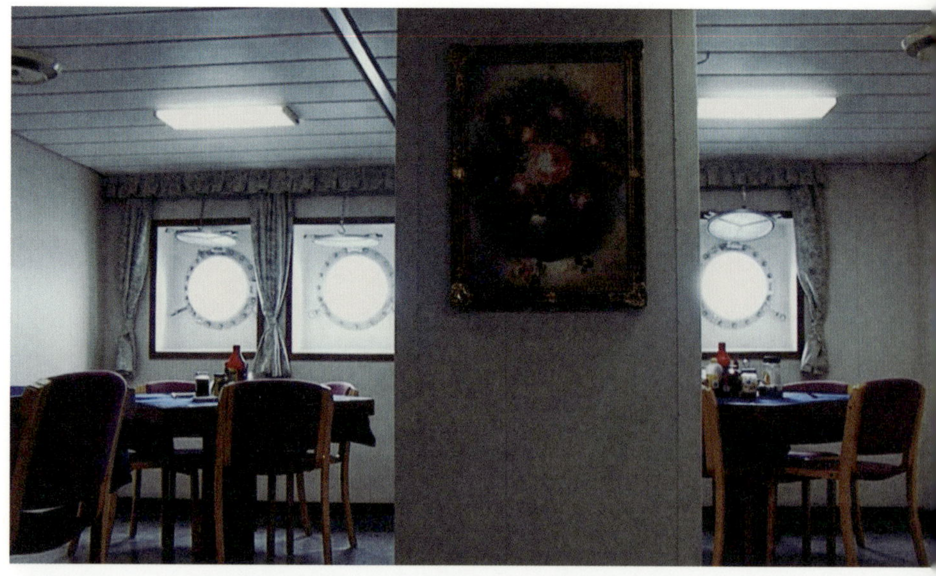

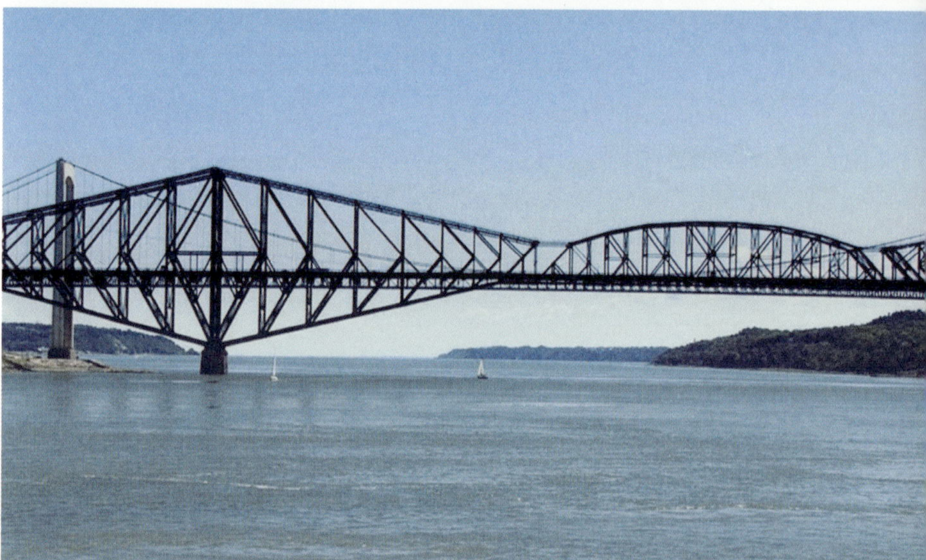

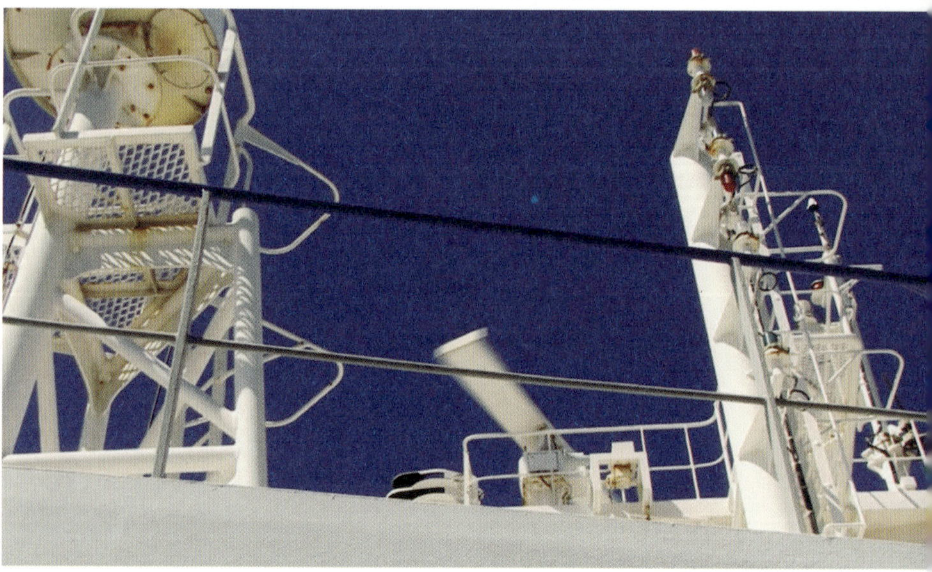

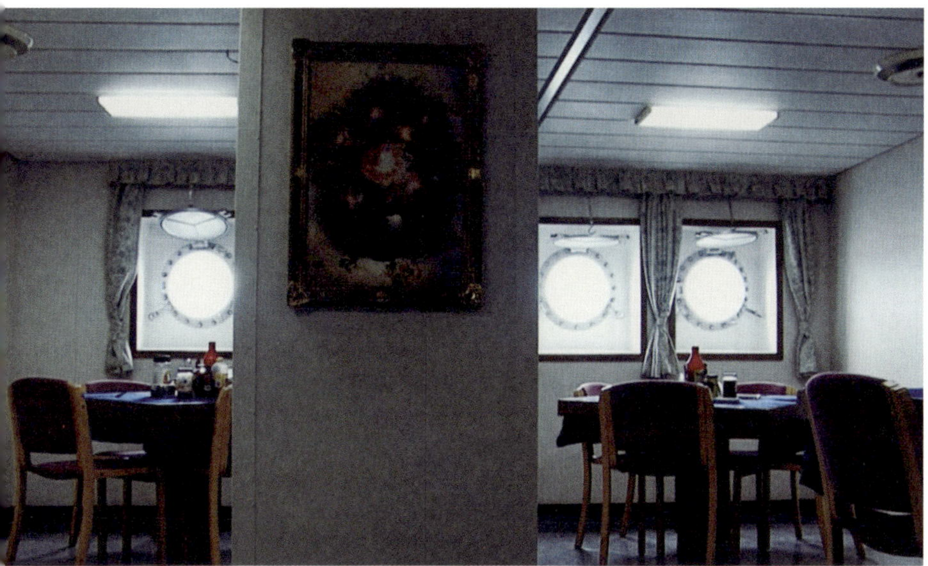

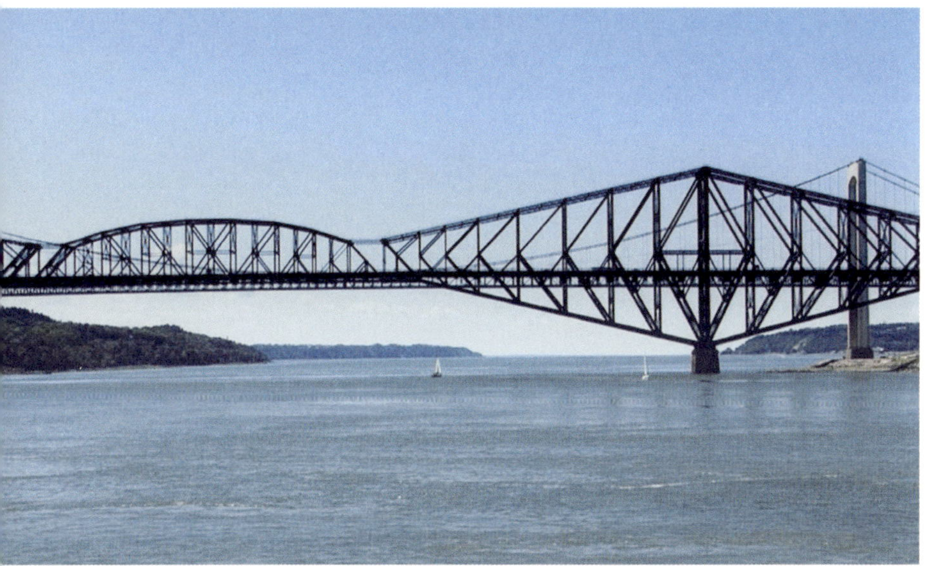

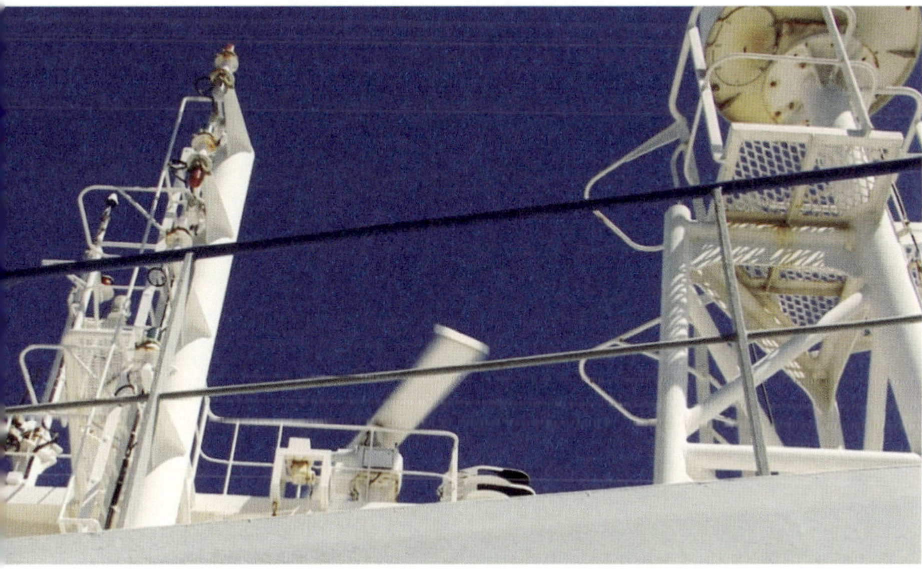

# Lawren

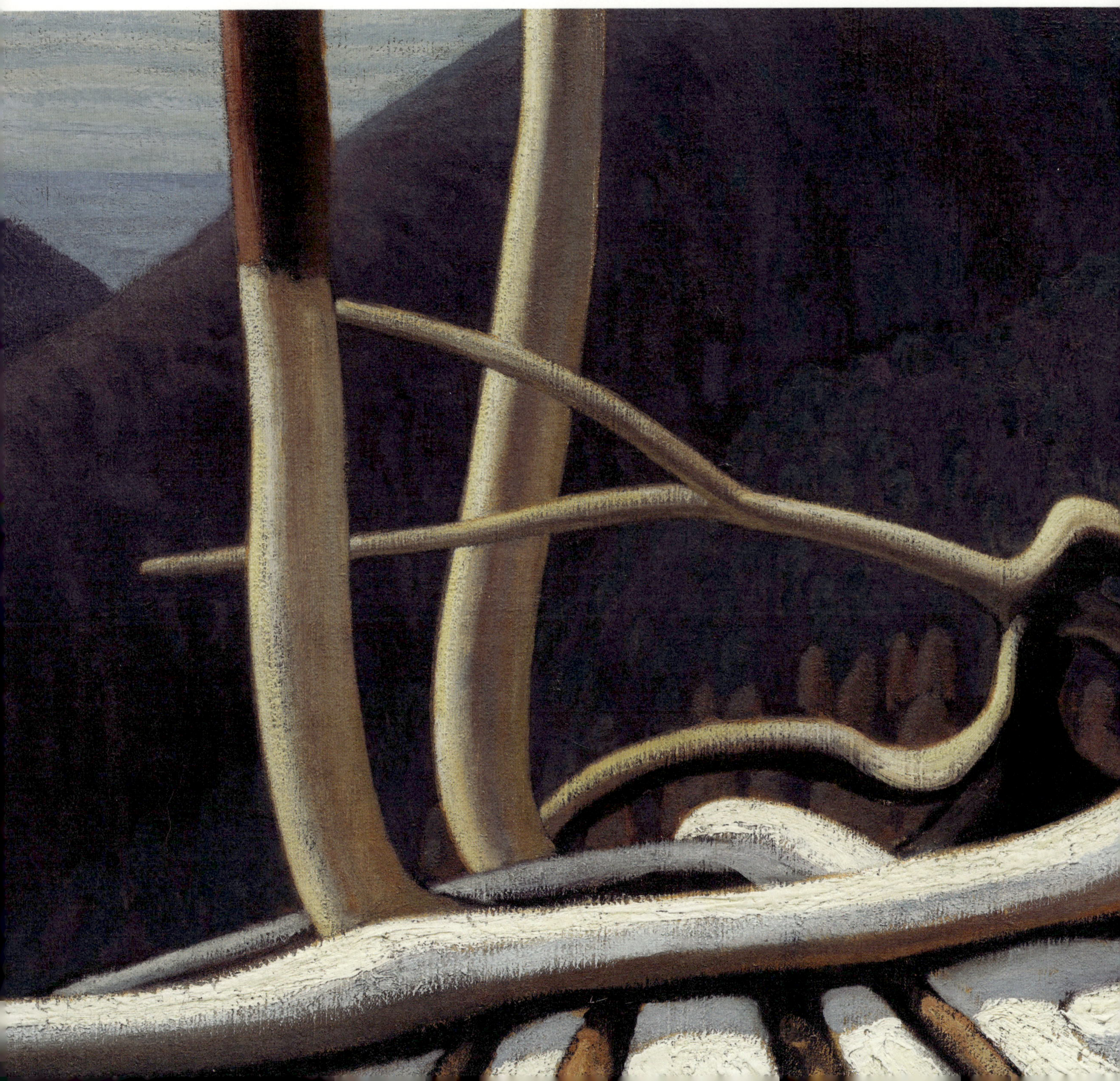

# Harris

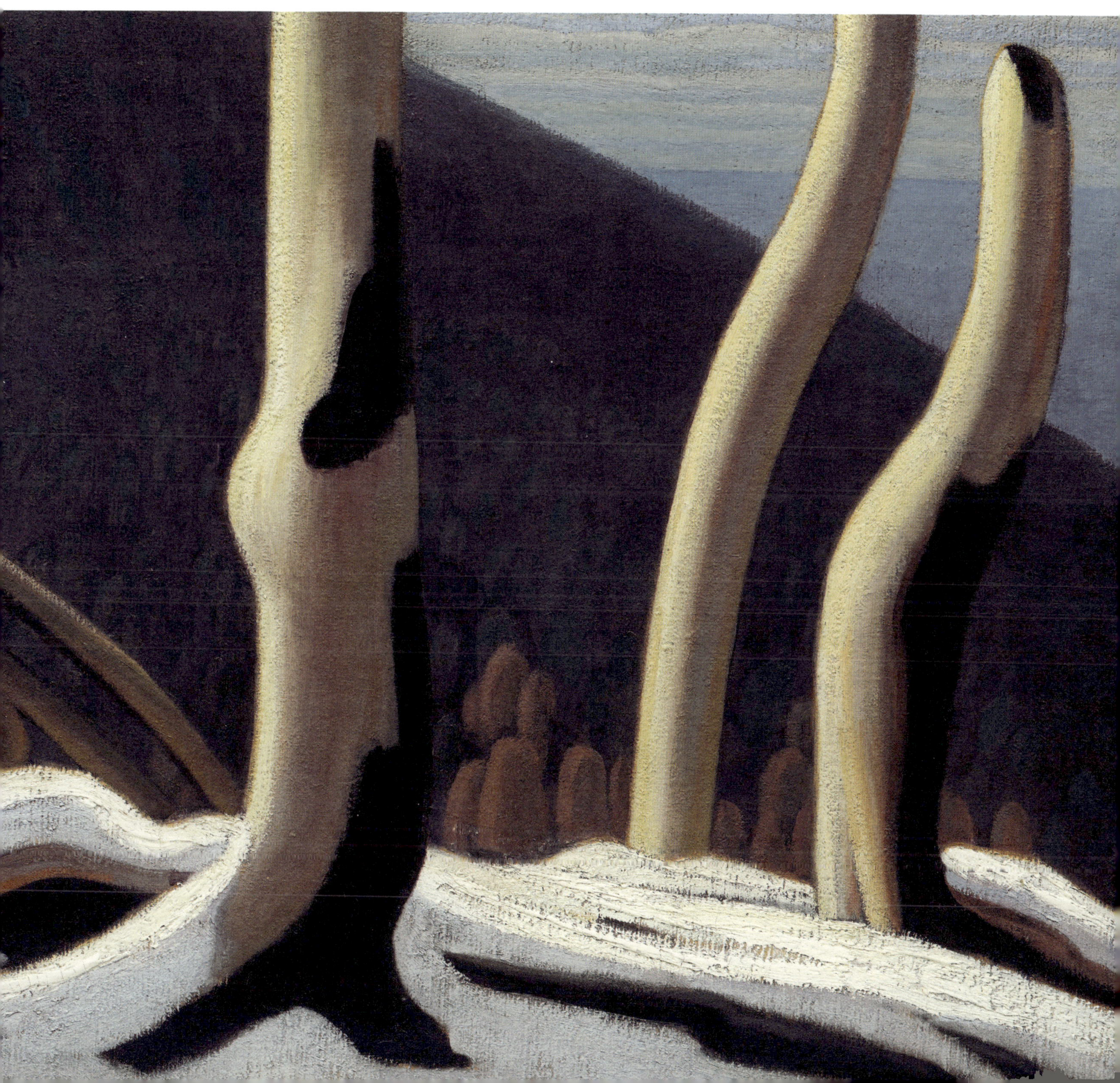

The landscapes of Lawren Harris captivate with their radical painting style displaying a reduced formal language and two-dimensional application of color. The artist sought a new visual vocabulary for the depiction of Canada; in articles and essays he would write about his desire to establish a specifically Canadian art, thus strengthening national identity in the process. Spirituality was likewise of central importance to Harris. In 1923, he joined the Toronto Theosophical Society dedicated to principles that included establishing a brotherhood of all men and investigating the higher forces operating in the world. Accordingly, paintings such as *Mt. Lefroy* (1930) or *Isolation Peak* (1929) not only testify to a heightened awareness of the beauty of the country as a source of artistic inspiration and national identity, but they also served to convey transcendental and, not least, religious content.

Over time, Harris increasingly moved away from a faithful depiction of reality, simplifying and abstracting his subjects instead. This approach is evident in his early 1920s paintings *Above Lake Superior* (ca. 1922) and *Lake Superior* (ca. 1924). Views of the Arctic created around 1930, in turn, such as *Grounded Icebergs (Disco Bay)* (ca. 1931) and *Icebergs, Davis Strait* (1930), reflect an interplay of the cool tonal range from icy blue to translucent white. Soon thereafter, Harris finally arrived at non-objective painting.

Lawren Harris, whose pictures received great attention and critical recognition, played a major role in shaping the genre of landscape painting in early twentieth-century Canada, as well as in igniting debates about abstraction and creating a form of national artistic expression. In the more recent reception, however, the nationalism inherent to his ideas has also drawn frequent criticism.[1] Not least, his "empty" landscapes support the colonial narrative of a *terra nullius.*

Rebecca Herlemann

1—See, for example, Lynda Jessup, "Bushwackers in the Gallery: Antimodernism and the Group of Seven," in *Antimodernism and Artistic Experience: Policing the Boundaries of Modernity,* ed. Lynda Jessup (Toronto: University of Toronto Press, 2001), pp. 130–52.

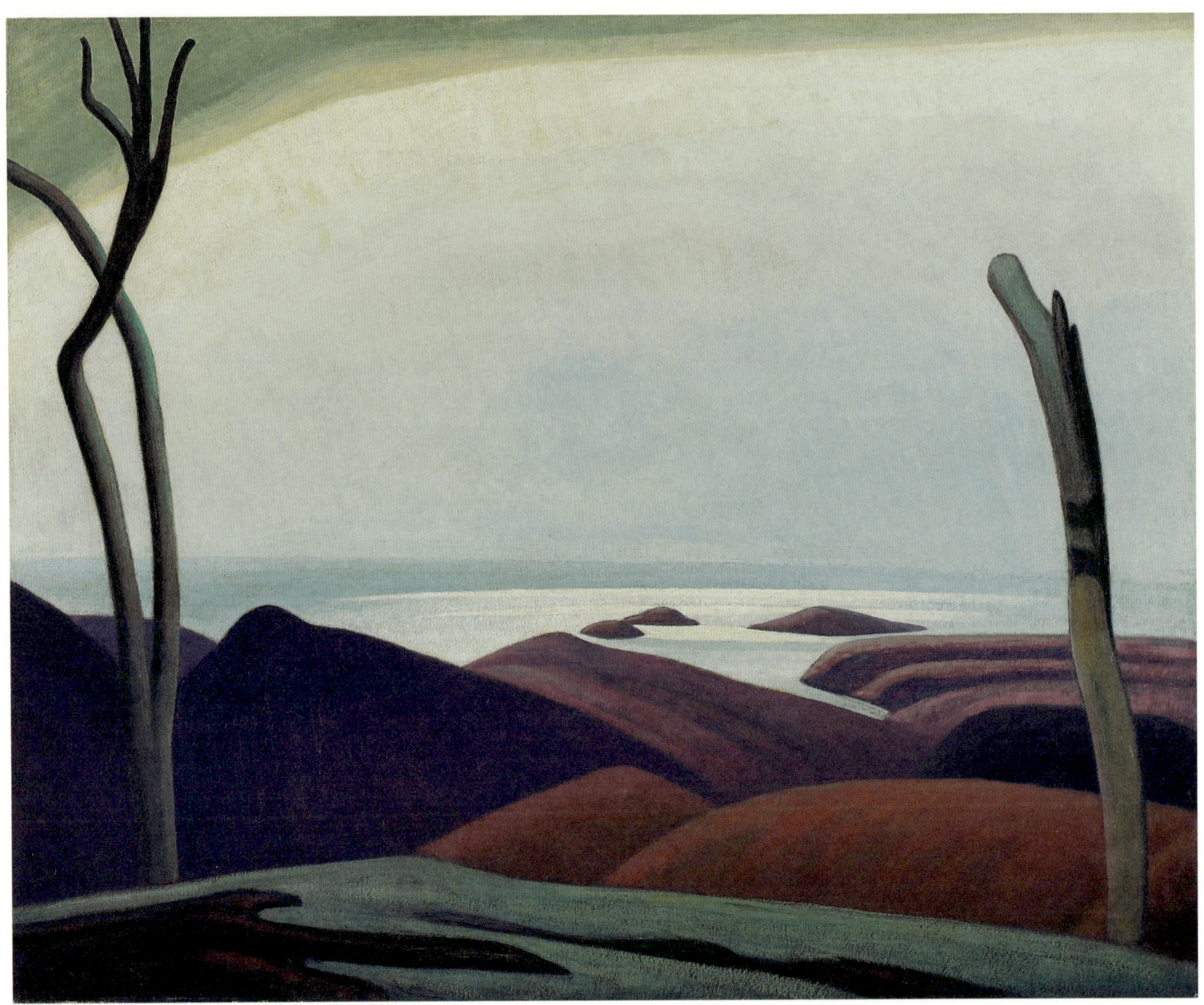

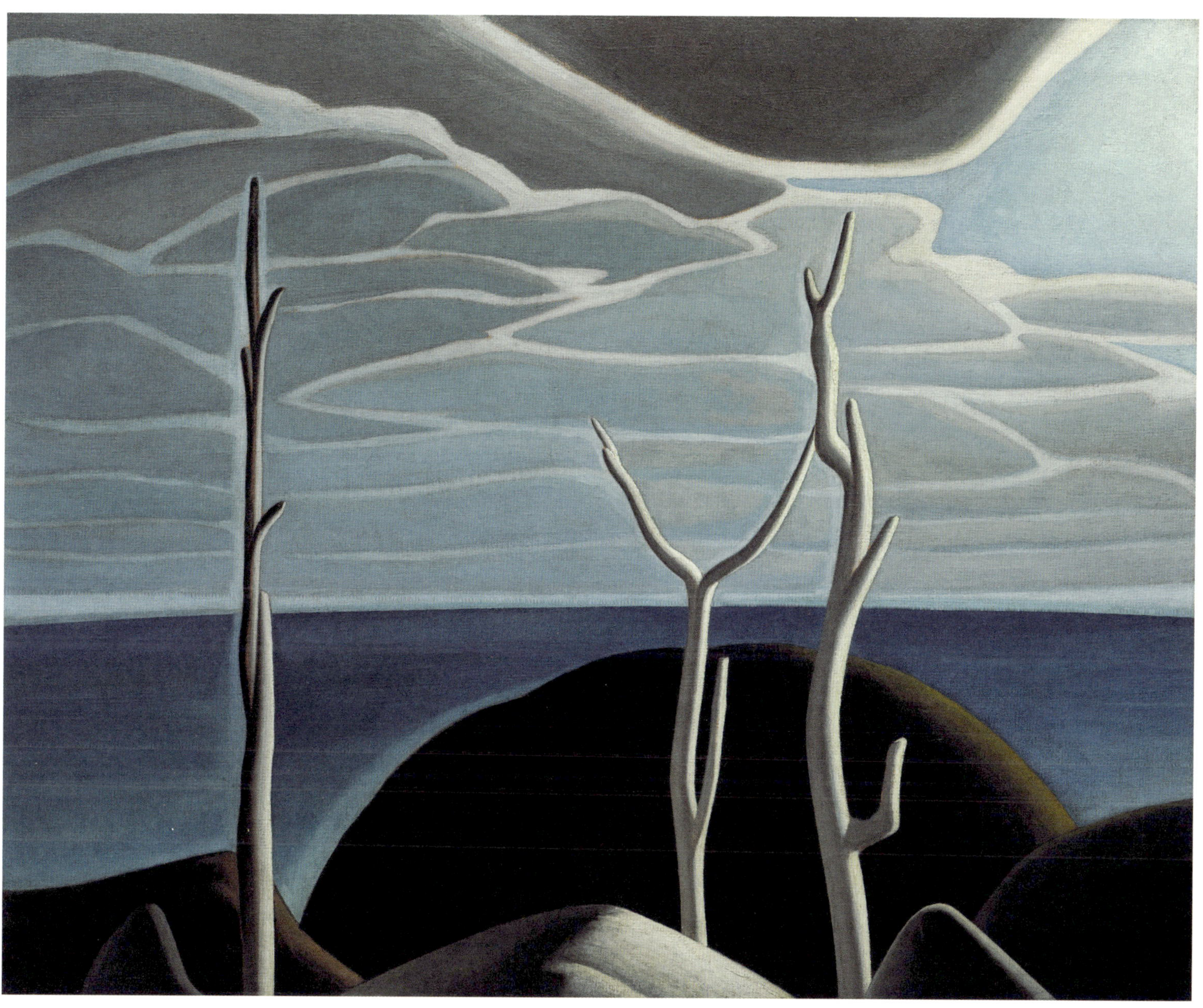

Lawren Harris
*Lake Superior,* n.d.
100.3 × 123.2 cm

Lawren Harris
*Lake Superior,* ca. 1924
101.7 × 127.3 cm

Lawren Harris
*Above Lake Superior,* ca. 1922
121.9 × 152.4 cm

In fall of 1921, Lawren Harris and A. Y. Jackson reached the northernmost point of Lake Superior for the first time. They traveled by freight train to Schreiber, Ontario, and then they walked 15 kilometers to Rossport, where they stayed for a few days.[1] Harris had seen enough of the lush landscape of the Algoma region and was looking for new inspiration, as Jackson reported: "The Algoma country was too opulent for Harris; he wanted something bare and stark."[2] A few years earlier, fires had raged along the North Shore of Lake Superior: patches of forest were burned and nature only slowly started to regenerate. These were the subjects he had been looking for.

Harris made a number of sketches and paintings of this scorched landscape, one of his most successful canvases being *Above Lake Superior.* From a snow-covered knoll with some bare, dead tree trunks rising up into the sky and others lying on the ground, the viewer gazes out over dark wooded hills, beyond which an endless expanse of water appears in the distance. A blanket of clouds in even, horizontal waves covers the sky above and provides a clear contrast to the vertical lines of the tree trunks in the foreground. Harris had been especially impressed with the sky over this landscape: "At times, there were skies over the great Lake Superior which, in their singing expansiveness and sublimity, existed nowhere else in Canada."[3]

The perspective the artist chose for this view is unusual. Five tree trunks that have lost most of their bark stand at the center of the composition and are cut off by the edge of the painting, thus rendering proportions unclear. Much of the landscape is shaded and visible only through the tree trunks which are bathed in warm light coming from the side. Rough, unadorned nature is foregrounded here and depicted in a very austere manner. Harris had stripped down the motif of his painting to its core, thus revealing its strength and beauty as he "sought to have no element in the work which did not contribute to a unified intense expression."[4]

The responses to the painting among contemporary viewers varied widely, ranging from great admiration to absolute rejection, according to the critic Fred Housser.[5] For Lawren Harris, the painting marked a turning point in his art. Having previously often adopted a decorative style of painting and also turning to cityscapes as subjects, he now focused on reduced landscapes in cool colors. It was a process of simplifying nature "to its fundamental and purest form,"[6] one that he would continue in subsequent years.

Rebecca Herlemann

1—Lawren Harris, "The Group of Seven in Canadian History," in *Canadian Historical Association Report of the Annual Meeting Held at Victoria and Vancouver June 16-19, 1948* (Toronto: University of Toronto Press, 1948), pp. 34-35.
2—A. Y. Jackson, *A Painter's Country: The Autobiography of A. Y. Jackson* (Toronto: Clarke Irwin & Company Limited, 1967), p. 57.
3—Harris, "The Group of Seven in Canadian History," p. 34.
4—Lawren Harris, quoted in Ann Davis, *The Logic of Ecstasy: Canadian Mystical Painting, 1920-1940* (Toronto: University of Toronto Press, 1992), p. 64.
5—F. B. Housser, *A Canadian Art Movement: The Story of the Group of Seven* (Toronto: The Macmillan Company of Canada, 1926), p. 189.
6—Lawren Harris, quoted in Christopher Jackson, *Lawren Harris: North by West; The Arctic and Rocky Mountain Paintings of Lawren Harris, 1924-1931* (Calgary: Glenbow Museum, 1991), p. 13.

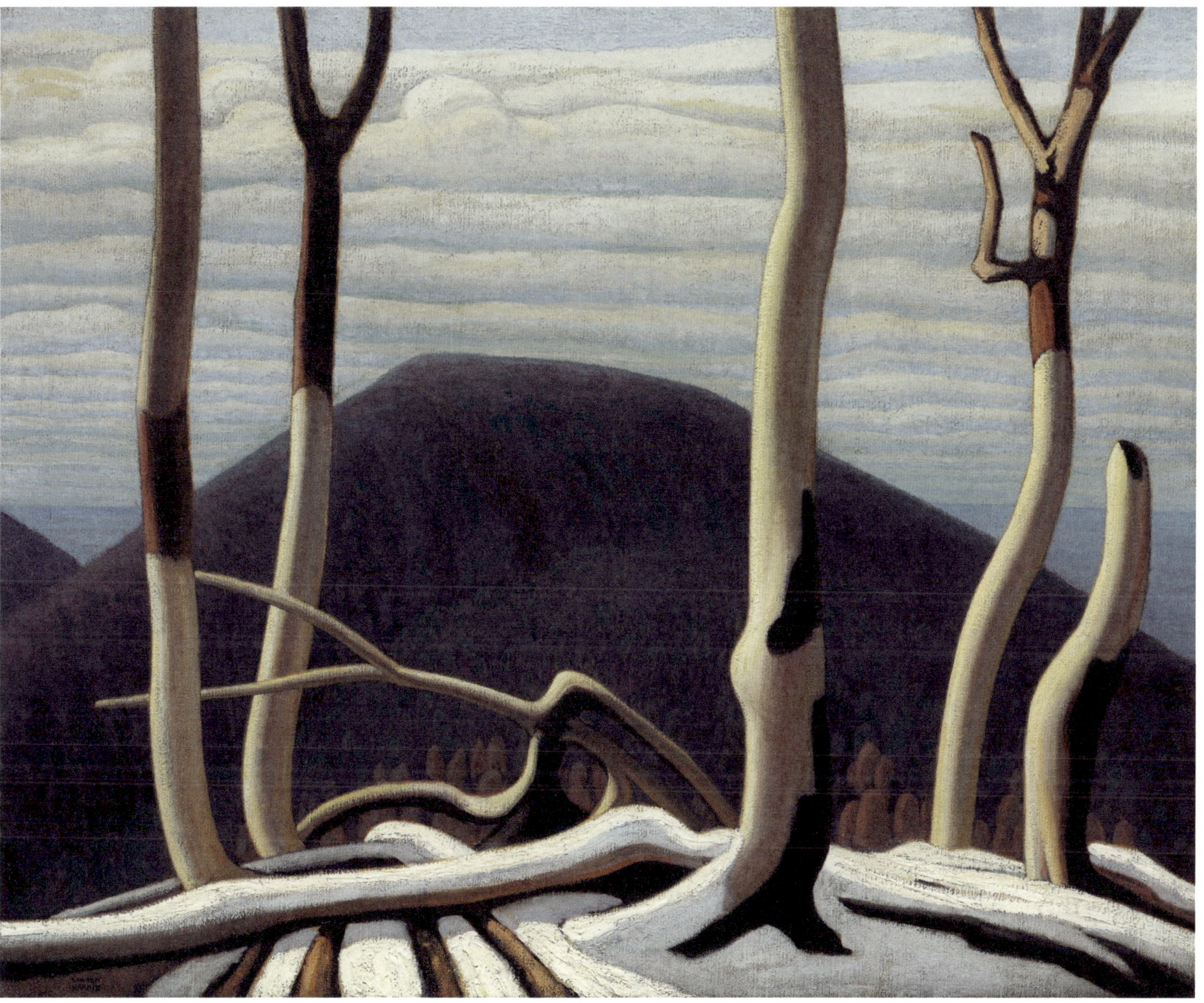

Lawren Harris
*Grounded Icebergs (Disco Bay)*, ca. 1931
80 × 101.6 cm

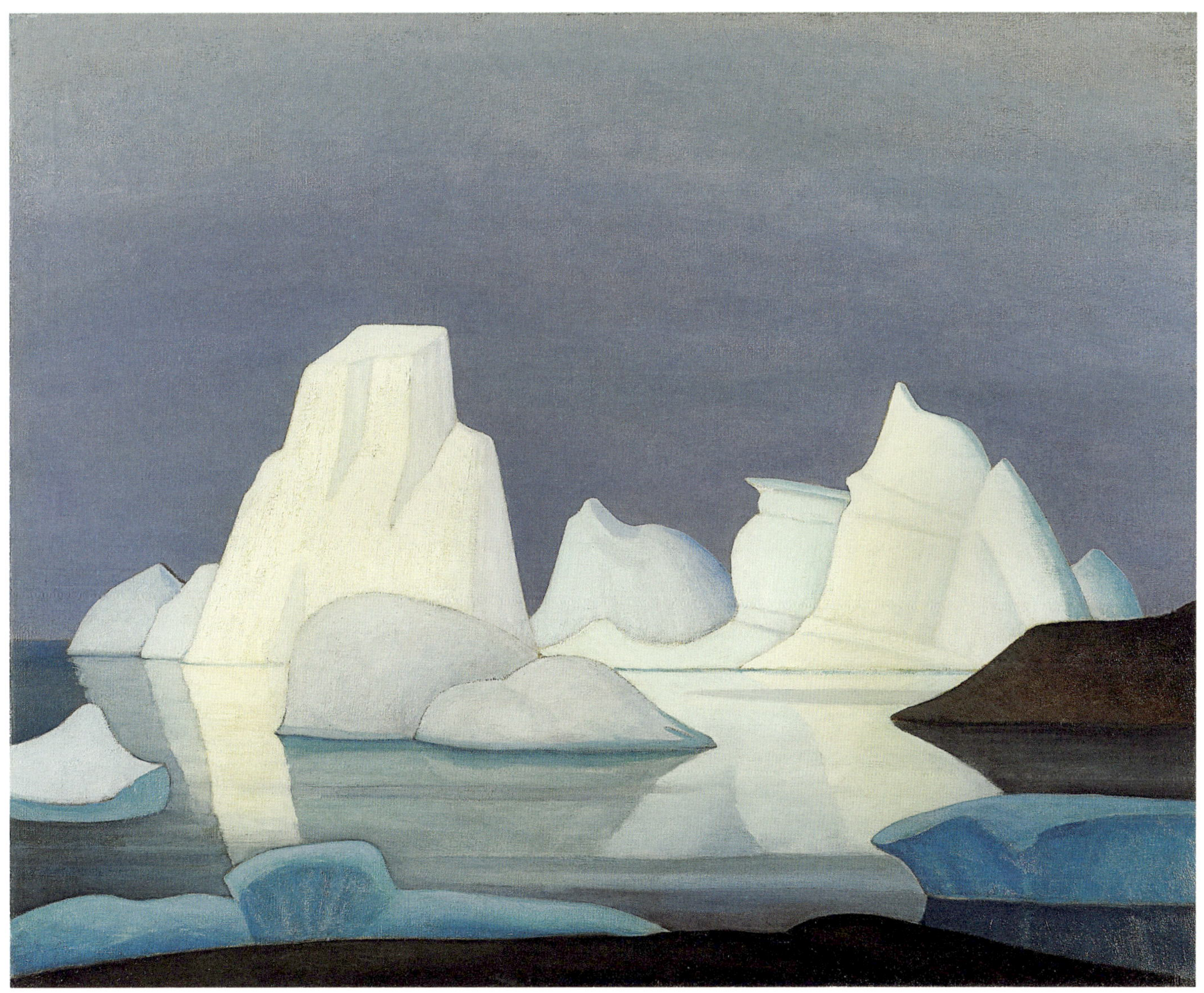

Lawren Harris
*Icebergs, Davis Strait,* 1930
121.9 × 152.4 cm

Securing an invitation from the Canadian government, Lawren Harris and A. Y. Jackson joined a two-month expedition to the Arctic in summer 1930.[1] Aboard the steamer *S. S. Beothic,* which supplied outposts of the Royal Canadian Mounted Police in the Arctic, the two artists sailed around Baffin Island and along the Davis Strait to the homeland of Inuit. Whenever possible, Jackson and Harris would go ashore and make sketches or take photographs of the impressive landscape that subsequently served as the basis for larger canvases.

The conditions were not always easy, as Harris recounted of his experiences: "While we were on this trip Jackson and I painted a large number of sketches, although painting was difficult as we usually saw the most exciting subjects while streaming through channels or while being bumped by pack ice. On many occasions we had time only to take rapid notes. These notes we worked up into sketches, crowded into our small cabin, seated on the edge of our respective bunks with only a port-hole to let in the light."[2]

For Harris, this trip yielded more than thirty oil sketches and six large-scale canvases.[3] *Icebergs, Davis Strait* is the largest of the series. In the middle of the composition, two monumental icebergs rise from a quiet expanse of water. The water surrounds this central image in concentric circles. Seemingly radiating from within, the icebergs stand out in shades of vibrant blue and turquoise against the gloomy sky and some wispy clouds. At the bottom, a piece of land, possibly the artist's and viewer's vantage point, juts into the image—a characteristic element in Harris' paintings.

The image evokes a sense of great calm and monumentality, indeed of transcendence. It seems to be charged with a special meaning that is conveyed by the cool colors and reduced forms. In his writings, Harris repeatedly emphasized the power and inspiration of the North for Canadian artists: "We are in the fringe of the great North and its living whiteness, its loneliness and replenishment, its resignations and release, its call and answer—its cleansing rhythms. It seems that the top of the continent is a source of spiritual flow."[4] He had now reached the most northern part of the country, but it was to remain his only trip to the Arctic. Soon after, he turned to abstract art as he sought more profound and universal artistic expression beyond nature.[5] His views of the Arctic marked the end of Lawren Harris's period as a landscape painter.

Rebecca Herlemann

1—A. Y. Jackson already had undertaken a similar trip in 1927. On the journeys of Canadian artists to the Arctic, see Agnes Elizabeth Ladon, "Art and Arctic Sovereignty: A. Y. Jackson, Lawren S. Harris and Canada's Eastern Arctic Patrols" (PhD diss., Queen's University, Kingston, 2012).
2—Lawren Harris, "The Group of Seven in Canadian History," in *Canadian Historical Association Report of the Annual Meeting Held at Victoria and Vancouver June 16-19, 1948* (Toronto: University of Toronto Press, 1948), p. 36
3—Cynthia Burlingham, "Notes to Self: The Drawings of Lawren Harris," in *The Ideas of North: The Paintings of Lawren Harris,* ed. Karen Jacobson, exh. cat. Hammer Museum, Los Angeles, Museum of Fine Arts, Boston, and Art Gallery of Ontario, Toronto (Munich et al.: Prestel, 2015), pp. 83-97, esp. p. 92.
4—Lawren Harris, "Revelation of Art in Canada," *The Canadian Theosophist* (July 15, 1926), pp. 85-86.
5—See Ann Davis, *The Logic of Ecstasy: Canadian Mystical Painting, 1920-1940* (Toronto: University of Toronto Press, 1992), p. 68.

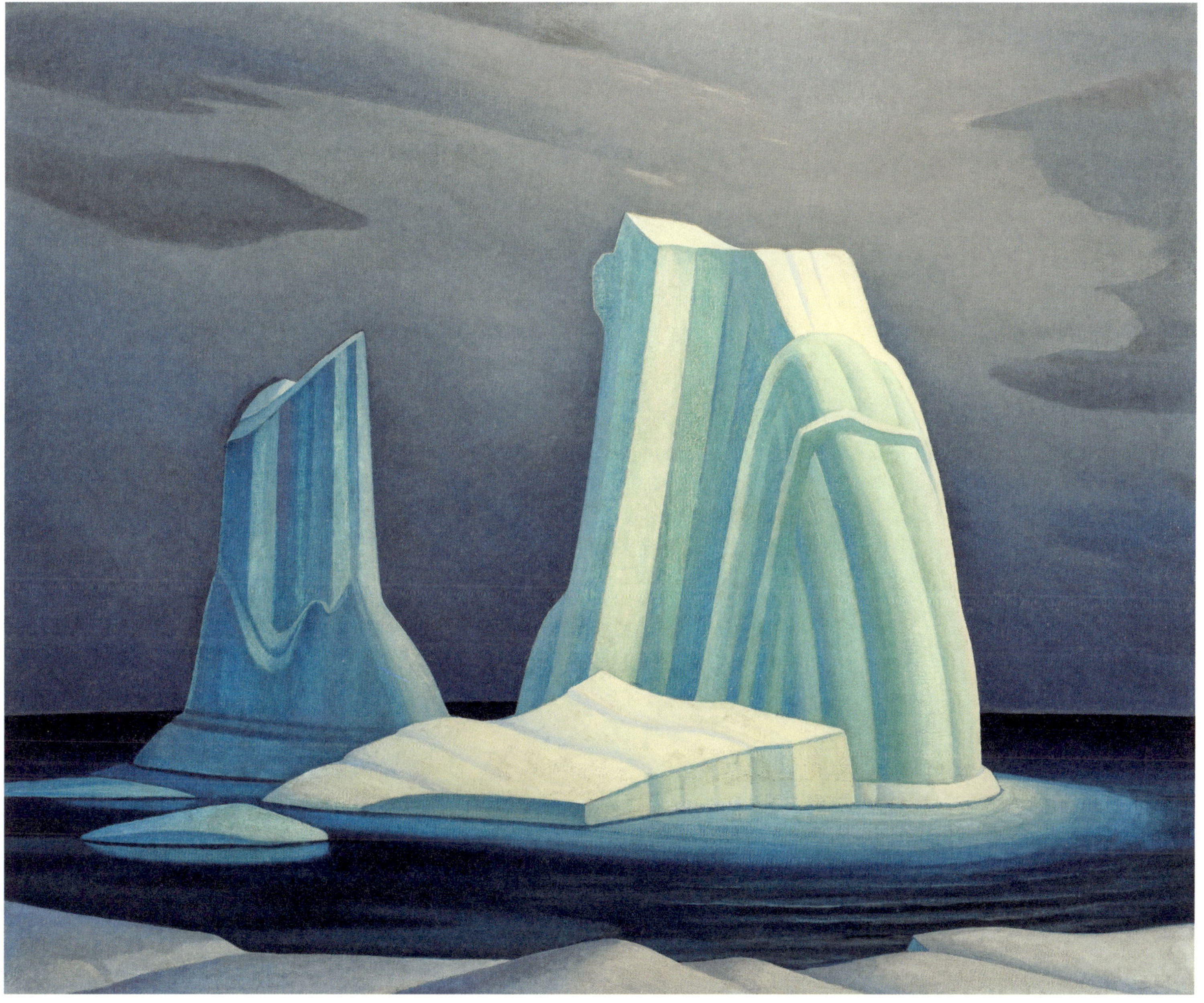

Lawren Harris
*Lake and Mountains*, 1928
130.8 × 160.7 cm

Lawren Harris

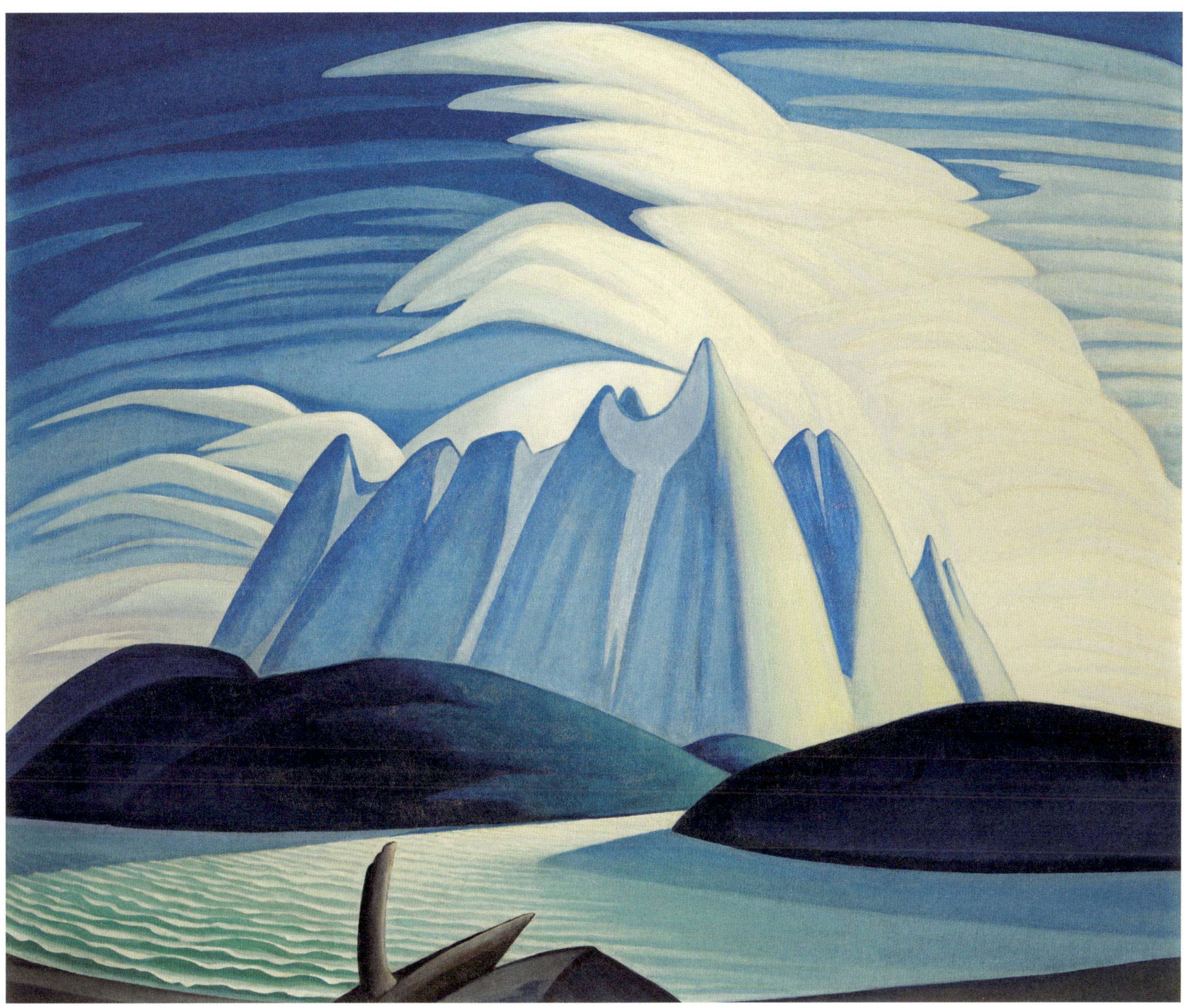

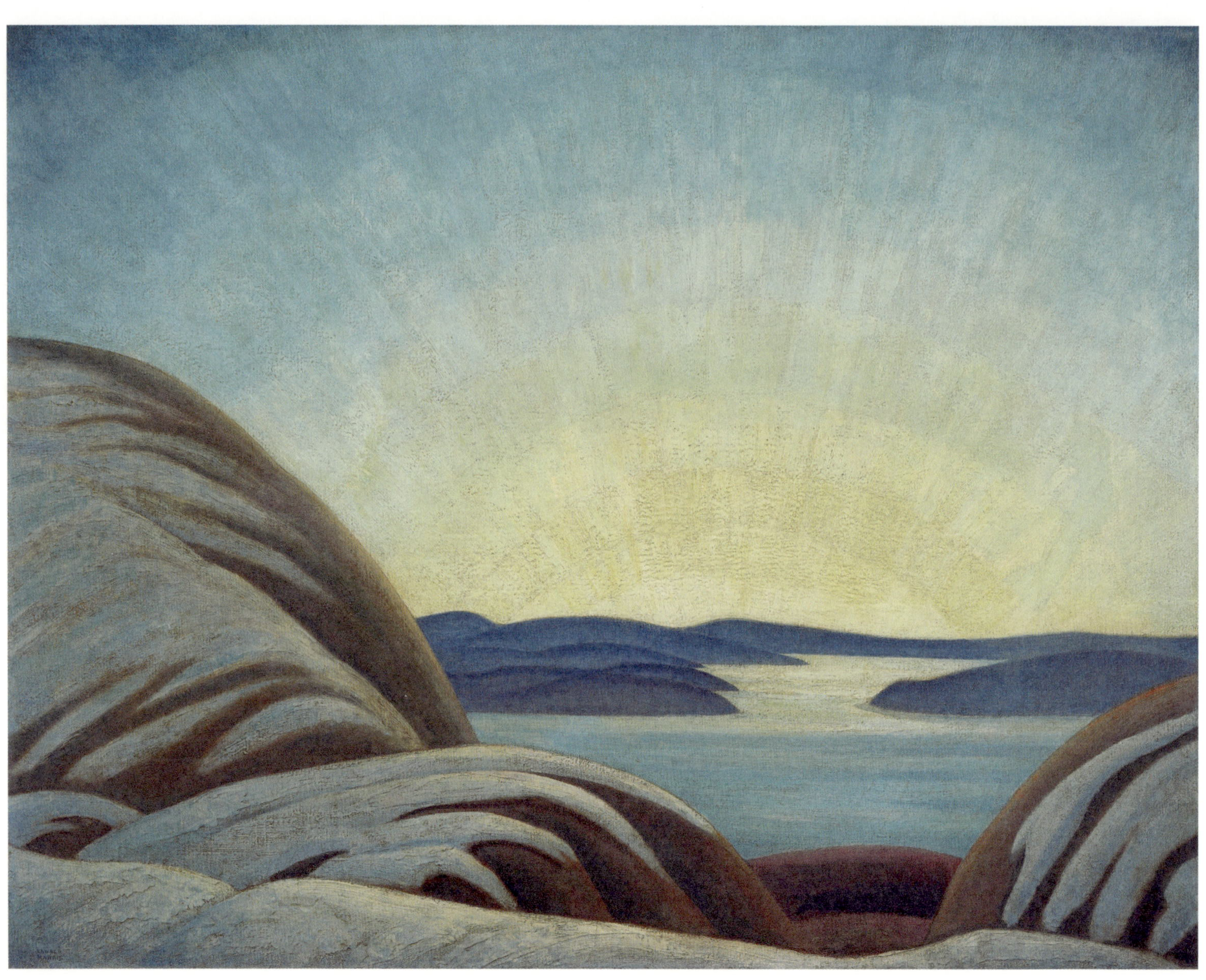

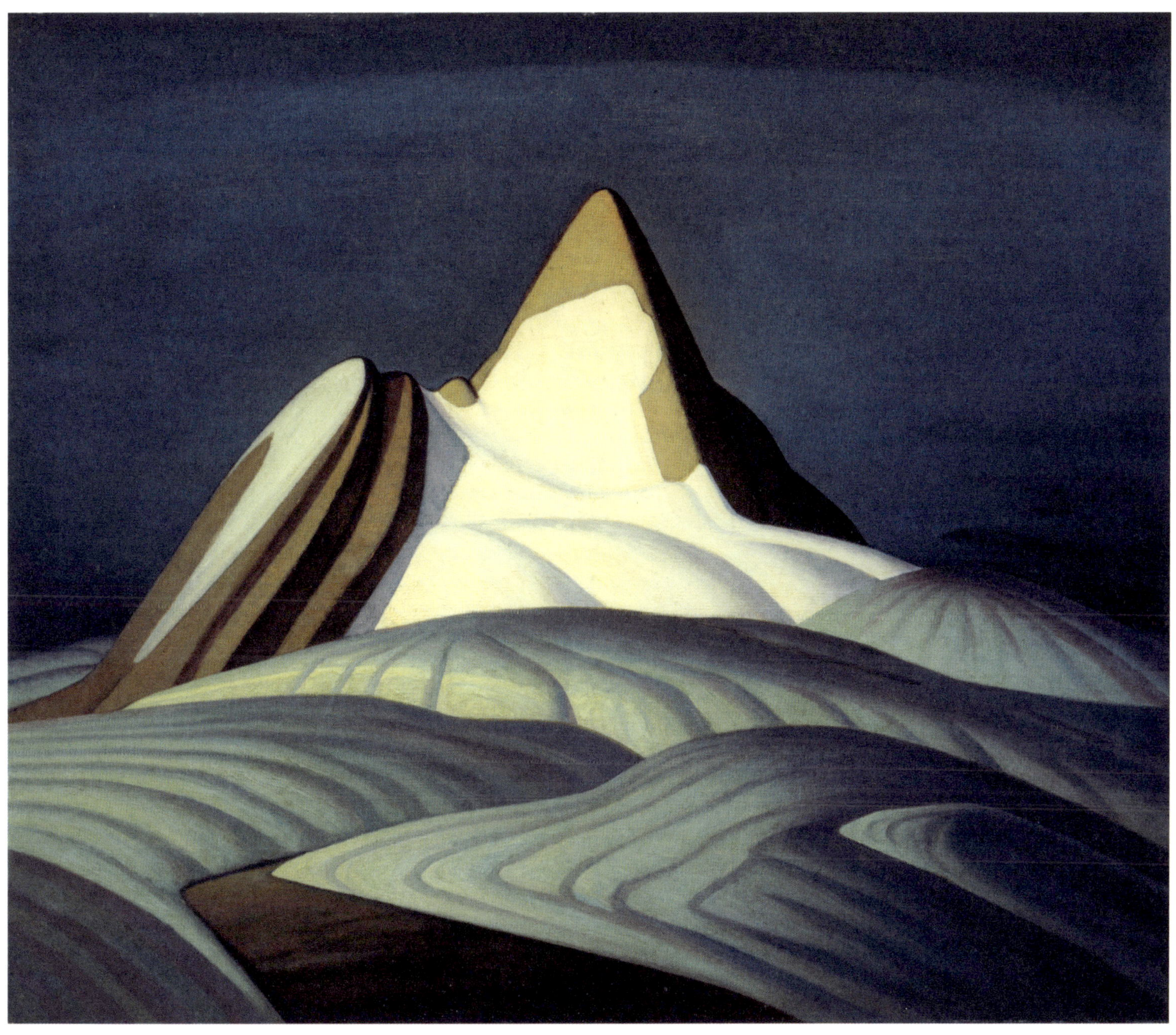

Lawren Harris
*North Shore, Lake Superior,* ca. 1924–26
102 × 132.5 cm

Lawren Harris
*Isolation Peak,* 1929
107.3 × 128 cm

# Tom Thomson

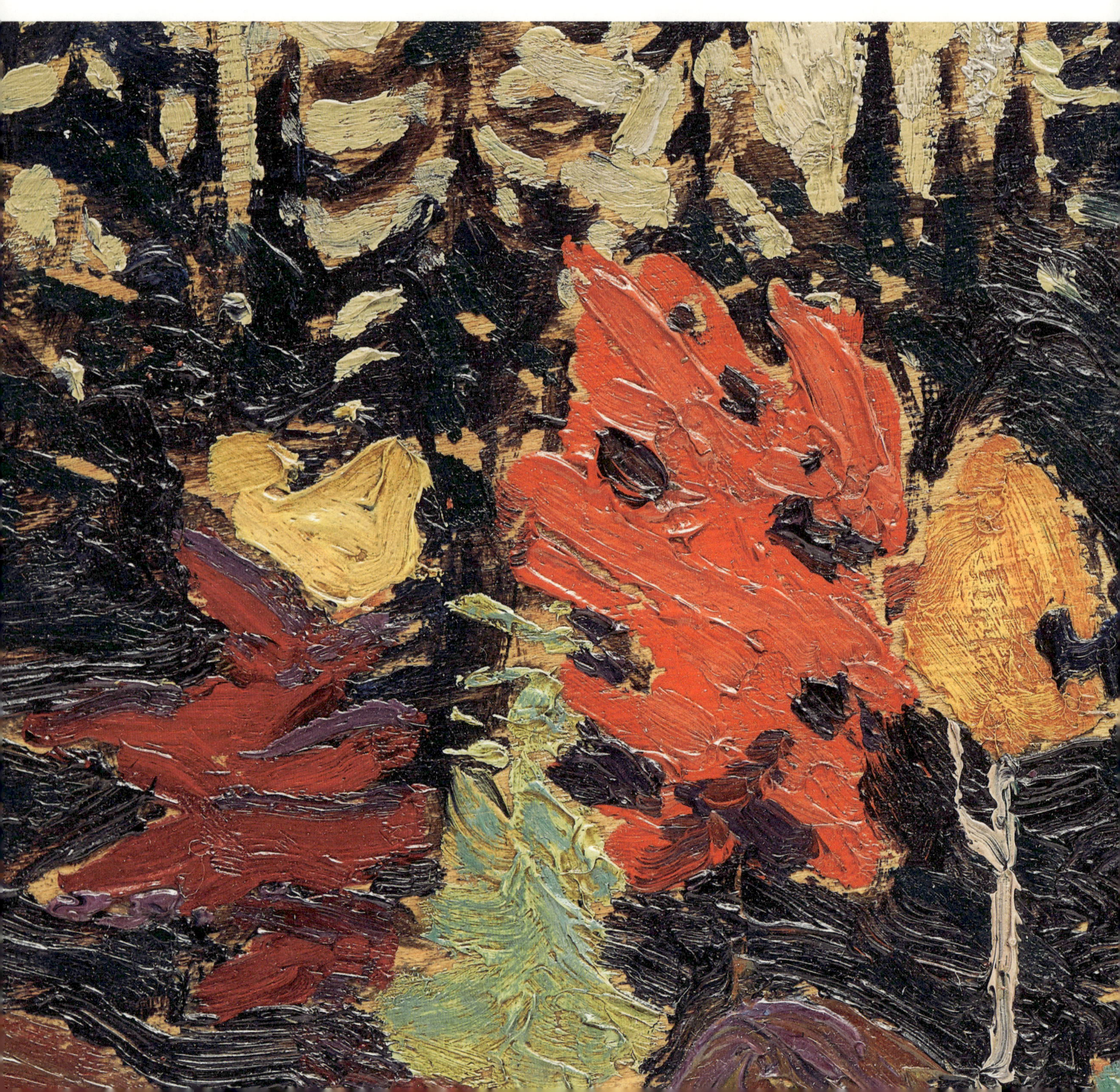

# Sketches

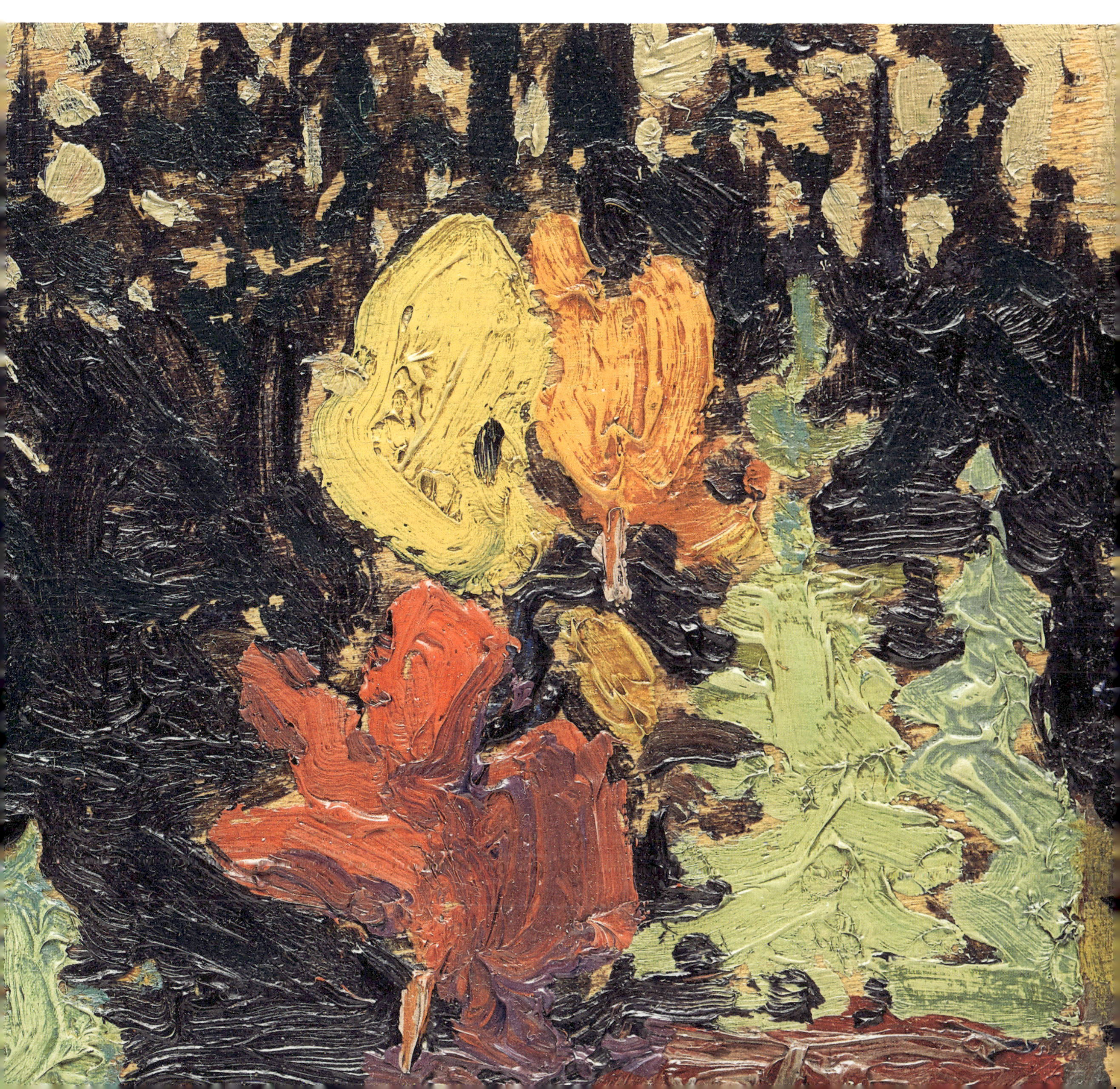

Tom Thomson achieved in his oil sketches a virtuosity and expressiveness that was unequalled in his Canadian contemporaries. He was regarded by his peers as the pioneer of a new, unconventional kind of landscape painting that is most apparent in his sketches. In the space of just five years (1912–17), Thomson created more than 300 oil sketches, only several of which he would rework as larger canvases.[1] The small-scale sketches on panel or cardboard were produced during extended stays in Algonquin Provincial Park. He would intensely draw and paint views he found compelling. Accordingly, his subjects range from dense forests and open lakes to night scenes with lone moose. From 1917 on, he would refer to the studies as "records," his way of documenting his surroundings in a journal-like manner.

As a matter of principle, Thomson painted the sketches outdoors. He had a wooden sketch box for this purpose into which multiple painting supports could be inserted to dry. At once easel and palette, the box was balanced on the knees while painting. The practical size allowed him to carry it on his backpack or in a canoe on trips farther afield.

Thomson would capture his subjects using quick lines and liberally applied paint, usually in just a few different colors. *Tamarack* (fall 1915), for example, is divided into four horizontal color fields at first glance. The impression of a row of trees standing out against the rest of the painting in vibrant orange is created only through jagged, vertical brushstrokes. *A Rapid* (fall 1915), by contrast, is a constellation of so many wild strokes and dabs of thick paint that a motif is only evident from a certain distance. The unpainted support shows through in many places and is also used to contour the pictorial elements. While his canvases are composed and ordered, the sketches have an intensity and immediacy in the way in which they play with variations in color and form. Their innovative approaches almost reach abstraction, which reveals an incredible modernity.

Rebecca Herlemann

1—Joan Murray, *Tom Thomson: Catalogue Raisonné,* https://www.tomthomsoncatalogue.org (accessed May 30, 2020).

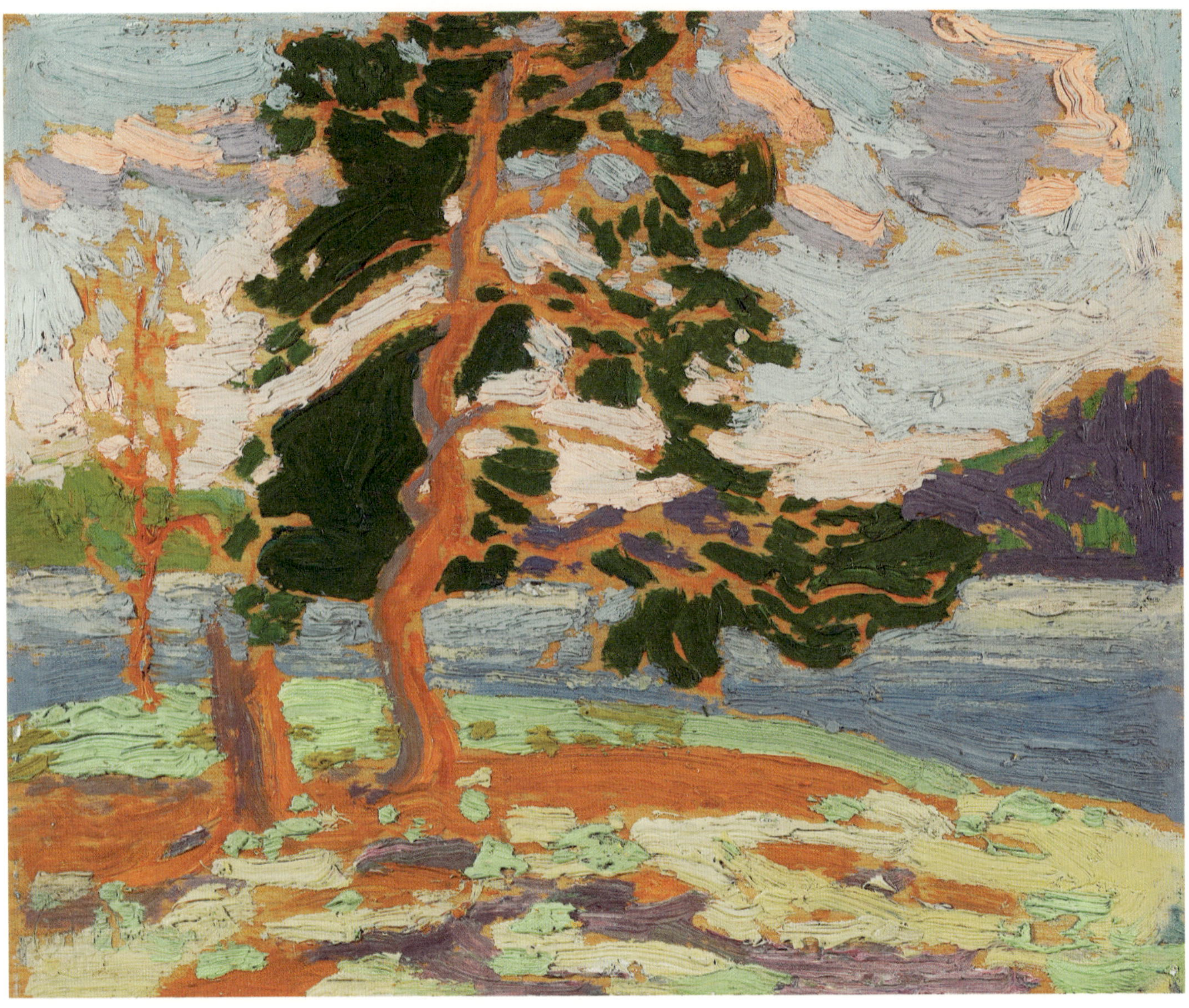

Tom Thomson
*Pine Tree,* summer 1916
21.6 × 26.7 cm

Tom Thomson
*Wild Cherry Trees in Blossom,* spring 1915
21.6 × 26.7 cm

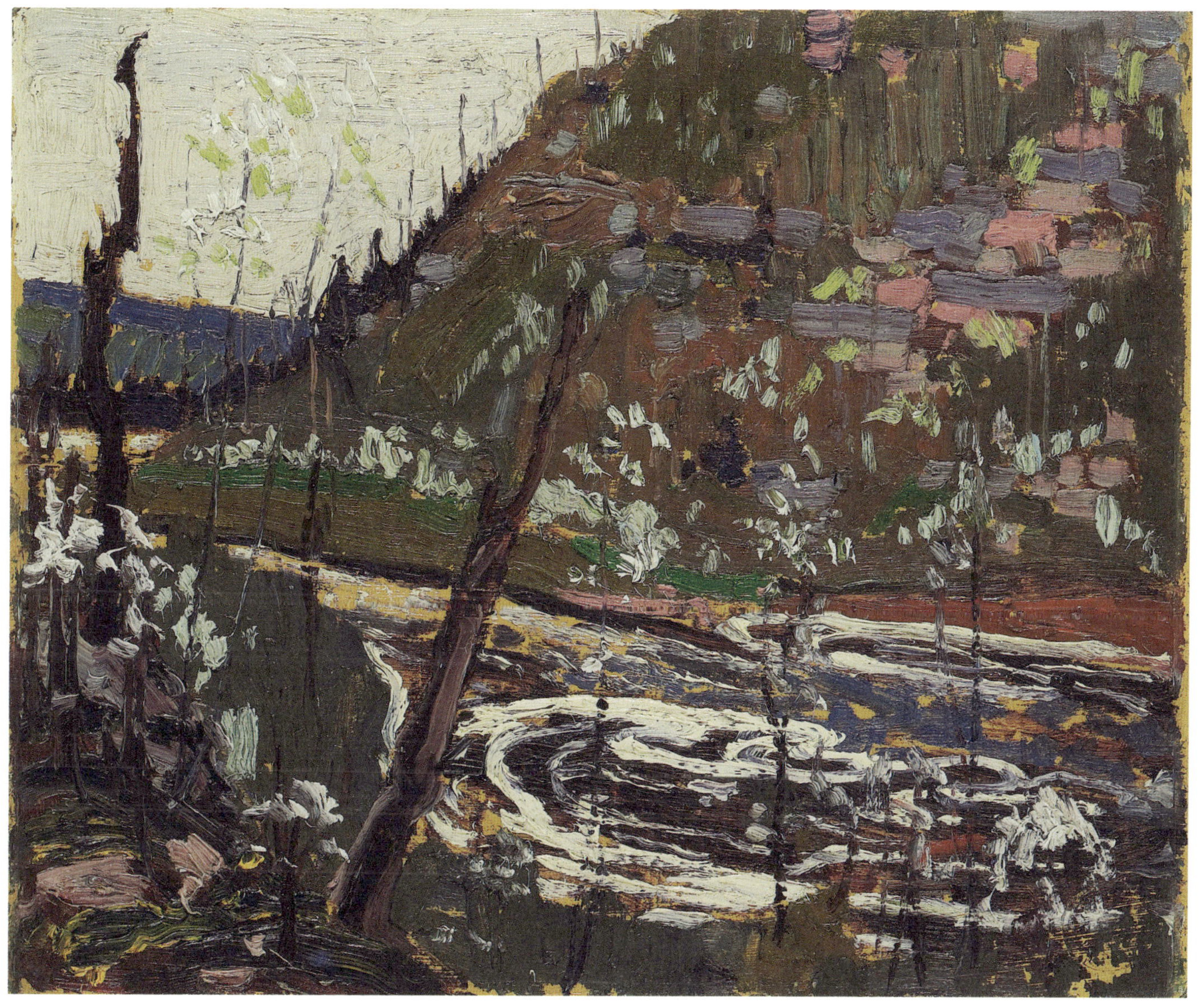

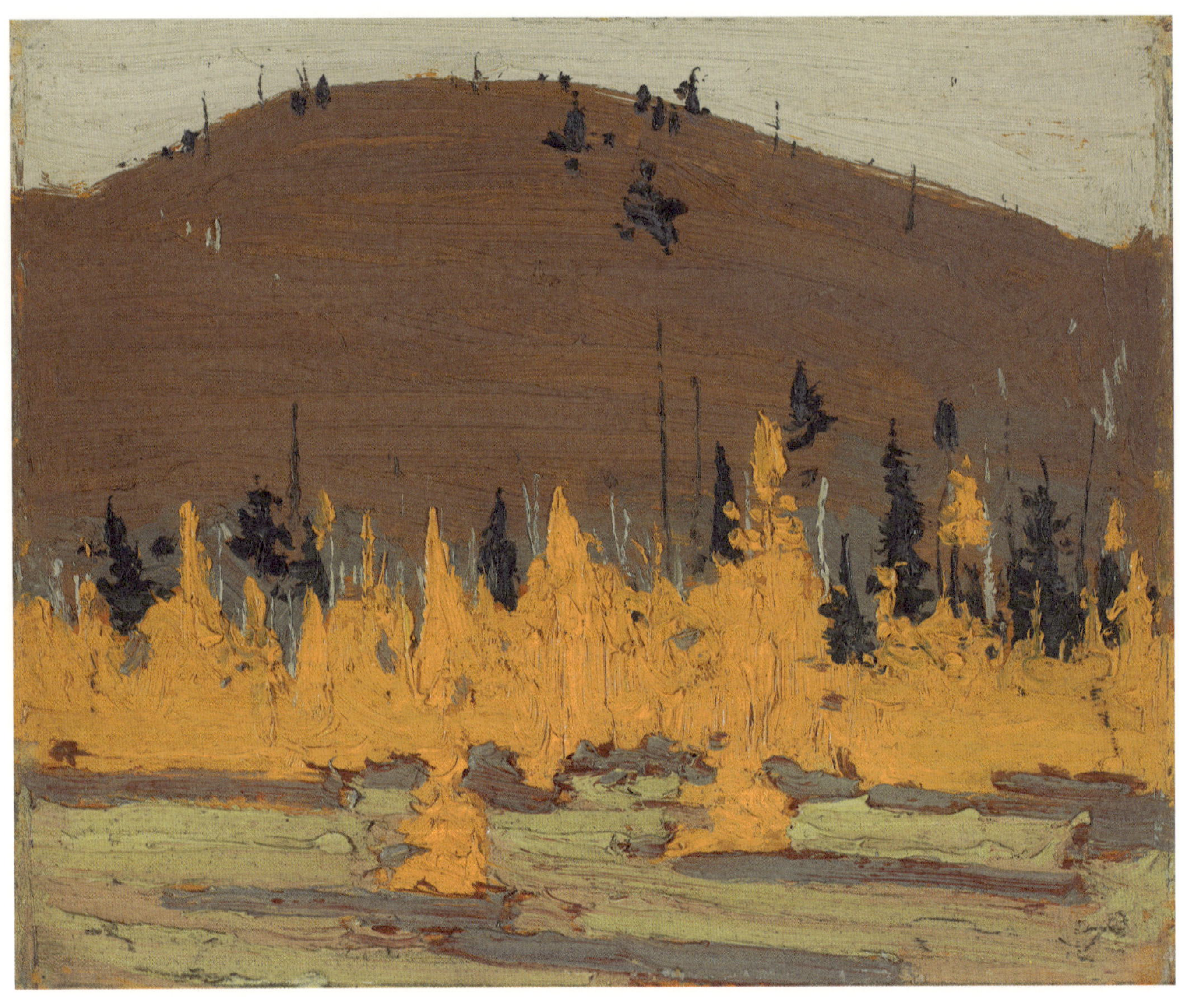

Tom Thomson
*Tamarack,* fall 1915
21.5 × 26.5 cm

Tom Thomson
*Forest, October,* fall 1915
21.3 × 26.9 cm

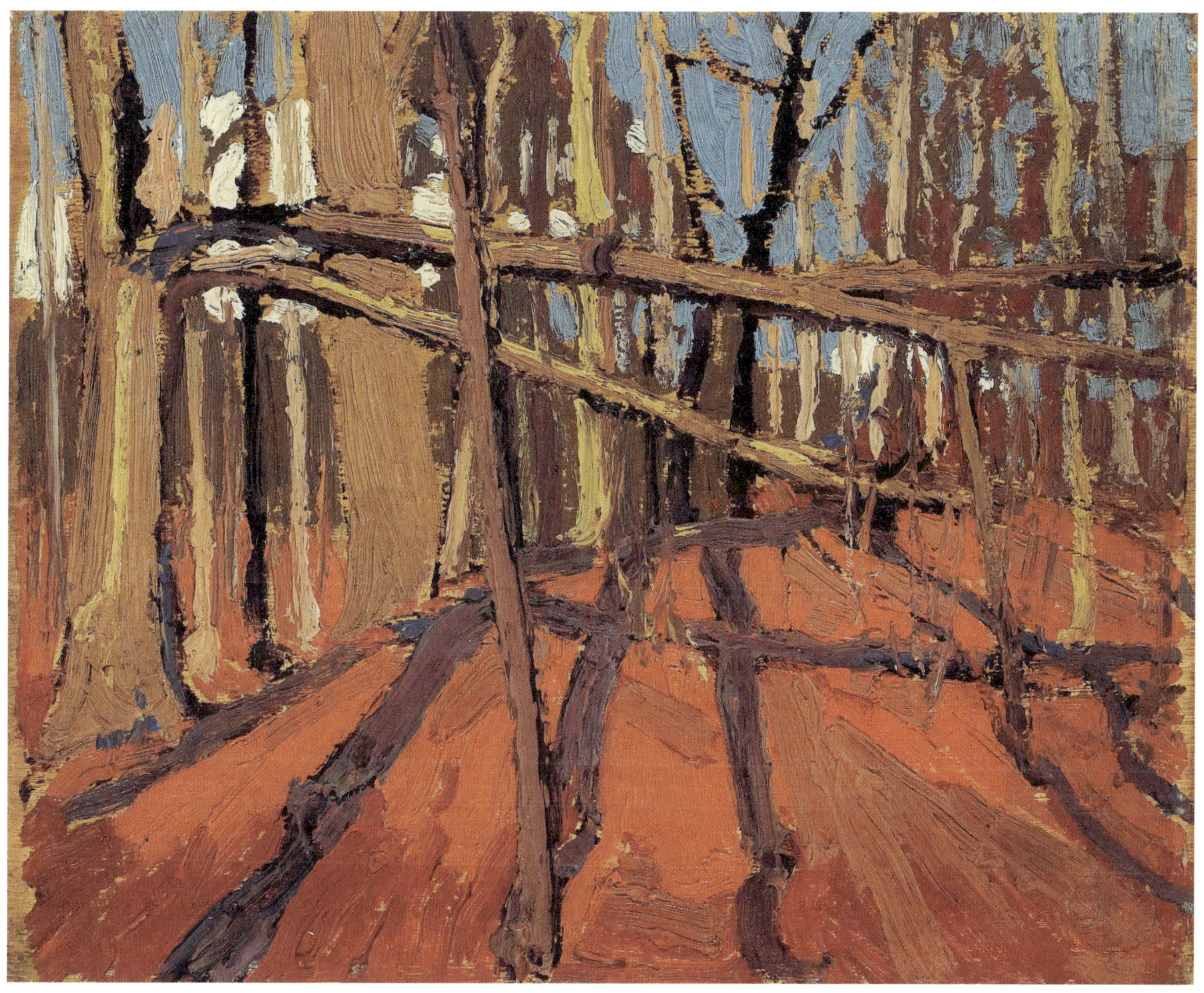

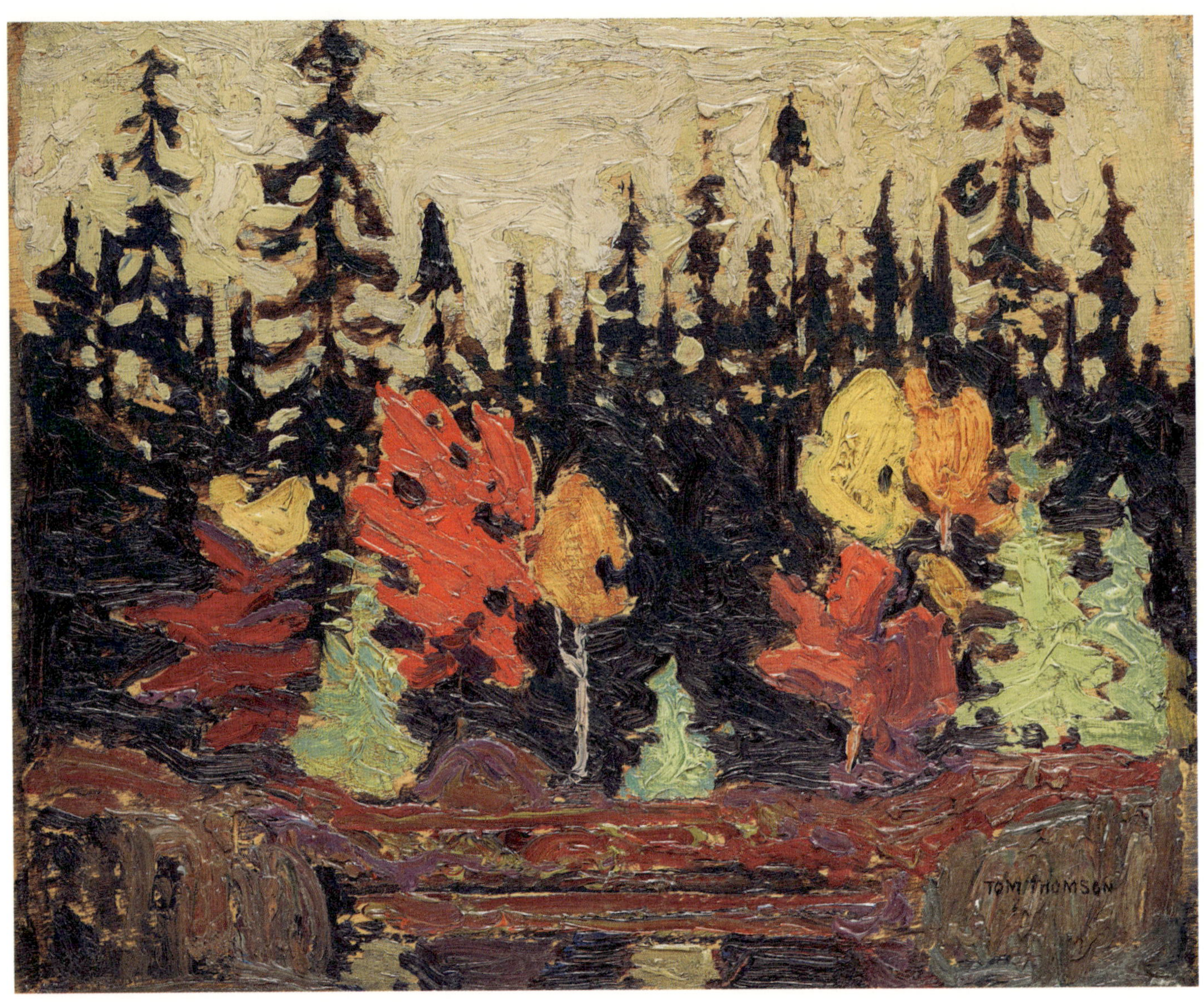

Tom Thomson
*Black Spruce and Maple,* fall 1915
21.6 × 26.7 cm

Tom Thomson
*Autumn Birches,* fall 1916
21.6 × 26.8 cm

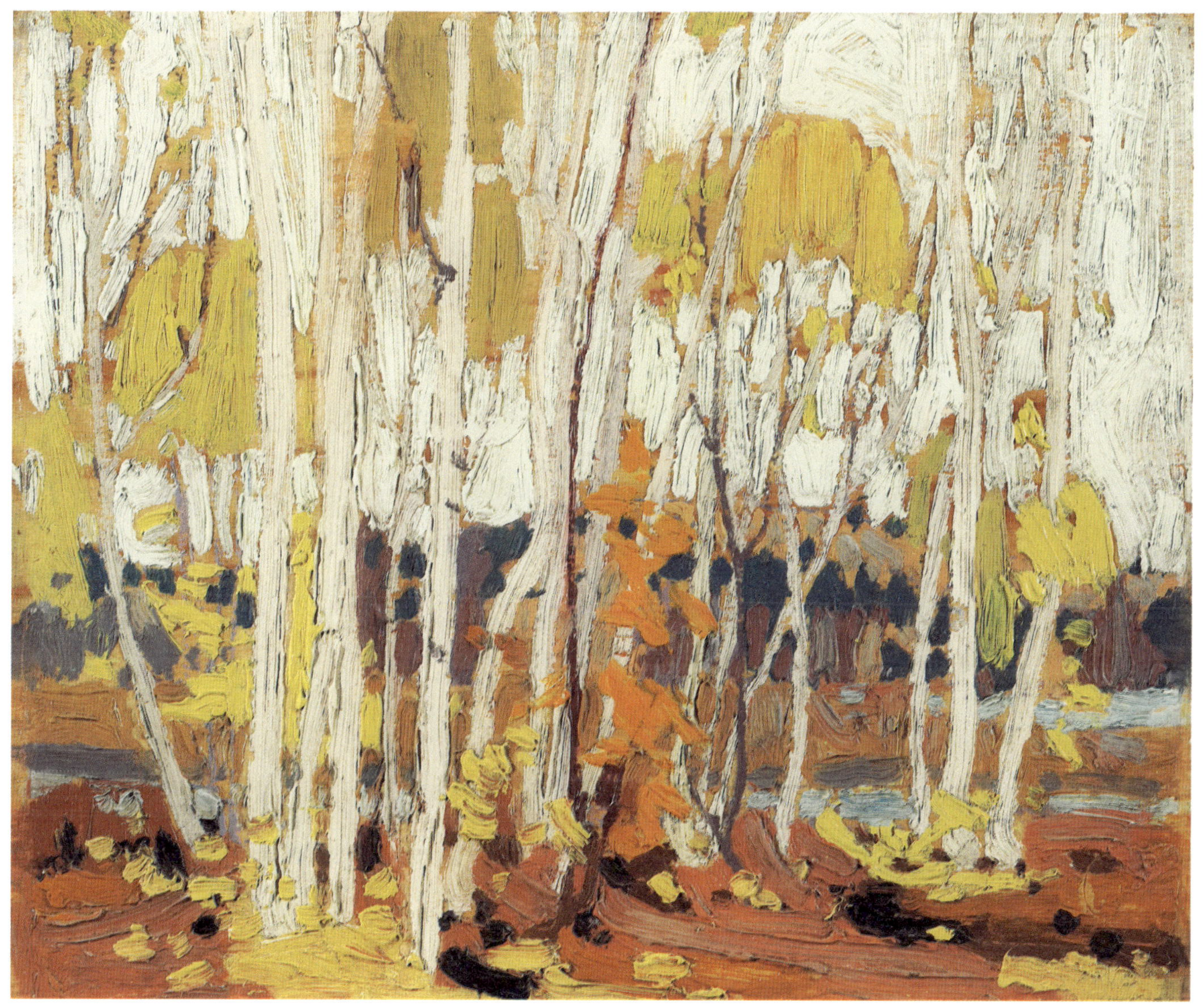

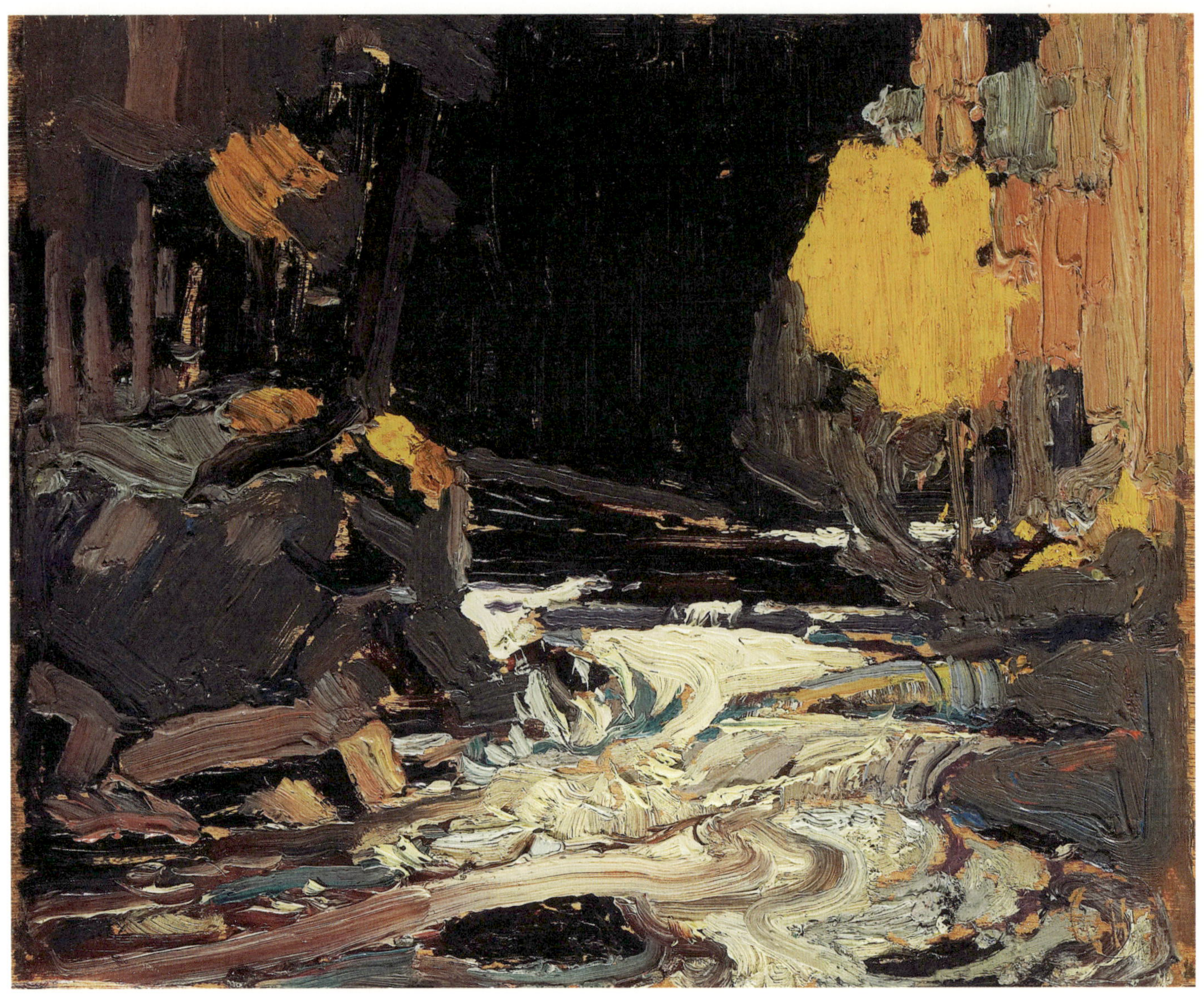

Tom Thomson
*A Rapid,* fall 1915
21.6 × 26.7 cm

Tom Thomson
*Autumn Foliage,* fall or winter 1915
21.6 × 26.8 cm

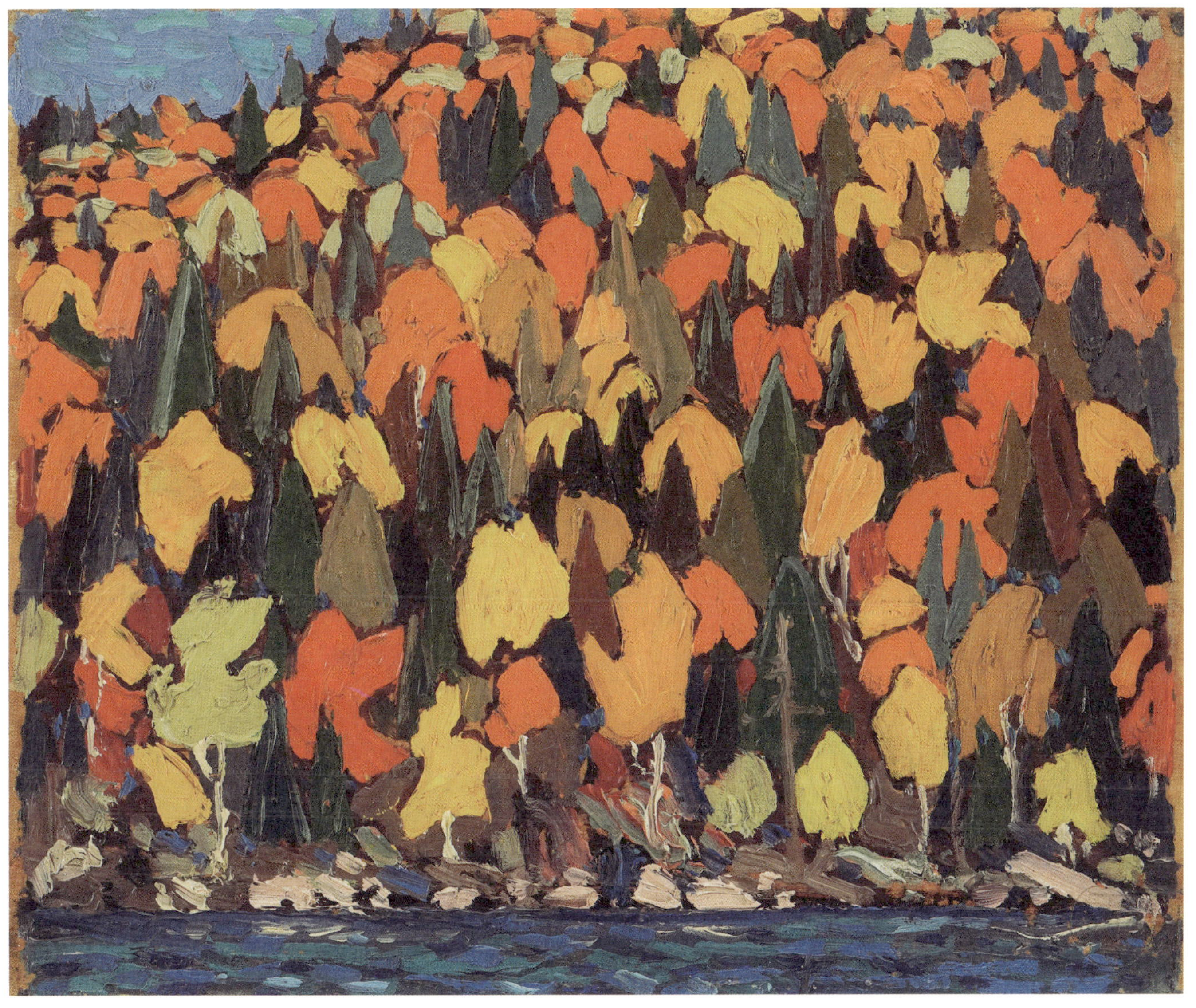

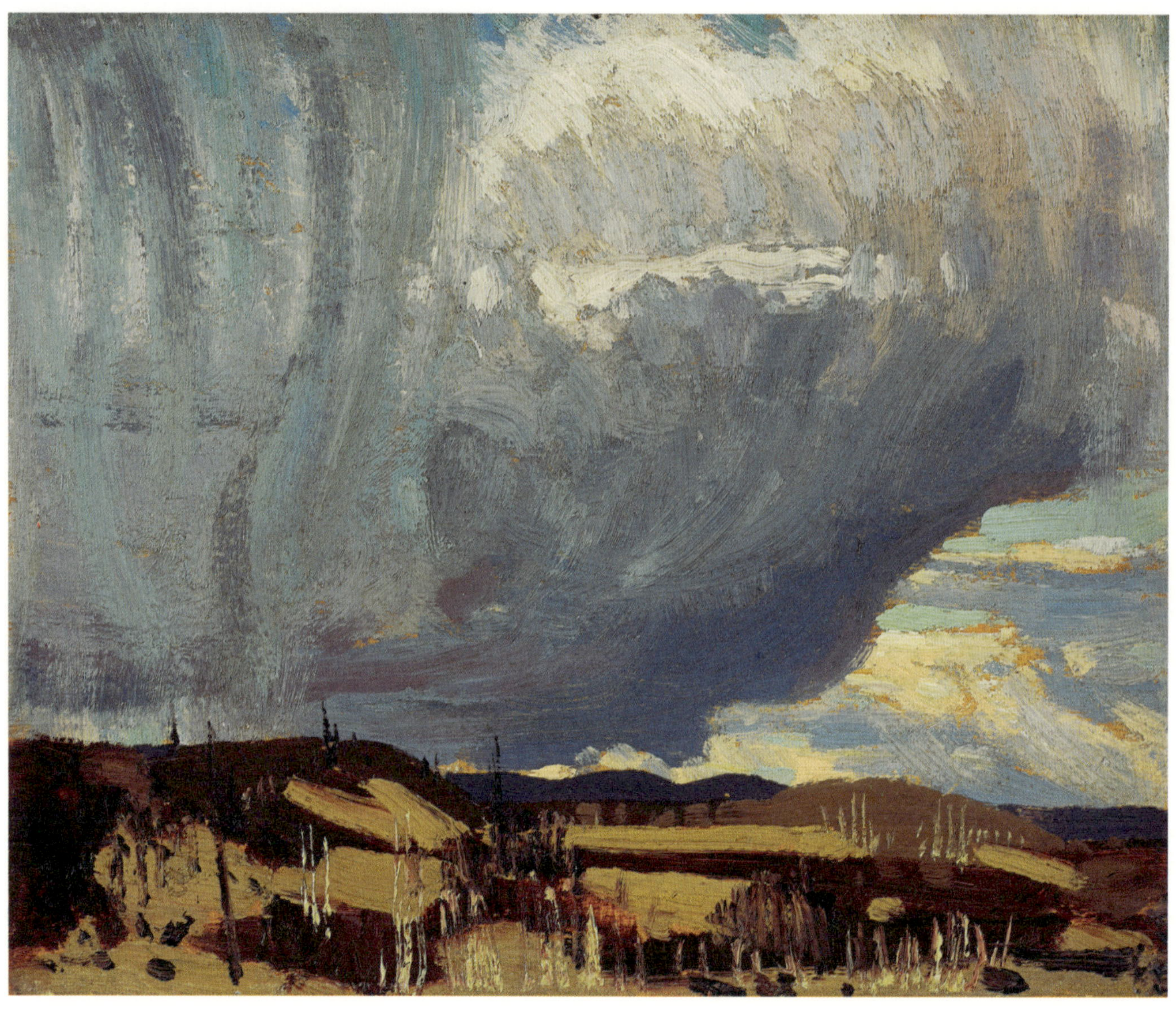

Tom Thomson
*Approaching Snowstorm,* fall 1915
21.3 × 26.6 cm

Tom Thomson
*Round Lake, Mud Bay,* fall 1915
21.5 × 26.8 cm

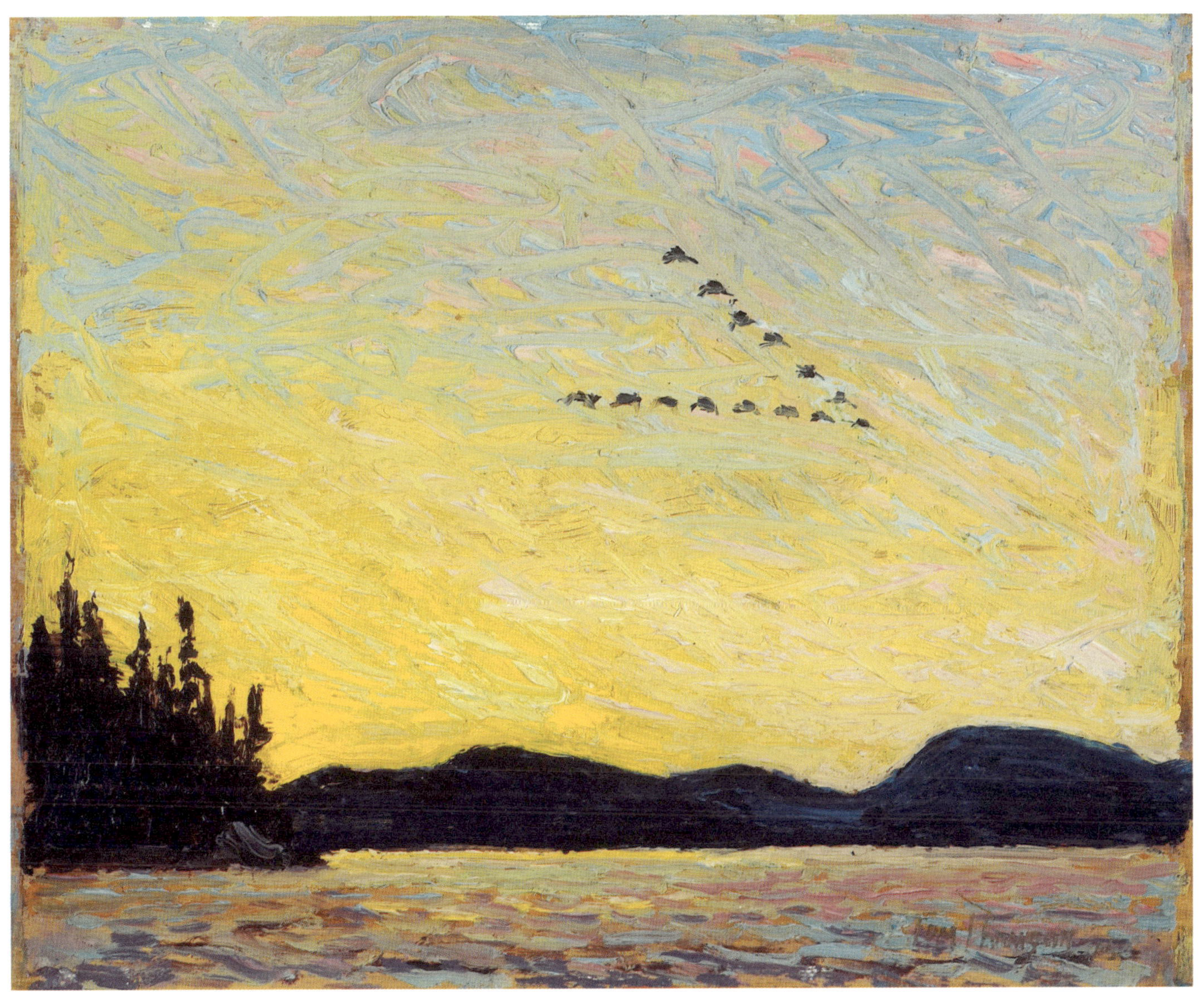

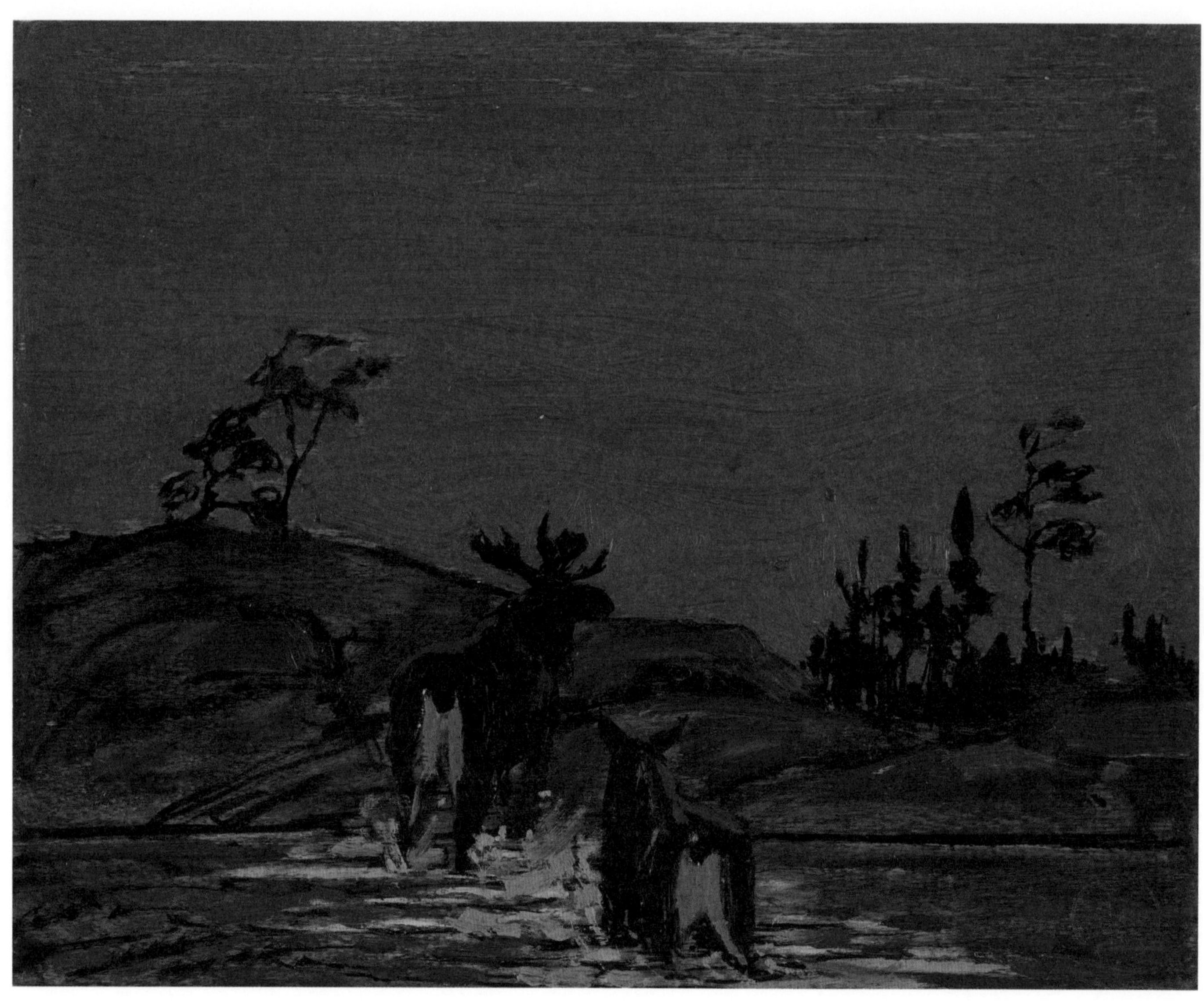

Tom Thomson
*Moose at Night,* winter 1916
20.9 × 26.9 cm

Tom Thomson
*A Northern Lake,* spring 1916
21.6 × 26.7 cm

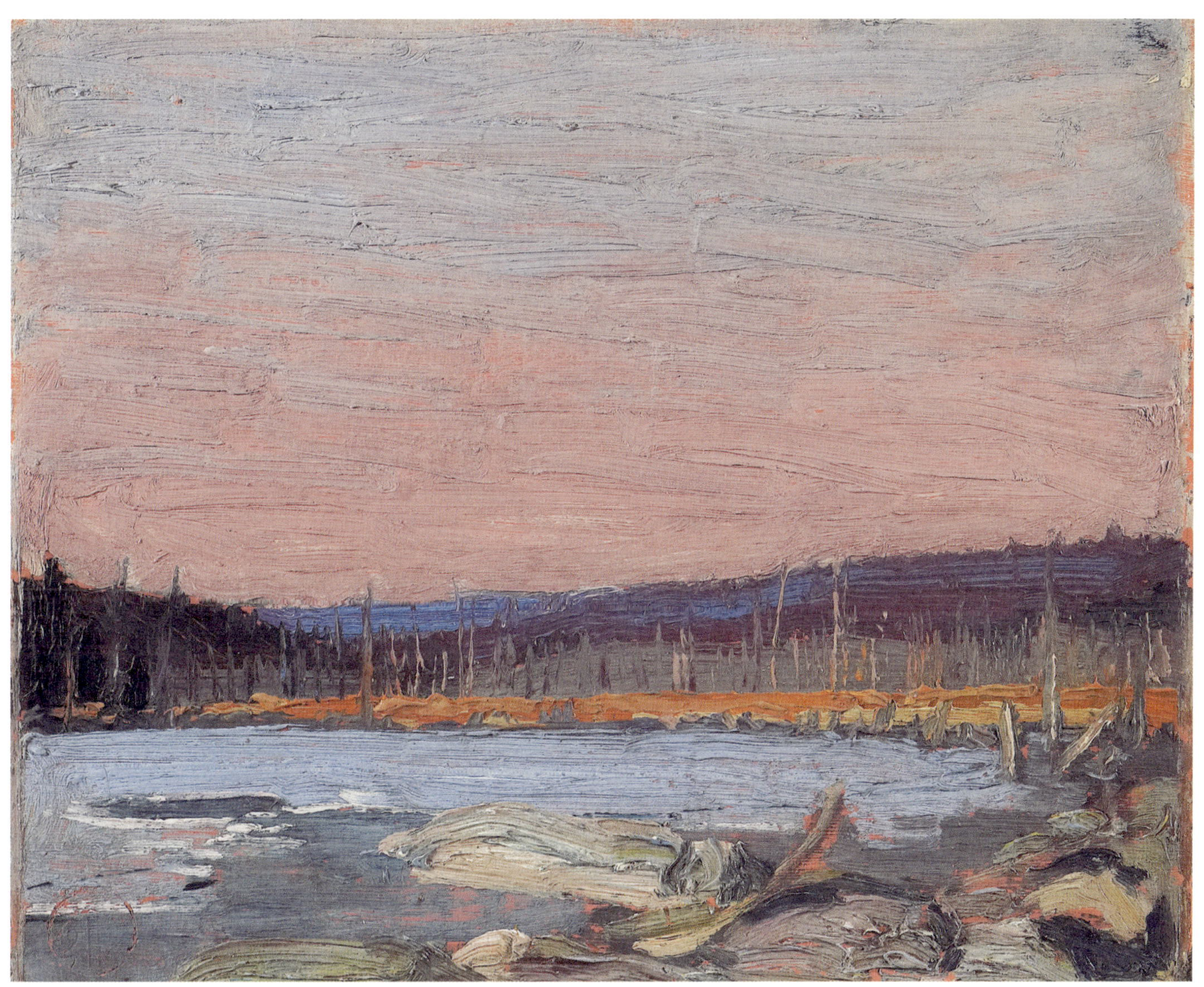

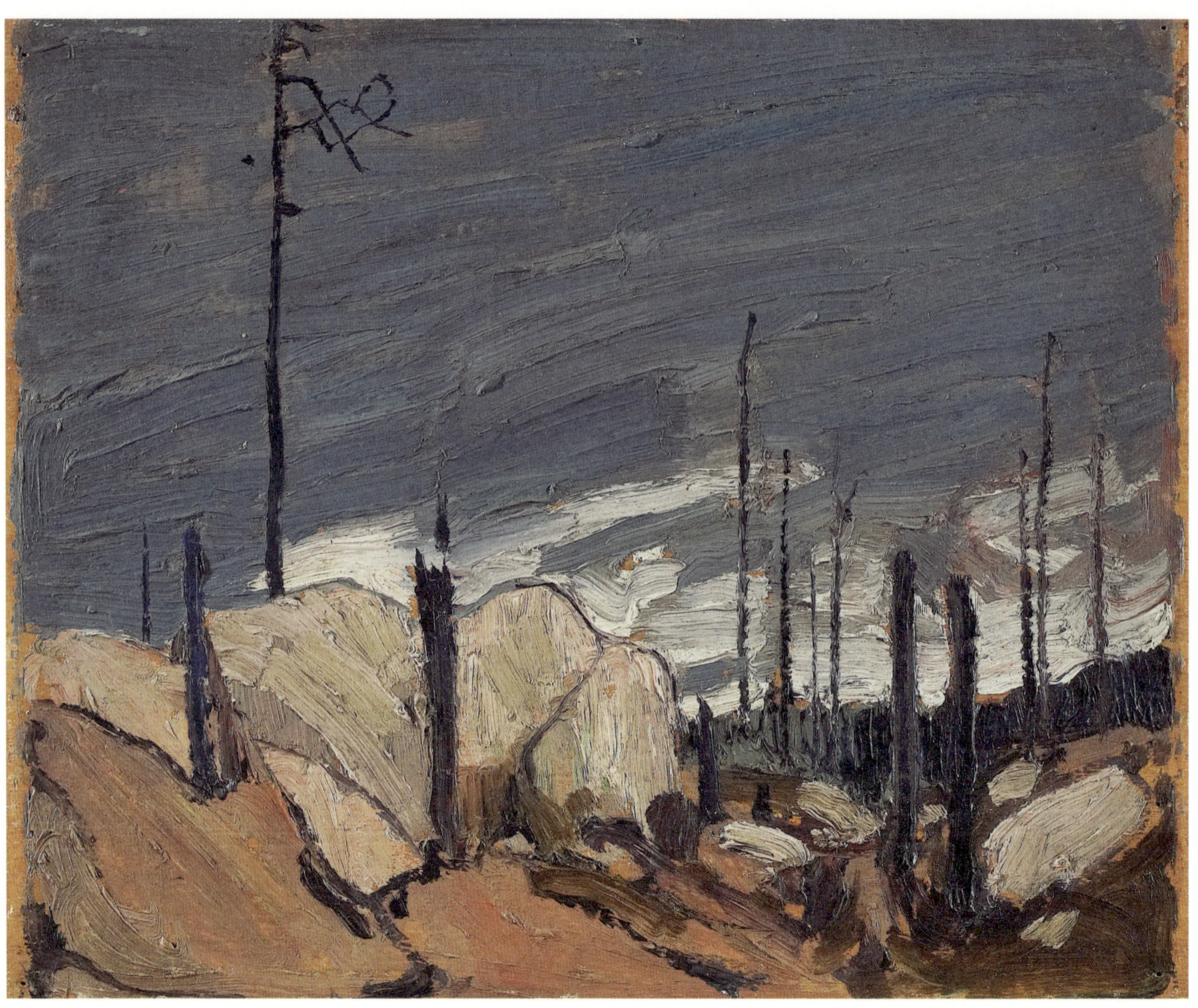

Tom Thomson
*Burnt Country,* spring 1915
21.6 × 26.7 cm

Tom Thomson
*Nocturne: The Birches,* spring 1916
21.6 × 26. cm

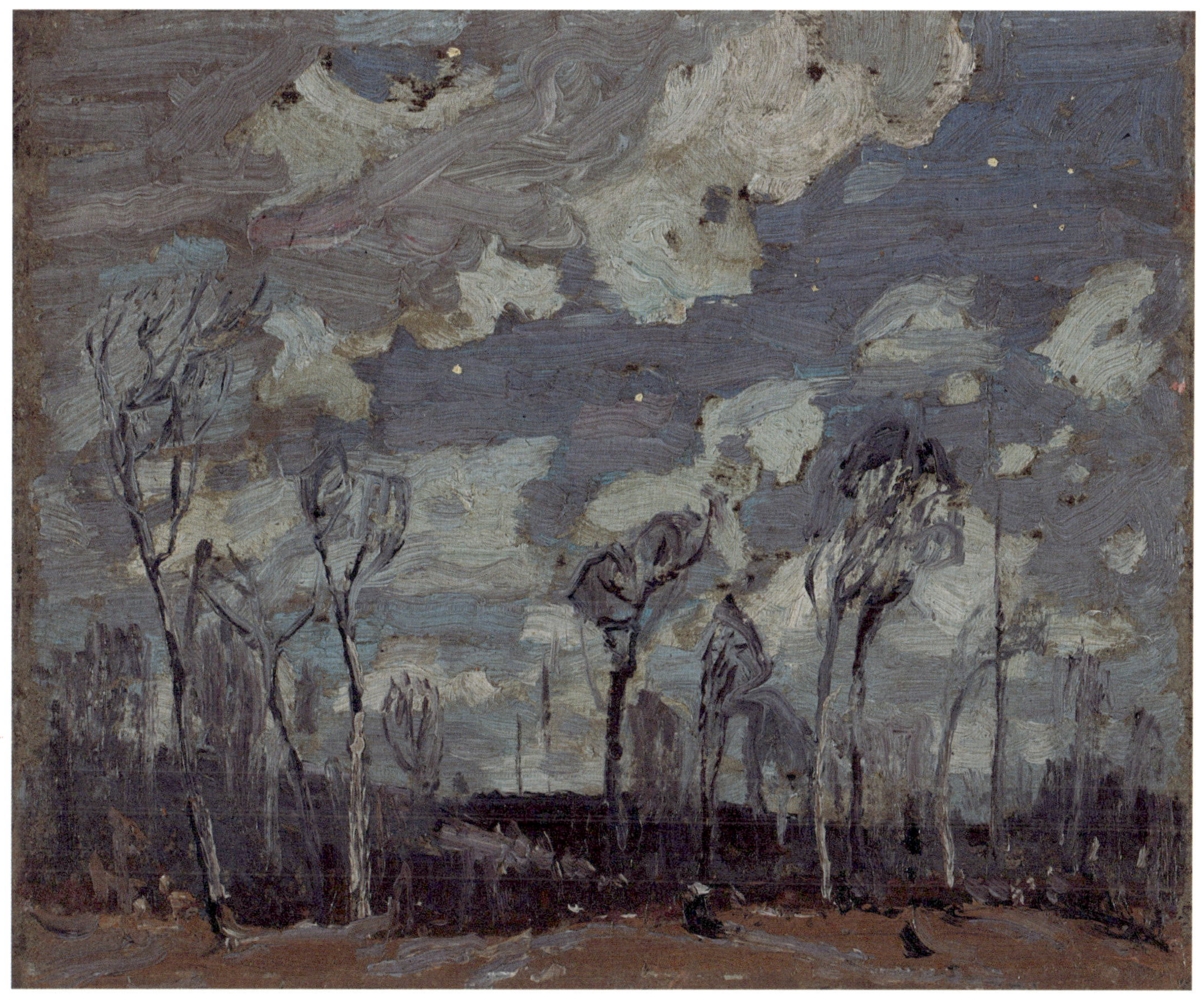

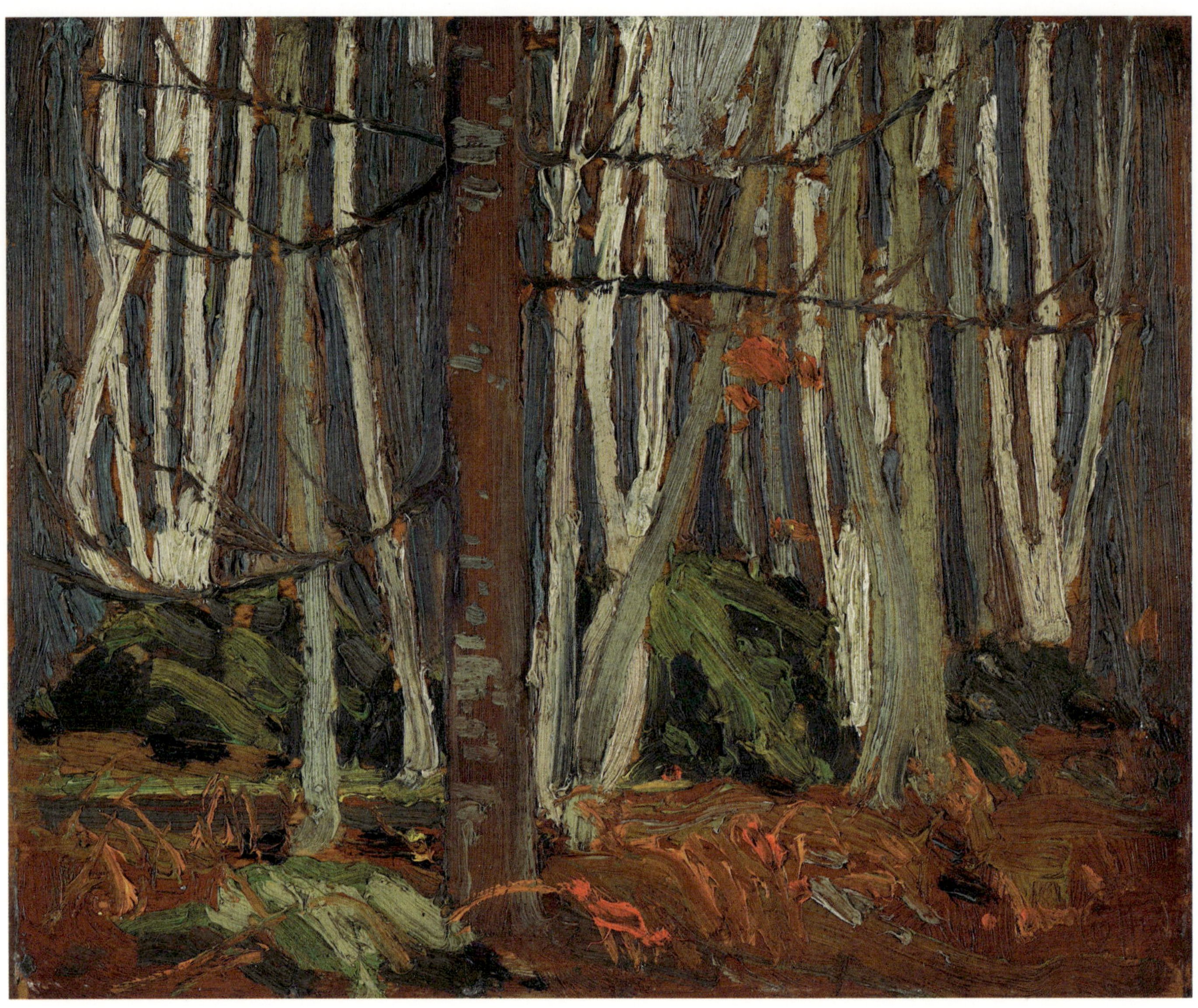

Tom Thomson
*Birch Woods in Autumn*, fall 1915
21.3 × 26.5 cm

Tom Thomson
*Trees, Red Hill, and Sunset Sky*, fall 1916
21.8 × 26.9 cm

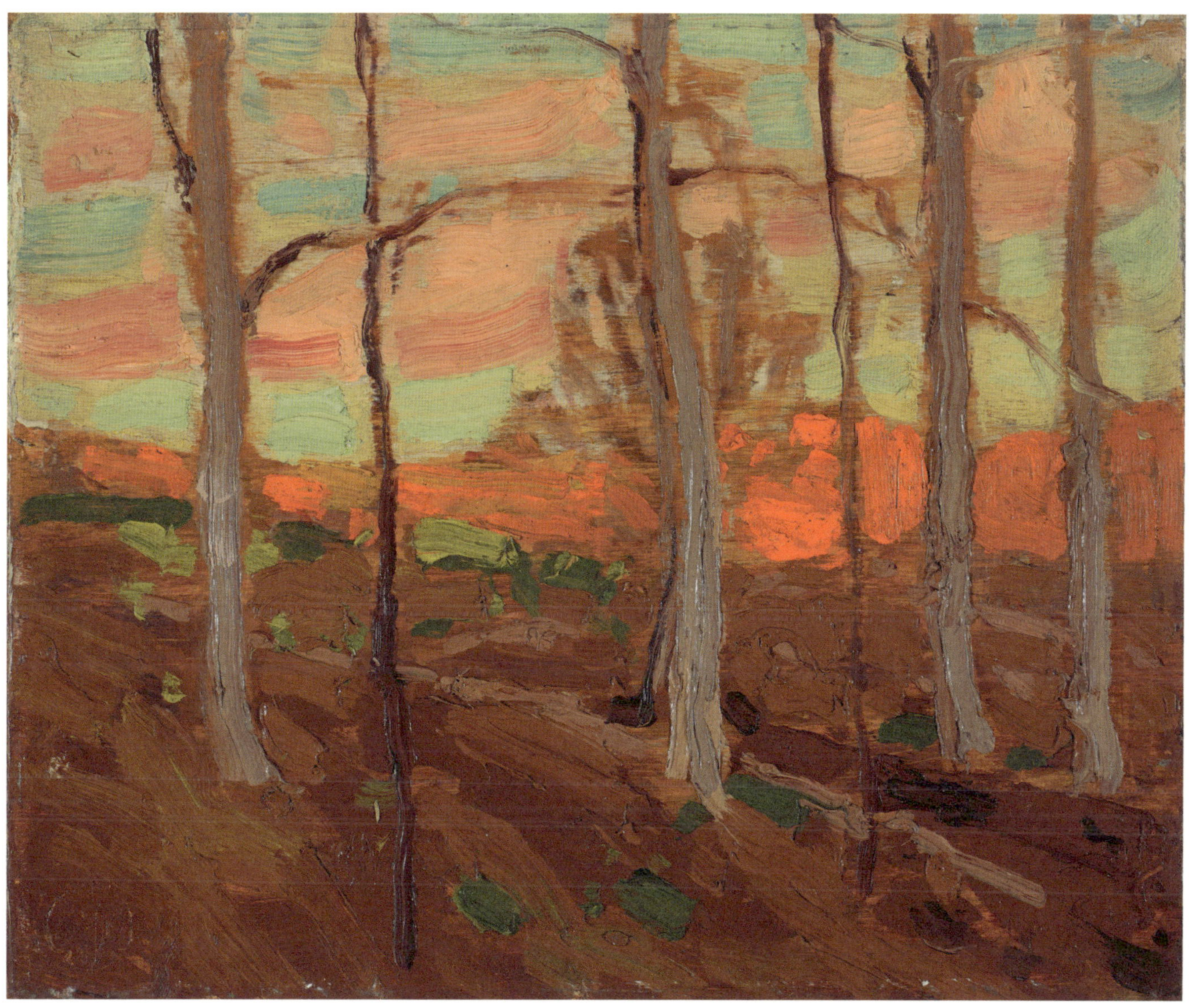

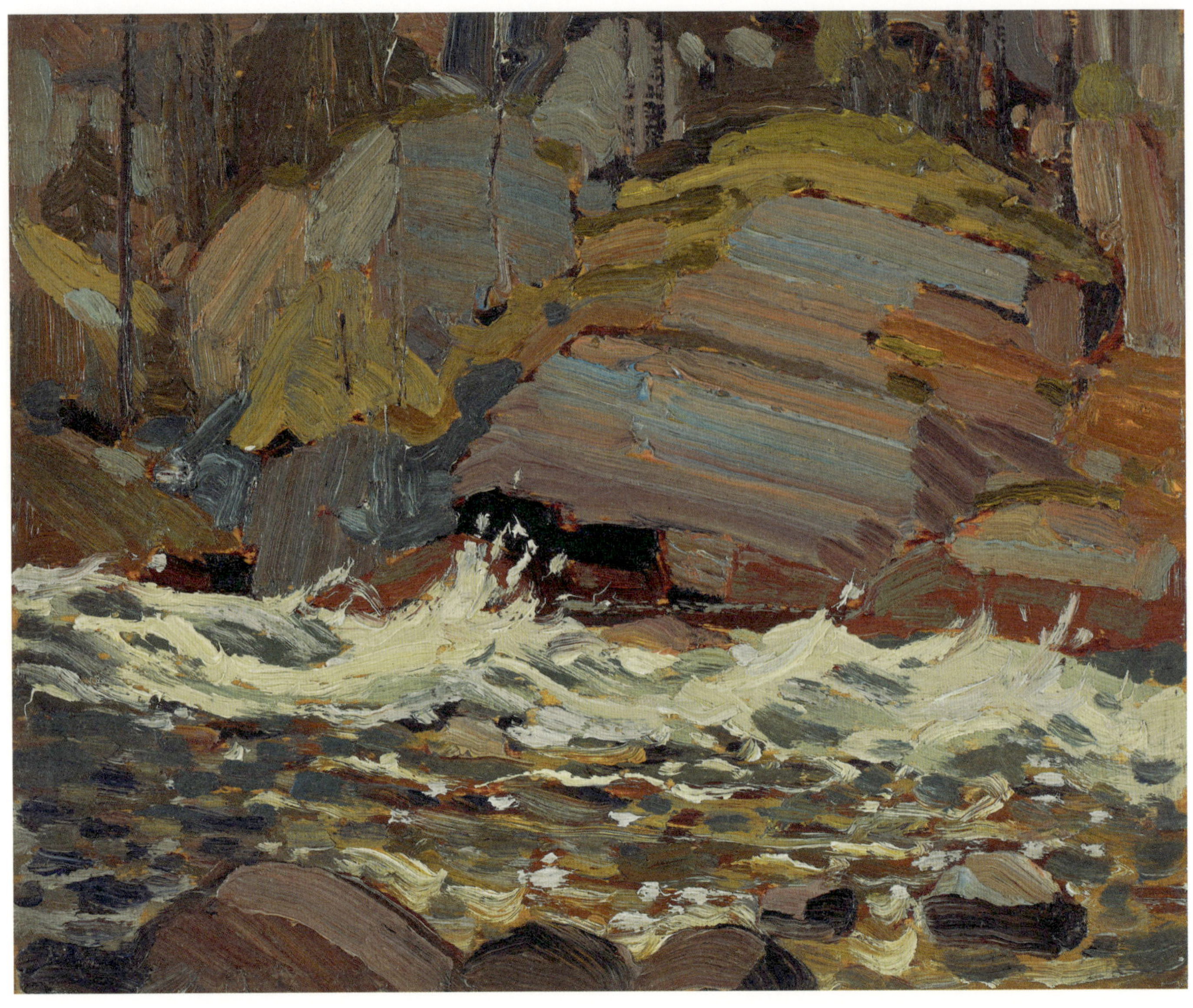

Tom Thomson
*Swift Water,* spring 1916
21.3 × 26.8 cm

Tom Thomson
*Snow and Rocks,* spring 1916
26.8 × 21.5 cm

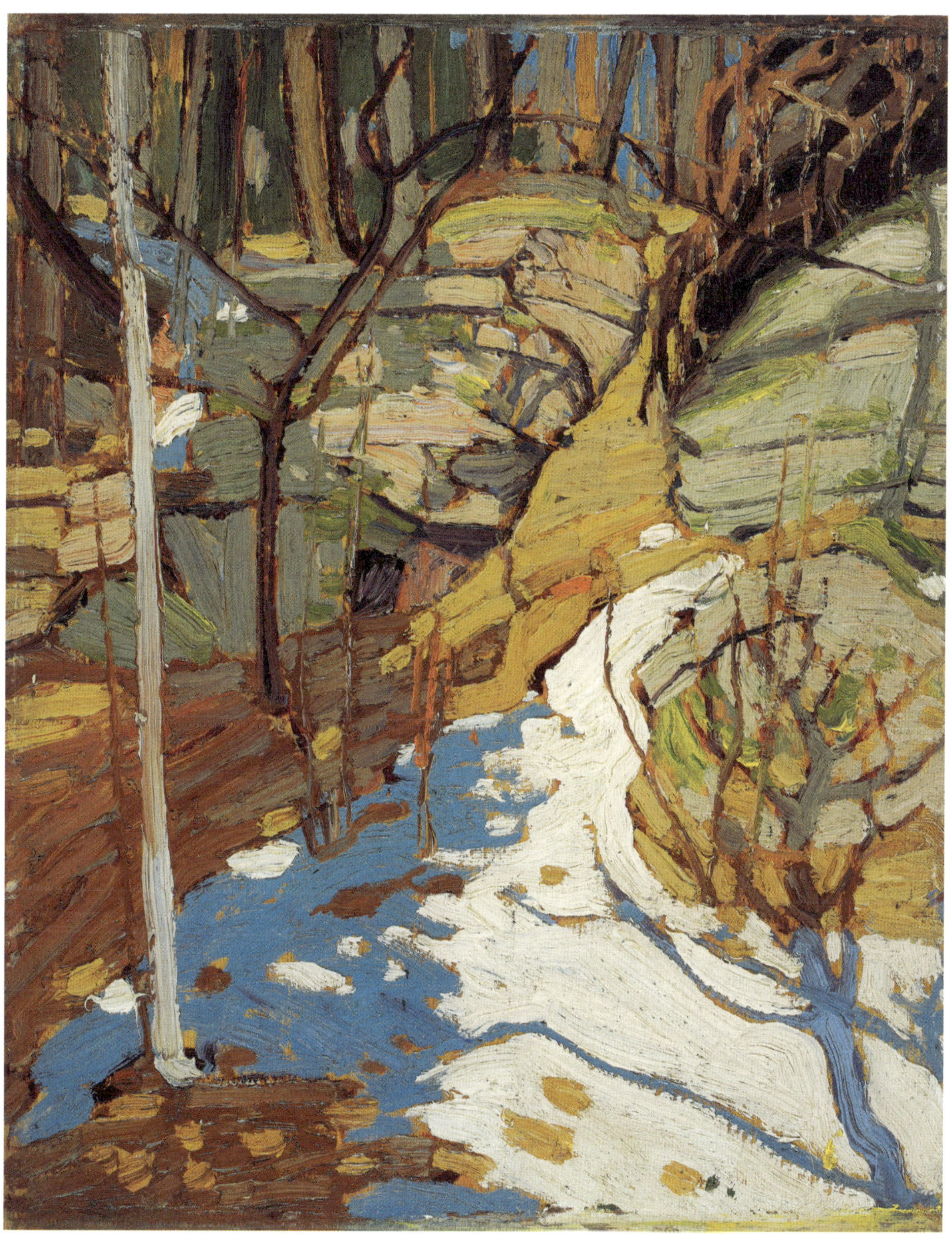

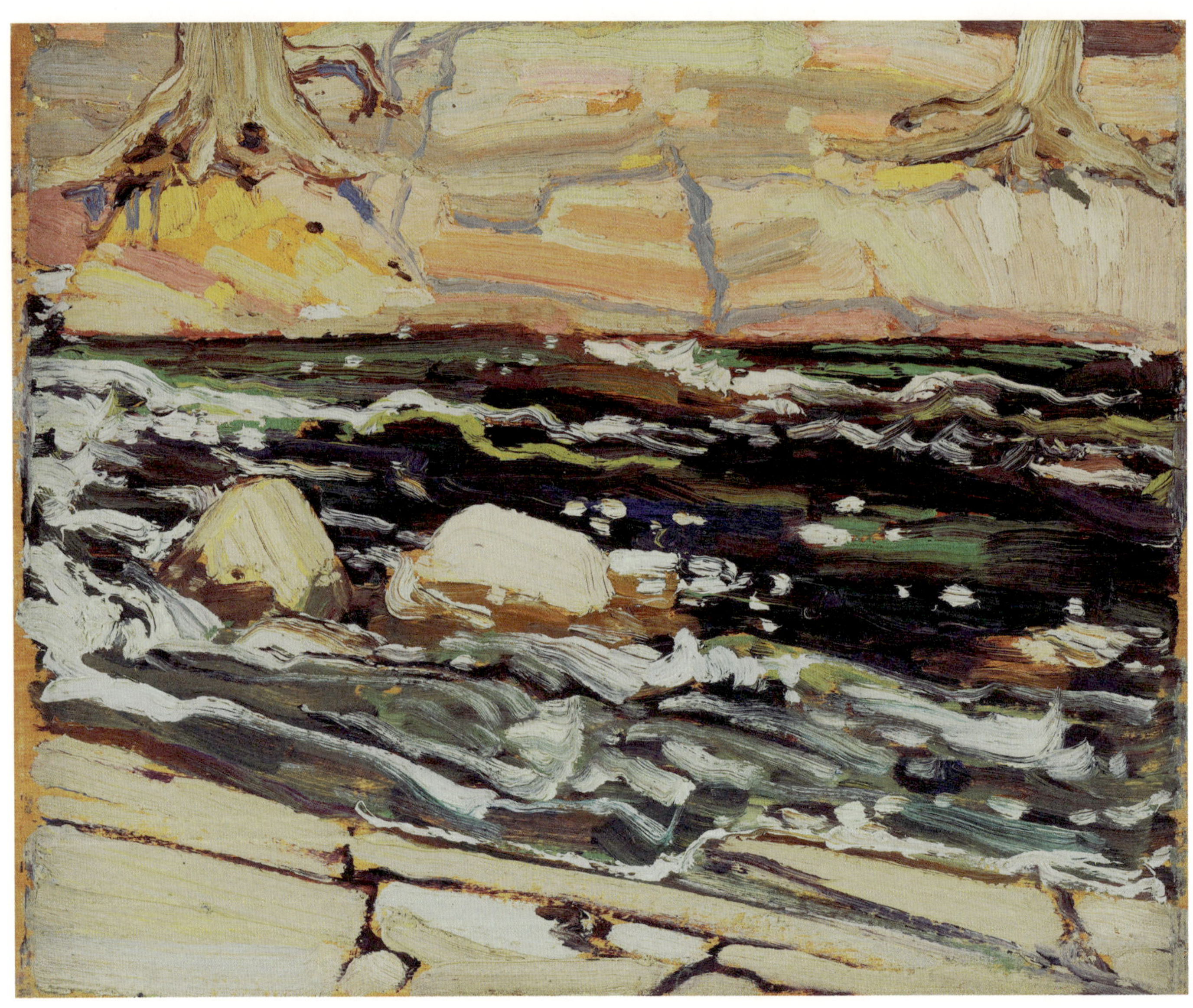

Tom Thomson
*Dark Waters*, spring 1917
21.3 × 26.8 cm

Tom Thomson
*The Enchanted Stream, Midnight,* summer 1916
21.5 × 26.7 cm

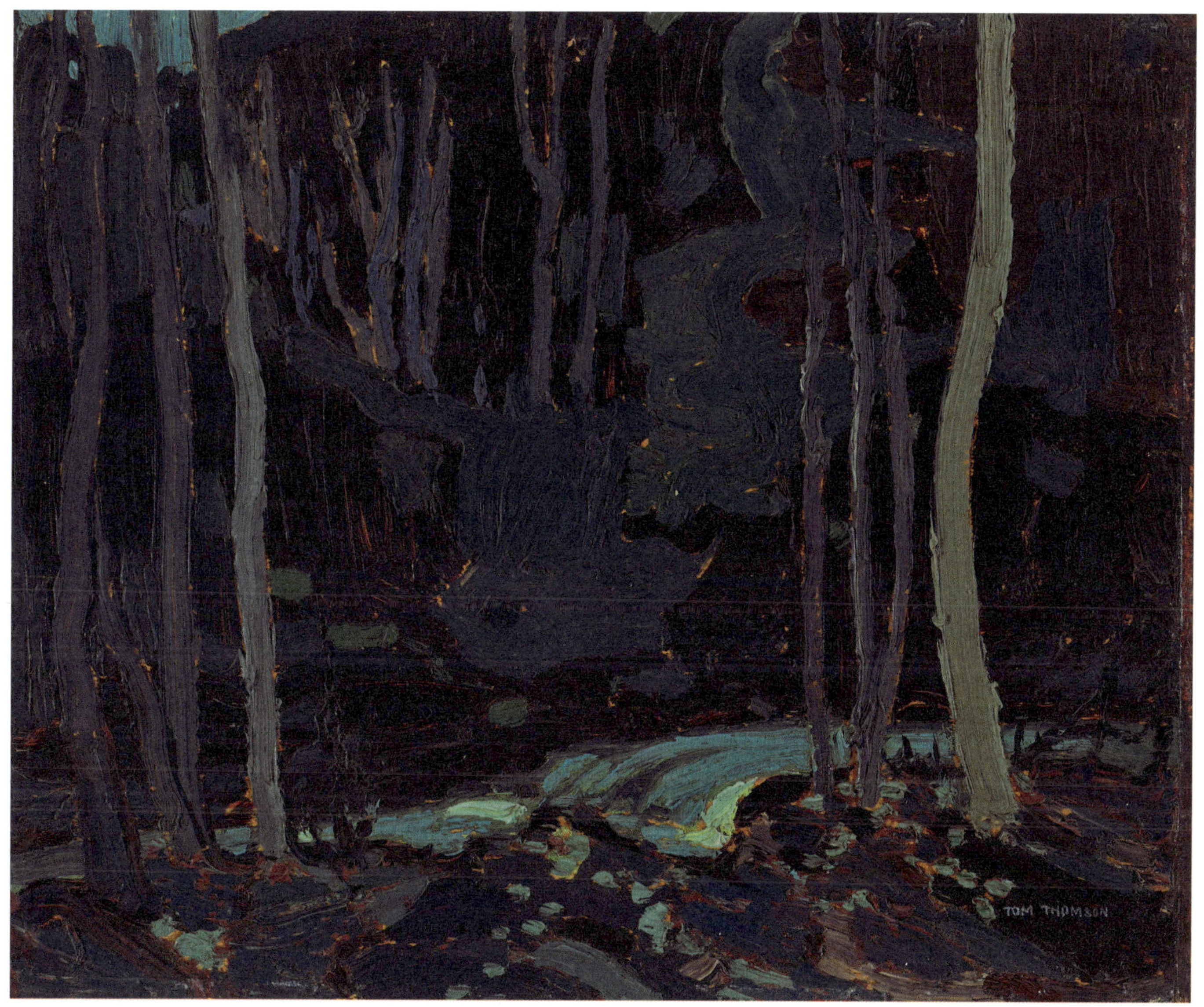

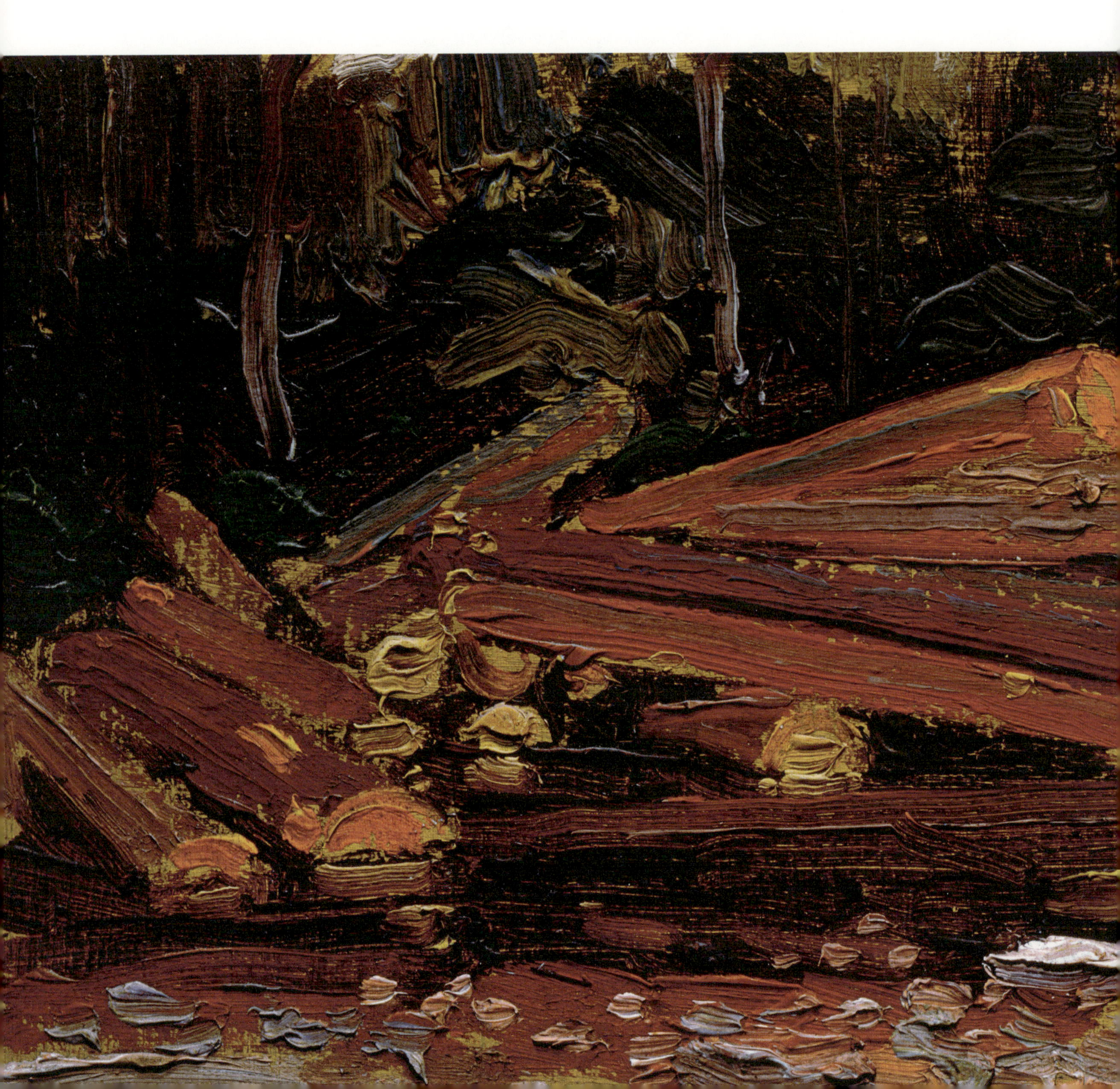

# Logging

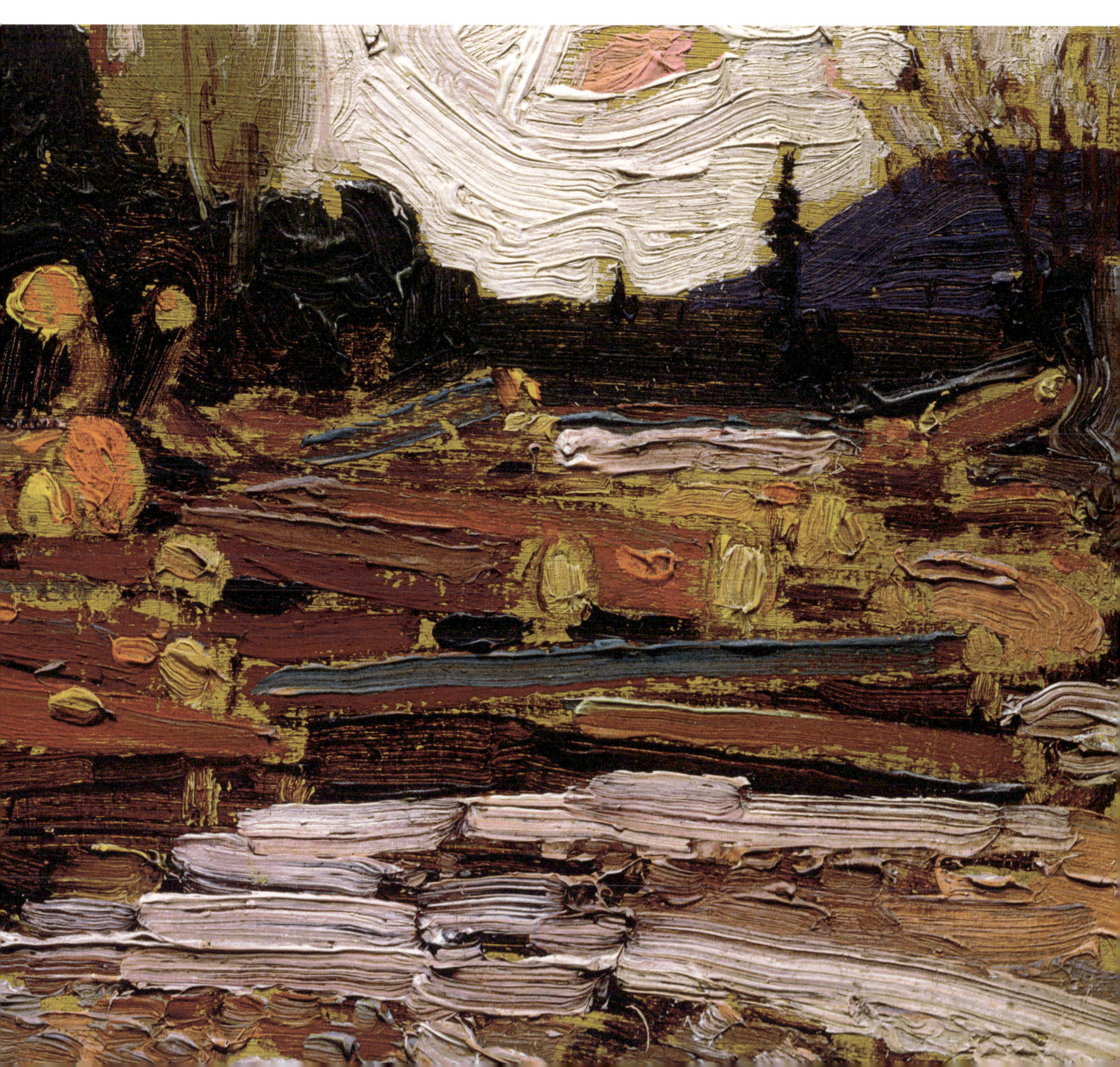

Today, with our perspective shaped by climate debates, global warming, the shrinking ice sheet, damage to forests, and various other environmental problems, we perhaps look with a certain sense of longing at the ostensibly unspoiled landscapes and regions painted by the Group of Seven, who came together based on their love of nature. Emily Carr thus wrote: "I spent all the time I could in the woods."[1] Canada truly impresses with the vastness of its landscape, and it is also one of the most densely forested countries in the world. But at the time of the Group of Seven, large portions of Canada had long since been subjected to industrial use. Logging boomed with enormous exports and the ongoing development of the production of paper and cellulose. The promotional film *Big Timber* (1935), commissioned by the Canadian government, reflects the enthusiasm for progress and prosperity that this branch of industry promised.

In Canada especially, wood is an almost immeasurable economic resource. But the great critic of civilization Henry David Thoreau, an important reference for the Group of Seven, was already concerned: "It is remarkable what a value is still put upon wood even in this age and in this new country, a value more permanent and universal than that of gold."[2] He called for "opening new channels, not of trade, but of thought"[3] and propagated a life in harmony with nature.

Numerous paintings by the Group of Seven "celebrate the wilderness," but traces of the use and exploitation of nature are at times also found in these works. Tom Thomson captured sawmills and chutes or dams for logs, for instance, in quite a number of sketches. Arthur Lismer portrayed the flotation of logs. Mary E. Wrinch did not paint a wilderness, but instead a landscape with a sawmill. Emily Carr dedicated herself to *Reforestation* (1936), even titling one of her works thus, while Edwin Holgate portrayed an earnest, virile, hardworking logger, who corresponded with the artist's image of himself. The critic Fred Housser thus wished for a "new type of artist; one who divests himself of the velvet coat and flowing tie of his cast, puts on the outfit of the bushwacker and prospector."[4]

Martina Weinhart

1—Emily Carr, *Growing Pains: The Autobiography of Emily Carr,* first published in Toronto in 1946 (Vancouver: Douglas & McIntyre, 2005), p. 306.
2—Henry David Thoreau, *Walden* (London: Penguin Classics, 2016), p. 233.
3—Ibid., p. 298.
4—F. B. Housser, *A Canadian Art Movement: The Story of the Group of Seven* (Toronto: The MacMillan Company of Canada Limited, 1926), p. 15.

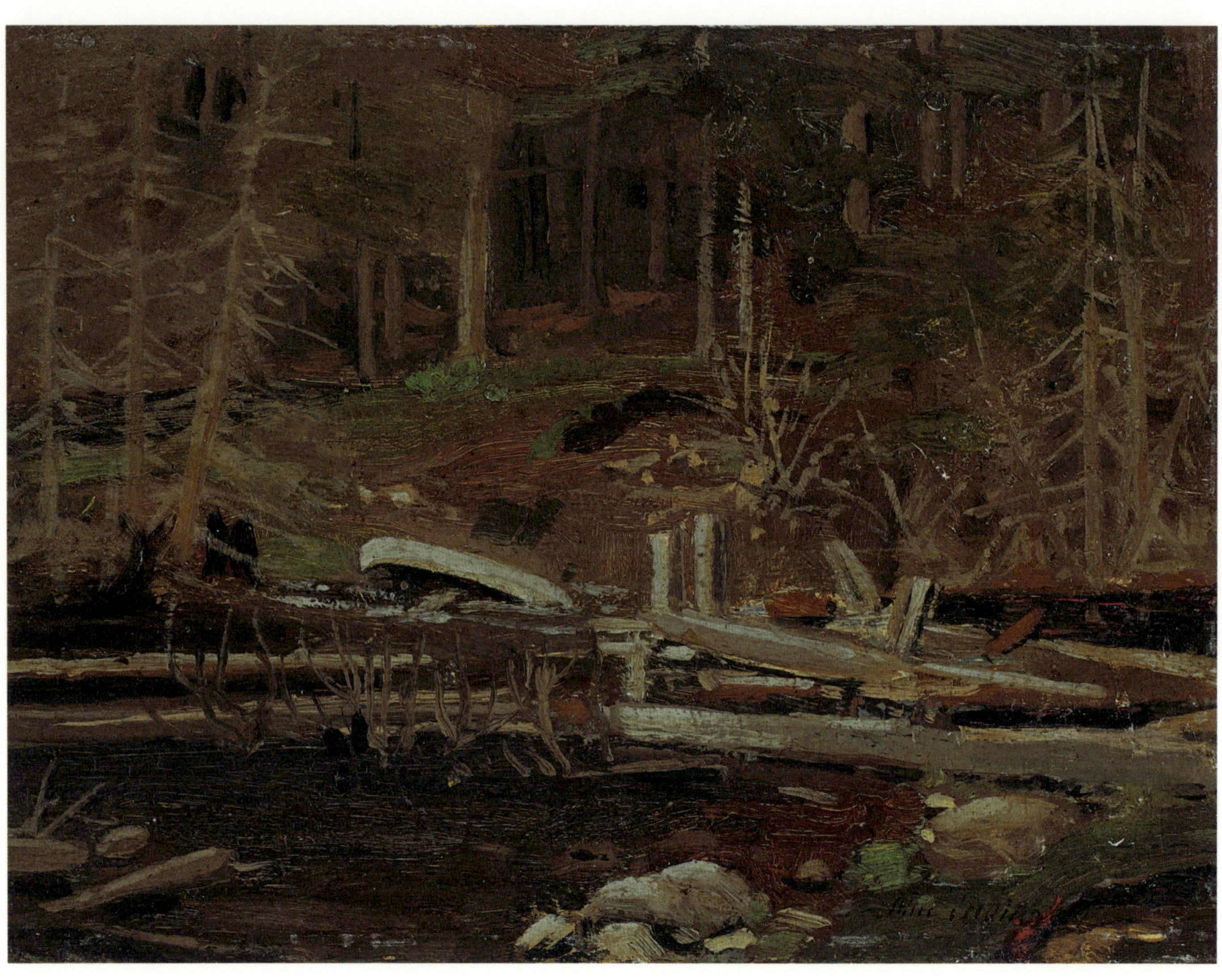

Tom Thomson
*Old Lumber Dam, Algonquin Park,* spring 1912
15.5 × 21.3 cm

Tom Thomson
*Timber Chute,* fall 1916
21.6 × 26.7 cm

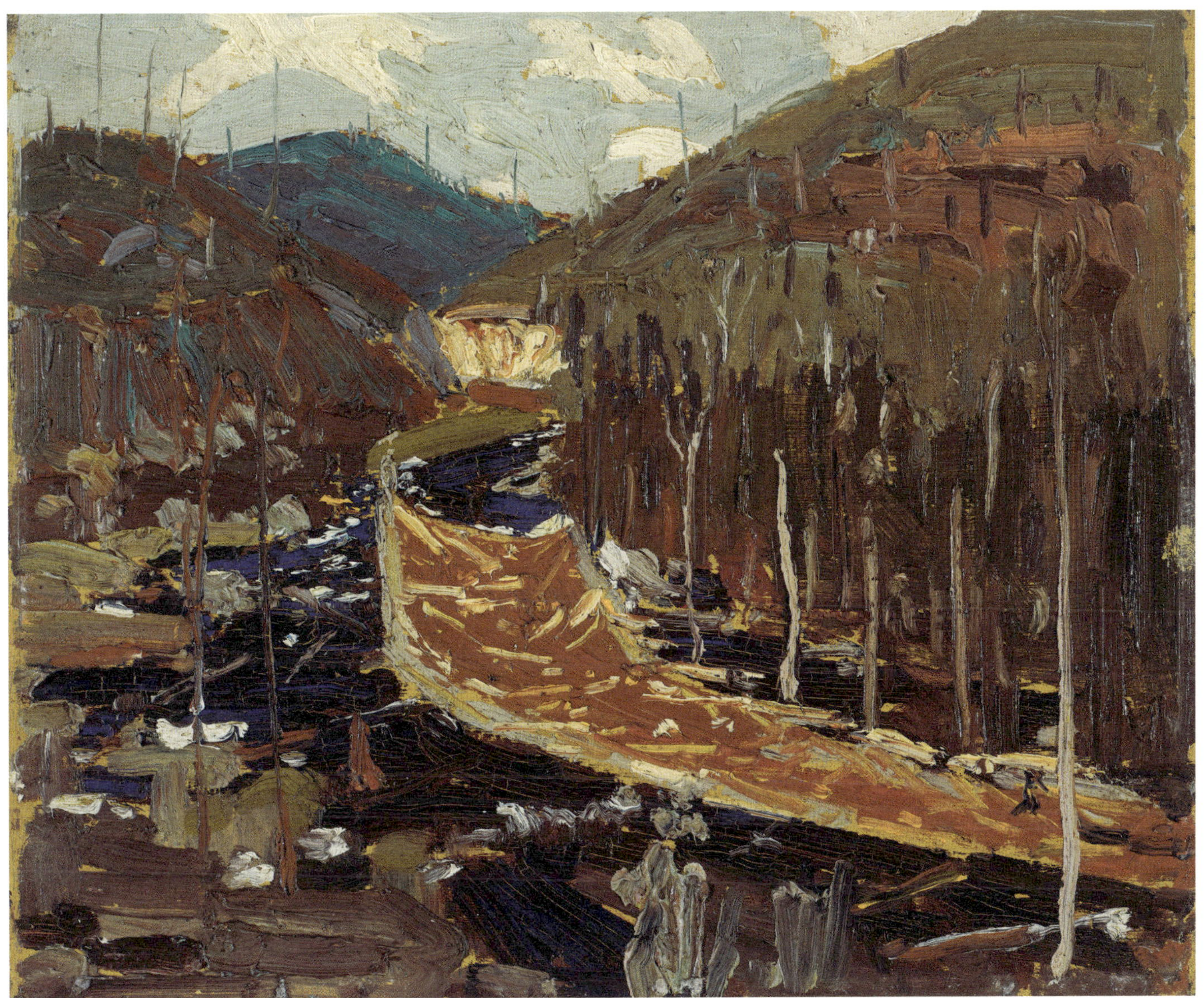

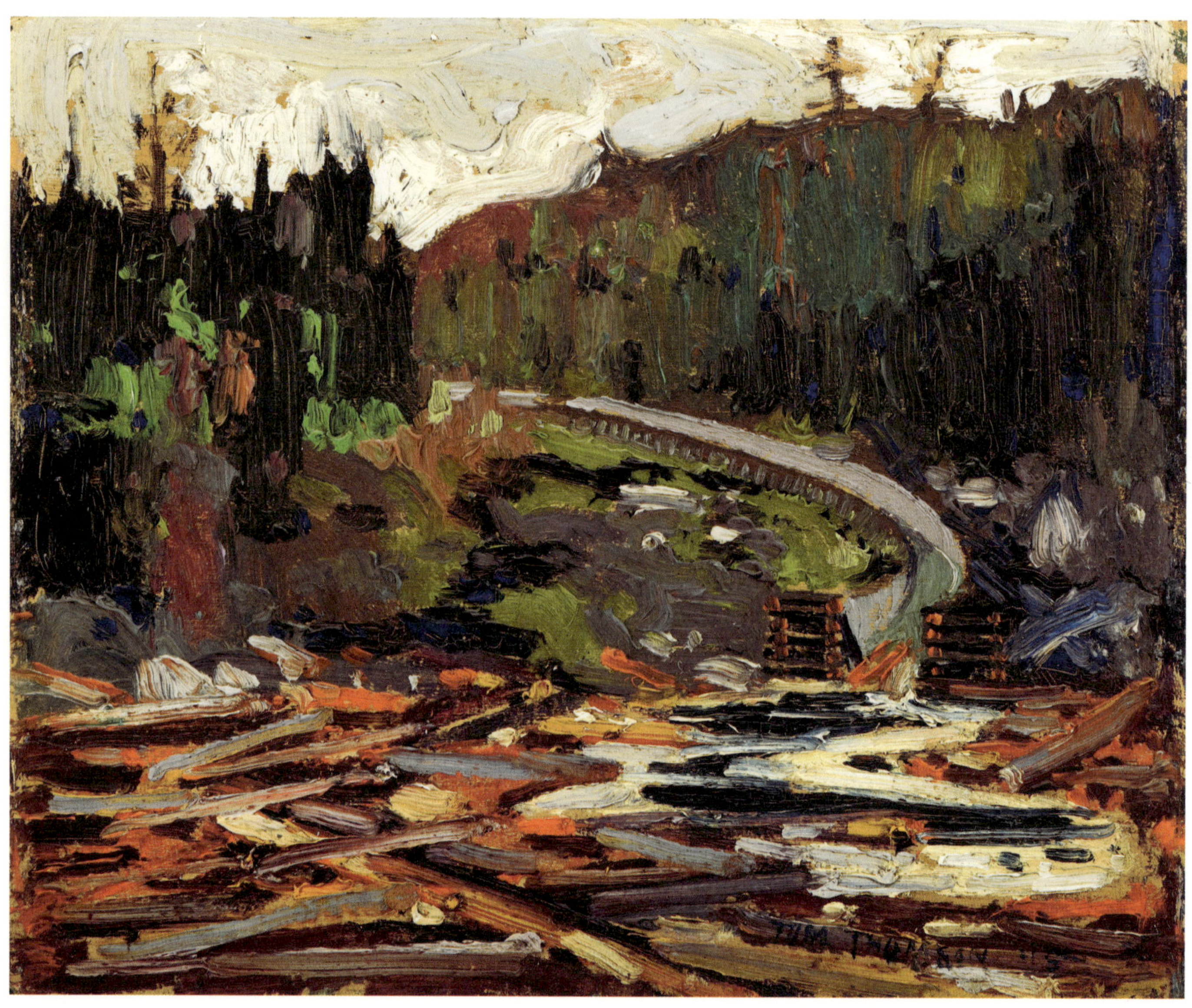

Tom Thomson
*The Log Flume,* spring 1915
21.7 × 26.8 cm

Tom Thomson
*Abandoned Logs,* fall 1915
21.6 × 26.6 cm

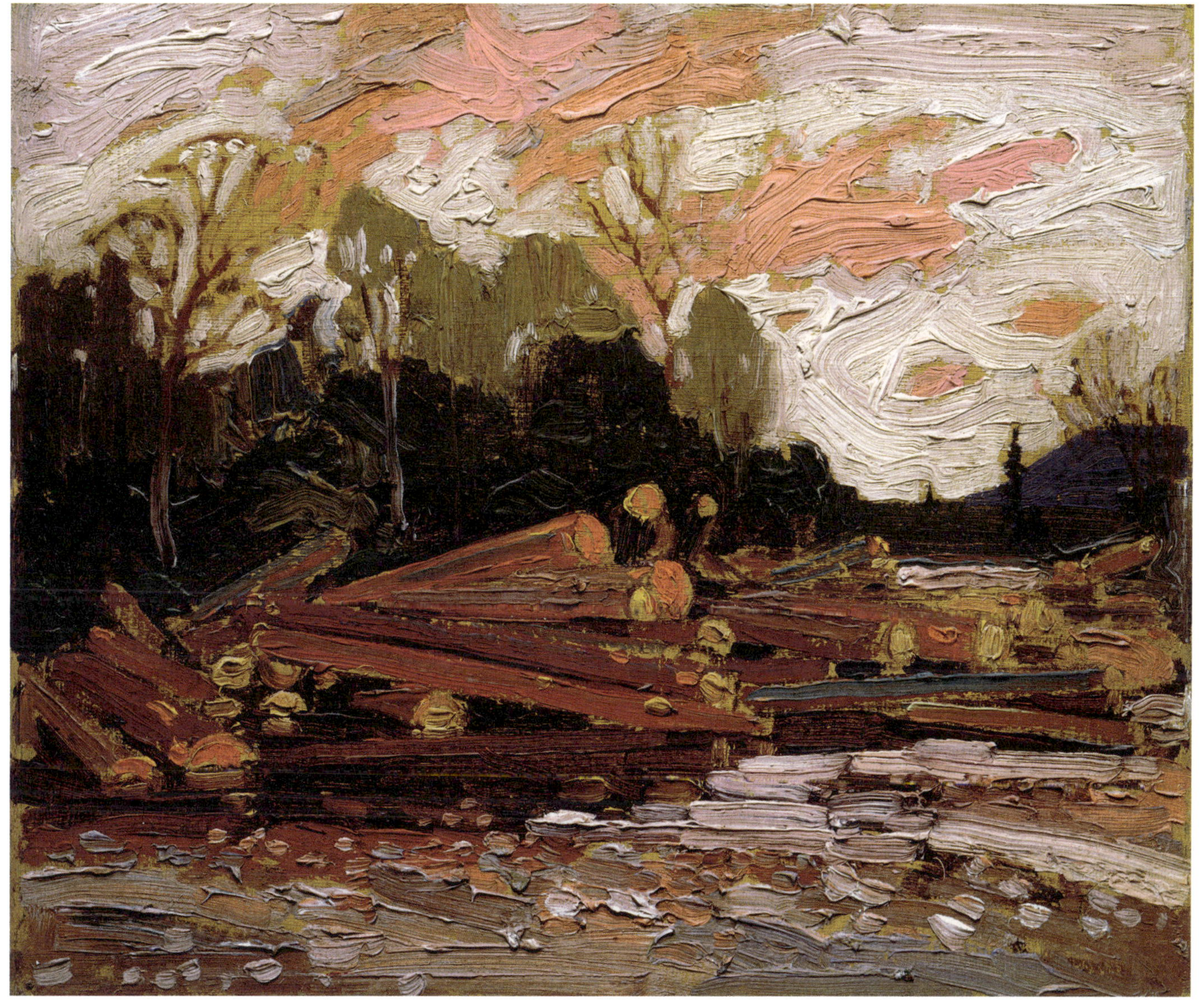

Tom Thomson
*Log Jam: Sketch for "The Drive,"*
fall 1916
21.6 × 26.7 cm

To help finance his painting career, Tom Thomson worked as a fire ranger in Algonquin Park. By the early 1900s, the park, located in Eastern Ontario, had already been subjected to extensive harvesting of its timber. Swaths of terrain were left bare and vulnerable to fires ignited by lightning or sparks from passing trains. As the Group of Seven painter A. Y. Jackson noted at one point, "Thomson was much indebted to the lumber companies,"[1] not only for his income, but also for his access to Algonquin Park via logging roads and railways. As a ranger, Thomson spent time in lumber camps and became familiar with the region's immense forests, and with the industry that rapaciously harvested them.

Forestry loomed large in Canadian capitalism at the turn of the century; its presence inflected the work of Thomson and his Group of Seven colleagues. Timber chutes, dams, lumberjacks, and fire-ravaged ground appear in a number of sketches and canvases from the Algonquin years.[2] As the art historians John O'Brian and Peter White observed, "in these works the artists chose to confront rather than elide the dystopian complexity of the new economic realities."[3] Curiously, in the canon of Canadian art history, logging paintings do not have the same blockbuster appeal as those featuring lush vistas, placid icebergs, or solitary windswept trees. The landscapes bereft of human presence have always had the most currency.

Nonetheless, Tom Thomson's *Log Jam: Sketch for "The Drive"* is undoubtedly a significant work. This sketch was painted on site and reflects the intense energy and immediacy of the river scene. It is one of the few panels that Thomson later translated into a large canvas composition, *The Drive* (fig. p. 177). Painted at the peak of Thomson's career, they are a powerful counterargument to the myth of Canada's north as an uninhabited, untouched land. Both the painting and the sketch richly contextualize a springtime log drive: agile lumberjacks usher logs through a dam and down a river toward a sawmill. Although they are diminutive in scale compared to the immense haul of logs and the surging river, these workers are celebrated for their heroism: their job was certainly a dangerous, occasionally fatal one. Though Thomson is known for compositions that are solid and contained, here he implicates the viewer in the treacherous action. Logs pour down around us with force, creating the sense that we are standing in the river itself; they spill into the foreground and threaten to pull us downstream with them. The upper part of the painting, by contrast, is still and quite peaceful. Even so, Thomson includes a stark cautionary note in the far distance: there, a massive clear-cut hilltop reveals the scale of such logging operations and the severe toll they take on the land.

Renée van der Avoird

1—Quoted in David P. Silcox, *The Group of Seven and Tom Thomson* (Richmond Hill, ON: Firefly Books, 2003), p. 210.
2—On various occasions between 1913 and 1917, A. Y. Jackson, Lawren Harris, Arthur Lismer, J. E. H. MacDonald, and F. H. Varley painted in Algonquin Park, alongside Tom Thomson.

Before the formation of the Group of Seven, these artists were unofficially named the "Algonquin School." After Thomson's death in 1917, his colleagues stopped going to the park to paint.
3—John O'Brian and Peter White, eds., *Beyond Wilderness: The Group of Seven, Canadian Identity, and Contemporary Art* (Montreal and Kingston: McGill-Queen's University Press, 2007), p. 137.

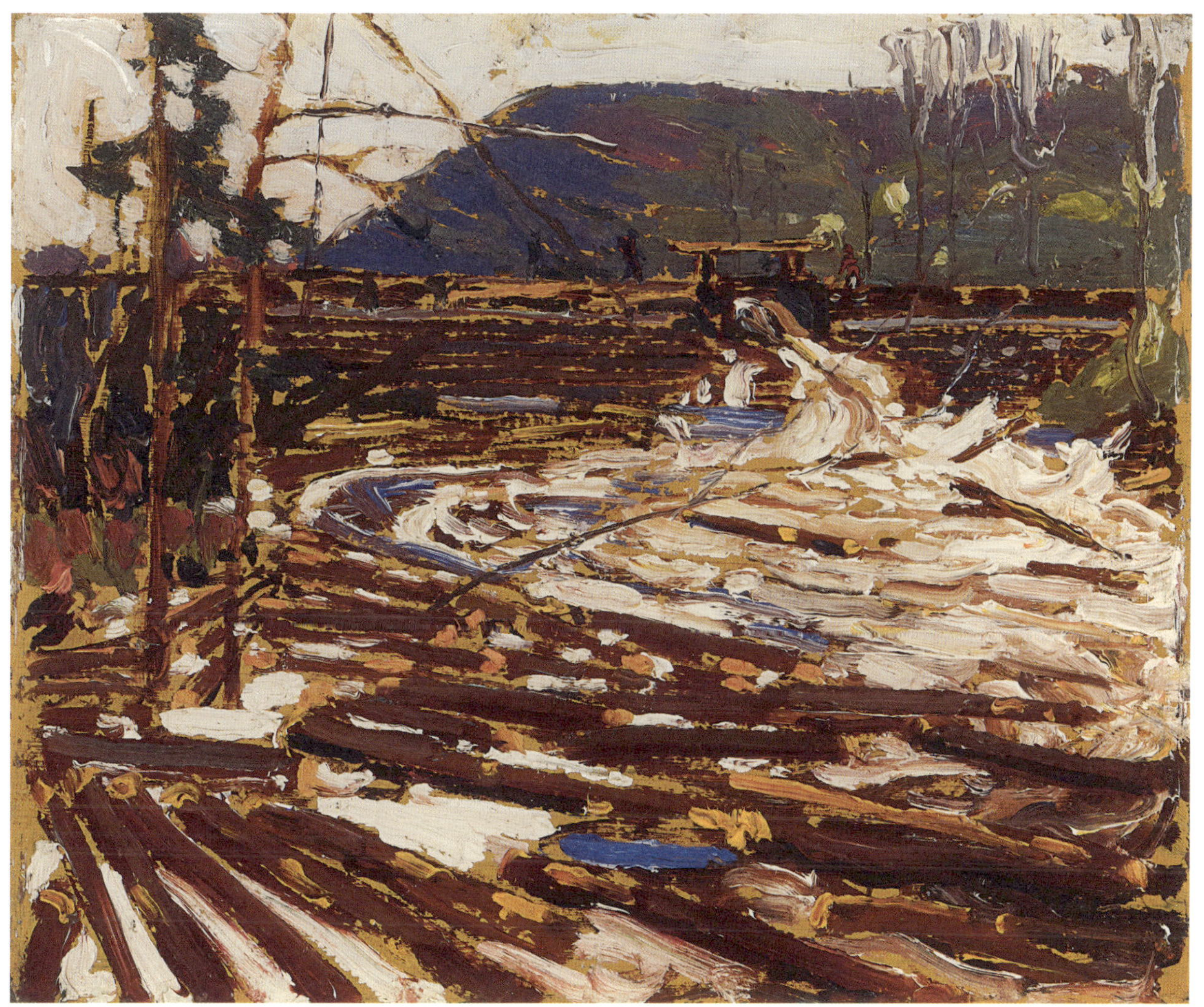

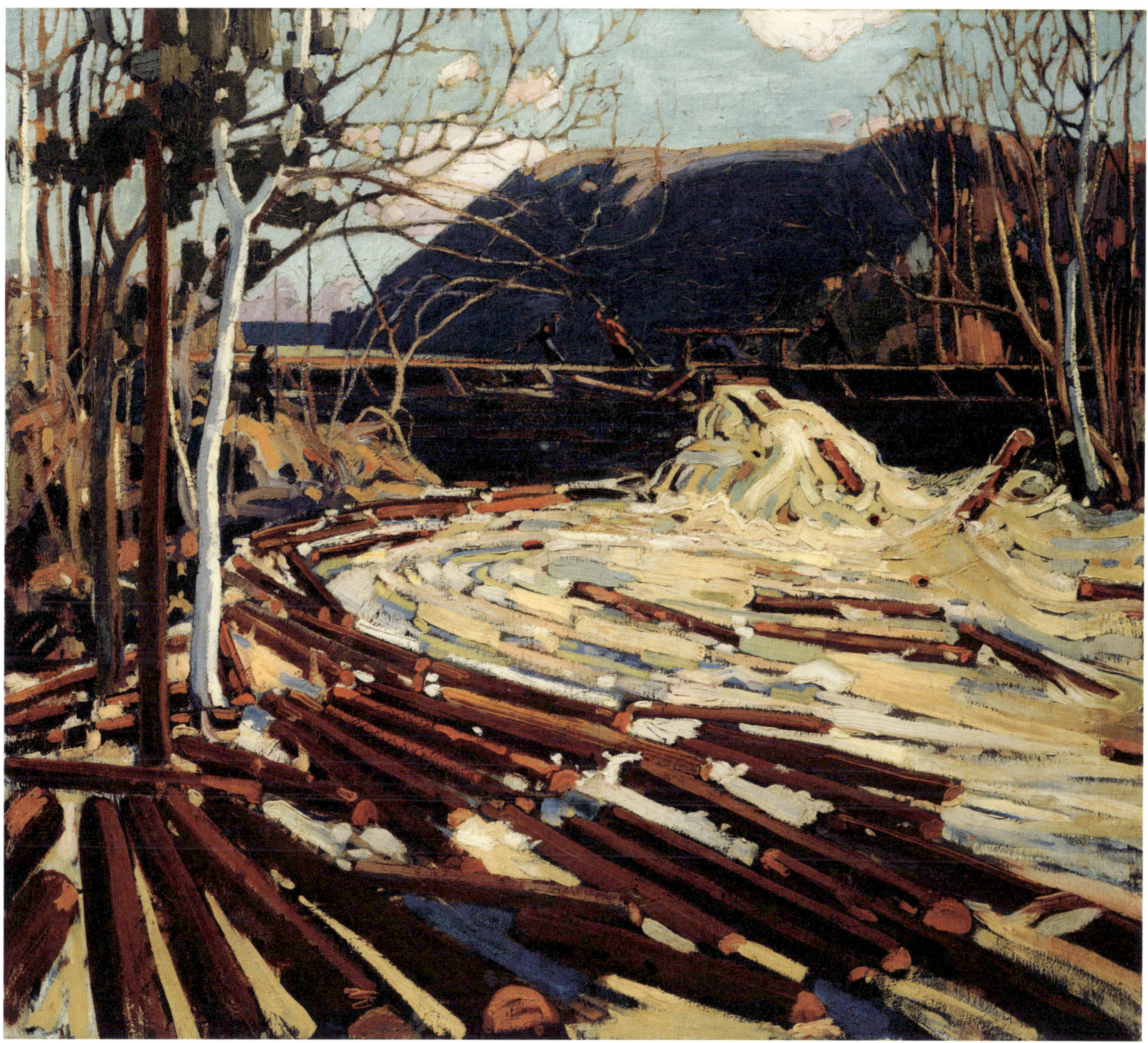

Tom Thomson, *The Drive,* winter 1916–17, oil on canvas, 120 x 137.5 cm
Ontario Agricultural College purchase with funds raised by students, faculty, and staff, 1926,
University of Guelph Collection at the Art Gallery of Guelph

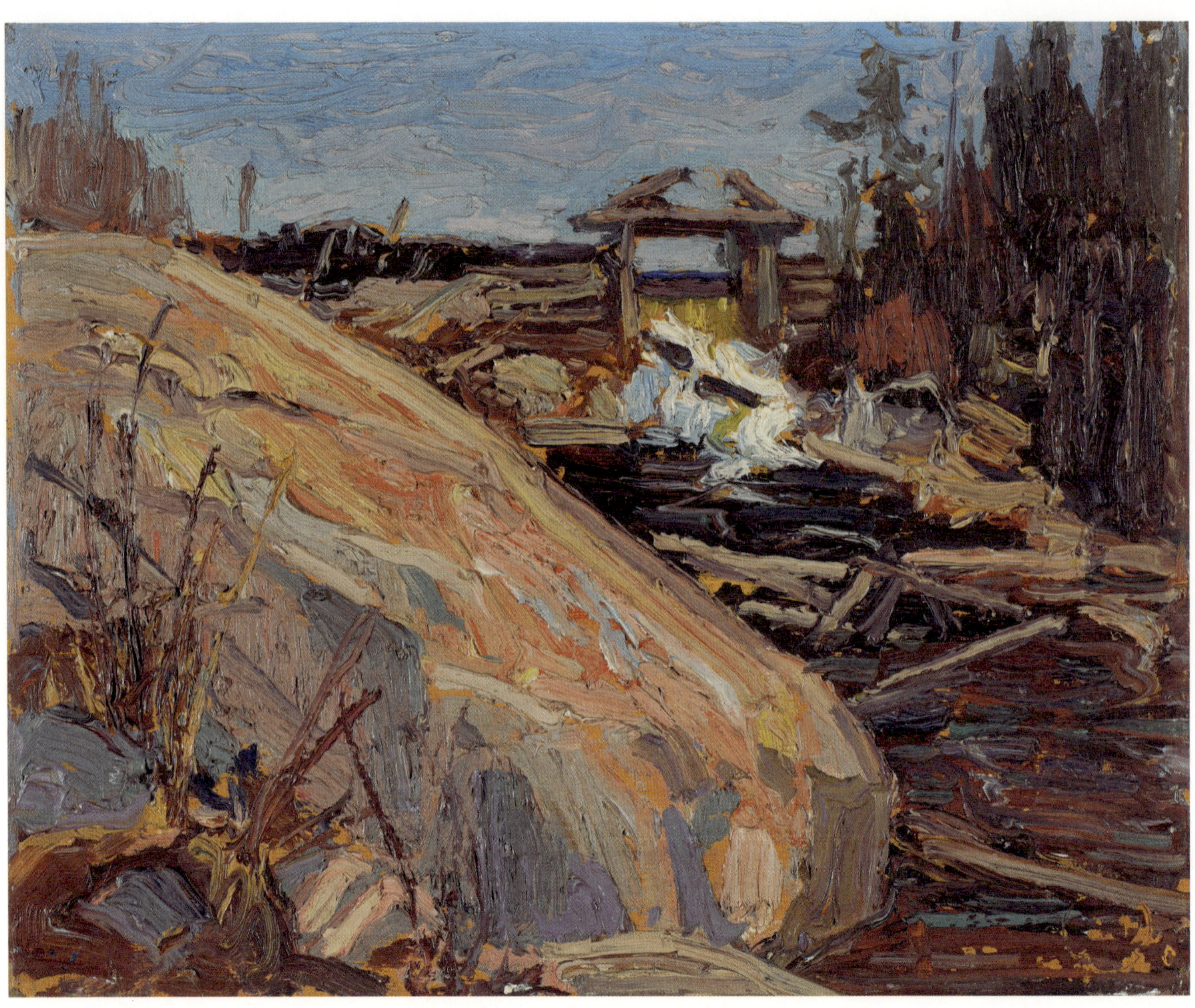

Tom Thomson
*Lumber Dam,* summer 1915
21.6 × 26.7 cm

Tom Thomson
*Timber Chute,* fall 1915
21.6 × 26.7 cm

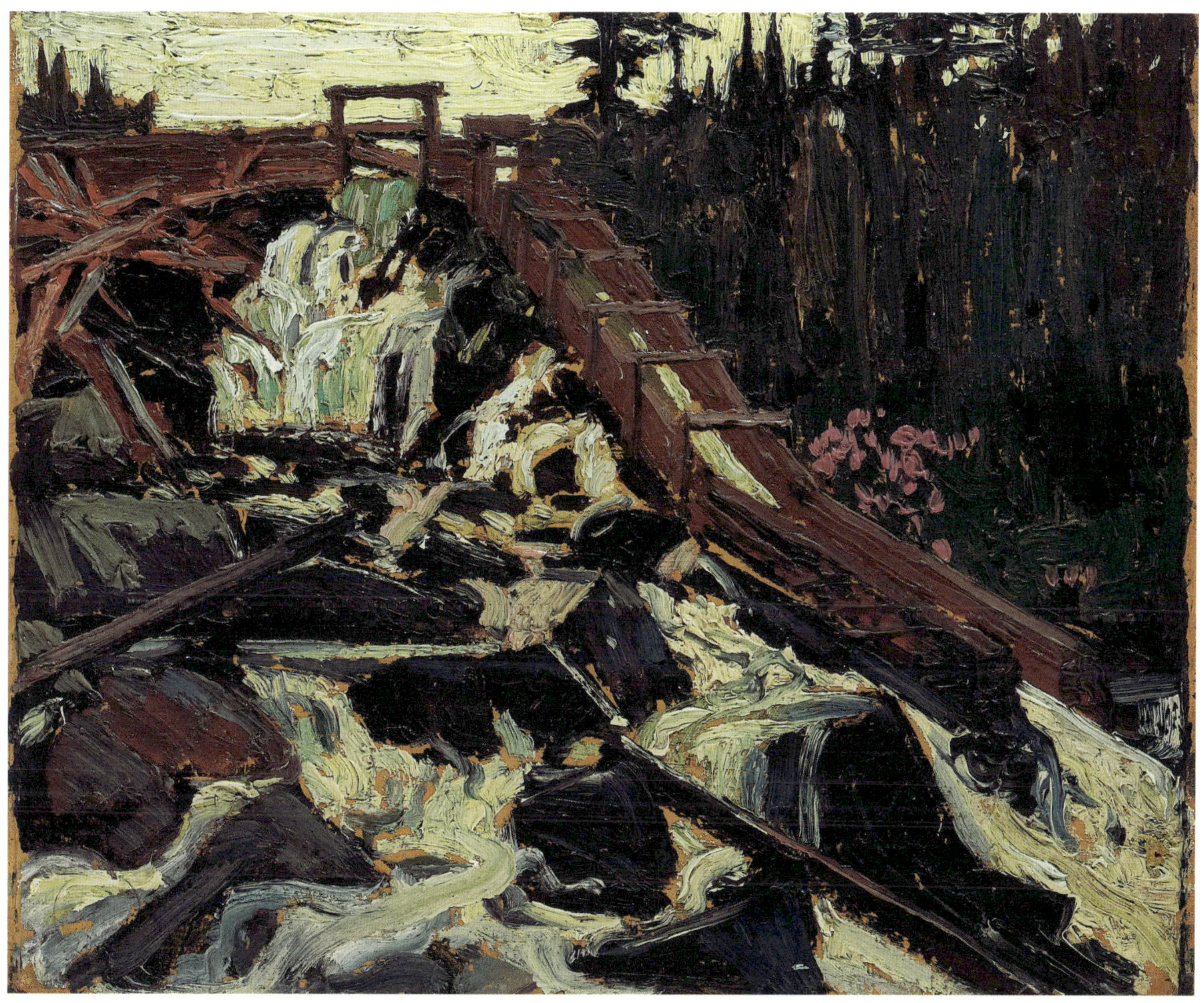

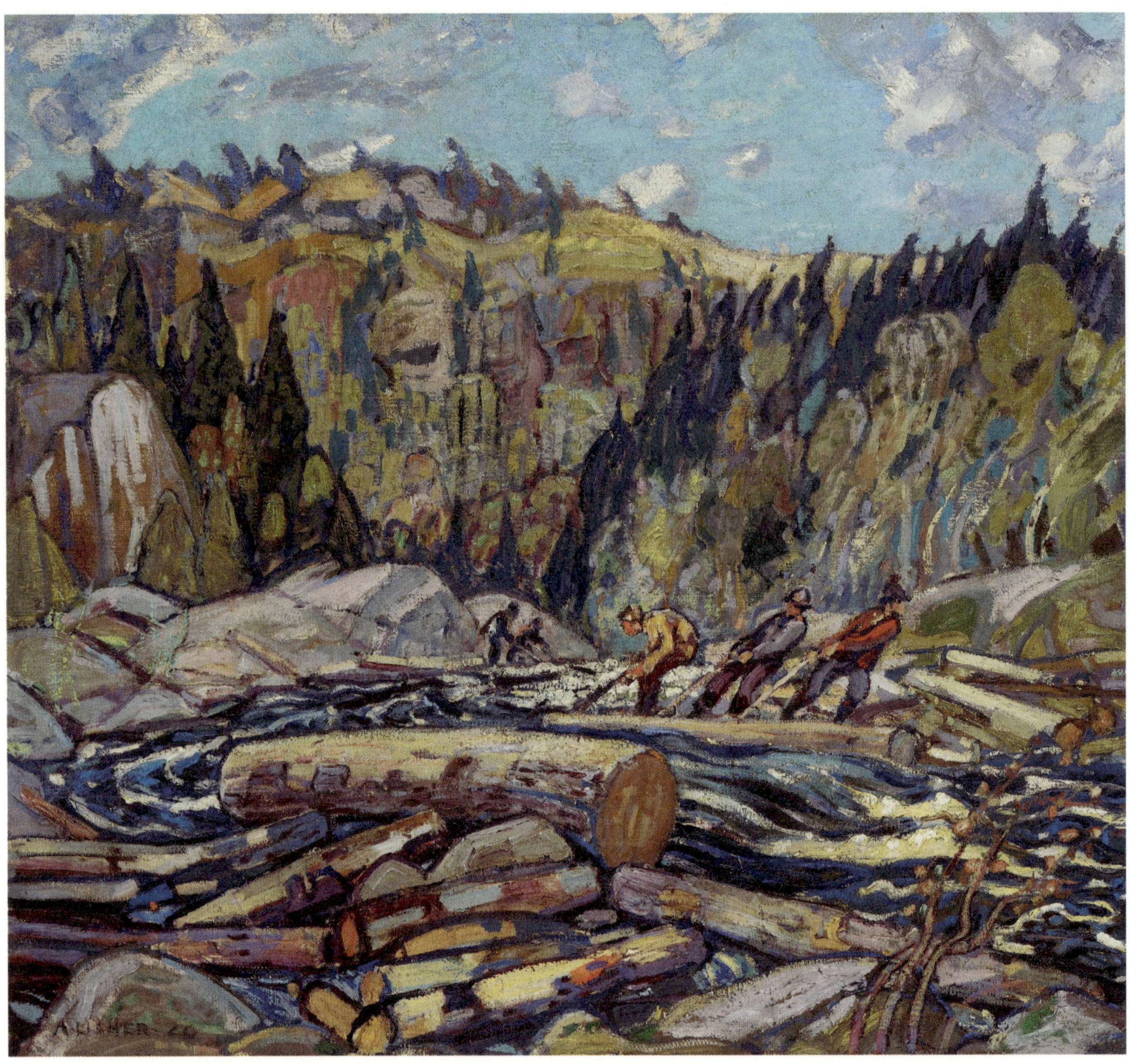

Arthur Lismer
*Logging in Nova Scotia*, 1920
91.4 × 101.5 cm

Edwin Holgate
*The Lumberjack*, 1924
64.8 × 56.6 cm

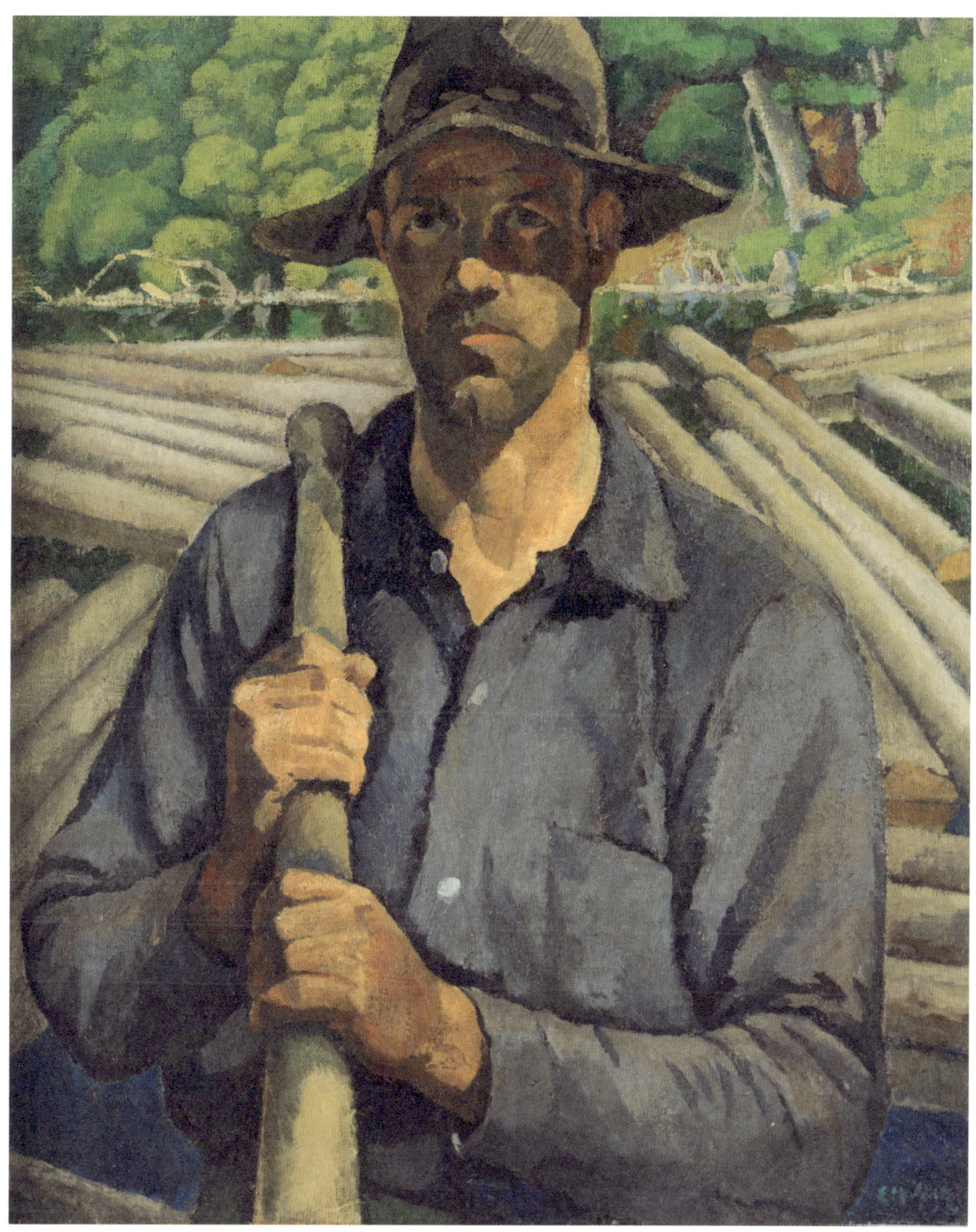

Mary E. Wrinch
*Saw Mills, Muskoka,* 1906
45.2 × 59.4 cm

A prominent Torontonian in the early 1900s, Mary Evelyn Wrinch was among the first women in the city to make a living from her art. The adventurous and independent Wrinch traveled to Ontario's northern regions a decade ahead of the Group of Seven. She drew on extensive formal training to develop her own vigorous, progressive style; this approach made her particularly influential in the landscape genre.

Wrinch painted *Saw Mills, Muskoka* during a trip to Gravenhurst, Ontario. The town is located on the southernmost point of Lake Muskoka, a body of water carved deeply into the Canadian Shield and surrounded by a dense forest of maples, hemlocks, and pines. Part of Anishinaabe territory and governed by the Williams Treaties,[1] Lake Muskoka has become a destination for luxury cottages in recent times. In the early twentieth century, however, it was the heart of Ontario's thriving lumber industry (at the time, Gravenhurst was known as Sawdust City). Sawmills occupied its shores, some running twenty-four hours a day, cutting timber in bulk and transporting it south via train.

Most modern Canadian landscape paintings include no evidence of human presence. Wrinch's *Saw Mills, Muskoka,* however, challenges the myth of an unspoiled, uninhabited country. In this sophisticated canvas, the artist directly tackles the industrial and environmental realities of the time. She painted the scene en plein air in an impasto style, captivated by the mill's stark, geometric forms, billowing steam, and plentiful piles of floating logs. This painting reveals Wrinch's interest in European styles of painting. In 1905, the young artist traveled to England and France, where she became energized by the light and atmosphere of British landscapes and the visual effects and industrial subjects of French Impressionism. After she returned home, her practice was viewed as more advanced than that of other local artists, catalyzing an aesthetic shift in Toronto painting.

Renée van der Avoird

1—Treaties in Canada are sacred covenants between Indigenous nations, or agreements between the government and Indigenous peoples on exchanges of ancestral lands in return for certain promises and payments. The Williams Treaties were signed in 1923 by the federal government and seven First Nations of the Chippewa of Lake Simcoe and the Mississauga of Lake Ontario. The government has since failed to recognize and respect the Indigenous rights of the Williams Treaties, leading to long-standing injustices, legal disputes, and unresolved land claims.

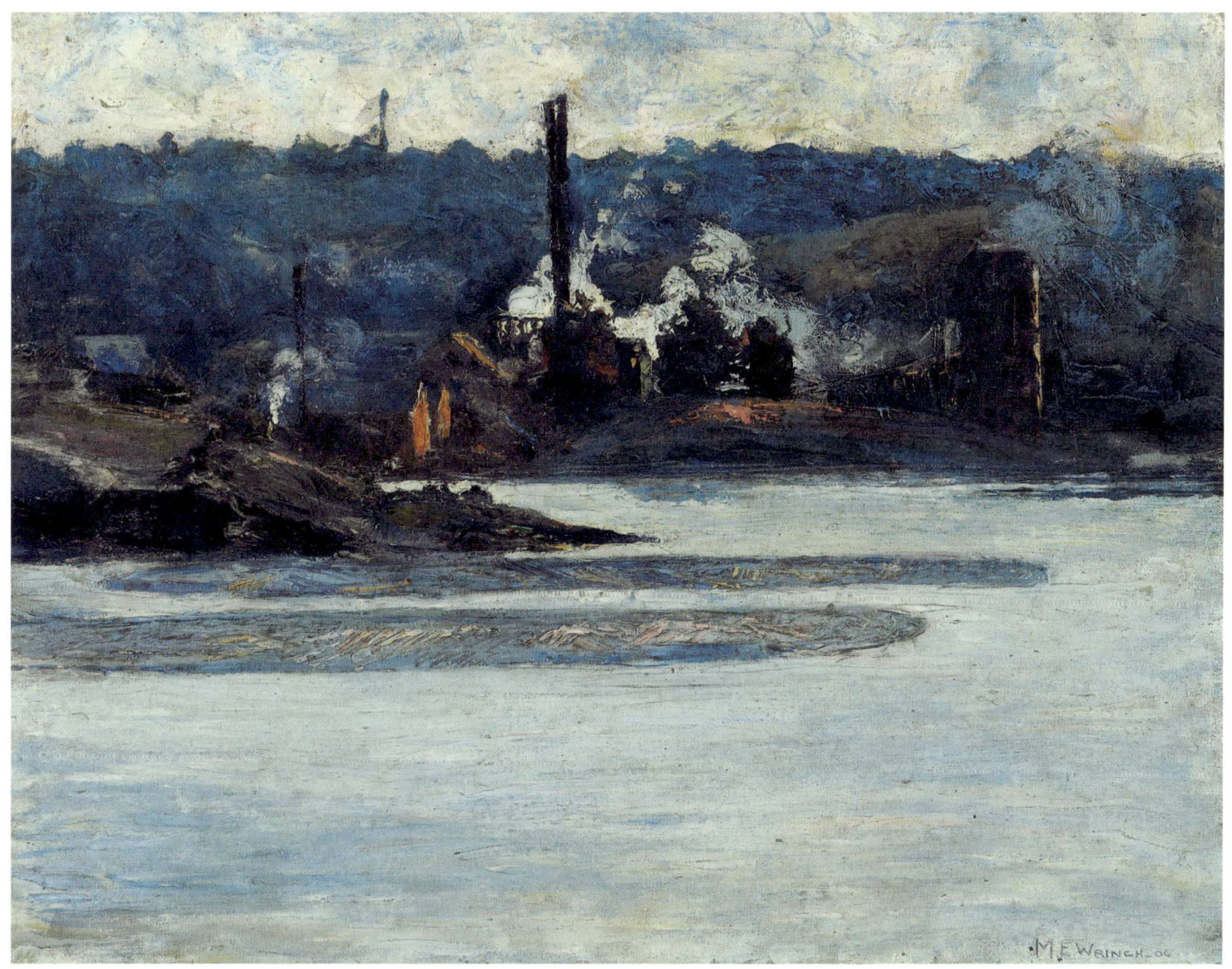

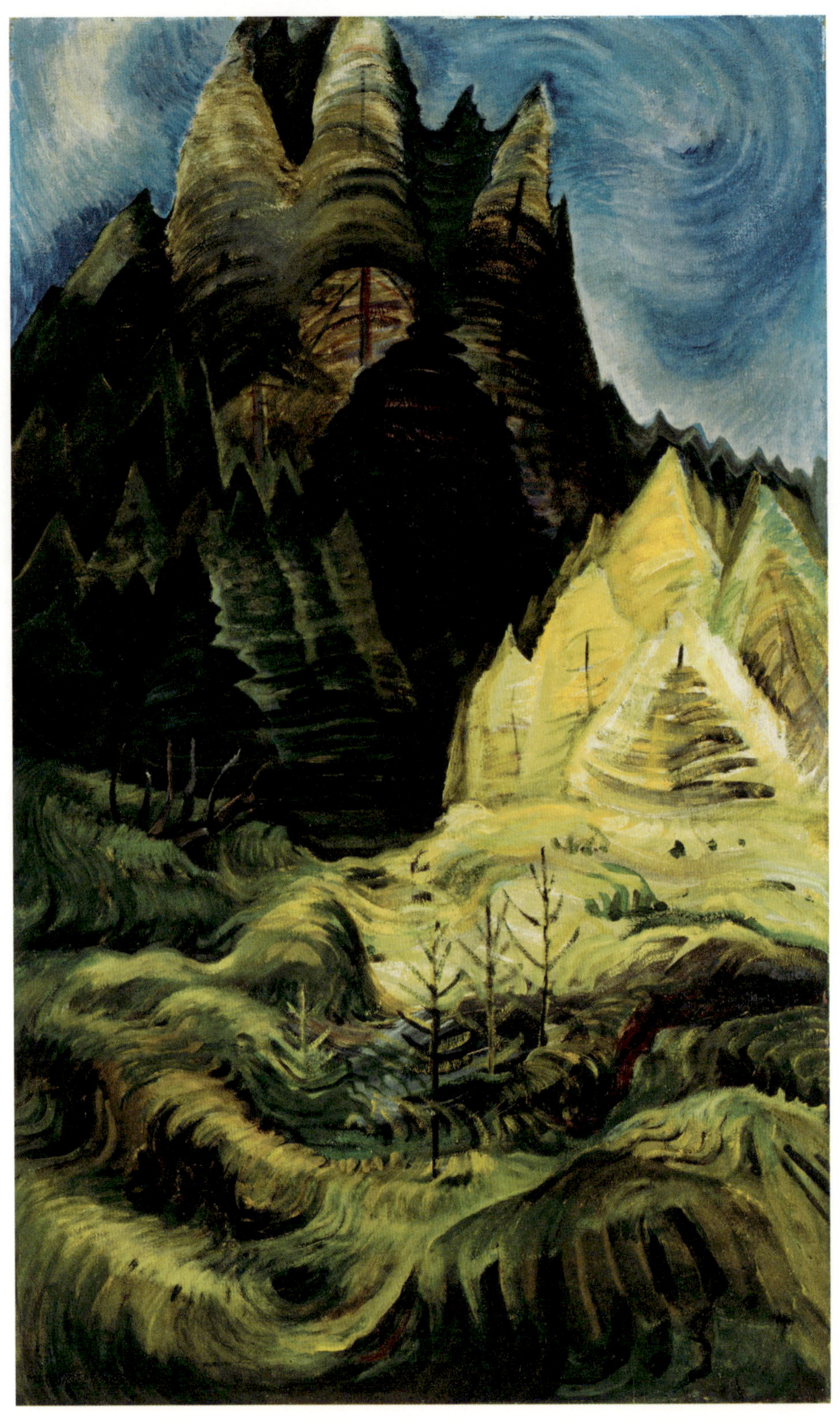

Emily Carr
*Reforestation,* 1936
110 × 67.2 cm

Emily Carr
*Trees in the Sky,* 1939
111.6 × 68.7 cm

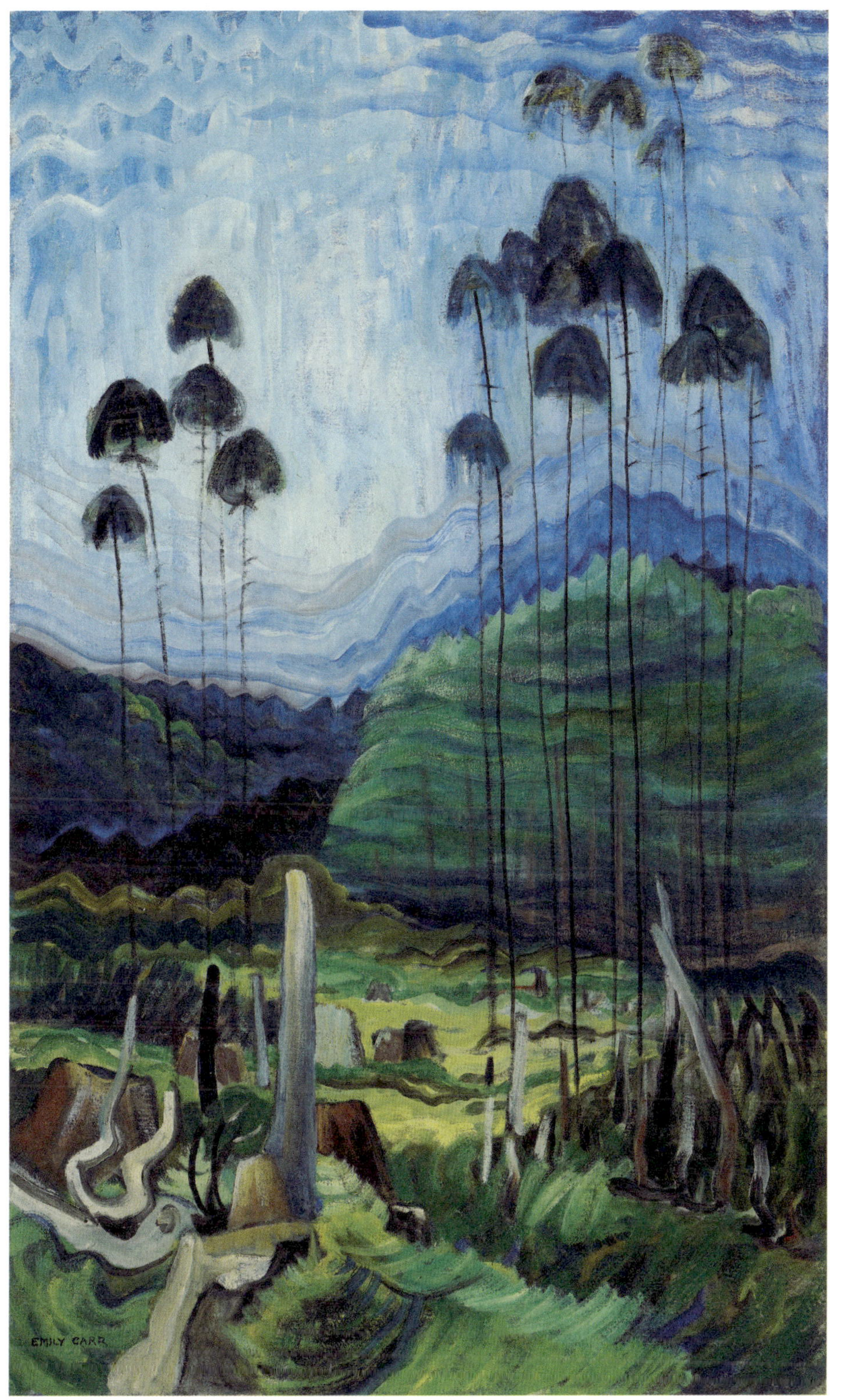

Canadian Government
Motion Picture Bureau
*Big Timber*, 1935
Film (digital video transfer, black and
white, sound, 11 min.)
W. Graham (photography),
David Gwydyr (scenario),
Rupert Caplan (narrator)

The industry film *Big Timber* was
commissioned by the Canadian
Government Motion Picture Bureau
(the first national film production
unit in the world, later absorbed by
the National Film Board) to promote the achievements and productivity of the logging industry in
British Columbia. The film enthu-
siastically describes the entire
process, from the felling of majestic Douglas firs to the cutting of
boards and their export across the
Pacific. In a typically 1930s style,
the film propagates the progress
that is found in exploiting the
resources of the forest. It had previously been "unknown land" and
now furnished "the world with one
of the basic commodities of civilization." The Picture Bureau, and
then the National Film Board (NFB),
produced films about Canada's
largest export industry for decades
to come with films such as *The
Story of Canadian Pine* (1938) and
*Pulp and Paper from Canada* (1949).

Martina Weinhart

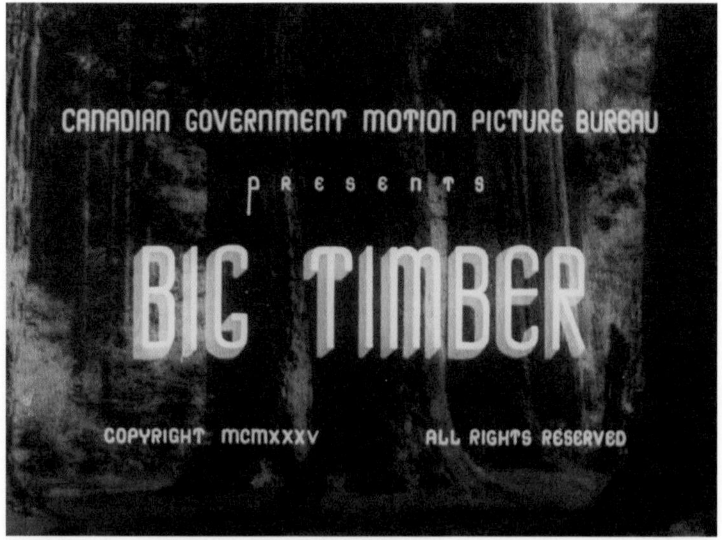


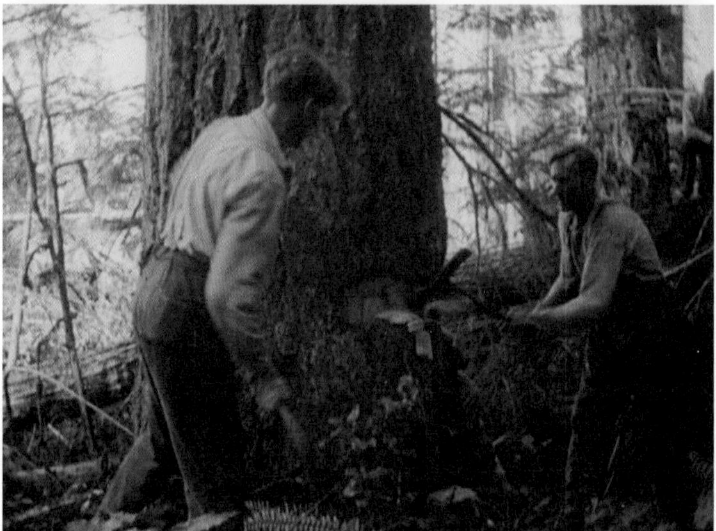

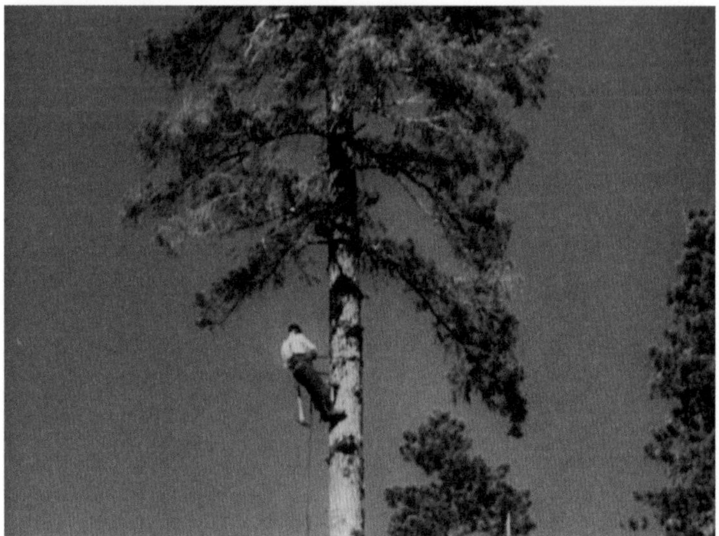

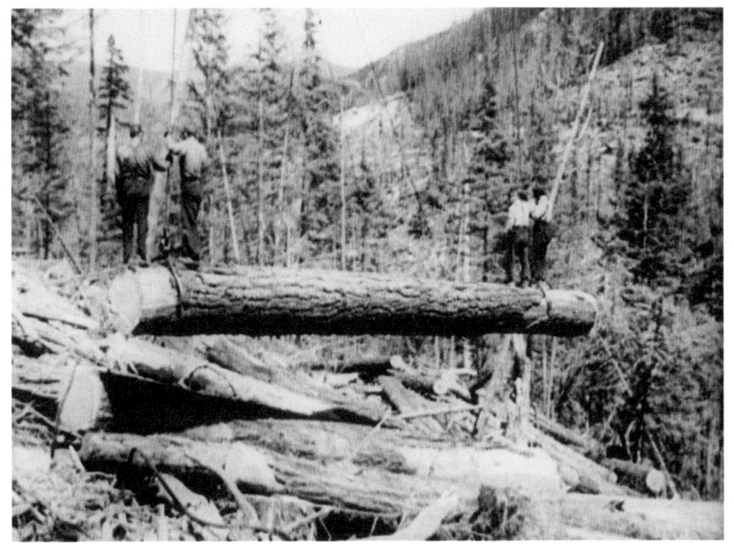
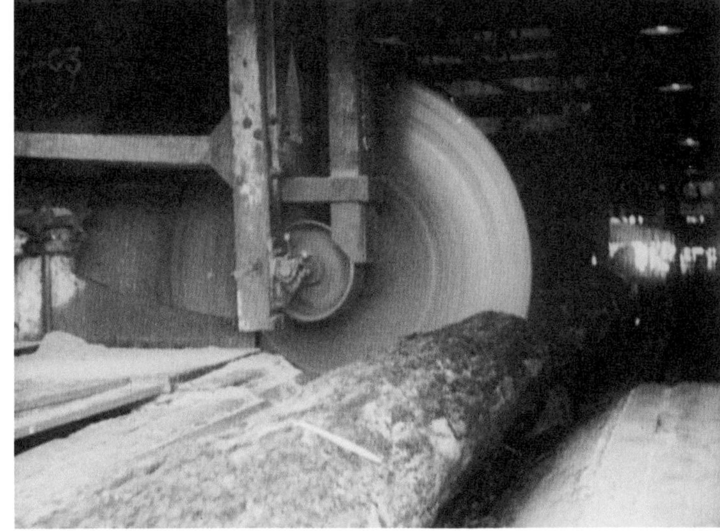
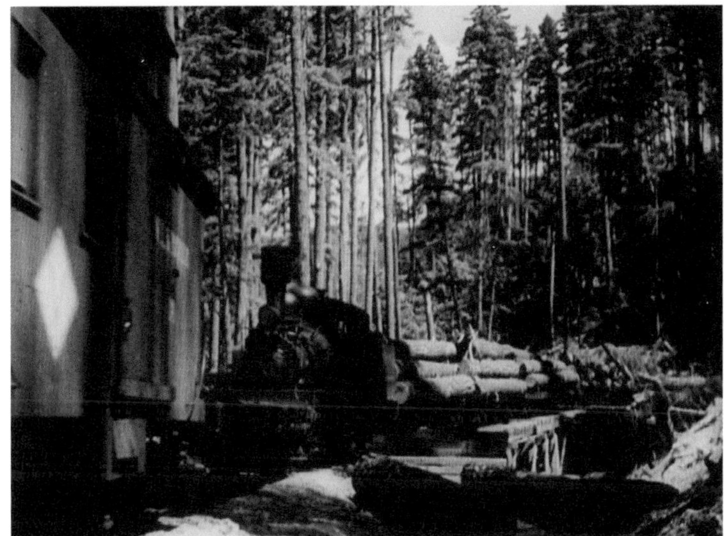
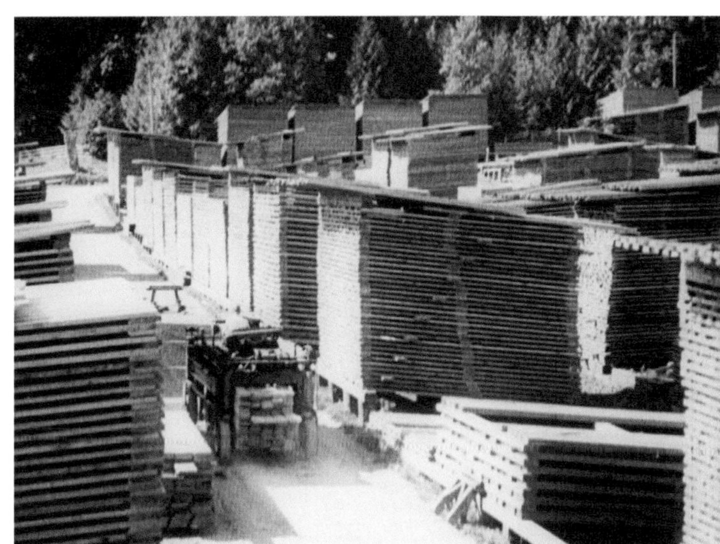
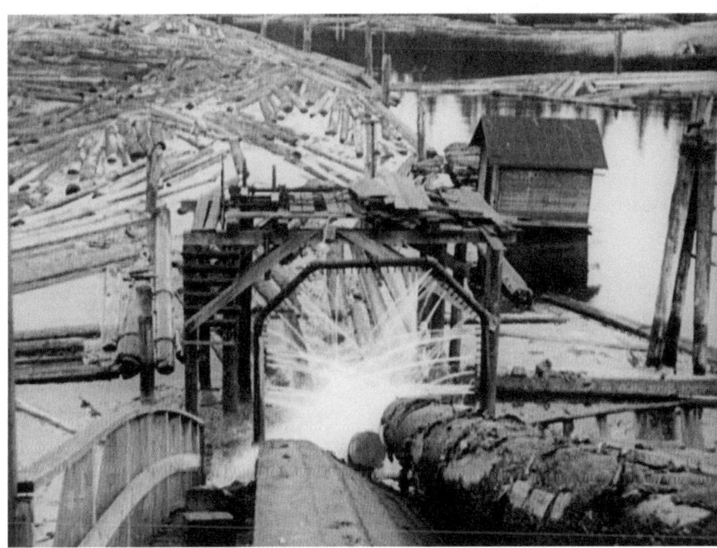
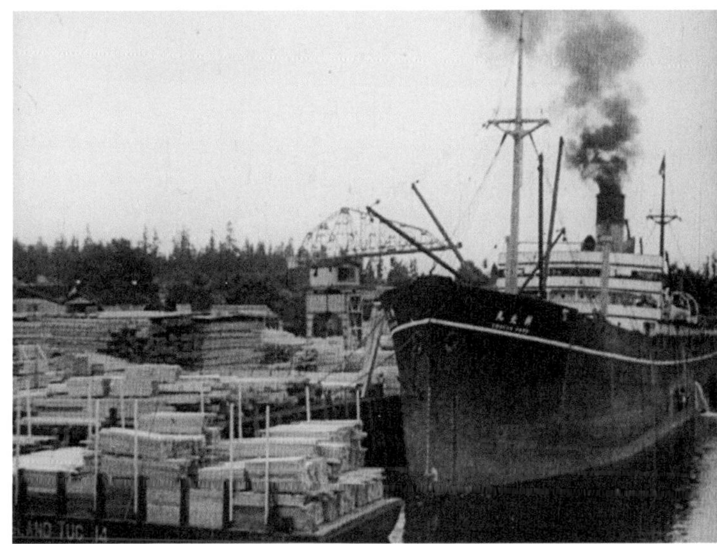

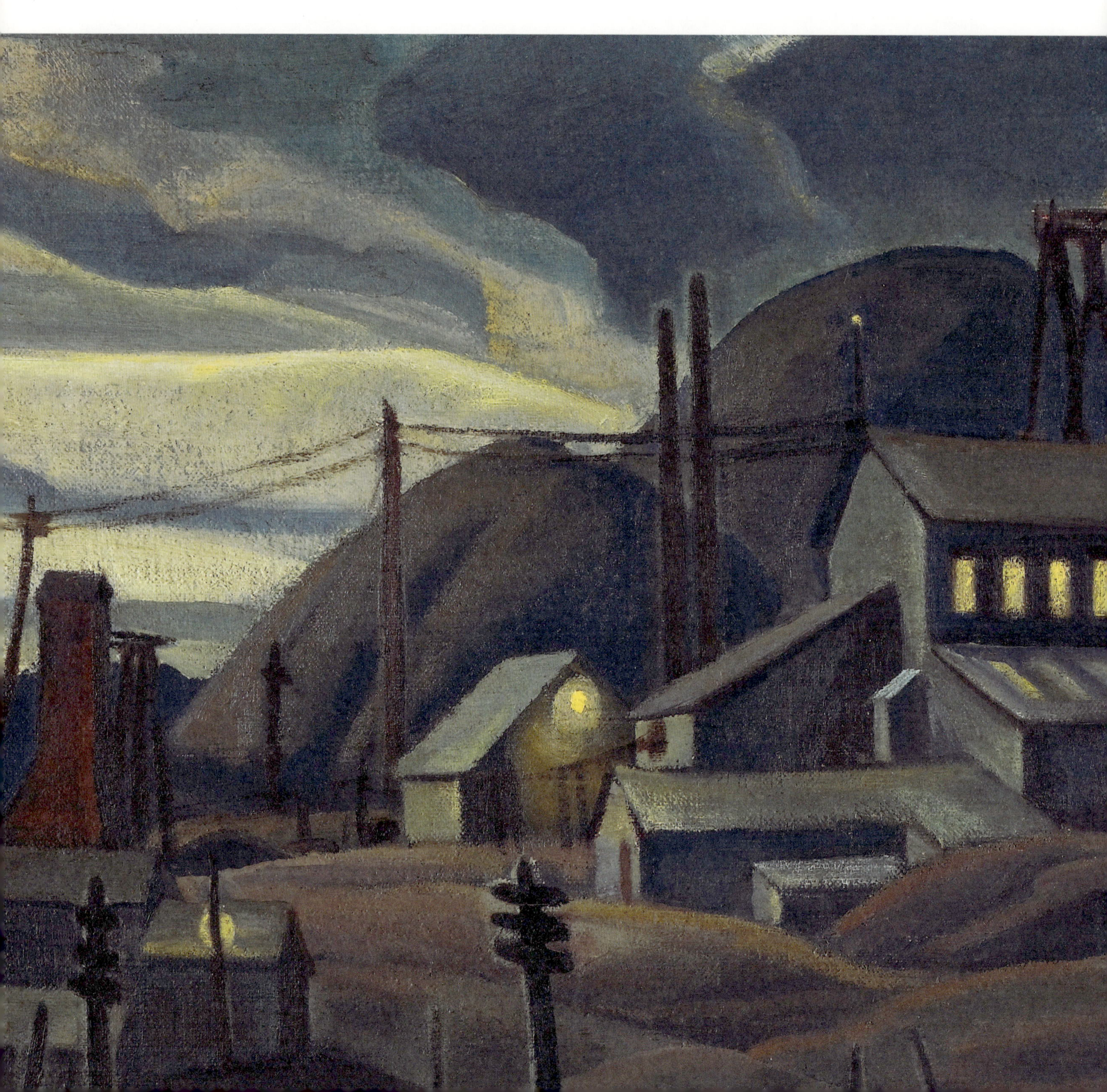

# Mining

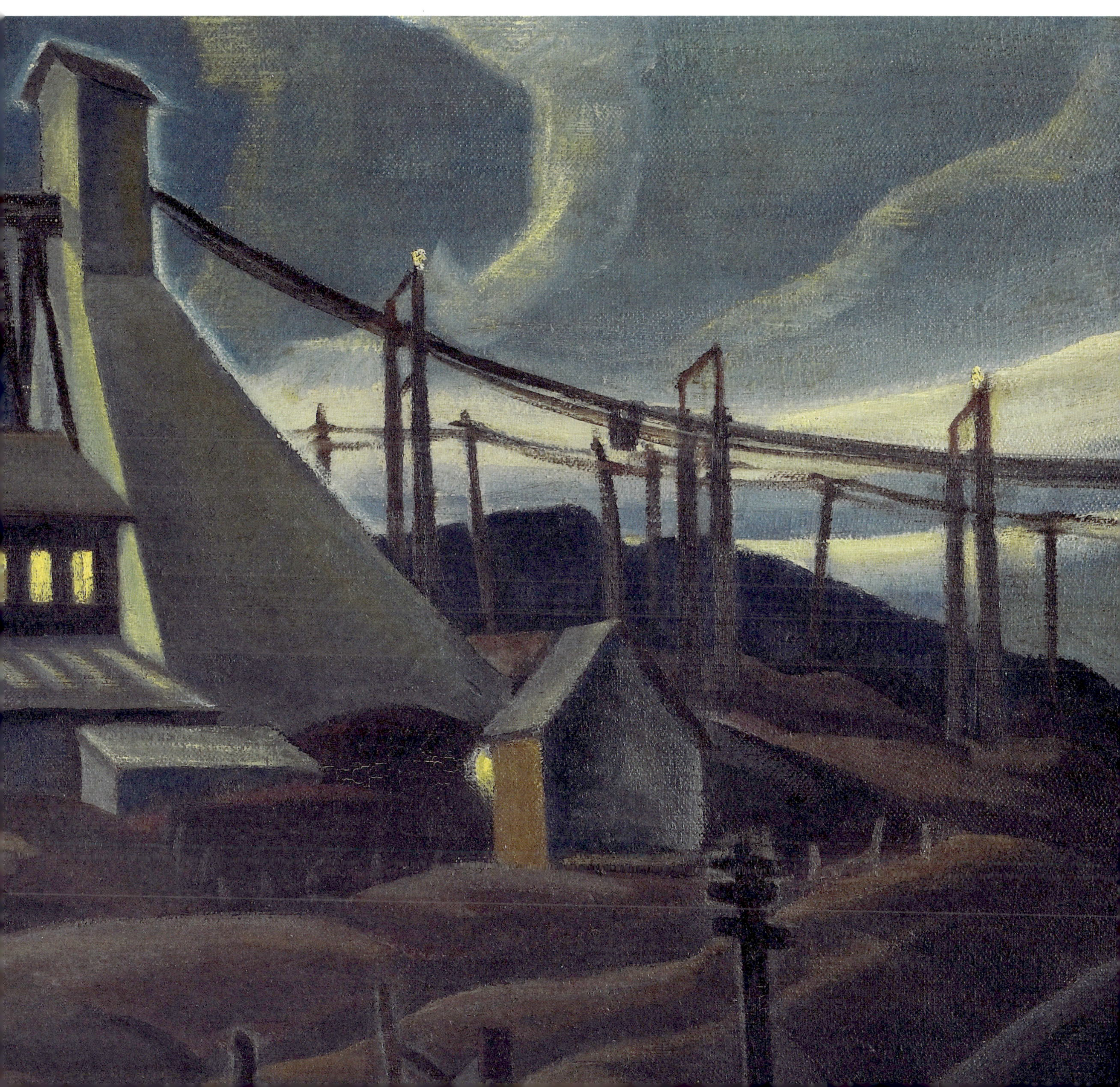

The industrialization of Canada was already undergoing a rapid boom at the end of the nineteenth century in the course of the second global wave of the Industrial Revolution. The mining of natural resources in particular accelerated the advent of a modern era that would guarantee the prosperity of society, while also signifying the shift from an agrarian to an industrial nation. Mining supplied industrial society with the raw materials of iron ore, copper, nickel, gold, and silver that it craved.

"This treasure-laden wilderness … will inform our literature and art with a spirit of its own … commerce and art are becoming allies," wrote a prominent supporter of the Group of Seven.[1] The pictures of this altered landscape, of mines and mining towns, to some extent belie the notion that Canada was characterized above all by vast, isolated regions and unspoiled wilderness—a myth that the Group was often accused of creating. The real irony is found in the imaginary quality of this vision, for: "Wilderness and capitalist modernity in Canada went hand in hand."[2]

Some pictures do actually reflect the complex role of art in the discrepancy between the myth of the wilderness and of industrialization. Yvonne McKague Housser captured the dreariness of abandoned cobalt mines following the legendary Silver Rush. Franklin Carmichael depicted *A Northern Silver Mine* (1930) as an almost cheerful scene with clear lines and cold precision. Little of the much-vaunted belief in progress and the trust in an inexhaustible wealth of the wilderness can be seen in Lawren Harris's paintings *Miners' Houses, Glace Bay* (ca. 1925) and *Ontario Hill Town* (1926). The dramatic scenes, with their strong contrasts and plunging lines, instead call to mind the stage sets of early Expressionist films. Harris, who began his career in 1908 with street scenes of the poorer districts of Toronto, here found his way back to social issues. In April 1925, during the bitter coal mining strike, he visited Glace Bay in Nova Scotia, at times to report for the *Toronto Star.* His stylized, theatrical pictures go beyond that idyll, yet they also avoid depicting the living conditions of miners in a realistic way. One thing unites the different genres: just like the pictures of nature, of the mountains and forests, the industrialized landscapes are generally also uninhabited.

Martina Weinhart

1—Vincent Massey, "Art and Nationality in Canada," in *Proceedings of the Royal Society of Canada,* 3rd series, XXIV (1930), p. lxif.
2—John O'Brian, "Wild Art History," in *Beyond Wilderness: The Group of Seven, Canadian Identity and Contemporary Art,* ed. John O'Brian and Peter White (Montreal: McGill-Queen's University Press, 2007), p. 22.

Franklin Carmichael
*In the Nickel Belt,* 1928
102.2 × 122.2 cm

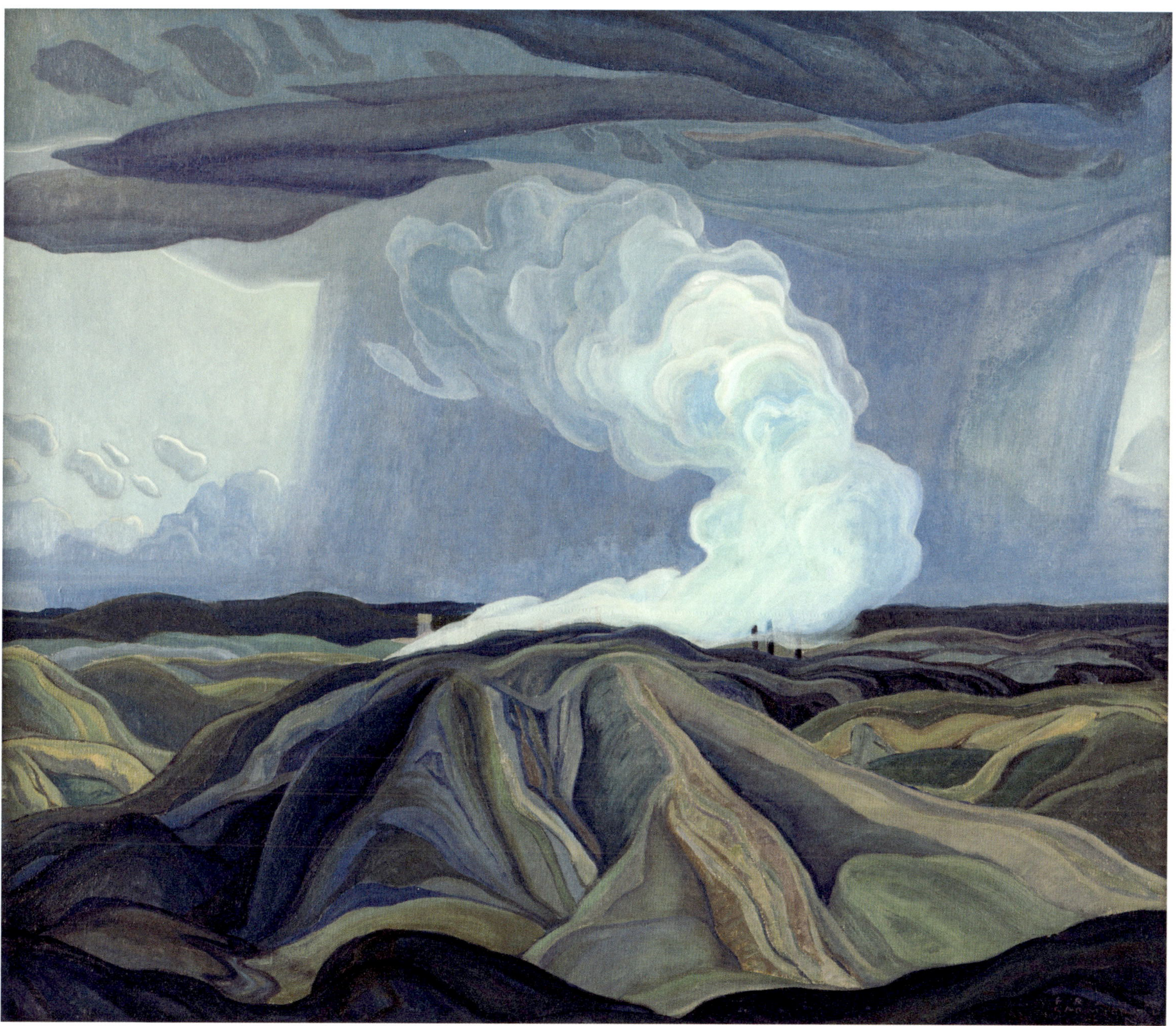

Franklin Carmichael
*A Northern Silver Mine,* 1930
101.5 × 121.2 cm

In his review of the Group of Seven's 1928 exhibition, the critic Fred Jacob wrote that Franklin Carmichael had "given up the purely decorative, in which he used to excel," choosing instead to interpret the "grim features of Canadian life," as evinced by *In the Nickel Belt* (p. 193), a work infused with "forbidding feeling."[1] Although Jacob was favorably commenting on the new direction in Carmichael's work, what he describes as the dark side of Canadian life was a key component of the nation's prosperity at the time. Indeed, the importance of mining was widely documented in a growing array of Canadian publications and promotional materials. Carmichael himself played a significant role in producing images promoting the country's advancing modernization and industrialization, both through his work at the advertising agency Grip Limited and, later, at the print company Sampson-Matthews. Yet in his paintings he offered a different view on the mining industry.

In the early twentieth century, mining in Canada epitomized industrial modernity, though the practice was also associated with greed, conflict, and environmental destruction.[2] Formed 1.85 billion years ago by the impact of an asteroid, the Sudbury Basin in Northern Ontario near Lake Huron is especially rich in metal deposits. It was here that large companies like the International Nickel Company of Canada and Falconbridge settled around 1900 to mine copper and nickel on a large scale. At the end of the 1920s,

Franklin Carmichael took several trips to this area and deftly captured the landscapes he found.

The artist chose an elevated point of view for his depictions of the region, which allows the viewer to gaze across smooth, rounded hills into the distance. Interventions in the landscape are evident only in a few elements. *In the Nickel Belt* shows a large plume of smoke rising from the distant smokestacks, yet the actual industrial site remains hidden. In *A Northern Silver Mine,* the mining towers and factories, grouped around a body of water, are quiet and deserted. The crystalline forms and sweeping view aestheticize a landscape into which the industry both blends and intrudes. The huge smoke cloud and the mining towers cut into the beautiful nature and offer some mild criticism of the impact on the environment in Carmichael's paintings.

Rebecca Herlemann

1—Fred Jacob, "In the Art Galleries," *Toronto Mail and Empire,* February 18, 1928, as quoted by Charles C. Hill, *The Group of Seven: Art for a Nation,* exh. cat. National Gallery of Canada, Ottawa, Art Gallery of Ontario, Toronto et al. (Toronto: McClelland & Stewart, 1995), p. 325, cat. 106.
2—See Rosemary Donegan, "Modernism and the Industrial Imagination: Copper Cliff and the Sudbury Basin," in *Beyond Wilderness: The Group of Seven, Canadian Identity, and Contemporary Art,* ed. John O'Brian and Peter White (Montreal: McGill-Queen's University Press, 2007), p. 146.

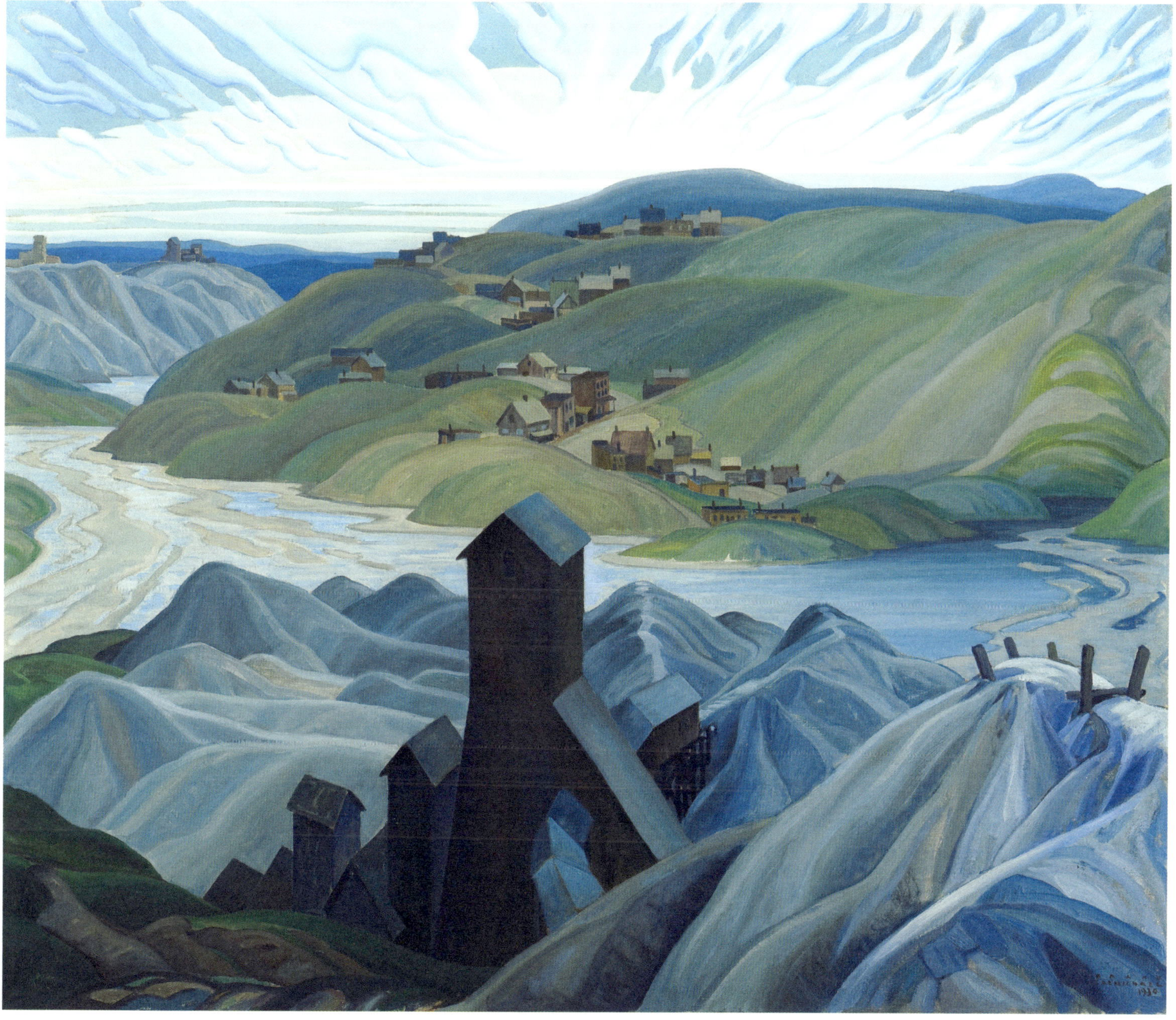

Yvonne McKague Housser
*Silver Mine, Evening,* 1932
61 × 76.2 cm

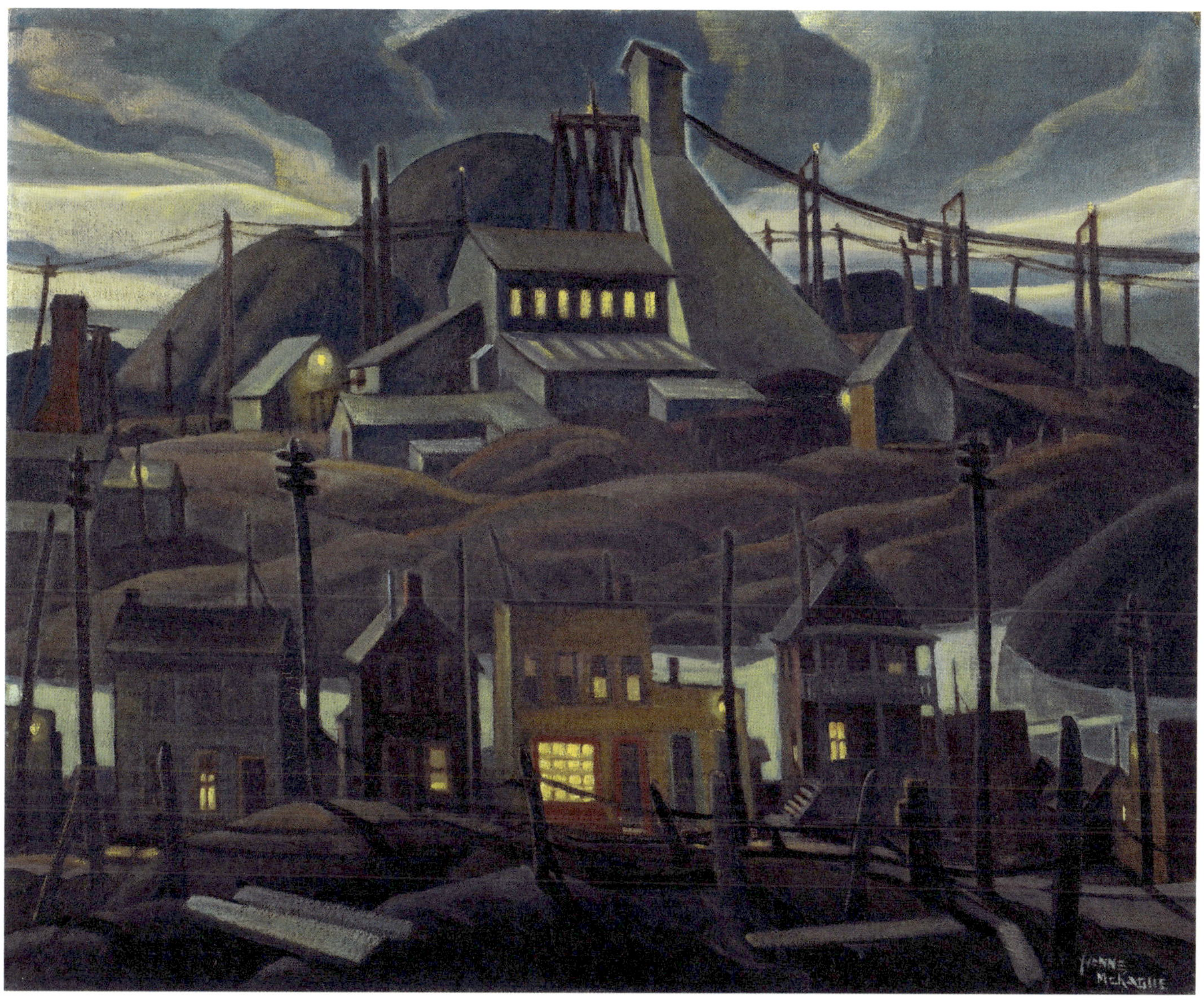

Yvonne McKague Housser
*Silver Mine, Cobalt,* 1930
77 × 89.5 cm

In the 1930s, when the artist Yvonne McKague Housser captured the town of Cobalt in her paintings, mining operations there had already come to an almost complete halt. As early as 1903, silver had been found in this area some 500 kilometers north of Toronto, and within a very short time numerous mines were established, with the town of Cobalt forming in their vicinity. Since the metal deposits were close to the surface, even inexperienced miners could try their luck here, and within a few years the area developed into the world's largest silver and cobalt mining region.[1] However, the worldwide economic crisis of 1929 caused the industry to falter, and Cobalt became a ghost town. Today, you can still visit the old, abandoned mines here.

Like many of her contemporaries, McKague Housser undertook numerous trips into the area north of Toronto looking for subjects. She visited Cobalt for the first time in 1917, becoming the first to discover its potential for artistic work.[2] She would return several times, including with her students from the Ontario College of Art where she taught from 1919 on. She portrayed Cobalt and other mining towns in many variations, in both day and night scenes (p.197). "For me, unlikely as it may seem, there is something romantic about a mining shaft against a northern sky with silver and black clouds racing by, and about the big, mountain-like slag heaps beside the buildings, and all reflected in a large pond or little lake. When dusk begins and the night shift carried [*sic*] lanterns whose tiny lights pinpoint the night, everything is mysterious and asks to be painted."[3]

In painterly terms, her canvases share similarities with those of the Group of Seven, with whom she exhibited from 1928 on.[4] She, too, went out in the field, painting landscapes in modern styles and vivid colors, but in her images of mining towns she eschewed depicting seemingly unspoiled nature, instead focusing on the industry's impact on the landscape. She also invariably hinted at the presence of people; the lit windows of the houses suggest that there is life behind them, and in some works individual miners can be seen. McKague Housser projected a romanticizing image of a once thriving industry, which earned her the appreciation of her contemporaries. One commentator even went so far as to identify her telephone poles and mine elevators as the objects that, in the 1930s, had replaced spruce, larch, and pine as symbols of the Nordic landscape.[5]

Rebecca Herlemann

1—S. A. Pain, *Three Miles of Gold: The Story of Kirkland Lake* (Toronto: Ryerson Press, 1960), pp.2-3.
2—Alicia Boutilier, "Mapping an Artist's Identity: The Life, Work and Writing of Yvonne McKague Housser" (master's thesis, Carleton University, Ottawa, 1998), p.73.
3—Yvonne McKague Housser, "Mining Country," *Northward Journal: A Quarterly of Northern Arts* 16 (June 1980), p.21, as quoted in Boutilier, "Mapping an Artist's Identity," p.141.
4—Charles C. Hill, *The Group of Seven: Art for a Nation,* exh. cat. National Gallery of Canada, Ottawa, Art Gallery of Ontario, Toronto et al. (Toronto: McClelland & Stewart, 1995), p.208.
5—John Flood, "Yvonne McKague Housser: Northern Moments," *Northward Journal: A Quarterly of Northern Arts* 16 (June 1980), pp.10-20, esp. p.14.

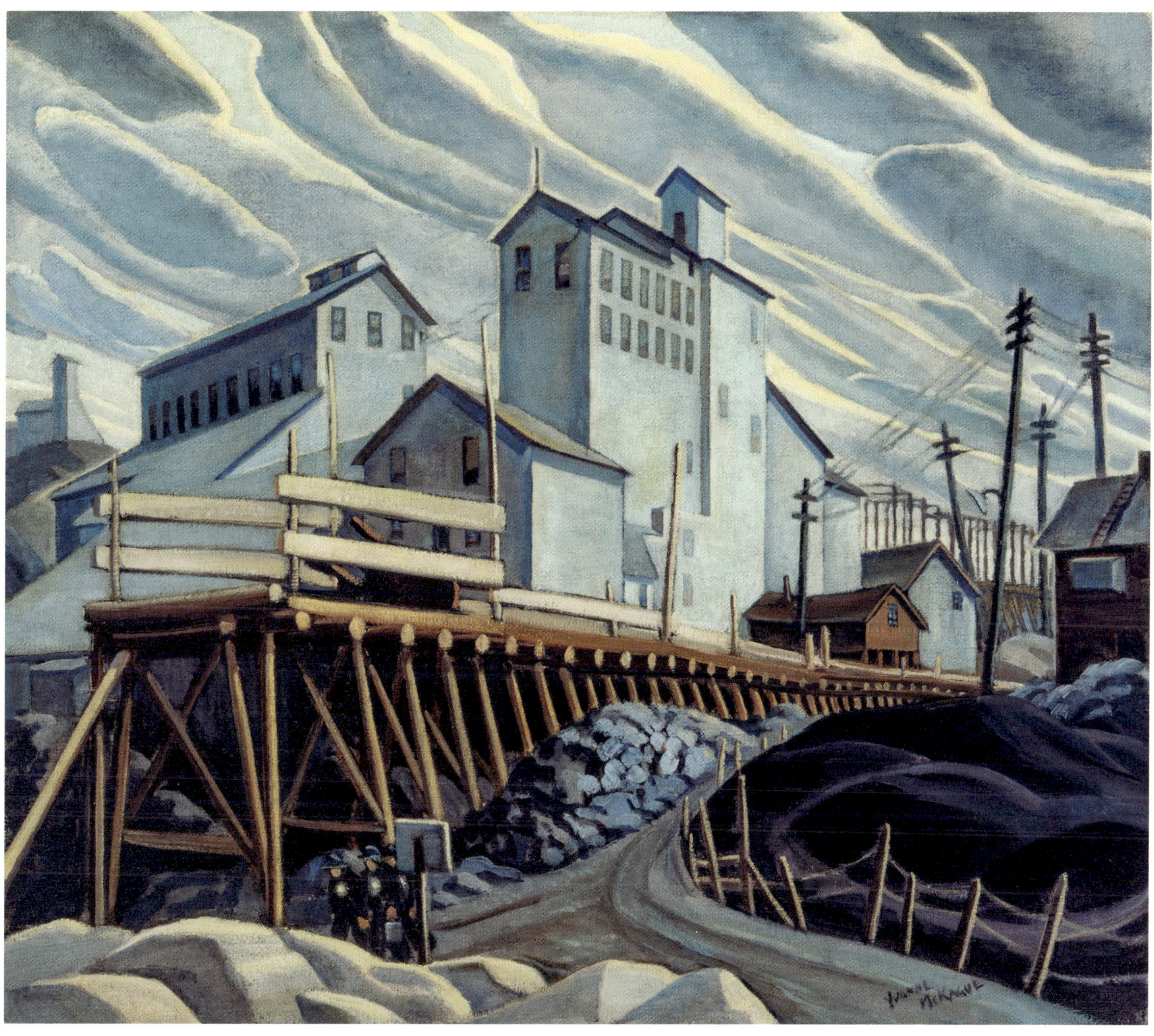

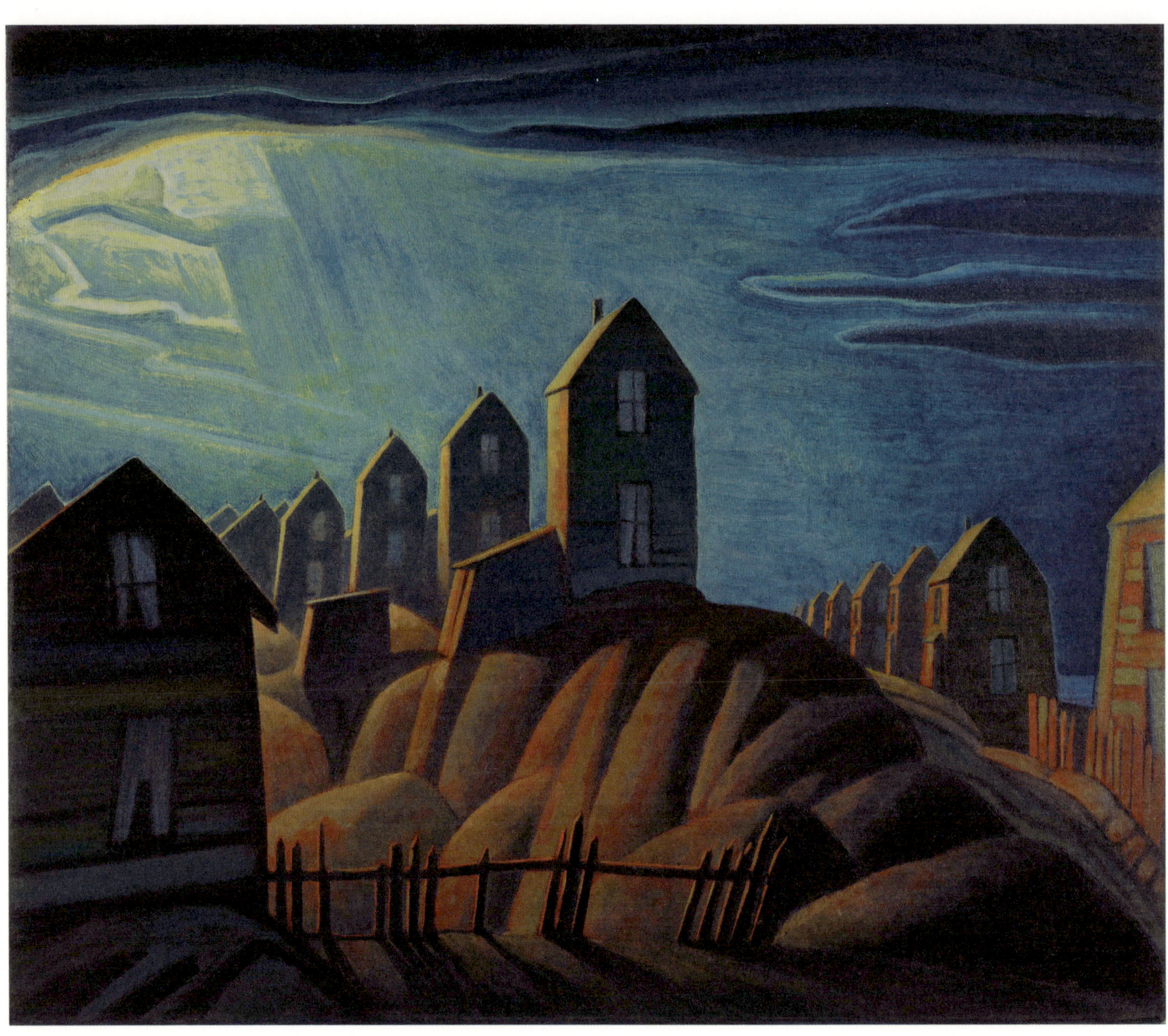

Lawren Harris
*Miners' Houses, Glace Bay*, ca. 1925
107.3 × 127 cm

Lawren Harris
*Ontario Hill Town*, 1926
85.7 × 102.8 cm

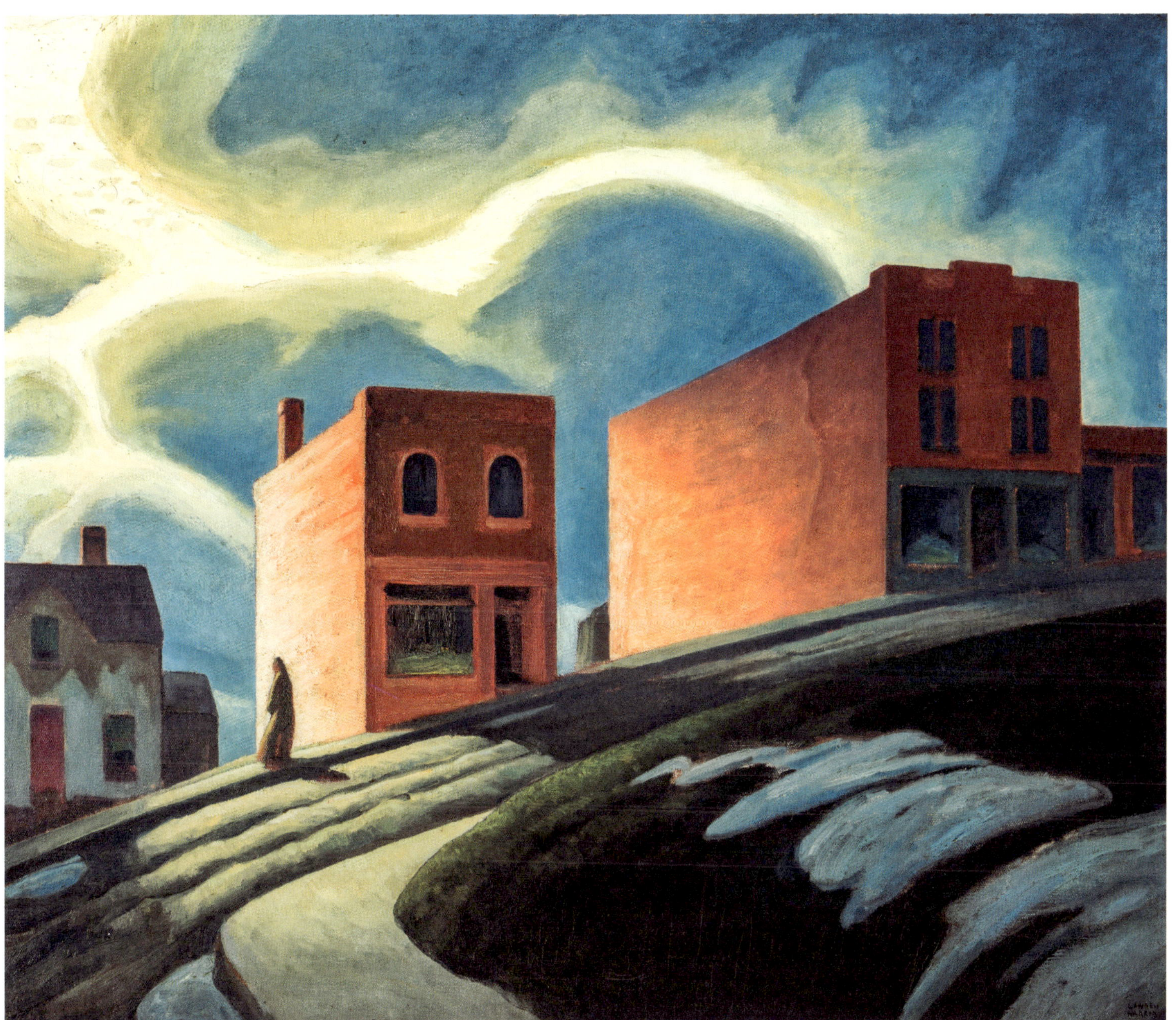

# Northern

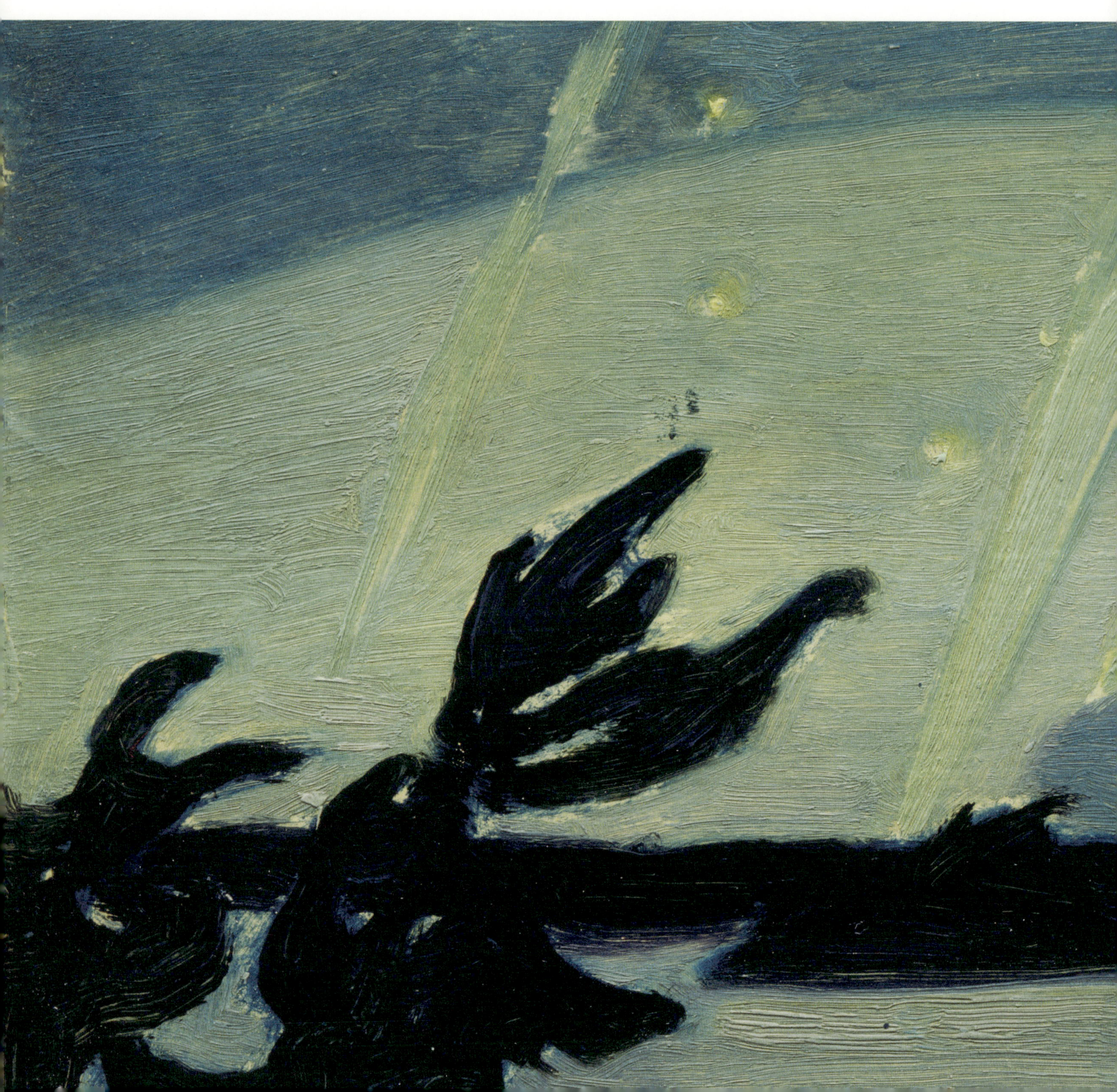

# Lights

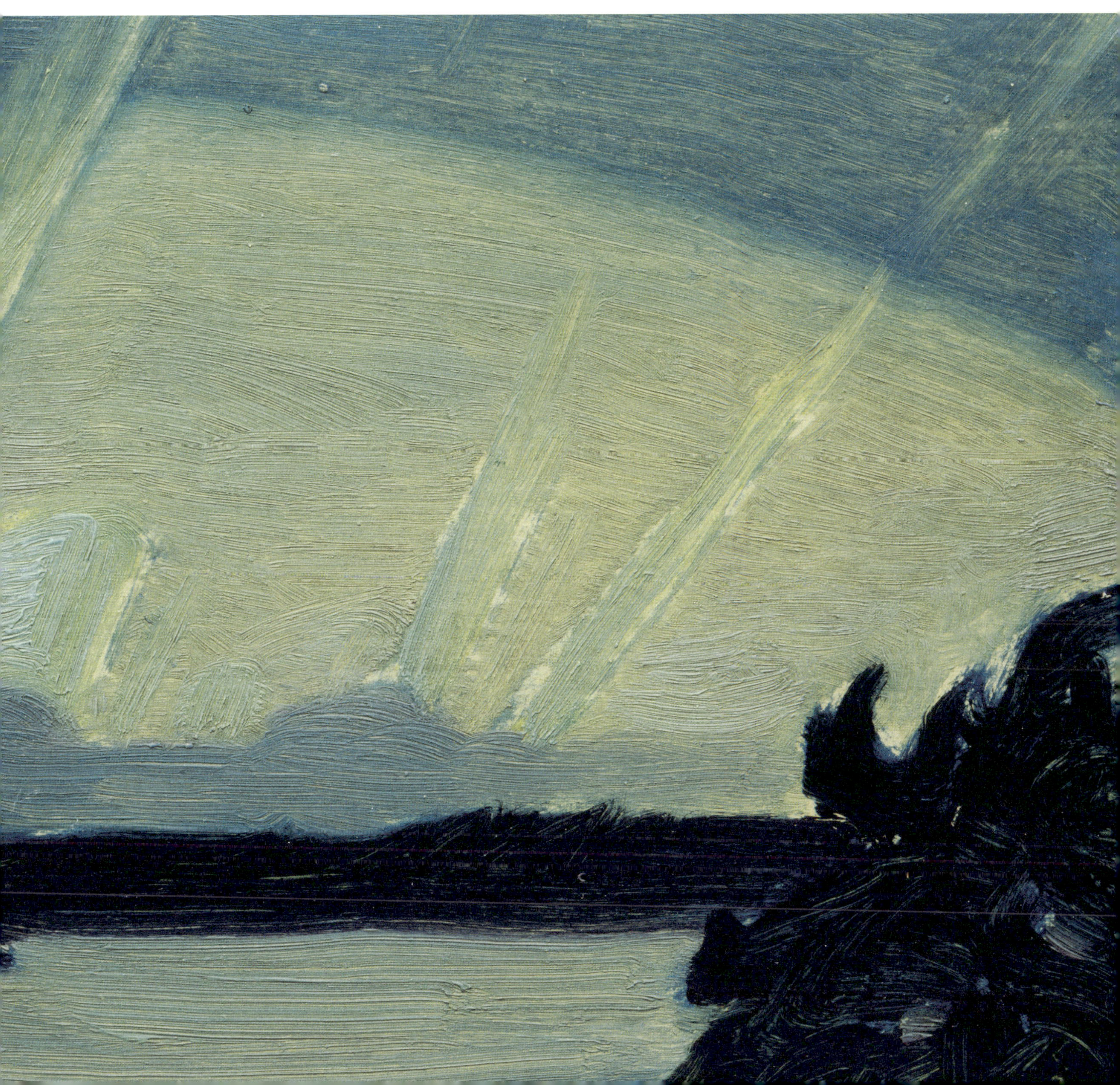

The concept of the North developed analogously to that of the Wild West in the United States and is central to a concept of Canadian identity based historically on a fascination with the remote regions of the country and, in terms of motifs, defined by the wilderness and the Arctic in particular. This fascination is expressed not least in pictures of the northern lights (aurora borealis). The northern lights occur due to the interplay of solar winds and the Earth's magnetosphere. Related scientific theories were developed in the nineteenth century, but the phenomenon, which can take on a wide range of forms, has not been rigorously examined until recently—an aspect that contributes to the almost mystic effect of the northern lights, around which numerous legends have sprung up. Some Inuit regarded them as spirits of the dead playing ball with a walrus skull. Others feared them as lanterns of demons pursuing lost souls, or they were believed to be a luminous, divine being, watching over the well-being of his people. The northern lights also frequently represent a bridge to the hereafter.

Painting's gaze into the cosmos also opens up the transcendental qualities of the northern lights. They play with the association of the otherworldly in a dramatic way, afford an opportunity for artistic experiments, and frequently verge on abstraction. Sometimes the northern lights seem to dance, yet other times they appear as green lights or hang curtains of light over the dark sky, such as in A. Y. Jackson's *Aurora* (1927). In turn, J. E. H. MacDonald cast his *Northern Lights* (1915–16) in various nuances of blue. These pictures of great simplicity can often barely be connected with the representational, and they search for the spiritual meaning behind the abstraction. Tom Thomson captured the northern lights in various versions again and again, for the first time in 1914. In Thomson's sketches, which bubble with the pleasure of experimentation—as well as in his oeuvre as a whole—pictures of the northern lights are arguably the most innovative ones. They develop a powerful expressiveness as a result of their bold, impasto brushstrokes. There also seems to be a particular kinship with German Romanticism, but they nonetheless speak of the feeling of being overwhelmed by the immeasurable. We encounter a radiance that virtually comes to us from the afterlife of the picture.

Martina Weinhart

A. Y. Jackson
*Aurora*, 1927
54 × 66.7 cm

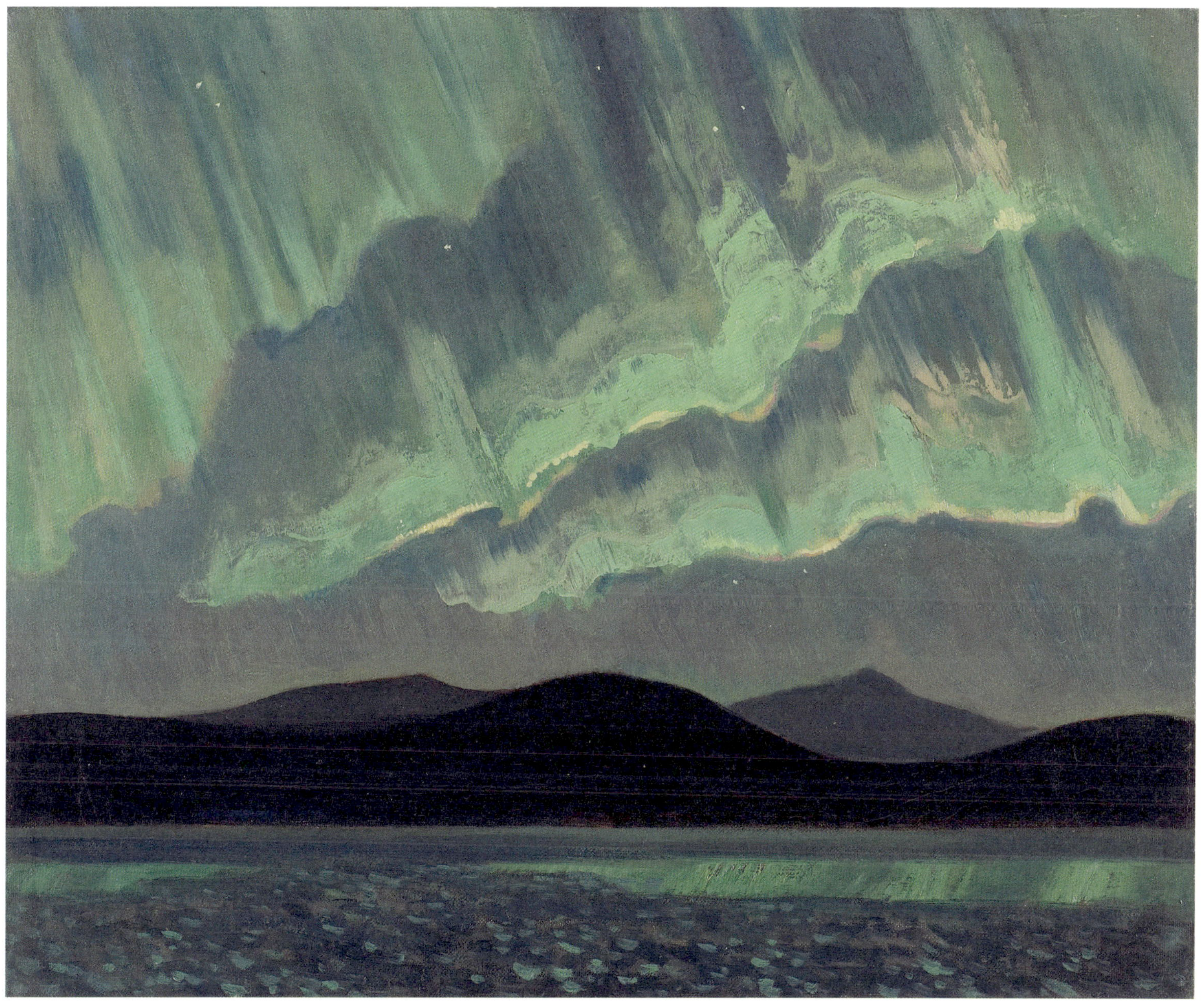

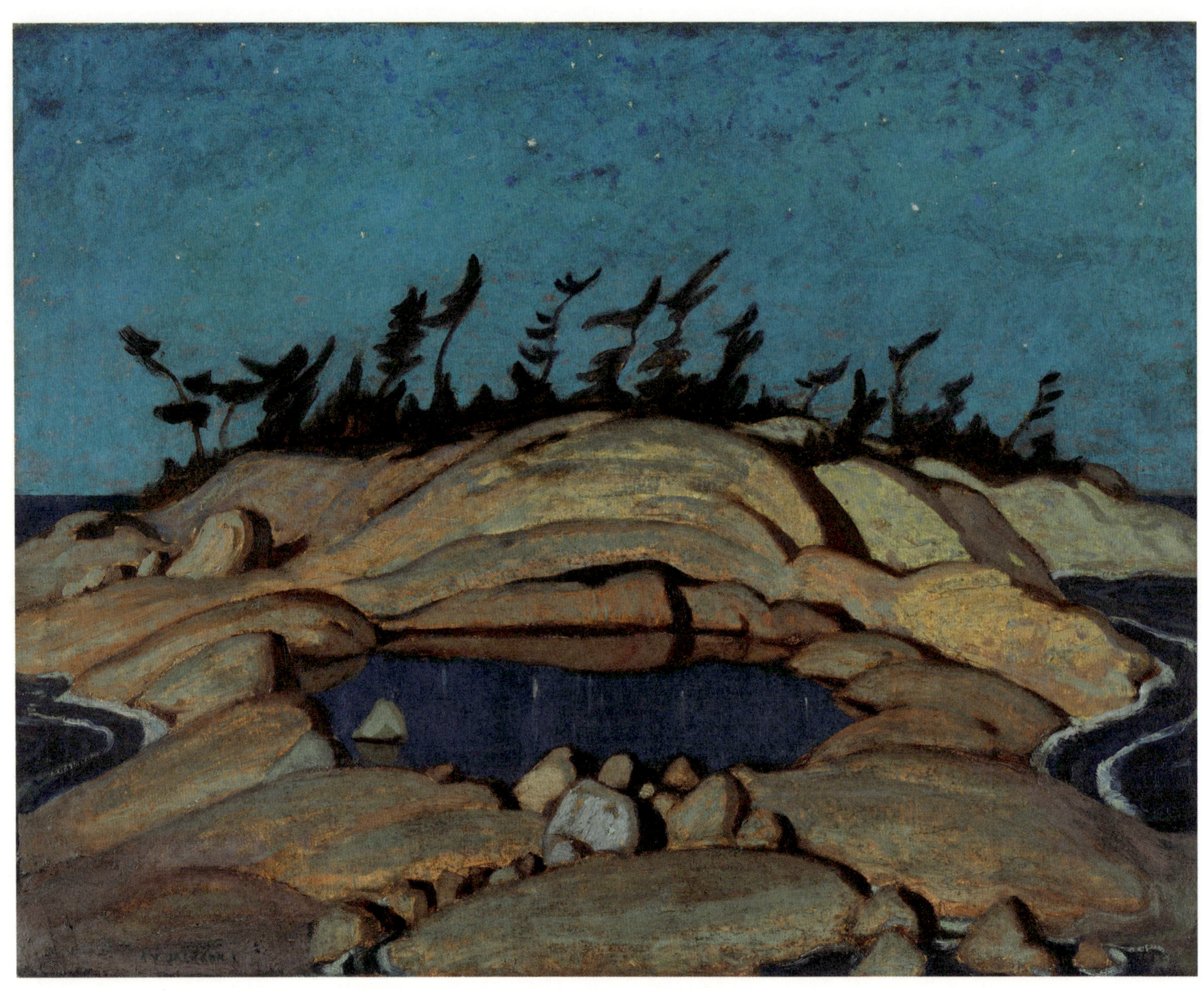

A.Y. Jackson
*Night, Pine Island*, 1924
64.2 × 81.5 cm

J.E.H. MacDonald
*Aurora, Georgian Bay, Pointe au Baril*, 1931
21.5 × 26.7 cm

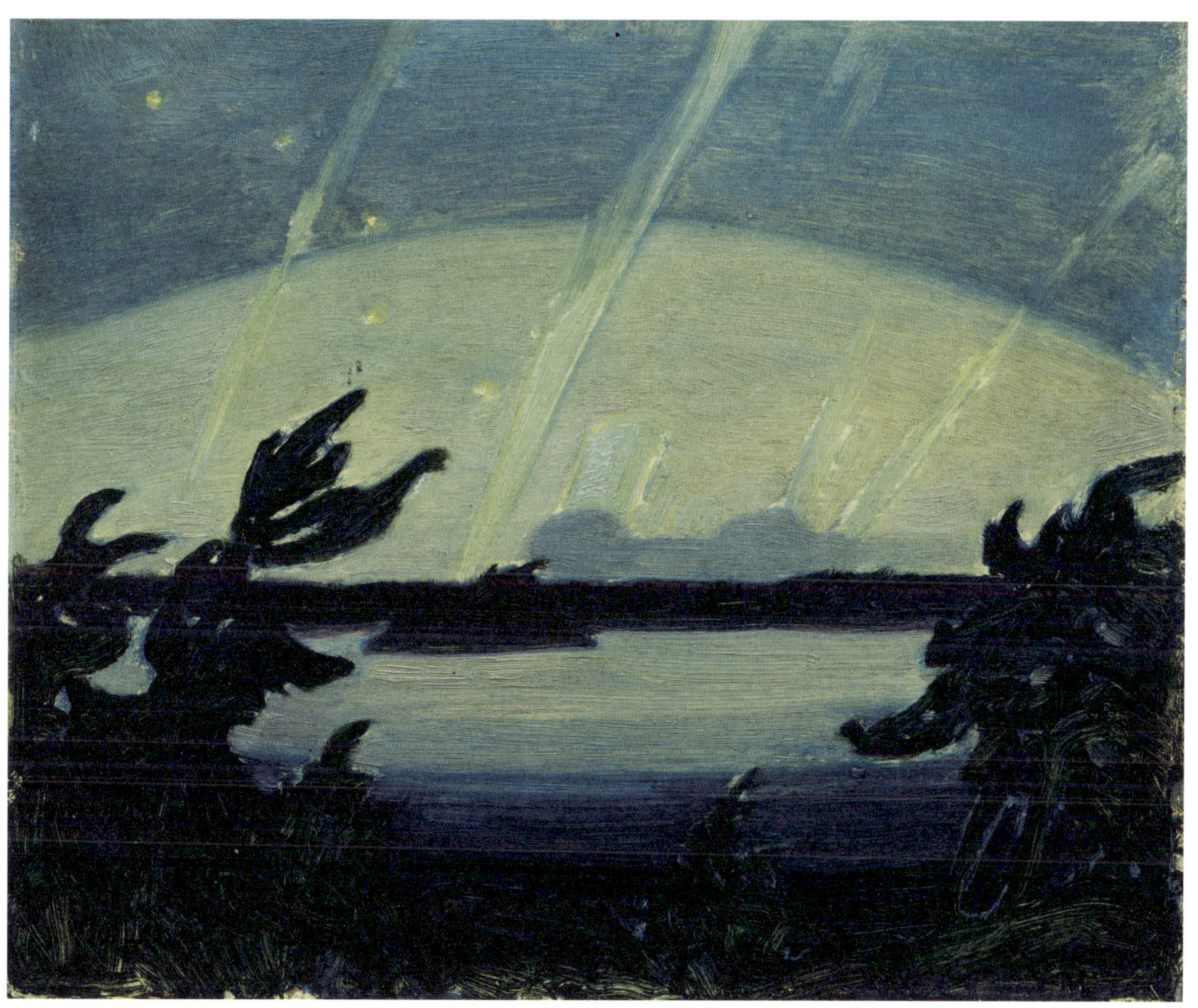

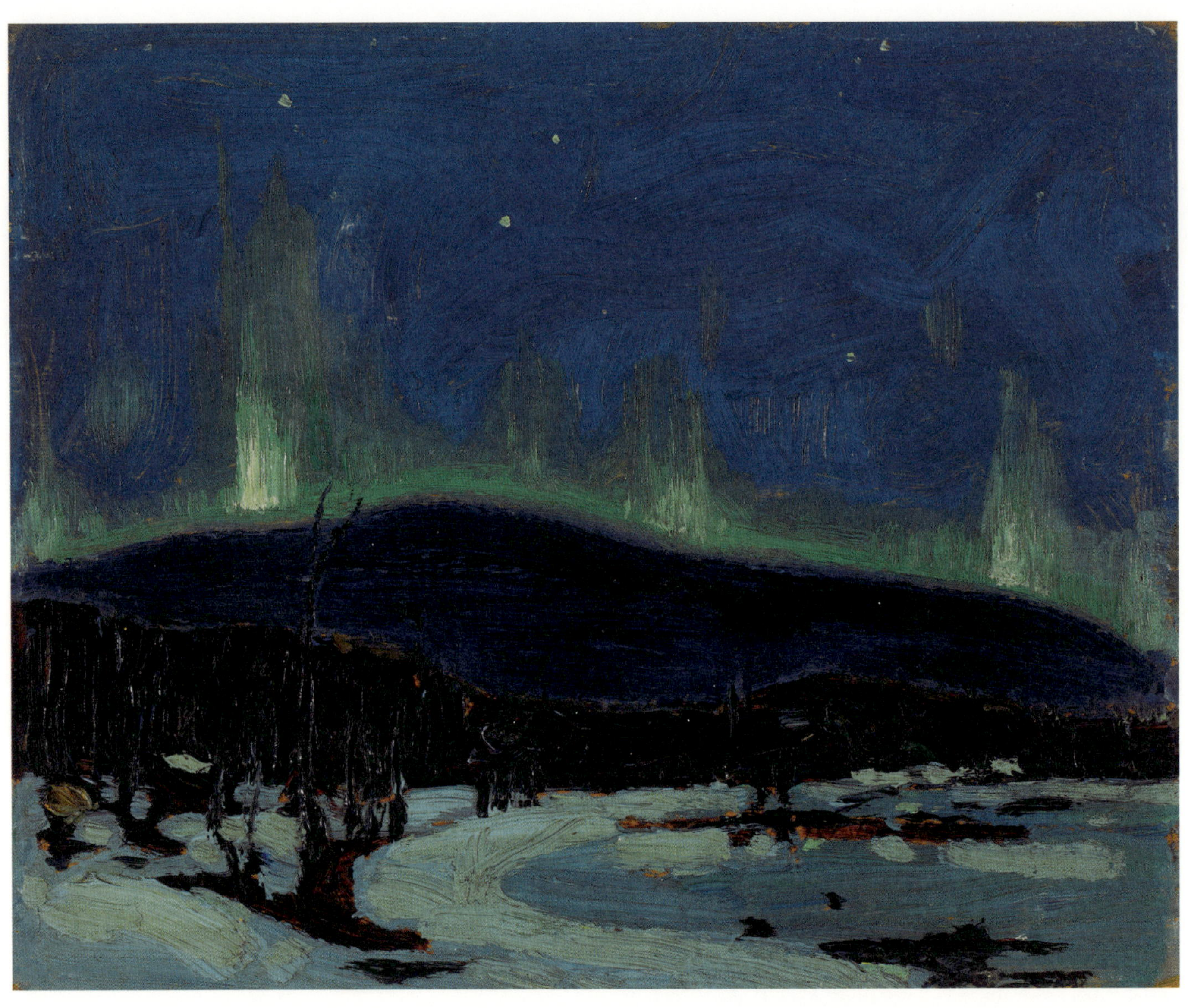

Tom Thomson
*Northern Lights,* spring 1917
21.5 × 26.7 cm

Tom Thomson
*Northern Lights,* summer 1915
21.6 × 26.7 cm

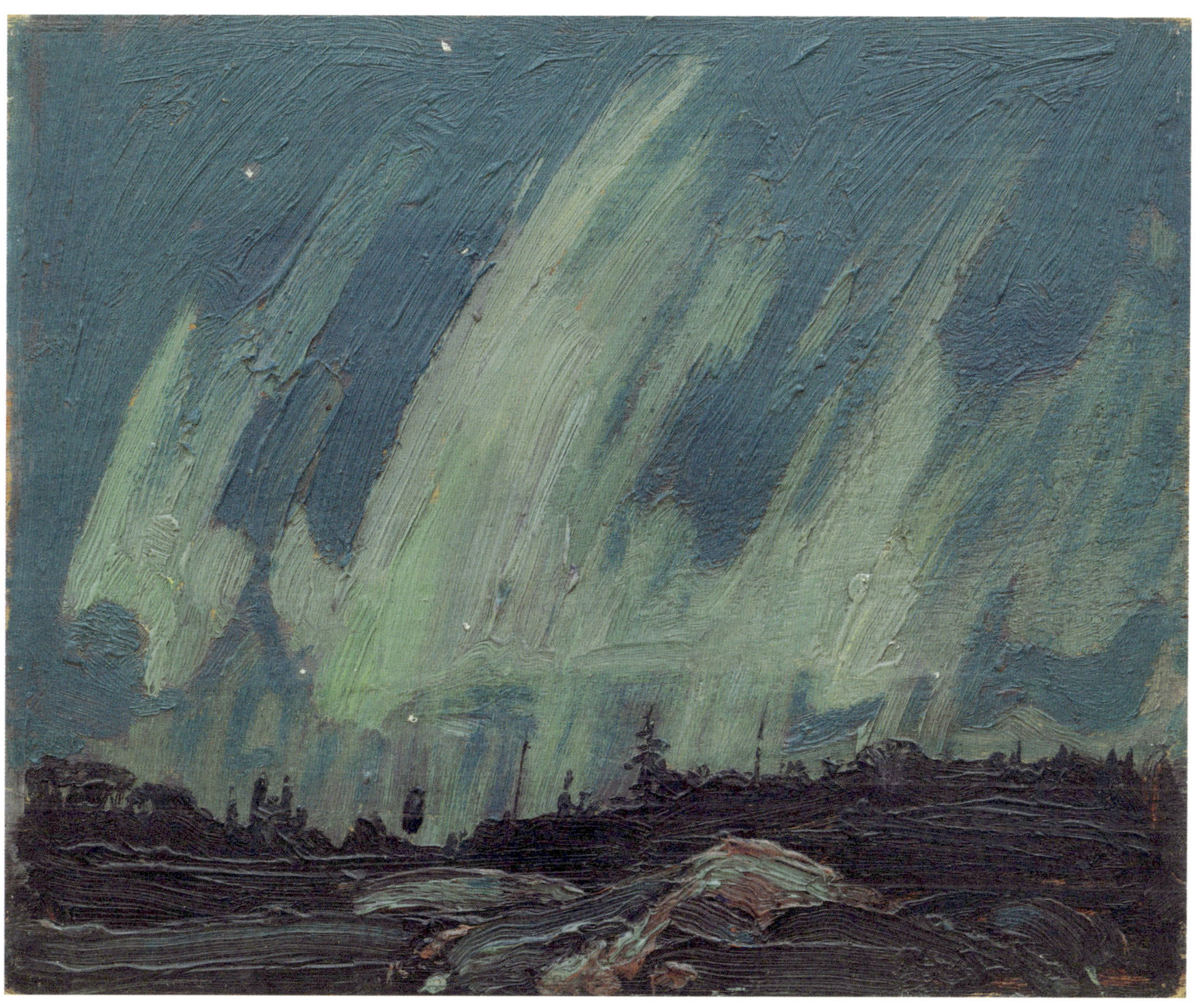

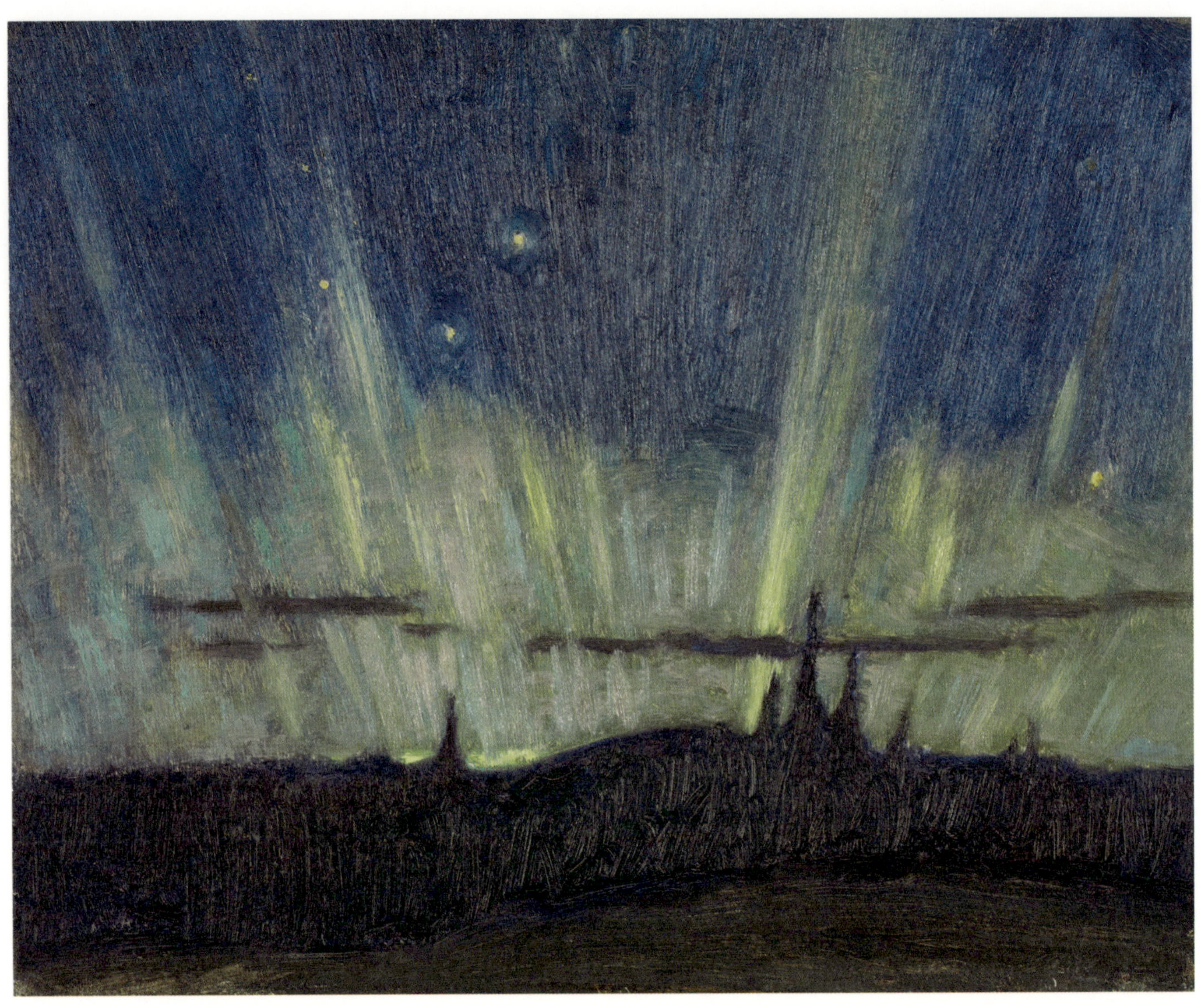

J. E. H. MacDonald
*Northern Lights,* 1915–16
20.2 × 25.4 cm

Tom Thomson
*Northern Lights,* spring 1916
21.6 × 26. cm

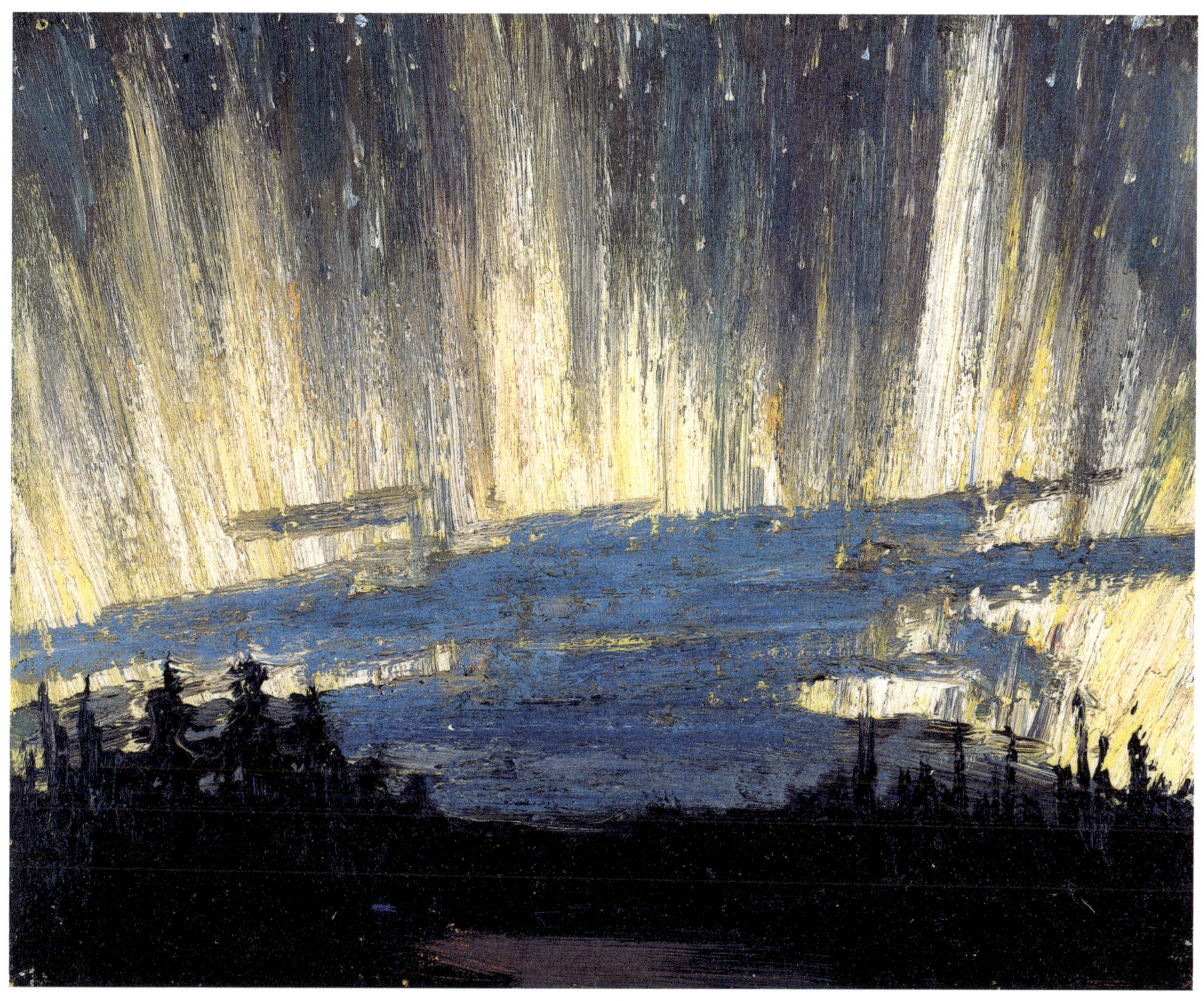

Northern Lights

# The Single

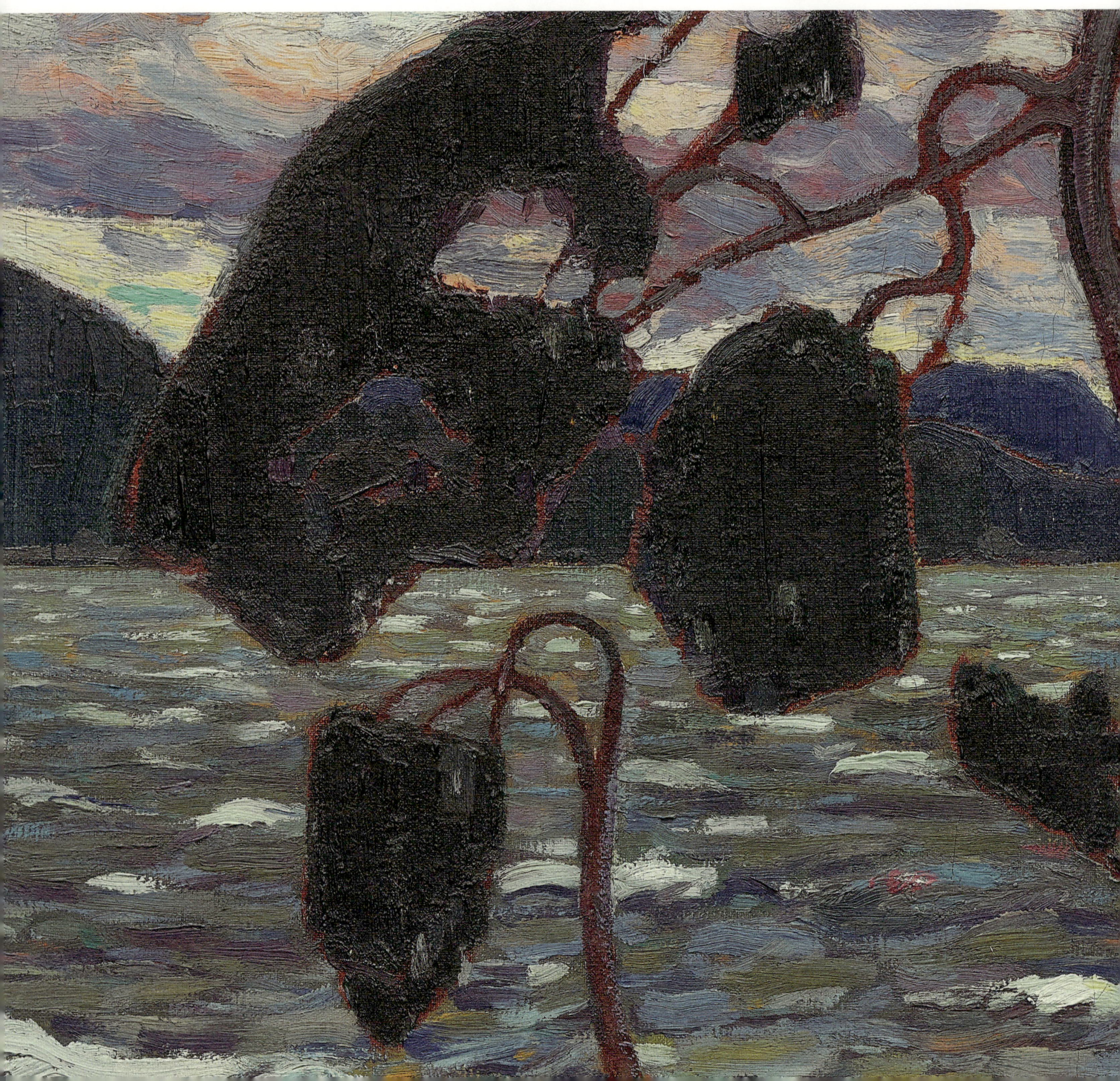

# Tree

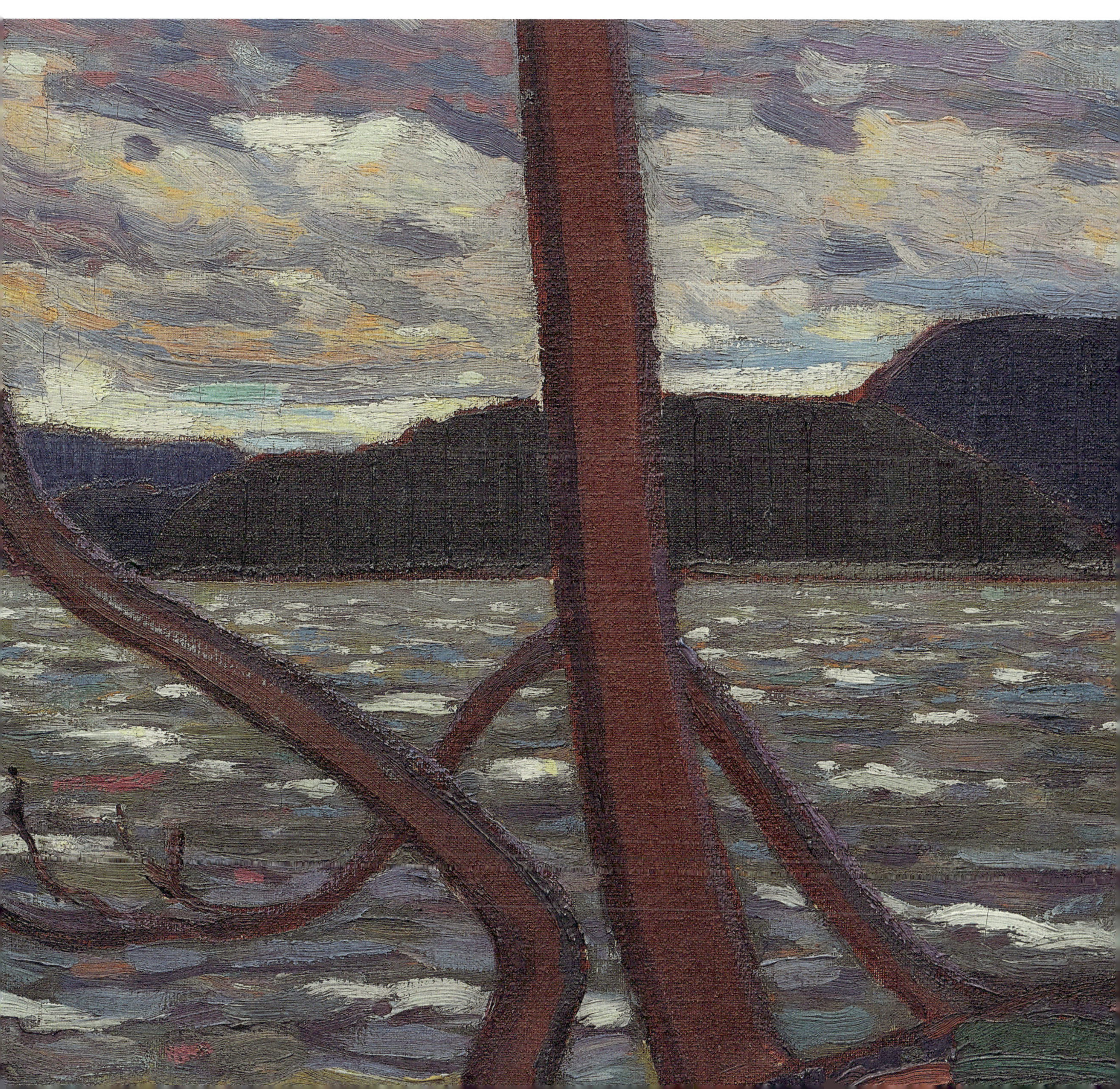

The image of a solitary tree silhouetted against a darkening sky and threatening clouds—its roots clinging to the archetypal granite rock of the Canadian Shield on the edge of a cold lake— has become emblematic of the rugged yet steadfast Canadian settler identity. Resilient and unyielding, the pine endures and thrives in its harsh setting. It bends in the wind but does not break. The romance of a single tree, rooted in a long European tradition, was reimagined in Canada in the 1910s and 1920s as a symbol of a young nation coming into its own cultural identity.

Seeking to capture the country's distinctive natural features, Canadian modern painters sought to create a new pictorial vocabulary that awakened a sense of authenticity and pride. Trekking across lakes and hills, the windswept tree emerging from a rocky shore was a familiar, inspiring sight. It was exemplified by Tom Thomson in one of his last canvases, *The West Wind* (winter 1916–17)—a painting that traveled extensively nationally and internationally. Over the past century, it has been reproduced in any given medium, solidifying the mythical status of the lone Canadian pine. Stylized nearing abstraction, Thomson's depiction of the tree introduced a seductive visual language and unmistakable emblem. After his death, Thomson's contemporaries further pursued this singular image, creating elegiac canvases such as Arthur Lismer's *Evening Silhouette Georgian Bay* (1928) and Franklin Carmichael's monumental jack pine in *The Upper Ottawa, near Mattawa* (1924).

Georgiana Uhlyarik

Franklin Carmichael
*The Upper Ottawa, near Mattawa*, 1924
101.5 × 123.1 cm

The Single Tree

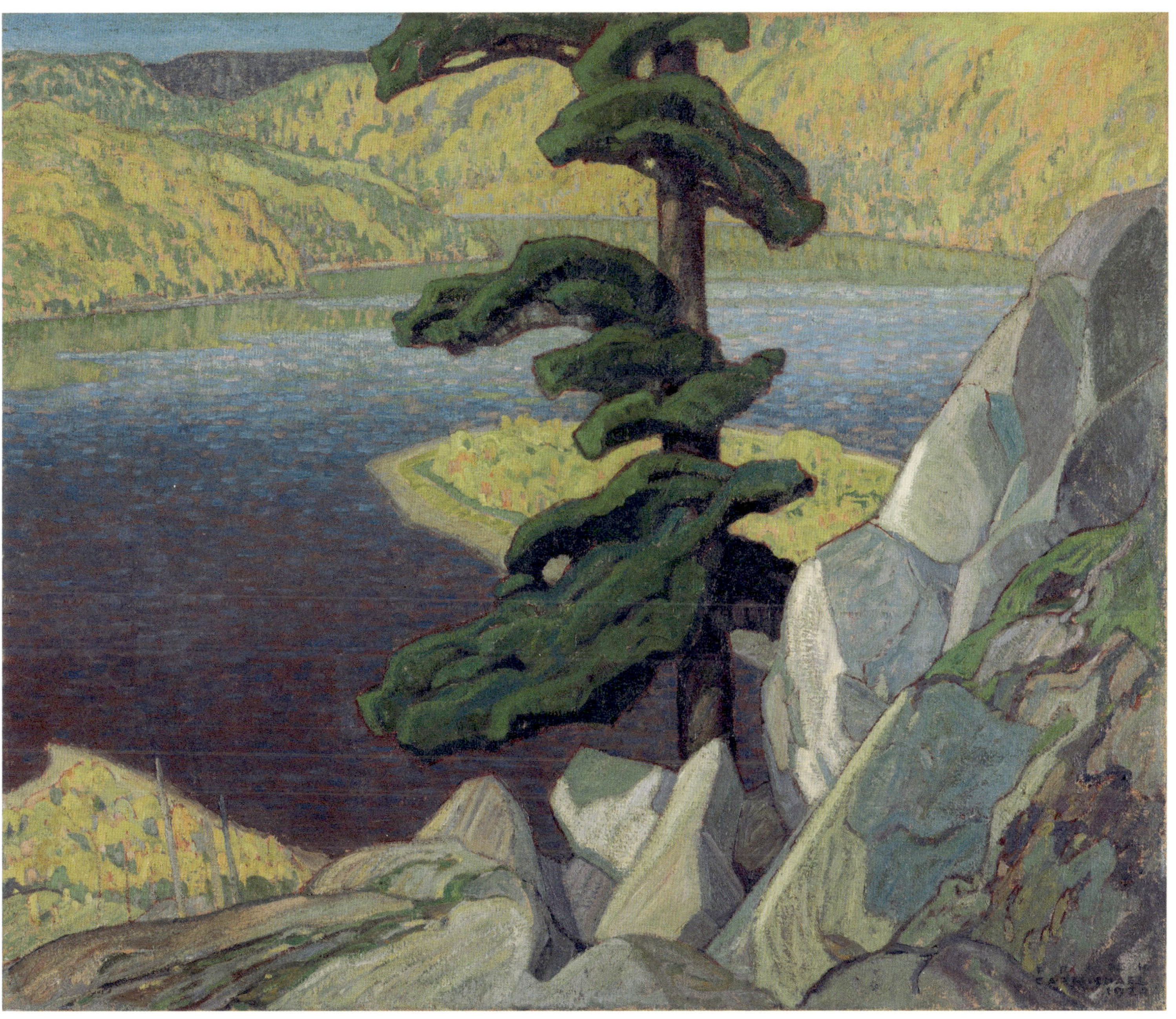

Arthur Lismer
*Evening Silhouette Georgian Bay,* 1928
80.3 × 100.8 cm

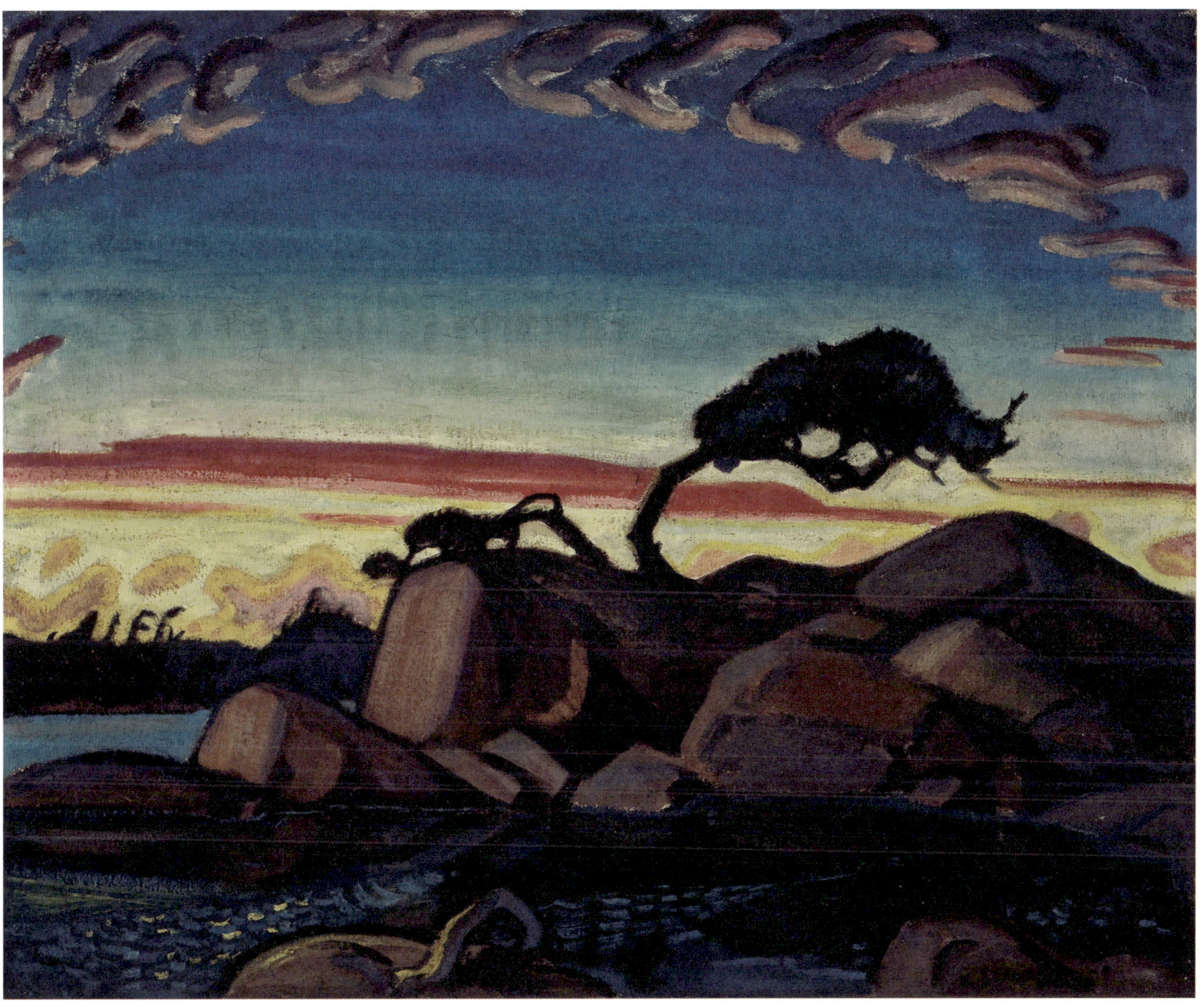

Tom Thomson
*The West Wind,* winter 1916–17
120.7 × 137.9 cm

One of Tom Thomson's last large-scale paintings, *The West Wind,* is based on a small sketch that he created in Algonquin Provincial Park, where he was known to spend his summers. It shows a single pine tree standing among the rocks along the edge of a lake. The cloudy sky and the whitecaps of the waves illustrate the windy weather. The artist used a variety of vibrant colors for the sky, the water is built up with small, broken strokes, and the rocks and mountains are styled as flat solids. The central pine winds decoratively with obvious Art Nouveau echoes. In some places, the primed canvas shines through and serves to contour the form of the pine.

The lone tree braving the storm is a very popular and charged symbol in Canadian art. In *The West Wind,* the figure of Tom Thomson is directly inscribed into this motif, as many considered him to be the quintessential landscape painter, facing the elements alone with his sketch box. His friend and fellow artist J. E. H. MacDonald stated the following in the emotional inscription of the memorial stone for Thomson that was erected at Canoe Lake in Algonquin Park: "He lived humbly but passionately with the wild. It made him brother to all untamed things of nature, it drew him apart and revealed itself wonderfully to him. It sent him out from the woods only to show these revelations through his art and it took him to itself at last."[1]

*The West Wind* quickly garnered a great deal of attention due to the circumstances of its making. In August 1917, shortly after its completion, the painter was found dead at Canoe Lake. To this day, theories and stories continue to swirl around his death and have likely contributed significantly to the painting's mythical status.[2] Due to his premature passing, Thomson was ultimately styled as a hero, and his painting *The West Wind* came to epitomize a new national sentiment: "the spirit of Canada made manifest in a picture," as Arthur Lismer put it.[3] Today, *The West Wind* is one of Thomson's most famous paintings and considered an icon of Canadian art.

Rebecca Herlemann

1—As quoted in Amy Concannon, ed., *Painting Canada: Tom Thomson and the Group of Seven,* exh. cat. Dulwich Picture Gallery, London, and National Gallery of Canada, Ottawa (London: Philip Wilson, 2011), p. 17.
2—See Gregory Klages, *The Many Deaths of Tom Thomson: Separating Fact from Fiction* (Toronto: Dundurn Press, 2016).
3—Arthur Lismer, "The West Wind," *The McMaster Monthly* 43 (January 1934), p. 163.

# The Single Tree

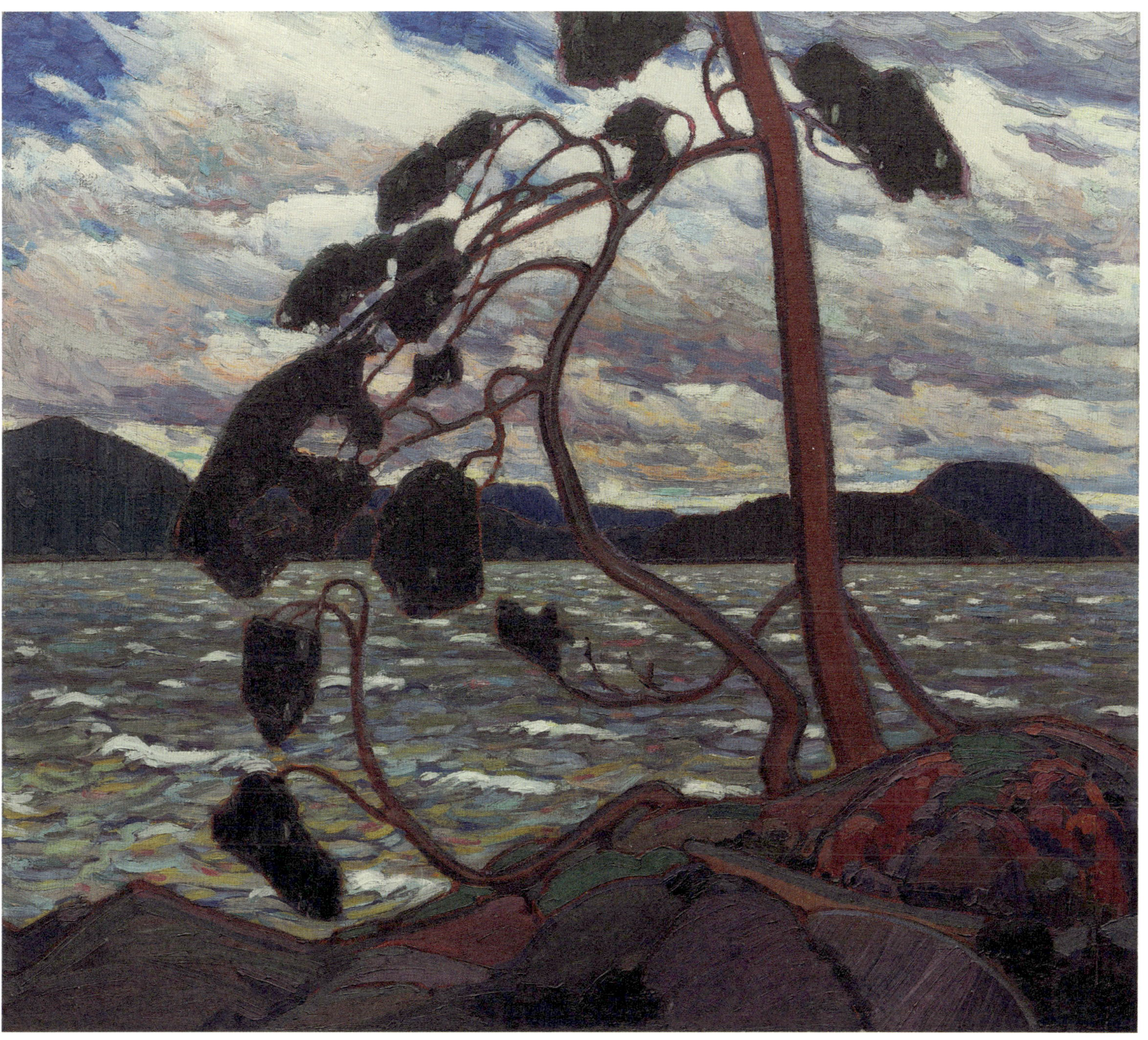

## Group of Seven

Established in Toronto in 1920, the Group of Seven was a collective of painters dedicated to a modern vision of the Canadian landscape. Their interpretations of the land were informed by Art Nouveau and post-Impressionism, and the belief that art-making should be inspired by direct contact with nature. Bold designs, lively rhythms, expressive brushwork, and energetic colors set their work apart from the academic style popular in Toronto at the time.

Three of the Group's original members were born and trained in England: Arthur Lismer, J. E. H. MacDonald, and Frederick Varley. The other four were born in Canada: Franklin Carmichael, Lawren Harris, A. Y. Jackson, and Frank Johnston. Two artists closely associated with (but not a part of) the Group of Seven were Tom Thomson and Emily Carr.

Although the Group members were primarily based in Toronto, their profound interest in nature propelled them northward. In 1918, several future members embarked on the famed boxcar trips to the Algoma Region in Northern Ontario, and later further along the north shore of Lake Superior. Traveling by train to remote painting locales, the artists lived out of an outfitted boxcar. These early trips fostered a kinship and collective enthusiasm for the land that led to the crystallization of the Group.

They were a highly organized and multifaceted collective, with economic prowess and international ambitions. Several members had a background in commercial art and understood the value of patronage and press. They lectured about and promoted their art, exhibiting extensively in Canada, as well as in England, France, and the United States, branding themselves with their own logo.

From the outset, public reaction to the Group was divided: their work garnered positive reviews as well as harsh criticism. To this day, there exists a divergence in opinion about the Group. While they remain highly popular in Canada, they are also scrutinized today for neglecting the realities of their time.

The Group of Seven's membership fluctuated over the years. A. J. Casson, Edwin Holgate, and Lionel LeMoine FitzGerald joined later, and many contemporaries, such as Yvonne McKague Housser, were invited to exhibit alongside them. After the Group disbanded in 1933, it was succeeded by The Canadian Group of Painters, a collective of twenty-eight painters from across the country, many of whom had exhibited with, or been members of, the Group of Seven in previous years.

## Biographies

### Franklin Carmichael
(1890, Orillia, Ontario –
1945, Toronto, Ontario)

A founding member of the Group of Seven, Franklin Carmichael was a celebrated watercolorist and a pioneer of commercial art. In 1911, he left his small hometown of Orillia to join Toronto's leading design firm, Grip Limited. As an office clerk, he was inspired by his older and more established colleagues, including Arthur Lismer, J. E. H. MacDonald, Tom Thomson, and Fred Varley. Evenings, he studied life drawing at the Ontario College of Art (OCA), and in 1913 he took courses in Antwerp, Belgium, at the Académie Royale des Beaux-Arts. Carmichael was a gifted draftsman, and upon returning to Toronto he embarked on a full-time career in design, specializing in commercial art and typography.

Carmichael frequented the all-men Arts and Letters Club, where he fraternized with fellow creatives. During this time, he had been painting with Grip colleagues on weekends and made his first trip to Lake Superior's north shore with the Group in 1925, accompanying Lawren Harris, A. Y. Jackson, and A. J. Casson. He was the only one to sketch in watercolor, and at the 1930 Group of Seven exhibition, Carmichael exhibited watercolors exclusively—a marked difference from the other Group members, who painted in oil. His work had a unique linear quality bridging it to graphic design; using rich and vibrant colors, he was interested in exploring the decorative aspects of painting.

In 1932, Carmichael was appointed head of the Graphic Design and Commercial Art Department at the Ontario College of Art, where he worked for the remainder of his life. Two years after his death, the Art Gallery of Toronto held a memorial exhibition of his work.

Biographies

### Emily Carr
(1871, Victoria, British Columbia –
1945, Victoria, British Columbia)

A leading figure in Canadian modern art, Emily Carr was inspired by the landscape and Indigenous cultures of the Pacific Northwest Coast. She is renowned for her powerful depictions of the Nuu-chah-nulth, Haida, Gitxsan, and Tsimshian peoples, their villages, carvings, and totems. In her time, she gained recognition when she shifted her subject matter to the landscapes of the Pacific Northwest Coast—particularly its old-growth forests.

Carr studied at the California School of Design in San Francisco in 1890 and traveled to England in 1899, where she enrolled at the Westminster School of Art in London, and at St Ives in Cornwall. In Paris a decade later, she took courses at the Académie Colarossi, where she became fascinated with Primitivism and Fauvism. These approaches influenced her paintings of Indigenous subjects, emphasizing painterly qualities, intense color, and personal expression—a style deemed radical in Canada at the time. Carr did not appropriate Indigenous motifs as a means of formal experimentation; rather, she sought to understand and document Indigenous cultural traditions that were facing rapid change in the face of racist government policies, as well as invasive fishing and lumber industries.

In 1927, a large selection of Carr's paintings was exhibited at the National Gallery of Canada in Ottawa, signifying her debut on the national art scene. Her work was well received, and it attracted the attention of the Group of Seven, and of Lawren Harris in particular. He influenced her immensely, and the two corresponded for years. Moving into her most prolific period, Carr began to focus on the land, painting forests with bolder, more sculptural forms, and capturing the divine quality, and deep sense of awe, she felt in nature.

### Edward S. Curtis
(1868, Whitewater, Wisconsin –
1952, Los Angeles, California)

Edward Sheriff Curtis was an American photographer known for chronicling the Indigenous tribes of North America. After apprenticing as a photographer in St. Paul, Minnesota, Curtis moved to Port Orchard, Washington, where he established a photography and photoengraving studio with Thomas Guptill. In nearby Seattle, he began photographing the Suquamish and Duwamish peoples living on the waterfront. He gained recognition for these early portraits and joined the Harriman expedition to Alaska as head photographer in 1899. This marked the first of numerous trips that Curtis would take throughout North America to photograph and film Indigenous tribes.

In 1907, Curtis began the project he is best known for: *The North American Indian* (1907-30), a twenty-volume compendium that was meant to be a comprehensive catalogue of Indigenous tribes across the continent. Curtis traveled with a crew of assistants, shooting portraits in a studio setting, and photographing events and activities on the land, which were generally staged or reenacted. While the project's scope was ethnographic, Curtis considered *The North American Indian* to be, above all, an artistic endeavor. He was familiar with photography's traditions, and its relationship to the fine arts. He posed his subjects in romanticized ways that reflected the pictorialist sensibilities of the day.

In 1935, the rights to *The North American Indian* and many of Curtis's unpublished photographs were sold to the Charles E. Lauriat Company in Boston, where they remained, untouched, until 1972. Once rediscovered, the photographs were reproduced widely and have since become a part of North American popular culture.

### Robert Gardner
(1925, Brookline, Massachusetts –
2014, Boston, Massachusetts)

Robert Gardner was an American filmmaker known for his work in the field of anthropological documentary film. Gardner began his career at the University of Puget Sound in Tacoma, Washington, where he taught and was enrolled in anthropology but did not complete a degree. During this time, he made *Blunden Harbour,* a short film about the Kwakwaka'wakw (Kwakiutl) people. He later returned to Massachusetts and helped to start a film production unit at Harvard's Peabody Museum. This eventually became the Film Study Center at Harvard University, of which Gardener was director from 1957 to 1997. During this time, he was also an undergraduate and graduate student in Harvard's Department of Anthropology and traveled extensively for film projects.

Gardner's films are celebrated for their sparse narration, refined visual language, and poetic sensibility. They have attracted wider audiences than most other anthropological films and have been screened at festivals across the globe. Gardner is the recipient of numerous awards; however, his work has also been criticized by anthropologists for othering subjects in a way that is more artistic than scientific. Among his films are *Dead Birds* (1964), on the Dugum Dani people in Indonesia; *Rivers of Sand* (1974), on the Hamar people of southwestern Ethiopia; and *Forest of Bliss* (1985), on the ancient city of Benares, India.

## Lawren Harris
(1885, Brantford, Ontario –
1970, Vancouver, British Columbia)

A leading member of the Group of Seven, and one of its best-known artists, Lawren Stewart Harris forged a distinctive painting career inspired by a mystical connection to nature. Born into one of Canada's wealthiest families, Harris studied art in Berlin and Munich from 1904 to 1908. Expressionism, Fauvism, and Symbolism enraptured the young artist. Upon his return to Toronto, he painted with fervor, embarking on a lifelong quest for spirituality in art. In 1913, Harris helped to finance the construction of a studio building in Toronto. The first structure of its kind in Canada, it provided artists with inexpensive or free workspace. When it opened, Harris, J. E. H. MacDonald, and A. Y. Jackson were the most progressive artists working in the studio building. It became a hub for artists willing to shun academic tradition in support of a new, characteristically Canadian art.

After the death of his brother during the First World War, Harris suffered a breakdown. During this fraught period, his theosophic beliefs intensified, leading to a shift in his artistic sensibilities. He turned to basic structures and underlying forms in the landscape, and he worked in an increasingly pared-down style, seeking "spiritual flow" in nature. After traveling through Northern Ontario in 1918–19 (together with other members of what would later become the Group of Seven), Harris ventured farther to Lake Superior's northern shore in 1921, where he would return for the next seven years.

Highly connected in Toronto's high society, Harris promoted the Group's progressive ideas about art and nationhood in periodicals, lectures, and private clubs. However, by the 1930s, after a trip to the Arctic, Harris's interest progressed beyond the landscape genre into abstraction. He left Canada to seek new transcendental subjects in New Hampshire, New Mexico, and eventually Vancouver, where he would spend the remainder of his life.

## Edwin Holgate
(1892, Allandale, Ontario –
1977, Montreal, Quebec)

Edwin Holgate is best known for his portraits of tradespeople, and for his female nudes in landscape settings. With simplified compositions that emphasize the character of his human subjects, Holgate's practice was distinct from that of other Group members. He also devoted his time to printmaking, illustration, and art education. As the Group of Seven strove to be a national school of painters, they invited Holgate to become a member. Representing the French-speaking province of Quebec, he was the ninth artist to join the Group in 1929.

Holgate enrolled in the Académie de la Grande Chaumière in Paris in 1912 and returned to France later in service of the Canadian Army during the First World War. In 1920, he traveled to Paris once again to study at the Académie Colarossi under the Russian-French Post-Impressionist Adolf Milman.

Back in Montreal, Holgate became a founding member of the influential Beaver Hall Group. The fellow Montrealer A. Y. Jackson joined Holgate on sketching trips in rural Quebec along the St. Lawrence River, where Holgate would produce his first landscape paintings. He continued to travel in the rural areas of Quebec, particularly the Laurentian hills where he painted farms and small villages throughout the seasons. It was through Jackson that Holgate began exhibiting with the Group of Seven. In 1933, the year the Group disbanded, Holgate was appointed a founding member of its successor group, the Canadian Group of Painters. A decade later, he served in England as an official artist during the Second World War.

## Yvonne McKague Housser
(1897, Toronto, Ontario –
1996, Toronto, Ontario)

Thanks to her intellectual curiosity, the work of Yvonne McKague Housser was continually reinvigorated by her artistic impulses. After graduating from the Ontario College of Art (OCA), she studied in Paris in the 1920s at the Académie Colarossi, the Académie de la Grande Chaumière, and the Académie Ranson, and in Vienna with the Austrian painter and educator Franz Čižek.

In France, McKague was inspired by Post-Impressionism, particularly by Paul Cézanne and Paul Gauguin, as by the Nabis member Maurice Denis, her instructor at Ranson. During this formative period, McKague began to emphasize volume, simplify design, and employ a vibrant palette—devices she would continue to hone throughout her career.

McKague was an influential instructor at OCA, where she worked alongside Arthur Lismer and hence became acquainted with the Group of Seven. She was invited to contribute work to the last three Group exhibitions in 1928, 1930, and 1931. Despite the opportunity for women to exhibit work, they never entered the official ranks of the Group, which remained tied to notions of masculinity and to the idea that only men could effectively paint the rugged landscape. Notwithstanding, her sketching trips took her through remote regions of Canada, including the Rocky Mountains, Lake Superior, and the mining town of Cobalt, where she made her most famous paintings.

In 1935, the artist married the renowned critic and author Fred Housser, but she was widowed the following year. Like Lawren Harris, Fred Housser was a devout theosophist, and Yvonne McKague Housser shared similar convictions. After the loss of her husband, she studied transcendental painting in New Mexico with the fellow theosophist Emil Bisttram. She later traveled to Provincetown, Massachusetts, to study with the pivotal Abstract Expressionist Hans Hofmann.

# Biographies

### A.Y. Jackson
(1882, Montreal, Quebec –
1974, Kleinburg, Ontario)

Alexander Young Jackson devoted himself to painting the Canadian landscape over a career that spanned six decades. An original member of the Group of Seven, and the only one born in Quebec, his paintings are characterized by rhythmic compositions, simplified forms, and precise hues and tones that evoke the mood of a place.

Jackson received education in drawing and graphic design at a young age at a Montreal lithography company. He later studied at the Art Institute of Chicago, and at the Académie Julian in Paris. By 1914, Jackson had moved to Toronto, where he met the painters with whom he would establish the Group of Seven. The Group's innovative spirit was also manifested in Montreal's Beaver Hall Group of modernist painters, of which Jackson was the inaugural president in 1920. This important role led him to be an influential figure in both English Canada and Quebec.

Appointed an official war artist, Jackson sketched on the front lines in northern France. In the mid-1920s, he established a regular routine of sketching in the villages along the St. Lawrence River in Quebec. In 1936, he became the president of the Canadian Group of Painters, a collective of painters from across Canada that formed after the Group of Seven's disbandment in 1933. Throughout his late career, Jackson traveled Canada to paint, adding Southern Alberta to his repertoire of locations. In his final years, Jackson was an artist-in-residence at the McMichael Canadian Art Collection in Kleinburg near Toronto, where he passed away and was buried alongside other Group of Seven members.

### Lisa Jackson
(born in Toronto)

Lisa Jackson is an Anishinaabe filmmaker based in Vancouver, British Columbia. Her projects range from documentaries, music videos, and experimental short films to virtual reality installations. After graduating from Simon Fraser University in Vancouver with a bachelor's degree in film production, she completed a Master of Fine Arts in film production at York University in Toronto. Her films have been broadcast across Canada and screened internationally at such major festivals as Toronto's Hot Docs, the Edinburgh International Film Festival, and the Berlin International Film Festival.

Jackson's debut short film *Suckerfish* (2004) combines animation, childhood photographs, and narration into a humorous and heartfelt reflection on her relationship with her mother, and her own identity. *How a People Live* (2013), Jackson's hourlong documentary on the forced removal of the Gwa'sala-'Nakwaxda'xw First Nations from their traditional coastal territories of British Columbia, was broadcast nationally by the Canadian Broadcasting Corporation. *Biidaaban: First Light* (2018) is Jackson's major interactive virtual reality project that portrays a future version of Toronto. The film, which was screened internationally and lauded by critics, illuminates Indigenous languages as frameworks for understanding place and facilitating reconciliation.

### Arthur Lismer
(1885, Sheffield, England –
1969, Montreal, Quebec)

Arthur Lismer is known for his boldly designed, rhythmic landscapes and his career as a visionary art educator. Born and educated in Sheffield, England, Lismer studied at the Académie Royale des Beaux-Arts in Antwerp and was inspired by the École de Barbizon and Post-Impressionist movements. A skilled draftsman and caricaturist, he emigrated to Toronto in 1911 and was hired at Grip Limited alongside fellow future Group artists. Exposure to their work, and that of other leading Canadian painters, led to an evolution in Lismer's style—he began to embrace more expressionistic paint handling and a vivid palette, propelled by a newfound, collective passion for the Canadian landscape.

In 1916, Lismer moved to Halifax, Nova Scotia, to work as president of the local art college. During the war, he painted naval vessels, notably dazzle camouflage ships, and was commissioned as an official war artist on the home front. Returning to Toronto three years later, he assumed a high-ranking role in education at the Art Gallery of Toronto (now Art Gallery of Ontario), and later at the Montreal Museum of Fine Arts. Lismer became a respected educator, lecturing internationally, all the while maintaining a robust painting practice. He traveled throughout Northern Ontario, making work that espoused the Group of Seven's mission to express a new people in a new land, and to seek spiritual values in art and nature. In later paintings, he focused on formal and technical aspects, studying the patterns of close-up forest interiors and land formations.

## J. E. H. MacDonald
(1873, Durham, England –
1932, Toronto, Ontario)

A founding member of the Group of Seven, James Edward Hervey MacDonald emigrated to Hamilton, Ontario, in his early teens and settled in Toronto shortly thereafter. He was influenced by Barbizonian, Romantic, and Arts and Crafts movements and also had a fascination with the hills and mountains of his childhood in North East England. Starting in 1895, MacDonald worked at Grip Limited in Toronto for almost a decade, except for a four-year stint at Carlton Studios in London, from 1903 to 1907. He painted his first landscapes in his Toronto neighborhood of High Park and exhibited them for the first time in 1911. The vivid oil sketches caught the attention of Lawren Harris, and a year later the two had their first joint exhibition.

In 1913, MacDonald and Harris visited an exhibition of Scandinavian art in Buffalo, New York. Decorative compositions, high-keyed colors, and simplified subject matter resonated with the duo, and their conviction that the art is essential for national identity was reinforced. By this time, MacDonald had resigned from Grip and relocated to the rural town of Thornhill, Ontario, as he felt a strong connection to nature. Later he traveled with other future members of the Group of Seven through the Algoma region. MacDonald's work from this period reveals an intense and mystical reaction to the land; his paintings are broader in design, with bold, more lively rhythms.

## Caroline Monnet
(b. 1985, Ottawa, Ontario)

Caroline Monnet is an artist of Algonquin-French heritage, who works in sculpture, installation, and film. Now based in Montreal, her childhood was spent between Brittany, France, and the Algonquin territory of Outaouais, Quebec. Her work often deals with her dual heritage, as well as with the ongoing colonial dynamics between Europe and North America, and the representation of Indigenous peoples and cultures in contemporary society.

Monnet has an academic background in sociology and communications from the University of Ottawa and the University of Granada in Spain. She debuted as a filmmaker in 2009 when she screened *Ikwé,* a five-minute experimental film at the Toronto International Film Festival. She has since presented her work internationally at venues including the Palais de Tokyo in Paris, Haus der Kulturen der Welt in Berlin, the Sundance Film Festival in Utah, and the National Gallery of Canada in Ottawa. In 2016, she was selected for the prestigious Cinéfondation residency in Paris.

Monnet's film *Transatlantic* and her large-scale installation *Proximal I, II, III, IV, V* (both 2018) were featured in the major group exhibition *Àbadakone | Continuous Fire | Feu continuel* at the National Gallery of Canada. Her work was included in the Whitney Biennial in New York and the Toronto Biennale of Art (both 2019).

## Jeff Thomas
(b. 1956, Buffalo, New York)

Jeff Thomas is a photographer, curator, and cultural theorist whose work confronts Indigenous stereotypes and enriches the representation of Indigenous peoples in contemporary art. Winner of a Governor General's Award in Visual and Media Arts in 2019, Thomas is based in Ottawa, Ontario, and has worked on curatorial projects at various cultural institutions, including the Canadian Museum of History in Gatineau, the Art Gallery of Ontario in Toronto, and the Library and Archives Canada in Ottawa. His photographs are in major public collections across Canada, the United States, and Europe. In 1997, the Canadian filmmaker Ali Kazimi produced a documentary film about Thomas's work entitled *Shooting Indians: A Journey with Jeffrey Thomas.*

Enrolled as a member of the Six Nations of the Grand River Reserve near Brantford, Ontario, Thomas is a self-described urban Iroquois man. His artistic practice largely concentrates on the ethnographic photographs of Indigenous peoples by the American photographer Edward S. Curtis. In contrast, Thomas's photographic work often depicts Indigenous subjects in urban environments. In his major series *Indians on Tour* (2000–18), Thomas posed plastic figurines of stereotypical "Indians" in front of urban scenes and landmarks. In these humorous and wryly critical images, the figurines visit popular non-Indigenous tourist attractions across North America and Europe, turning the typical conception of tourism on its head.

Biographies

## Tom Thomson
(1877, Claremont, Ontario –
1917, Canoe Lake, Algonquin Park, Ontario)

Tom Thomson's childhood in scenic Grey County, Ontario, sparked his early fascination with rugged terrain. Known as a keen woodsman, his innate passion for the Ontario landscape would emerge during a remarkable but short painting career that peaked in 1917, the year of his drowning in Canoe Lake, Algonquin Park.

Despite being highly regarded as a painter, Thomson had no formal training in the medium. In his early twenties, he traveled to Seattle to work as a commercial artist, and later worked at Grip Limited in Toronto along with future Group of Seven artists. Thomson's skill as a designer permeated his painting technique, derived from Impressionist and post-Impressionist trends, as well as Art Nouveau design principles.

From 1913 to 1917, the artist spent most of his time in Algonquin Park, 300 kilometers north of Toronto. Of his contemporaries who also painted there—Lawren Harris, A. Y. Jackson, Arthur Lismer, and J. E. H. MacDonald—Thomson was most familiar with the region. His naturalistic treatment of the land evolved into freer design and form, and a more expressive use of color.

Thomson spent winters in Toronto to work on canvases in his studio, a shack near Lawren Harris's studio building. He has been mythologized after his death, his work touted as a vital expression of love for his country. The Art Gallery of Toronto held his memorial exhibition a few months before the first Group of Seven exhibition. His major canvases, such as *The West Wind* and *The Jack Pine,* entered public collections soon after his death and have become icons of Canadian identity, signaling strength and resilience.

## F. H. Varley
(1881, Sheffield, England –
1969, Unionville, Ontario)

In 1912, after completing studies at the Académie Royale des Beaux-Arts in Antwerp, Frederick Horsman Varley emigrated to Canada at the suggestion of his friend, the fellow Sheffielder Arthur Lismer. The two worked at Grip Limited in Toronto alongside Tom Thomson and J. E. H. MacDonald. In 1914, Varley took his first and only trip to Algonquin Park with Tom Thomson, A. Y. Jackson, and Arthur Lismer. His paintings of the rugged region were rich and vibrant; however, unlike the other Group members, he often incorporated figures as a main element of the work. Varley did not follow Group members farther north to the shores of Lake Superior.

In 1918, the same year that Lawren Harris financed the first Algoma boxcar trip, Varley accompanied Canadian troops to Europe as an official war artist. In the trenches between Amiens, France, and Mons, Belgium, he painted visceral scenes of destruction and violence; the experience of war had profound psychological effects on the artist.

In 1926, Varley moved to Vancouver to teach at the recently opened Vancouver School of Decorative and Applied Arts. Enamored by the Rocky Mountains and the coast, he turned his attention to landscape painting. In 1928, he sent four strikingly rich British Columbian landscape paintings to the Group of Seven exhibition in Toronto. No Group members had explored the West Coast as Varley did—it was in the west that he found his spiritual home, and his most productive and inspired period.

## Mary E. Wrinch
(1877, Kirby-le-Soken, England –
1969, Toronto, Ontario)

Born into a farming family in a small Essex village, Mary Evelyn Wrinch moved to Ontario at the age of seven. As a student in Toronto, she is known to have skipped school to attend a china-painting class, gravitating to its delicate style. A promising and independent young artist, Wrinch studied watercolor miniatures in both London and New York City. After several years of painting intricate miniature portraits, she turned her focus to the wooded landscape of Muskoka, Ontario. As with her miniatures, Wrinch was drawn to contrast and the play of colors. In a lively, impasto style, she painted natural and industrial Muskoka scenes nearly a decade before the Group of Seven formed.

In the early 1900s, Wrinch made her home in Wychwood Park, a Toronto artists' colony, with her husband and fellow artist George A. Reid. She continued to use her given name, which was uncustomary at the time and demonstrative of her commitment to maintaining her own professional identity. She exhibited her works nationally and internationally, and in 1924, Wrinch was the first woman to be elected to the executive committee of the Ontario Society of Artists. Two years later, she exhibited at the Art Gallery of Toronto alongside other leading Canadian artists, such as Lawren Harris and Tom Thomson. Later in her career, inspired by Japanese woodcut prints, Wrinch took up printmaking and received critical acclaim for her exquisite prints of flora and fauna.


Compiled by Renée van der Avoird

List of Works

## Franklin Carmichael

*Autumn Hillside,* 1920
Oil on canvas
76 × 91.4 cm
Art Gallery of Ontario, gift of the J. S. McLean
Collection, Toronto, 1969, donated by
the Ontario Heritage Foundation in 1988
p. 39

*The Upper Ottawa, near Mattawa,* 1924
Oil on canvas
101.5 × 123.1 cm
National Gallery of Canada, Ottawa,
purchased in 1936
p. 219

*In the Nickel Belt,* 1928
Oil on canvas
102.2 × 122.2 cm
Firestone Collection of Canadian Art, Ottawa
Art Gallery, donated to the City of Ottawa by
the Ontario Heritage Foundation
p. 193

*A Northern Silver Mine,* 1930
Oil on canvas
101.5 × 121.2 cm
McMichael Canadian Art Collection,
gift of Mrs. A. J. Latner
p. 195

## Emily Carr

*Heina, Q.C.I.,* 1928
Oil on canvas
129.6 × 91.2 cm
National Gallery of Canada, Ottawa,
purchased in 1937
p. 85

*Inside a Forest II,* 1929–30
Oil on canvas
109.9 × 69.8 cm
Art Gallery of Ontario, bequest of
Charles S. Band in 1970
p. 84

*Wood Interior,* 1929–30
Oil on canvas
106.9 × 70.2 cm
Collection of The Robert McLaughlin Gallery,
Oshawa, gift of Isabel McLaughlin in 1987
p. 81

*Blunden Harbour,* ca. 1930
Oil on canvas
129.8 × 93.6 cm
National Gallery of Canada, Ottawa,
purchased in 1937
p. 77

*Guyasdoms D'Sonoqua,* ca. 1930
Oil on canvas
100.3 × 65.4 cm
Art Gallery of Ontario, gift of
the Albert H. Robson Memorial
Subscription Fund in 1942
p. 75

*Forest,* ca. 1930–39
Oil on canvas
111.7 × 68 cm
Victoria University, Toronto, Canada,
purchased by the Women's Art Committee,
Victoria University, in 1944
p. 78

*Big Raven,* 1931
Oil on canvas
87 × 114 cm
Collection of the Vancouver Art Gallery,
Emily Carr Trust
p. 9

*Western Forest,* ca. 1931
Oil on canvas
128.3 × 91.8 cm
Art Gallery of Ontario,
purchased in 1937
pp. 70–71 (detail), 83

*Old Tree at Dusk,* ca. 1932
Oil on canvas
112 × 68.5 cm
McMichael Canadian Art Collection,
gift of Colonel R. S. McLaughlin
p. 79

*Reforestation,* 1936
Oil on canvas
110 × 67.2 cm
McMichael Canadian Art Collection, gift of
the Founders, Robert and Signe McMichael
p. 184

*Red Tree,* ca. 1938
Oil on paper mounted on paperboard
91.8 × 61.2 cm
Art Gallery of Ontario, gift of the J. S. McLean
Collection by Canada Packers Inc. in 1990
p. 74

*Trees in the Sky,* 1939
Oil on canvas
111.6 × 68.7 cm
Art Gallery of Ontario,
gift of Richard M. Ivey in 2008
p. 185

Arthur Lismer

*Tom Thomson's Camp,* 1914
Oil on wood panel
30.8 × 23.4 cm
McMichael Canadian Art Collection, gift of
the founders, Robert and Signe McMichael
p. 67

*Logging in Nova Scotia,* 1920
Oil on canvas
91.4 × 101.5 cm
The Thomson Collection at the Art Gallery of
Ontario, 2017
p. 180

*Evening Silhouette Georgian Bay,* 1928
Oil on canvas
80.3 × 100.8 cm
University College Art Collection, University
of Toronto, gift of H. S. Southam in 1947–48,
in memory of Major Gordon H. Southam (B.A.
UC 0T7), who was killed at the Somme in 1916
p. 221

*Sunlight in a Wood,* 1930
Oil on canvas
91.4 × 101.6 cm
Art Gallery of Ontario, bequest of
John M. Lyle, Toronto, in 1946
p. 45

*Pine Wrack,* 1933
Oil on canvas
92.1 × 106.9 cm
National Gallery of Canada, Ottawa,
Royal Canadian Academy of Arts diploma work,
deposited by the artist, Montreal, in 1948
p. 47

J. E. H. MacDonald

*Northern Lights,* 1915–16
Oil on paperboard
20.2 × 25.4 cm
McMichael Canadian Art Collection, gift of
the founders, Robert and Signe McMichael
p. 212

*The Elements,* 1916
Oil on wood-pulp board
71.1 × 91.8 cm
Art Gallery of Ontario, gift of Dr. Lorne Pierce,
Toronto, in 1958, in memory of Edith Chown
Pierce (1890–1954)
p. 59

*The Beaver Dam,* 1919
Oil on canvas
81.6 × 86.7 cm
Art Gallery of Ontario, gift of the Reuben and
Kate Leonard Canadian Fund in 1926
pp. 54–55 (detail), 65

*Falls, Montreal River,* 1920
Oil on canvas
121.9 × 153 cm
Art Gallery of Ontario, purchased in 1933
p. 61

*Aurora, Georgian Bay, Pointe au Baril,* 1931
Oil on paperboard
21.5 × 26.7 cm
McMichael Canadian Art Collection,
gift of Mr. R. A. Laidlaw
pp. 202–03 (detail), 209

Yvonne McKague Housser

*Silver Mine, Cobalt,* 1930
Oil on canvas
77 × 89.5 cm
Collection of Museum London, London, Ontario,
F. B. Housser Memorial Collection, 1945
p. 199

*Silver Mine, Evening,* 1932
Oil on canvas
61 × 76.2 cm
Art Gallery of Ontario, gift of the estate of
J. Kemp Waldie, Toronto, in 1989
pp. 188–89 (detail), 197

*Autumn's Garland,* winter 1915–16
Oil on canvas
122.5 × 132.2 cm
National Gallery of Canada, Ottawa,
purchased in 1918
p. 51

*A Northern Lake,* spring 1916
Oil on composite wood-pulp board
21.6 × 26.7 cm
Art Gallery of Ontario, gift of the Reuben and
Kate Leonard Canadian Fund in 1927
p. 157

*Nocturne: The Birches,* spring 1916
Oil on grey wood pulp board
21.6 × 26.8 cm
National Gallery of Canada, Ottawa, bequest
of Dr. J. M. MacCallum, Toronto, in 1944
p. 159

*Northern Lights,* spring 1916
Oil on wood
21.6 × 26.7 cm
The Montreal Museum of Fine Arts, purchase,
A. Sidney Dawes Fund
p. 213

*Snow and Rocks,* spring 1916
Oil on wood
26.8 × 21.5 cm
National Gallery of Canada, Ottawa, bequest
of Dr. J. M. MacCallum, Toronto, in 1944
p. 163

*Swift Water,* spring 1916
Oil on wood
21.3 × 26.8 cm
National Gallery of Canada, Ottawa, bequest
of Dr. J. M. MacCallum, Toronto, in 1944
p. 162

*Bateaux,* summer 1916
Oil on wood
21.5 × 26.8 cm
Art Gallery of Ontario, gift of the Reuben and
Kate Leonard Canadian Fund in 1927
p. 69

*Pine Tree,* summer 1916
Oil on wood
21.6 × 26.7 cm
Art Gallery of Ontario, gift of the Reuben and
Kate Leonard Canadian Fund in 1927
p. 146

*The Enchanted Stream, Midnight,* summer 1916
Oil on wood
21.5 × 26.7 cm
National Gallery of Canada, Ottawa, bequest
of Dr. J. M. MacCallum, Toronto, in 1944
p. 165

*Autumn Birches,* fall 1916
Oil on wood panel
21.6 × 26.8 cm
Art Gallery of Ontario, gift of Mr. and Mrs.
Lawren S. Harris, Toronto, in 1927
p. 151

*Log Jam: Sketch for "The Drive",* fall 1916
Oil on composite wood-pulp board
21.6 × 26.7 cm
The Thomson Collection at the
Art Gallery of Ontario
p. 175

*Timber Chute,* fall 1916
Oil on cardboard
21.6 × 26.7 cm
National Gallery of Canada, Ottawa, bequest
of Dr. J. M. MacCallum, Toronto, in 1944
p. 171

*Trees, Red Hill, and Sunset Sky,* fall 1916
Oil on wood
21.8 × 26.9 cm
National Gallery of Canada, Ottawa,
bequest of Vincent Massey in 1968
p. 161

*Moose at Night,* winter 1916
Oil on wood
20.9 × 26.9 cm
National Gallery of Canada, Ottawa,
purchased in 1918
p. 156

*The West Wind,* winter 1916–17
Oil on canvas
120.7 × 137.9 cm
Art Gallery of Ontario, gift of the
Canadian Club of Toronto in 1926
pp. 214–15 (detail), 223

*Dark Waters,* spring 1917
Oil on wood
21.3 × 26.8 cm
National Gallery of Canada, Ottawa, bequest
of Dr. J. M. MacCallum, Toronto, in 1944
p. 164

*Northern Lights,* spring 1917
Oil on wood
21.5 × 26.7 cm
National Gallery of Canada, Ottawa, bequest
of Dr. J. M. MacCallum, Toronto, in 1944
p. 210

List of Works

F. H. Varley

*Magic Tree,* 1924
Oil on canvas
52.7 × 52.7 cm
Hart House Permanent Collection,
University of Toronto, purchased by the
Art Committee in 1924–25
p. 53

*Mountain Portage,* 1925
Oil on canvas
50.5 × 61 cm
McMichael Canadian Art Collection, gift of
the founders, Robert and Signe McMichael
p. 63

*Mountain Sketching,* ca. 1929
Oil on plywood
30.5 × 38.1 cm
Art Gallery of Ontario, gift of Mrs. Doris
Huestis Mills Speirs, Pickering, Ontario, in 1971
p. 62

*Open Window,* 1933
Oil on canvas
102.9 × 87 cm
Hart House Permanent Collection,
University of Toronto, purchased by the
Art Committee in 1944 with funds from the
Harold and Murray Wrong Memorial Fund
p. 3


Mary E. Wrinch

*Saw Mills, Muskoka,* 1906
Oil on canvas
45.2 × 59.4 cm
Art Gallery of Ontario, gift of Sylvia and
Irving Ungerman and Family in 2010
p. 183

Films

Edward S. Curtis
*In the Land of the Head Hunters /*
*In the Land of the War Canoes,* 1914
Film (restoration with original musical score,
tinted, sound, 66 min.)
Courtesy of Milestone Film & Video,
Harrington Park, New Jersey
pp. 90–93

Canadian Government Motion Picture Bureau
*Big Timber,* 1935
Film (digital video transfer, black and white,
sound, 11 min.)
W. Graham (photography), David Gwydyr
(scenario), Rupert Caplan (narrator)
Library and Archives Canada / Bibliothèque
et Archives Canada
pp. 186, 187

Robert Gardner
*Blunden Harbour,* 1951
Film (digital video transfer, black and white,
sound, 22 min.)
Richard Selig (casting), W. H. Heick,
P. Jacquemin (camera), M. E. Dowd (sound)
Courtesy of Documentary Educational
Resources, Watertown, Massachusetts
pp. 100–103

Lisa Jackson (Dir.)
*How a People Live,* 2013
HD video (color, sound, 59 min., 5 sec.)
Courtesy Moving Images Distribution Society
pp. 110, 111

Caroline Monnet
*Mobilize,* 2015
Single-channel video (color, sound, 3 min.)
Courtesy of the National Film Board of Canada
pp. 86–87 (detail), 116, 117

Colophon

This catalogue is published in conjunction with the exhibition
*Magnetic North: Imagining Canada in Painting 1910–40*

An exhibition organized by
SCHIRN KUNSTHALLE FRANKFURT, the Art Gallery of Ontario, and the National Gallery of Canada

Schirn Kunsthalle Frankfurt
February 5 – May 16, 2021

Kunsthal Rotterdam
June 12 – October 17, 2021

Editor
Martina Weinhart
with Georgiana Uhlyarik

Editing
Martina Weinhart
Rebecca Herlemann

Schirn Publication Management
Antonia Lagemann
Anuschka Berthelius

Copyediting
Dawn Michelle d'Atri
Sarah Liss

Translation (German-English)
Susie Hondl
Amy Klement
Bram Opsteiten

Graphic Design
Moiré: Marc Kappeler,
Dominik Huber, Simon Trüb,
Max Fingerhuth, Zurich

Editorial Project Management, Prestel
Andrea Bartelt-Gering

Production Management, Prestel
Andrea Cobré

Separations
Schnieber Graphik, Munich

Printing and Binding
Eberl & Koesel GmbH &. Co. KG

© 2021 Schirn Kunsthalle Frankfurt, authors and artists, and Prestel Verlag, Munich · London · New York
A member of Penguin Random House Verlagsgruppe GmbH
Neumarkter Strasse 28
81673 Munich

In respect to links in the book, the publisher expressly notes that no illegal content was discernible on the linked sites at the time the links were created. The publisher has no influence at all over the current and future design, content, or authorship of the linked sites. For this reason, the publisher expressly disassociates itself from all content on linked sites that has been altered since the link was created and assumes no liability for such content.

Library of Congress Control Number: 2020950763

A CIP catalog record for this book is available from the British Library.

ISBN 978-3-7913-5994-6
(English trade and museum edition)

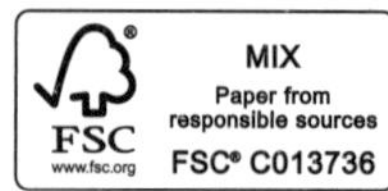


Penguin Random House Verlagsgruppe FSC® N001967

Printed on 130g Schleipen Fly 06

Printed in Germany

www.prestel.com

Cover Illustration
Lawren Harris, *Icebergs, Davis Strait,* 1930 (detail, p.137)

The assertion of all claims according to Article 60h UrhG (Copyright Act) for the reproduction of exhibition/collection objects is carried out by VG Bild-Kunst.

Image Credits
Art Gallery of Ontario, pp. 23 (fig.12), 39, 59, 61, 65, 69, 74, 75, 84, 146, 147, 149, 151–53, 155, 157, 158, 179, 183, 185, 223; photo: Craig Boyko, pp. 66, 83, 150; photo: Ian Lefebvre, p. 211
Arthur Lismer papers, Edward P. Taylor Research Library and Archives, Art Gallery of Ontario, Toronto, gift of Marjorie Lismer Bridges (file 19), p. 21 (fig. 5)
Collection of the E. P. Taylor Library and Archives, Art Gallery of Ontario, p. 29 (fig.1)
commons.wikimedia.org, photo: Dmitry Rozhkov, p. 19 (fig.1)
Courtesy Library of Congress/LC-USZC4-11256, p. 97 (fig.1)
Courtesy Moving Images Distribution Society, pp.110, 111; photo: Colleen Hemphill, p. 111 (fig. 5)
Courtesy of Caroline Monnet, pp. 116, 117, 122–25
Courtesy of Documentary Educational Resources, Watertown, Massachusetts, pp.100-03
Courtesy of Milestone Film & Video, Harrington Park, New Jersey, pp. 90–93; photo: Edward S. Curtis, p. 93 top
E. P. Taylor Library and Archives, Art Gallery of Ontario, gift of Marjorie Lismer Bridges, 1976, photo: Art Gallery of Ontario, LA.ALF.S5.1, p. 23 (fig. 11)
Estate of A.Y. Jackson, © VG Bild-Kunst, Bonn, 2020, photo courtesy of AGO, p. 207
Estate of Arthur Lismer, photo courtesy of AGO, p. 45; photo: Michael Cullen, p. 180
Estate of Yvonne McKague Housser, photo courtesy of AGO, p.197
Family of Lawren S. Harris, p. 23 (fig. 9); photo courtesy of AGO, pp. 43, 130, 131, 133, 135, 200; photo: Ian Lefebvre, p. 139; photo: Pat Keatley, p. 23 (fig. 10)
Firestone Collection of Canadian Art, Ottawa Art Gallery, p.193
Hart House Collection, University of Toronto, photo: Toni Hafkenscheid, pp. 3, 53, 141

Jeff Thomas, p. 97 (fig. 2); courtesy of Library
and Archives Canada/C-019972, p. 97 (fig. 3
middle); courtesy of the Library of Congress/
LC-USZ62-106767, p. 99 (fig. 4 middle); courtesy
of the Library of Congress/LC-USZ62-108465,
p. 99 (fig. 5 left); courtesy of the Library of
Congress/LC-USZ62-112234, p. 99 (fig. 5 right)
Judith & Norman Alix Art Gallery, p. 181
Library and Archives Canada / Bibliothèque et
Archives Canada, pp. 186, 187
McMichael Canadian Art Collection, pp. 11, 41,
63, 67, 68, 79, 137, 172, 173, 184, 195, 209, 212;
Archives, p. 21 (figs. 7, 8); photo: Joachim
Gauthier, p. 21 (fig. 6)
Museum London, p. 199
National Gallery of Canada, Ottawa, pp. 7, 19
(figs. 2–4), 29 (fig. 2), 42, 47, 49, 51, 77, 85, 148,
154, 156, 159–65, 170, 171, 178, 208, 210, 219;
Library and Archives, photo: Elliott & Fry
Limited, London, p. 29 (fig. 3)
The Montreal Museum of Fine Arts, photo:
Jean-François Brière, p. 213
The Robert McLaughlin Gallery, p. 81
The Thomson Collection at the Art Gallery of
Ontario, photo: Michael Cullen, p. 175
University College Art Collection, Art
Museum at the University of Toronto, photo:
Toni Hafkenscheid, pp. 201, 221
University of Guelph Collection at the Art
Gallery of Guelph, p. 177
Vancouver Art Gallery, photo: Rachel
Topham, p. 9
Varley Art Gallery of Markham / City of
Markham, photo courtesy of AGO, p. 62
Victoria University, Toronto, Canada, photo
credit: Thomas Moore and photographer:
Sean Weaver, p. 78; photo: Craig Boyko, p. 140



Exhibition
Schirn Kunsthalle Frankfurt

Director
Philipp Demandt

Deputy Director & Head of Exhibitions
Esther Schlicht

Curator
Martina Weinhart

Curatorial Assistant
Rebecca Herlemann

Registrars
Karin Grüning
Elke Walter
Luise Leyer

Supervision of Installation Crew
Andreas Gundermann

Conservators
Stefanie Gundermann
Susanne Silbernagel

Technical Services
Christian Teltz, Oliver Taschke

Exhibition Architecture
Marc Ulm, buero.us

Exhibition Design
VERY, Frankfurt

Press
Johanna Pulz
Julia Bastian
Elisabeth Pallentin
Isabelle Hammer

Schirn Magazine
Antonia Lagemann
Anuschka Berthelius

Marketing
Luise Bachmann
Heike Stumpf
Isabel Reiche
Angelika Schäfer

Engagement
Julia Lange
Hannah Ruiz

Education
Chantal Eschenfelder
Simone Boscheinen
Laura Heeg
Olga Schaetz
Anna Haag

Events & Visitor Management
Ute Seiffert
Alena Flemming

Administration
Heike Berndt
Tanja Mayer
Boris Deckelmann

Assistant Head of Exhibitions
Anna Noll

Assistant to the Director
Samira Koch

Administrative Assistant
Andrea Canthal

Cleaning Supervision
Rosaria La Tona

Reception
Bettina Beyermann
Josef Härig

In cooperation with:

Art Gallery of Ontario

Michael and Sonja Koerner Director, and CEO
Stephan Jost

Managing Editor
Jim Shedden

Production and Copy Editors
Laura Cameron
Sarah Liss

Publishing Coordinator
Kathryn Yuen

Fredrik S. Eaton Curator, Canadian Art
Georgiana Uhlyarik

Assistant Curator, Canadian Art
Renée van der Avoird

Curatorial Administrative Assistant,
Indigenous + Canadian Art
Chloé Wittes

Chief Curator
Julian Cox

Chief, Exhibitions and Collections
Christy Thompson

Senior Director, Strategic Initiatives
Jessica Bright

Associate Director of Exhibitions
Laura Comerford

Project Manager, Exhibitions
Melissa Ramage

Registration and Collections
Donna Austria
Alison Beckett
Cindy Brouse
Jerry Drozdowsky
Tim Hardacre
Joel Herman
Doug Moore

Julie Seddon
Curtis Strilchuk

Collection Information
Tracy Mallon-Jensen
Liana Radvak
Olga Zotova

Conservators
Maureen Del Degan
Christina McLean
Meaghan Monaghan
Fiona Rutka
Maria Sullivan

Logistics and Art Services
Scott Cameron
Corinne Carlson
Iain Hoadley
Matthew Thors-Waples
Craig Whiteside

National Gallery of Canada

Director & CEO
Sasha Suda

Deputy Director, Collection & Research,
and Chief Curator
Kitty Scott

Deputy Director & Exhibitions and Outreach
Isabelle Corriveau

Senior Exhibition Manager
Christopher Régimbal

Exhibitions Officers
Bianca Fortier
Rosanne Boileau

Manager, Art Transit and Loans
Ceridwen Maycock

Registrar
Alana Topham

Chief, Collections Management
Sonya Dumais

Senior Curator, Canadian Art
Katerina Atanassova

Acting Senior Curator, Canadian Art
Adam Welch

Curatorial Assistants, Canadian Art
Christopher Davidson
Krista Broeckx

Chief, Publications & Copyright
Ivan Parisien

French Editor
Valérie Mandia

Conservator of Paintings
Susan Walker

Assistant Conservator of Paintings
Tasia Bulger

Senior Framer
Robert Roch

Framer, Prints, Drawings, and Photographs
Heather McLeod

Manager, Technical Services
Patrick Arcudi

Crating
Julie Drapeau